THE ROUGH GUIDE TO
The Velvet Underground

by
Peter Hogan

ROUGH
GUIDES

www.roughguides.com

Credits

The Rough Guide to The Velvet Underground

Design and layout: bounford.com
Editor: Andrew Heritage
bounford.com for Rough Guides Ltd.

Rough Guides Reference

Series editor: Mark Ellingham
Director: Andrew Lockett
Editors: Peter Buckley, Duncan Clark, Tracy Hopkins,
Sean Mahoney, Matt Milton, Joe Staines, Ruth Tidball

Picture Credits

Corbis: 13, 18, 23, 32, 40, 47, 51, 68, 70, 83, 89, 90, 93, 95, 99, 102, 105, 112, 120, 128, 129, 130, 133, 172, 176, 188, 199, 205, 235, 239, 290
Getty: 21, 26-27, 34, 35, 37, 39, 86
Moviestore Collection: 277, 278
Pearson: 9
Redferns: 3, 28, 44, 53, 57, 61, 65, 75, 78, 79, 80, 114, 117, 119, 123, 163, 268
Rex Features: 126, 170

Publishing Information

This first edition published August 2007 by
Rough Guides Ltd, 80 Strand, London WC2R 0RL
345 Hudson St, 4th Floor, New York 10014, USA
Email: mail@roughguides.com

Distributed by the Penguin Group:
Penguin Books Ltd, 80 Strand, London WC2R 0RL
Penguin Putnam, Inc., 375 Hudson Street, NY 10014, USA
Penguin Group (Australia), 250 Camberwell Road, Camberwell, Victoria 3124, Australia
Penguin Books Canada Ltd, 10 Alcorn Avenue, Toronto, Ontario, Canada M4P 27E
Penguin Group (New Zealand), 67 Apollo Drive, Mairangi Bay, Auckland 1310, New Zealand

Printed in Italy by LegoPrint S.p.A

A catalogue record for this book is available from the British Library

ISBN 13: 978-1-84353-588-1
ISBN 10: 1-84353-588-2

1 3 5 7 9 8 6 4 2

Contents

Contents cont.

Introduction

"Rock and roll is as valid as any other art form" – John Cale

Forty years on from the year it was recorded, *The Velvet Underground & Nico* sounds as fresh, as dazzling and as socially relevant as ever – a claim that very few other records of that era could make. As the late Lester Bangs once observed: "Modern music begins with the Velvets, and the implications and influence of what they did seem to go on forever". Yet Andy Warhol's 'Peel Slowly And See' slogan on the cover of that first album proved to be a prophetic phrase, since it took literally decades for the Velvets to become what Lou Reed would accurately describe in the early 1990s as "a big cult band".

Brian Eno once famously quipped something to the effect that although not many people had bought the Velvets' debut album, those who did all promptly formed bands of their own. There's more than a grain of truth in that, and the Velvets' influence visibly extends through glam-rock and punk to grunge and beyond. The timelessness of their appeal is almost certainly related to the fact that back in the 1960s The Velvet Underground were completely and radically out of step with their times, and usually ahead of them. For example, when Lou Reed met John Cale at the beginning of 1965, he had already written 'Heroin' and 'I'm Waiting For The Man'. It's worth noting that at this point The Beatles were just starting to record their *Help* album, and Bob Dylan was still thought of as simply a "protest singer".

But the social and musical movements of the 1960s largely passed The Velvet Underground by. They had no interest in protest, or folk-rock. They thought the whole hippie movement was shallow and absurd, and while most of their contemporaries were extolling the virtues of psychedelic drugs, the Velvets (apart from Moe Tucker) embraced narcotics that were much harder and darker. They had far more in common with the Beat generation that had preceded them, and with the punks who would follow a decade later; they almost fit the profile of what Danny Fields called "Mole People": "they only seemed to come out at night; they all wore black – black turtlenecks, pants. Some leather. Their skins were light, and they were very intense". Visually, John Cale had a fashion sense that verged on the bizarre – while the other Velvets have usually dressed in basic black throughout their careers, Cale has frequently been seen in garments that lead you to believe he's just wandered in from another dimension. For a man to wear a rhinestone necklace in public in 1965 – as Cale did – was, to put it mildly, extremely unusual.

Artistically, The Velvet Underground was a place where widely differing ideas collided – and whatever Lou Reed may have later claimed, there's no doubt at all that the Velvets were a true collaboration, a synthesis of four (or five) very talented people. Lou Reed's love of doo-wop, and his and Sterling Morrison's grounding in the blues were by no means unusual for the time – but they became something far greater when wedded to the ingredients brought to the table by Cale (a man later described by Brian Eno as "a fountain of musical ideas… and very original ones, too"). Cale's background in both classical and avant garde music made him a unique figure in rock at this time, and no other rock band in 1965 would even have dreamt of using as unusual an instrument as the electric viola. Nor should the input of Morrison and Moe Tucker – as musicians and as people – be underestimated.

But perhaps most importantly, the band provided an outlet for Lou Reed's literary ambitions. More than any other contemporary songwriter, Reed has explored the possibilities of fiction, with lyrics that he'd later describe as "personalized short stories". These were often peopled by characters from the darker side of the tracks: junkies, drunks and losers. People about whom, as Lester Bangs once observed, "nobody else gives a shit" – but Reed did, and his work is steeped in that compassion. That anybody should write rock songs about this territory was deemed outrageous at the time, since pop music was still almost universally thought of as merely entertainment for empty-headed teenagers. As Reed told Barney Hoskyns in 1996: "That's why, in a sense, it was so easy to do. It was like uncharted waters. Which made it so absurd to be told you were doing something shocking, with *Howl* and *Naked Lunch* and *Last Exit To*

Brooklyn already out. There was such a narrow-minded view of what a song could be … And ironically, now we have rap and stuff, people say to me, 'Oh, your stuff's not so shocking.' And I'm saying, 'I never said it was.' The point is, I wanted those songs really to be *about* something that you could go back to thirty years later. And in fact, you can: they're not trapped in the 60s, they're not locked into that zeitgeist". In fact, Reed's lyrics took a factual, reportage approach to their subject matter. 'Heroin' is neither explicitly for nor against the drug, merely descriptive – but the fact that there was a song called 'Heroin' at all still caused waves.

All of these ingredients were wrapped up with three chords and an attitude, and overlaid with the sensibility and lessons they learned from Andy Warhol. At least some of the Velvets' long-term intellectual cachet springs from their association with Warhol – a man who was either a great artist or a great con-artist, and probably both. Today, Warhol's talent is still somewhat overshadowed by his image as 'party Andy', a seemingly shallow creature dazzled by celebrity and puzzled by pretty much everything (Gore Vidal once acidly described him as "the only genius with an IQ of 60"). Yet it was Warhol's unquenchable curiosity, and his uniquely child-like view of the world, that led him to experiment constantly in his art – and to encourage others to do likewise. While he may not have known much about music, and had little to do with what the Velvets actually produced, there is no doubt that they all took Warhol's opinions extremely seriously. Andy undoubtedly knew about style, and recognized it in others. Not

vi

only did he gain The Velvet Underground exposure on a scale undreamt of by most of their contemporaries (even if it also backfired on them), but he also paired them with Nico for their debut album – against their wishes, but to their ultimate profit. Would that first album have attracted as many people without those wistful ballads, sung in that breathless voice? If only for making them more user-friendly, Warhol's role in this story should not be underestimated. "It seemed almost fated", commented Gerard Malanga on the marriage of the Velvets and Warhol. Certainly, no other band of that era would have fitted so well into Warhol's half-formulated plans for a multi-media spectacle – compared to most of their rock contemporaries, the Velvets looked like fine artists in the first place. It was also Warhol's death which instigated the coda to the Velvets' career, inspiring Reed and Cale to patch up their differences with a masterful tribute to their mentor ... which, in turn, led to the unexpected 1993 reunion of the band.

Astonishing as it may seem today, back in the 1960s The Velvet Underground were pretty much ignored, and what little success they had came mainly via word of mouth. They attracted few reviews, got little or no radio airplay. They weren't invited to play at Woodstock (and if they had been, they probably wouldn't have gone), and few mourned when they broke up after recording just four studio albums. This may have been at least partly because there were many who identified the Velvets with their subject matter – which for many others was of course part of their appeal – but confusing the teller with the tale is usually a foolish thing to do. In later years

Reed's material has become more confessional, seemingly more personal, but even there the lines blur. "I'm interested in writing a book, but not about me", he once asserted.

It is true that Reed's sexuality has always been somewhat fluid, and that both Cale and Reed inflicted an enormous amount of self-destruction through alcohol and hard drugs ("I was really fucked up. And that's all there is to it", Reed candidly admitted in 1989). However, it's also true that both Reed and Cale – and the vast majority of the Factory crowd – gave up drugs for good in the 1980s. Even Nico, the queen of the junkies, was seriously attempting to quit heroin and methadone at the time of her death (which was not drug-related).

Surprisingly, the Velvets managed to survive the weight of their own legend, resulting in solo careers that have been – at the very least – interesting. Some of that solo work is truly great, some of it truly awful – but for all of their excesses and failures, the output of both Reed and Cale mainly displays intelligence, craft, maturity and compassion. Throughout, both have followed the dictates of art and conscience rather than those of the marketplace, and – to paraphrase Reed – have grown up in public. Their story is far from over.

The *NME*'s Mary Harron once called The Velvet Underground "the first *avant-garde* rock band, and the greatest". As Lou Reed pointed out in 1993: "The proof is in the work, and the work is on record".

Peter Hogan, London, 2007

Acknowledgements

I'm indebted to the writings of those who have explored this territory before me, notably Lester Bangs, Victor Bockris, John Cale, Diana Clapton, Peter Doggett, Nat Finkelstein, David Fricke, Mary Harron, Joe Harvard, Clinton Heylin, Nick Kent, M.C. Kostek, Olivier Landemaine, Gerard Malanga, Legs McNeill, Tim Mitchell, George Plimpton, Lou Reed, Chris Roberts, Jean Stein, Dave Thompson, Lynn Tillman, Andy Warhol, Steven Watson, Gillian Welch, Mary Woronov, Michael Wrenn, Richard Witts, James Young and Albin Zak III. Inevitably, many of these accounts contradict each other – as do the faulty and selective memories of the story's protagonists. In every instance, I've weighed the available evidence and used my discrimination to select the version of events that seemed the most probable.

Special thanks to: Ken Clark and Bill Allerton, who tracked down quite a few rarities for me. Bill's record shop Minus Zero is well worth a visit (2 Blenheim Crescent, London W11; Fridays and Saturdays only); Patrick Humphries and Sue Parr, who let me raid their library and provided the occasional moment of sanity; William Higham and Mailan Henning, who both helped with research.

I'd also like to thank the following for sharing their thoughts about the Velvets with me down through the decades, which has undoubtedly influenced the way I've viewed the band: Lawrence Ball, Peter Buck, Chris Carr, Fred Dellar, Steve Ehrenberg, Mick Farren, Neil Gaiman, Debbie Geller, Charles Hayward, Allan Jones, Michael Jones, Nick Kent, Bill MacCormick, Phil Manzanera, Glenn Marks, Dave Marsh, Alan Moore, Charles Shaar Murray, Nico, John Tobler, Pete Townshend and Carol Whitaker. And a few more, sadly no longer with us: Susan Hill, Sean Hogan, Ian MacDonald/MacCormick and John Platt.

General support and maintenance: Tim Broadbent, Murshida Carol Conner, David and Ruth Hogan, Maureen Hughes (and the entire Hughes clan), Paul Johnson, David and Petra Manley-Leach, Matt Martin, Vanessa Morgan, Andrew Sumner, John Tomlinson and Kathy Woods. Special thanks to Andrew Lockett at Rough Guides, for his understanding and patience, and to my editor Andrew Heritage for helping to iron out the bugs and nailing the whole thing together.

Finally, I'd like to thank Ellie and Quinn, for being my mirrors – and for putting up with hearing a lot of music they'd probably rather have avoided.

About The Author

Peter Hogan has written about music, film and other aspects of popular culture for numerous British magazines, including *Melody Maker*, *i-D*, *Vox* and *Uncut*. He is also the co-author (with Alan Moore) of the critically acclaimed graphic novel series *Terra Obscura*. He lives in South London with his wife and son, and numerous imaginary friends.

Part One:
The Story

Prominent Men:
The Early Years

"What we did was unique. It was powerful."

John Cale

Prominent Men: The Early Years
1942–1965

Born during World War II, and raised during the Eisenhower years of the 1950s, the core individuals who would form The Velvet Underground were in many ways typical of their generation in reacting against the cosy assumptions that had determined their parents' world. The countercultural allure of the Beat Generation lifestyle – jazz, drugs, nightclubs, slumming it – was irresistible to Lou Reed and his peers. But, on the other hand, both Reed and John Cale went through extraordinary and often painful experiences in their adolescent years which were to colour their particular form of rebellion, and influence their artistic lives for decades.

Shock Factors

Lewis Alan Reed was born on 2 March 1942 in Brooklyn, New York. His father, Sidney Reed (originally Rabinowitz), was a tax accountant, his mother Toby was a former beauty queen; a few years after Lou's birth they had a daughter, and another son a decade later. The family moved to Freeport, Long Island, when Lou was 11 years old. He'd had some classical piano lessons, but it was at this point that he discovered rock'n'roll via the radio and he demanded that his guitar tutor show him the three chords necessary to play a **Carl Perkins** song, rather than the typical novice's tune 'Twinkle Twinkle Little Star'. By 12 he'd mastered enough guitar

to begin writing his own songs, and his high school doo-wop group The Jades (who later changed their name to The Shades) released a single when Lou was still only 16: he played rhythm guitar on a recording of two of his songs, 'So Blue' and 'Leave Her For Me'. He later claimed his total royalty earnings from the record amounted to 78 cents.

Reed had a suburban middle-class upbringing, attending public school in both Brooklyn and Long Island and, like most Jewish boys, he was bar mitzvahed at the age of 12. But Lou hated his school education, and had a problem with authority from an early age. He argued with his father frequently; when Lou was 17 the fights grew worse, and his parents – suspecting that he might be homosexual (which Lou himself had suspected since his early teens) and concerned about Lou's violent mood swings – sought medical advice. The Reeds' doctor prescribed the then-popular solution of a course of electroshock therapy, three times a week for eight weeks, at **Creedmore State Psychiatric Hospital**. Lou later described the treatment as being "like a very prolonged bad acid trip, with none of the benefits". The treatment failed to cure the mood swings, caused memory loss and badly affected Lou's sense of empathy and identity – all of which may well explain (though not excuse) some of his more anti-social personality traits, and his destructive behaviour towards anyone with whom he became closely involved. It certainly didn't help his family situation – he felt betrayed by his parents, and their relationship took decades to heal. Most witnesses from the time have expressed the view that the Reeds were basically nice people who wanted the best for their son, who had trusted the bad medical advice they were given. On the other hand, Sterling Morrison has said that while he and Lou were at university together Lou's parents were constantly threatening to have him "thrown in the nut-house".

In the autumn of 1959 Lou escaped his family by going to college – to NYU's campus in the Bronx, where he studied music theory for two semesters. He went there simply because he was undergoing postshock therapy nearby. Four times a week he was medicated with tranquilizers, and he was utterly miserable until he transferred to Syracuse University in the autumn of 1960, joining his childhood friend

Allen Hyman (with whom he'd form a band called LA and The Eldorados to play bars and parties). At Syracuse, Reed studied Journalism for one week before switching to Liberal Arts to study music, philosophy and literature, as well as taking courses in directing and the history of theatre. He was expelled from the (compulsory) Reserve Officers' Training Corps after a few weeks, having refused to obey orders from his commanding officer. He cultivated the image of a rebel-cum-poet, one who had been through electroshock and was (to quote a fellow student) "very shocking and evil".

Lou also contributed to a quarterly poetry magazine and operated as a DJ three nights a week for the college radio station, naming his show 'Excursion On A Wobbly Rail' after an improvisational Cecil Taylor piece. He played everything from doo-wop, soul and rockabilly to the free jazz of Ornette Coleman, but his show was too radical for the times and was cancelled within months. As well as his band with Hyman, Reed – heavily influenced by **Bob Dylan** – took up the harmonica and played in a couple of folk groups.

Reed also became friends with another musician, a student from Long Island who'd discovered the guitar at age 12 (already being a proficient trumpet-player), and who shared Reed's passion for electric blues and streetcorner doo-wop: **Holmes Sterling Morrison** (born 29 August 1942). Morrison recognized Reed as a kindred spirit, part of the college's "one percent lunatic fringe". Morrison had played in numerous Long Island bar bands (which he described as "some of the shittiest bands that ever were"); he and Lou occasionally jammed together, but neither took the association too seriously. Morrison soon transferred from Syracuse to New York's City College and he and Reed lost touch; they would meet again in 1965, by accident.

Another big influence on Reed's thinking and personality was his roommate, **Lincoln Swados**, who was highly intelligent, witty and literary – but also agoraphobic, hygienically-challenged and socially inept. Though no one realized it at the time, Swados was actually schizophrenic, and later hospitalized. In a failed suicide attempt in 1964 Swados threw himself under a subway train, losing an arm and a leg in the process. He died in 1990.

Reed also had an active sex life at Syracuse, and had several girlfriends, of whom **Shelley Albin** was the most significant. Their relationship lasted several years, but Reed eventually drove her away. He was frequently unfaithful with other women, and had also begun to experiment with homosexuality. 'I'll Be Your Mirror' is said to have been written for Shelley, though it would be Nico who supplied the title.

At the end of his first year at Syracuse, Lou was placed on academic probation – partly for achieving low grades, partly because the college knew he was smoking marijuana (and had been for years). In addition to this, Lou was being prescribed the tranquilizer Placidyl, and drinking a lot of alcohol; while at Syracuse he also reportedly tried peyote, LSD, magic mushrooms, cocaine, the Codeine-laced cough syrup Turpenhydrate and heroin. He is also said to have sold drugs to other students.

According to Sterling Morrison, prior to the Velvets discovering speed through their association with Angus MacLise, they were primarily "pill people", using downers like Seconal and Thorazine. Reed's drug of choice for many years was amphetamine – in the mid-1970s specifically injectable liquid methedrine. He also claims to have injected himself, in 1966, with "a drug" that made all his joints freeze (doctors suspected that he had terminal lupus).

Reeding And Writing

In one of his professors at Syracuse, Lou found a mentor. **Delmore Schwartz** was a natural-born storyteller who spent as much time teaching in the local bar, the Orange, as he did in the classroom. Lou, who studied creative writing under Schwartz, later called him "the first great man that I had ever met". Schwartz taught his students the value and beauty of language, and in Lou he found an eager student – and a talented one – whom he encouraged to write.

But Reed would never show Schwartz his writing, because the poet hated rock music and although Lou was writing poetry and short stories (and had been since high school), Reed was most interested in writing rock songs. He wanted to see if the medium could be infused with the kind of literary writing he loved, his favourite authors including William Burroughs, Allen Ginsberg, Raymond Chandler, Hubert Selby Jr. and Edgar Allan Poe. (Reed has been known to register in hotels as "Joe Salinger" and "Philip Marlowe".)

Delmore Schwartz (1913–1966)

Delmore Schwartz was a poet, short story writer and essayist, whose Kafkaesque short story "In Dreams Begin Responsibilities" (1937) earned him praise from T.S. Eliot. He edited *The Partisan Review* from 1943 to 1955, and taught the creative writing course at Syracuse from 1962. He apparently told Reed: "You can write, and if you ever sell out and there's a Heaven from which you can be haunted, I'll haunt you". A larger-than-life figure, Schwartz was sadly prone to serious alcohol and amphetamine abuse, and his teaching days were always numbered. Reed tried to contact him a few years after leaving college, but was refused entry to Schwartz's apartment as, by this time, the poet was suffering from acute paranoia. Schwartz died of a heart attack in a cheap hotel in July 1966, aged 53. The failed poet Von Humboldt Fleisher in Saul Bellow's 1975 novel *Humboldt's Gift* is said to be based upon Schwartz. "The smartest, funniest, saddest person I ever met", was how Reed later described him. Reed was to dedicate several songs to Schwartz, including 'European Son'; even years later the poet's ghost featured in 'My House'. When Lou married Sylvia Morales in 1980, their wedding vows were adapted from two of Schwartz's poems.

The subject matter of Reed's short stories included dysfunctional families and gay subculture. One of his stories, "The Gift", the Velvets later accompanied with music at the suggestion of John Cale. Before leaving college Lou had also written both "Heroin" and "Waiting For The Man", their concerns being subjects about which he obviously knew a great deal. It's worth noting that there were no overt pop songs about drugs being written at all at this point – even The Byrds' "Eight Miles High" from a few years later is very vague – and certainly none about addiction outside of old blues songs.

Reed graduated from Syracuse in June 1964 with a BA in English, and two weeks later found himself facing the draft board. He probably avoided military service on medical grounds (having just had his first bout of drug-related hepatitis), but would later claim to have been judged psychologically unfit for the army after requesting a gun and telling the board he was "ready to kill". At the end of that summer, Lou got a job at **Pickwick International Records**, based in their office on Staten Island, as one of the label's in-house songwriters – "a poor man's Carole King", as he later put it. Basically, Pickwick was a copycat label. Whatever the hit vogue of the time was – be it surf music, girl groups or motorcycle songs – Pickwick would churn out a string of records in that style until the fad passed; Lou Reed was one of a small team employed to write the material. In retrospect it seems strange that he would embrace a posture so cynical, but Lou genuinely enjoyed the job and gained a lot of studio experience in the process. He was happy to be working in the music business at all, and hoping it might lead to something more serious.

One of the numerous songs Reed co-wrote for Pickwick was a dance number titled "The Ostrich" (inspired by a fashion revival of ostrich feathers), which was released in late 1964 under the group name **The Primitives**. Pickwick thought the song could be a real hit (the lyrics are great: "you put your head on the floor and have someone step on it"), but they needed to form an actual band that could promote the record for an *American Bandstand*

TV performance. At a party in January 1965, Pickwick executive **Terry Phillips** met two people with long hair he thought might fit the bill: they turned out to be avant garde musicians Tony Conrad and John Cale.

The Welsh Prodigy

John Cale was born one week after Reed, on 9 March 1942 in the mining village of Garnant, South Wales. He was a classical music student and child prodigy – he'd started on piano at the age of seven, and he gave his first performance

At Pickwick International

There are a number of songs known to have been co-written by Lou Reed while at Pickwick, including:

YOU'RE DRIVING ME INSANE – THE ROUGHNECKS
THIS ROSE – TERRY PHILLIPS
FLOWERS FOR THE LADY – TERRY PHILLIPS
WILD ONE – RONNIE DOVE
JOHNNY WON'T SURF NO MORE – JEANNIE LARIMORE
I'VE GOT A TIGER IN MY TANK – THE BEECHNUTS
CYCLE ANNIE – THE BEECHNUTS
THE OSTRICH' B/W SNEAKY PETE – THE PRIMITIVES
TELL MAMA NOT TO CRY B/W MAYBE TOMORROW
– ROBERTHA WILLIAMS
WHY DON'T YOU SMILE B/W DON'T PUT ALL YOUR EGGS
IN ONE BASKET – THE ALL NIGHT WORKERS
DON'T TURN MY WORLD UPSIDE DOWN – ARTIST
UNKNOWN
OH NO, DON'T DO IT – ARTIST UNKNOWN
HELP ME – ARTIST UNKNOWN
BABY YOU'RE THE ONE – ARTIST UNKNOWN
WHAT ABOUT ME – ARTIST UNKNOWN
BAD GUY – ARTIST UNKNOWN

SAY GOODBYE OVER THE PHONE – ARTIST UNKNOWN
I'M GONNA FIGHT – ARTIST UNKNOWN
LOVE CAN MAKE YOU CRY – ARTIST UNKNOWN
MAYBE TOMORROW – ARTIST UNKNOWN
SOUL CITY – ARTIST UNKNOWN
TEARDROPS IN THE SAND – ARTIST UNKNOWN
YA RUNNIN' BUT I'LL GET YA – ARTIST UNKNOWN

According to Reed, another Pickwick song of his, entitled 'Let The Wedding Bells Ring', ended with the characteristically Reedian jet black twist of the song's romantic hero dying in a car crash.

The Story

on the radio aged only twelve. At home, John and his mother Margaret spoke Welsh, though his father Will spoke only English; John always thought of his mother as warm and his father as distant. He eventually learned English in school. Will Cale was a miner in the local colliery, while Margaret was a schoolteacher who stressed the importance of education, particularly as a means of escaping having to work in the mines. She wanted John to be a doctor or lawyer when he grew up; he preferred music as an option. John practised piano every evening, played the organ in the village church and discovered the viola – "the saddest of all instruments" – at grammar school, simply because it was the only instrument free. At the age of twelve he was molested by his organ tutor in the local church, and at around the same age had his first sexual encounter with a local girl, and was also recorded playing one of his own compositions by BBC Radio Wales; at the age of thirteen he toured Wales and Holland playing with the Welsh Youth Orchestra.

At night he educated himself in other kinds of music by listening to Alan Freed playing rock'n'roll on The Voice of America, as well as to Radio Moscow and Radio Luxembourg; his heroes were **John Coltrane** and **John Cage**, yet he dressed like a teddy boy. He'd experienced serious childhood bronchial problems, for which he was given an opium-based sedative and he suffered a nervous breakdown at the age of sixteen. His ambition was to become an orchestral conductor – anywhere but Wales, but preferably in New York.

His first stop was London. Having failed to gain a place at a musical academy, Cale gained a teaching scholarship to Goldsmiths College, which he accepted, even though he had no plans to become a music teacher. Frustrated by the formal classical approach, Cale found himself drawn to more experimental composers such as **Stockhausen** and **John Cage**. He began a correspondence with the latter, and also with **Aaron Copland**. Cale left Goldsmiths College in the Summer of 1963, having won a Leonard Bernstein scholarship to study for eight weeks at the Berkshire Music Center in Tanglewood, Massachusetts, under the tutorship of **Iannis Xenakis**. As his farewell performance at Goldsmiths, Cale performed an experimental piece by LaMonte Young.

Arriving in New York, Cale was surprisingly granted a Green Card by the immigration department, which allowed him to stay in the US indefinitely and also to work there. When his eight-week scholarship was over, Cale inevitably gravitated towards Manhattan, cashing in his return air ticket to pay for a lease on a loft apartment, and working in a bookshop called Orientalia.

On 9–10 September 1963 Cale was one of a relay team of pianists taking part in an eighteen-hour marathon event of John Cage's, each pianist playing the 180-note **Erik Satie** piece 'Vexations' for a total of 840 times (Cale later learned that Andy Warhol had been in the audience for part of the concert, perhaps attracted by the idea of repetition that echoed his own work). Cale and Cage were photographed

LaMonte Young

One of the leading lights of avant garde music in the 1960s, LaMonte Young (b.1935) had been a jazz saxophonist in California in the late 1950s before returning to New York and discovering Arabic and Indian music at the turn of the decade. He'd had an affair with Yoko Ono, and was one of the first musicians to deliberately destroy an instrument on stage. Prior to Cale's joining Young's group, the members included Young, Angus MacLise on percussion (sculptor Walter De Maria also occasionally drummed), Tony Conrad on violin and Young's wife Marian Zazeela on vocals (she also provided "calligraphic light art projections"). This line-up's major piece was entitled 'Second Dream Of The High Tension Line Stepdown Transformer', which experimented with both drone and extremely loud volume. The key piece they worked on after Cale joined was titled 'The Tortoise (His Dreams & Journeys)', an improvisation with parameters which were set each time by Young. One of these was the time factor – the group would already be playing before the audience was allowed to enter the auditorium. Cale does not appear on Young's *Theater Of Eternal Music* album, but the Young archives contain tapes of eighteen months of daily rehearsals, all featuring Cale. Throughout 1965 Cale continued to play with Young, as well as rehearsing with Reed and making his own experimental tapes. He played his last performance with Theater Of Eternal Music in December 1965, the same month the Velvets went public. After Cale's departure, Terry Riley joined Young's group. LaMonte Young's most famous piece is probably 'The Well Tuned Piano': a key work of American minimalism, it is often extended to six hours in performance.

together (which did much for Cale's reputation when the photo appeared in *The New York Times*), and Cage suggested Cale contact LaMonte Young. A few days later Cale took his viola along to his meeting with Young, and was promptly invited to join Young's group, **Theater Of Eternal Music.**

Discovering The Drone

Cale also formed a spin-off duo with Young's violinist Tony Conrad, nicknamed **The Dream Syndicate** (and certainly not to be confused with the 1980s rock group of the same name). The pair experimented with their instruments, adding electric pickups. Cale went a step further, adding electric guitar strings (Conrad was to follow suit, with metal strings) and flattening the viola's bridge to allow three or four strings to be played simultaneously. It allowed him to play a very rich, thick drone – one that could sound like an aeroplane taking off.

The ideal of Young's group was, as Cale later explained, "to sustain notes for two hours at a time". Young's drone-inspired experiments would have a lasting impact on Cale, who would go on to employ similar techniques with The Velvet Underground. "If they were three-chord songs, I could just pick two notes on the viola that really fit for the whole song," he said. "It would give a dream-like quality to the whole thing". Young's group rehearsed seven days a week, six hours a day for the

The Story

duration of Cale's involvement (approximately eighteen months). The newly amplified instruments forced Young to abandon his saxophone in favour of amplified vocals, and the music moved away from its blues/raga direction towards something much louder and harsher. At a private party for Metropolitan Museum curator **Henry Geldzahler**, Young's Theater Of Eternal Music played for an audience that included Jackie Kennedy and Andy Warhol. Cale and Conrad also worked on soundtracks for underground films by their friend, the art-house experimental director **Jack Smith**.

According to Cale, Young funded his music by dealing marijuana – an enterprise that Cale was briefly involved in, and which led to his arrest. He spent one night in prison, but nothing could be proved and charges were dropped. He also narrowly avoided having to go to **Vietnam**, since his Green Card status made him eligible for the draft. Fortunately, at his examination in Spring 1964 he was dismissed as unsuitable on medical grounds – hepatitis, according to biographer Tim Mitchell.

Artistically, Cale quickly grew frustrated with the avant garde. He liked the sense of urgency he had discovered in modern rock'n'roll through listening to Tony Conrad's record collection, once the two began sharing an apartment on **Ludlow Street** on the Lower East Side. (Angus MacLise and underground actor Mario Montez lived in the same building, and underground filmmaker **Piero Heliczer** lived next door.) Cale also avidly listened to Murray the K's radio shows, being especially impressed by **Phil**

Spector's signature "Wall of Sound" production style. It was the time of the **"British Invasion"**, and The Beatles and the Rolling Stones were already rocking America. When he met Lou Reed, Cale was ripe and ready to join them.

The First Outing

The day after meeting Pickwick executive and future Spector collaborator Terry Phillips (real name Philip Teitelbaum), Cale and Conrad turned up at the offices of Pickwick International Records. They brought along sculptor **Walter De Maria**, whom they had recruited to play drums. De Maria was actually a jazz drummer on the side, but he was to gain most acclaim as a sculptor for his 1977 piece *Lightning Field*. It was that day that John Cale and Lou Reed met for the first time. Cale was amazed to discover that the open tuning of 'The Ostrich' – with all the instruments tuned to one note – was effectively the very same approach he'd been using with Young. Cale, Conrad and De Maria refused to sign the slave-labour contracts they were offered by Pickwick, but agreed to play a few East Coast promotional gigs with Reed as The Primitives. This they did, but the *American Bandstand* appearance failed to materialize, and the record flopped.

Meanwhile, Reed had played Cale some of the songs he'd already written that Pickwick weren't interested in, including 'Heroin' and 'Waiting For The Man'. Cale was initially sceptical, since Reed used an acoustic guitar and the songs sounded to Cale's ears like folk music

West Greenwich Village resembled the Parisian Left Bank by the early 1960s, a hangout for artists, musicians, writers and Beatniks, with impromptu gatherings on street corners. Though based in the East Village, Cale and Reed were inevitably drawn towards it

– something in which he had no interest. But he couldn't help but be impressed by both Reed's lyrics and by his ability to improvise intelligent lyrics on the spot. "They were very different, very literate, and he was writing about things other people weren't" Cale observed. He and Conrad had quickly worked out that Reed was the most talented person they had met at Pickwick, Conrad commenting that rock'n'roll "came out of him like sweat".

Though Tony Conrad wasn't really interested in playing rock in the long term himself, he sensed the potential of this meeting and was aware that both Reed and Cale were deeply impressed with each other. For Reed, the discovery that a classical musician from the avant garde would take him seriously was a vindication, and it was clear that the duo's association would last beyond The Primitives.

At this point Reed was still living at home, under strict parental discipline. He was still taking the tranquilizer Placidyl, subject to bouts of depression and still indulging himself in antisocial behaviour – such as trying to provoke drunks into fights. Cale tried to boost his confidence, assuring him that they could make groundbreaking music together.

Shortly afterwards, Tony Conrad moved out of the **Ludlow Street** apartment, and Reed moved in. The two men began to create more music that Pickwick wouldn't have touched with a bargepole, funding themselves with (very) odd jobs: they modelled for photographs of supposed criminals to illustrate sensational and fictitious stories in the supermarket tabloids and sold their blood. Reed did carry on working at Pickwick until September, even though the pay wasn't great.

Ludlow Street was then a rough, drug-dealing neighbourhood. It runs from Canal Street north to East Houston, crossing the Manhattan end of the Williamsburg Bridge on Delancey. The landlord carried a gun when collecting the rent. Electricity came via an extension cable to another apartment. Cale and Reed scavenged the streets for wood to burn as fuel, and lived on oatmeal and, occasionally, chicken giblets for weeks on end. Reed was given to experimentation with what Morrison termed "mad diets" anyway, which may well have had as big an effect on his mental state as any drugs.

Cale had early on rejected the possibility of a sexual relationship with Reed, and was soon beginning to suspect that sharing an apartment with him wouldn't work out. Meanwhile, Reed had introduced Cale to heroin, giving him his first injection (since Cale was too squeamish to shoot up alone). Soon the pair were both suffering from hepatitis as a result of sharing dirty needles, and decided to christen their act **The Falling Spikes**. For both of them, poverty made heroin a weekend pastime only – though both would have recurring bouts of hepatitis over the years.

Improbably, the duo had some success performing Reed's songs as buskers up in Harlem, in front of the **Club Baby Grand** on 125th Street. Reed played acoustic guitar, Cale played viola and recorder. In the course of these adventures they recruited a female vocalist named **Electra,** but it didn't work out (she was unstable, and Cale had an affair with her). Cale claimed that Electra played the sarinda (a stringed Indian lute) so hard that her knuckles bled, because she enjoyed the pain. She was soon replaced by another female vocalist named Daryl, who was another disaster (she was a junkie, who had affairs with both Cale and Reed). The pair were consequently wary of working with women again – something that would overshadow their initial meetings with both Moe Tucker and Nico. The pair were clearly incorrigible, however, as both Reed and Cale had affairs with Nico and also with Warhol superstar **Susan Bottomley,** aka International Velvet.

In April 1965, Reed ran into his old friend Sterling Morrison on the subway, and soon persuaded him to join them, renaming the band The Warlocks in the process. Cale now played bass guitar as well as viola. Shortly afterwards, they added **Angus MacLise** on drums. MacLise was very interested in Asian music and the possibilities of tablas and hand drums; he had, according to Morrison, "radically different ideas about rhythm and percussion". By the sound of it, MacLise would have made the band sound jazzier and more beatnik-orientated. Regardless, it was clear from the start that the music they were making was hardly ordinary pop music and, despite Reed and Morrison's blues grounding, they were determined not to rely on standard blues riffs if they could avoid it. Reed later cited his main guitar influences as being Carl Perkins, Ike

Turner and James Burton; the only one of his contemporaries he'd admit to admiring was The Byrds' **Roger McGuinn.**

They made a demo tape – long since lost – with MacLise, featuring 'Heroin', 'Venus In Furs', 'The Black Angel's Death Song', 'Wrap Your Troubles In Dreams' and an otherwise unknown song titled 'Never Get Emotionally Involved With Man, Woman, Beast Or Child'. On a brief return to London that year, Cale tried to raise interest in the tape – without success – from Marianne Faithfull (who declined to pass a copy on to boyfriend Mick Jagger) and **Miles Copeland.** Cale returned to NYC laden with new records by The Kinks and The Who.

There's also a tape from this era made without MacLise (which would eventually be released on the *Peel Slowly And See* boxed set), simply because Angus had forgotten to turn up that day. MacLise had a particularly fluid concept of time, and was apparently incapable of following any kind of schedule. According to Sterling Morrison, at one gig MacLise carried on playing for half an hour after the rest of the band had left the stage, which to his mind compensated for the fact that he'd arrived on stage half an hour late.

What strikes you most about the Ludlow Street demos on the boxed set is just how folky they are. Despite John Cale's avowed hatred for folk music, the versions of early Velvets songs here sung by him all sound like old English ballads and laments. And the influence of **Bob Dylan** on Reed's vocals is also undeniable.

The Story

Angus MacLise (1938–1979)

A native New Yorker, Angus MacLise graduated from high school in 1956 and went on to study geology at New York University. During vacations he played bongos with jazz groups at resort hotels in the Catskills "Borscht Belt". After a short period in the army he moved to Paris, and founded a small publishing company – The Dead Language Press – with friends Piero and Olivia Holiczer. It published their own poetry, including several books of MacLise's, as well as some by celebrated Beat poet Gregory Corso. MacLise returned to New York in 1960, and the following year joined the LaMonte Young Trio as a drummer, being particularly drawn towards oriental music. He was also a member of New York's neo-Dadaist group Fluxus – a loose collective of experimental artists of all types – and collaborated with fellow Fluxus member Yoko Ono on her piece 'Music For Dance'.

After leaving the Velvets, Angus MacLise remained involved with LaMonte Young for some years, as well as creating his own music. With his wife Hetty and son Ossian, MacLise travelled to India in 1971, moving to Kathmandu in Nepal in 1973.

MacLise released numerous albums of widely varying experimental music throughout his career, now available on compilations such as *The Cloud Doctrine* (2002)

Here he started another small publishing company – Dreamweapon Press – to produce his poetry. He and Hetty also provided the music for a film titled *Invasion Of The Thunderbolt Pagoda* by photographer Ira Cohen (best known for the cover shots on Spirit's 1970 album *Twelve Dreams Of Dr Sardonicus*).

MacLise had long been interested in the kabbalah, and the works of Aleister Crowley. One of his last projects was to write a film adaptation of Crowley's book *Diary Of A Drug Fiend*. He spent most of his last year alive in New York, recording a soundtrack to Sheldon Rochlin's film *Hymn To The Mystic Fire*. MacLise then returned to Kathmandu, where his health worsened. An "intestinal malady" exacerbated by years of drug abuse led him to be hospitalized, but he reportedly ripped out his feeding tubes in the last days of his life. He died of malnutrition on 21 June 1979. In one of the strangest footnotes to the entire Velvet Underground story, MacLise's son Ossian (aka OK) was recognized at a young age as being a *tulku*, the reincarnation of a Tibetan lama. He is now known as Sangye Nyenpa Rinpoche.

Going Underground

Throughout 1965, the band practised and experimented almost constantly, working on arrangements for the songs that would comprise their first album. There was no doubt in Cale's mind that this material was going to last.

"What we did was unique, it was powerful," he stated. It would later surprise him that Reed would claim sole composing credit, as if Cale had been merely an arranger. This would cause many arguments in the years to come. Sterling Morrison maintained that the Velvets' music "evolved collectively". "Lou would walk in with some sort of scratchy verse and we would all develop the music" he explained. "We'd all thrash it out into something very strong. John was trying to be a serious young composer, he had no background in rock music, which was terrific – he knew no clichés. You listen to his bass lines, he didn't know any of the usual riffs, it was totally eccentric". Cale wanted to see if Spector's "Wall of Sound" approach could be re-created with a four-piece band – but in fact, the music they were beginning to make was like no rock music ever heard before. They were also idealistic, intending that no performance should be the same, and that any records they might make should all be recorded live. Throughout that year Cale had also been playing with **LaMonte Young**, and making his own experimental tapes, sometimes with Tony Conrad and MacLise (and, on at least one occasion, Sterling Morrison).

As a band they also played live behind the screen at arthouse cinemas such as the Lafayette Street Cinémathèque, providing improvised film soundtracks for the silent underground movies of director Piero Heliczer, as well as for **Kenneth Anger**'s *Scorpio Rising* and Barbara Rubin's *Christmas On Earth*. At the Cinémathèque, the proto-Velvets also performed in two mixed media "ritual happenings" – 'The Launching Of The Dreamweapon' and 'The Rites Of The Dreamweapon' – which involved movies, slide projections, poetry and music, with the band playing stripped to the waist with their chests painted. In short, they were well-versed in multi-media presentations long before they ever met Andy Warhol.

They gave each other nicknames (Reed was "Lulu", Cale was "Black Jack"), but collectively they remained The Warlocks until they found a better name on the cover of a cheap paperback that Tony Conrad had found in the street. Anyway there were at least two other bands using the Warlocks name at the time, one of which would soon become the **Grateful Dead**. *The Velvet Underground* was the title of a 1963 book by Michael Leigh; the cover would lead one to assume it concerned sadomasochism, but according to Morrison it was about "wife-swapping in suburbia". The cover blurb boasted: "It will shock and amaze you. But as a documentary on the sexual corruption of our age, it is a *must* for every thinking adult". Much the same could be said of the band who adopted its title. But they did so largely because the word "underground" resonated with the world they inhabited in New York – a world of underground films and art – not because of the S&M connotations.

Later in 1965 journalist **Al Aronowitz** – the man who had introduced Allen Ginsberg to Bob Dylan, and Dylan (and marijuana) to The Beatles – became interested in managing the Velvets, and booked them what was their debut gig proper on 11 December 1965 at Summit High School in New Jersey, as support for a band called The Myddle Class. Shortly before the gig, Angus MacLise – dismayed to learn that they were going to be paid (albeit a mere $75 for the whole band) and that his art would thus be corrupted by capitalism – quit the group.

The Café Bizarre on West 3rd Street in Greenwich Village was a major draw for new acts

The Velvets found a last-minute replacement drummer for the Summit gig in the sister of one of Morrison's college friends, Jim Tucker. Her name was **Maureen Anne Margaret Tucker** (b. 26 August 1945). She had grown up with Morrison in his hometown of Levittown, New York, and had known him since the age of ten. Having studied clarinet and guitar, she had eventually decided to try her hand at drumming. When the Velvets approached her, the local band she'd been drumming with – The Intruders – had just broken up. "At that point I was the only one they could grab – the only one with a drum kit", she later recalled. As it turned out, the group had lucked out: Maureen (or "Moe", as she soon became known) had a solid rhythmic approach, inspired by **Bo Diddley**, **Charlie Watts** and the Nigerian drummer **Babatunde Olatunji**. Throughout the early days of the Velvets she continued to work as a data-entry clerk, living in Levittown and commuting into the city to play music in the evenings.

In 1998, Reed described Tucker "one of the greatest drummers in the entire world", but at the time he had his doubts about her ability, as did Cale. They were nervous about having a woman in the band again – and female drummers were a distinct rarity in rock at this point – but the self-confessed "tomboy" Tucker felt totally at home playing pool and drinking beer in all-male company. The fact that she could drive and had the use of her parents' car were also factors in her favour – and the fact that many people who saw the band early on were unsure whether Moe was a boy or a girl added

some real novelty value, according to Warhol film director **Paul Morrissey**.

Supposedly it was Cale who insisted on the need for continued experimentation by making Moe discard the cymbal from her drum kit and play standing up – which gave her a striking visual presence on stage. Her simple but unorthodox approach to rhythm radically affected the Velvets' sense of timing, and was as important a factor as any other in the Velvets' creation of a totally new kind of beat music. In the end, all concerned were utterly convinced: the Velvets had found their drummer. Moe would also become their emotional anchor, a calm centre around which the three men could argue and rage and storm without actually killing each other. In the years after the band broke up, when the others were barely speaking to each other, all of them stayed in touch with Moe. As Lou Reed later put it: "Maureen Tucker is so beautiful. She has to be one of the most fantastic people I've ever met in my life. She's so impossibly great".

The Summit gig went badly. They played 'Venus In Furs', 'Heroin' and 'There She Goes Again'. There was a lot of booing, two girls fainted and, according to Cale, the crowd "fled screaming out of the room". Later that month Aronowitz got them a two-week residency playing the **Café Bizarre** on West 3rd Street in Greenwich Village. The building had once been Aaron Burr's livery stable, and was now a beer and wine joint with a small stage in the back where folk singers would play – as Bob Dylan had done a couple of times when he was first

starting out. The club had an anti-rock group policy, which meant that Tucker wasn't allowed to use a drum kit – just a tambourine. The Velvets played six sets a night (at $5 per member), performing Chuck Berry and Jimmy Reed covers as well as their own material (just before starting the residency they wrote 'Run Run Run' to pad out their set).

They played right through Christmas, but deliberately got themselves booted out shortly afterwards in order to avoid having to endure New Year's Eve there. Having been told not to play another song like 'Black Angel's Death Song' or else they'd be fired, they played it again to open their next set, and got fired. During the residency the underground film-maker **Barbara Rubin** made plans to film the Velvets playing live, and asked her friend **Gerard Malanga** to assist her. Malanga drafted in filmmaker Paul Morrissey to help as well; after both men had been duly impressed by seeing the band play, they returned the next night with Malanga's boss, whose name was **Andy Warhol**. The Velvets were about to become a key part of Warhol's universe.

Andy Warhol (1928–1987)

Andy Warhol (born Andrew Warhola) was already a highly successful and celebrated artist by the time he met the Velvets. The son of Czech immigrants, Warhol suffered numerous childhood ailments, including rheumatic fever and scarlet fever. At the age of eight his already pasty complexion grew worse when his skin lost pigmentation; combined with the dark glasses necessary for his poor eyesight and his fair hair, he appeared practically albino. This was heightened further when he started to go bald at the age of 25 and began wearing a wig (they ranged from brown with grey streaks through grey and silver to pure white).

Warhol graduated from the Carnegie Institute of Technology in 1949, and quickly found work in New York as a commercial artist, illustrating stories for magazines and record covers. This led to work for the advertising world, much of it fashion-related – though Warhol's artfully downtrodden apparel caused him to be known as "Raggedy Andy" on Madison Avenue. His first gallery show took place in 1952, but the fine art world didn't take Warhol seriously until he stopped imitating the Abstract Expressionists and – inspired by Jasper Johns and Robert Rauschenberg – began to develop his own style, around the spring of 1960. He quickly attracted the attention of collectors and gallery owners. By late 1962 – when he had his first New York show – Warhol was producing the work for which he'd become most famous: silkscreened paintings of Campbell's soup cans, Brillo boxes, Elvis Presley and Marilyn Monroe – in short, Pop Art. His choice of such iconic images was no accident: Warhol was fascinated by both the mundane and by celebrity, and in his youth had become obsessed with author Truman Capote to the point of virtually stalking him. Ironically, Warhol soon became as famous as the iconic stars he'd painted. At the opening of his 1965 retrospective exhibition in Philadelphia, he and his entourage were mobbed by a crowd of screaming fans, to the point that all the paintings had to be removed from the museum's walls before it even opened, thus making it an art exhibit without any art. Eventually, Warhol and retinue had to escape the mob via a fire exit to the floor above. The Pop Artist had become a pop star. In the Spring of 1963, Warhol bought a 16mm camera and started making underground movies. His early films were usually plotless and unedited – experimental celebrations of the mundane created by simply training a camera on the subject and leaving it running. Thus *Sleep* (1963) showed Beat poet John Giorno sleeping for six hours; the *Kiss* series (1963–1964) portrayed various couples kissing; *Blow Job* (1963) was a continuous shot of the face of someone supposedly receiving oral sex; whilst *Empire* (1964) showed the same view of the Empire State Building over an eight-hour period. Warhol grew enthusiastic about the possibilities of film, and talked of leaving painting behind.

As a person, some found Warhol manipulative, cold and downright bitchy; yet he inspired enormous affection and loyalty in others. Warhol was gay – though he'd remained a virgin till he was 25, and according to most accounts was more of a voyeur than a participant. His writings reveal a man of genuine wit, warmth and charm, who loved life and people. And there's no doubt at all that he was a hugely talented graphic artist, who was constantly experimenting with new media (hence the films) though not always successfully. Many find his movies unwatchably dull. Warhol's credo at this point was that: "The Pop idea, after all, was that anybody could do anything, so naturally we were trying to do it all. Nobody wanted to stay in one category, we all wanted to branch out into every creative thing we could". And that included rock music.

All Tomorrow's Parties:
The Warhol Years

"*What happens when the Daddy of Pop Art goes Pop Music? The most underground album of all! It's Andy Warhol's new hip trip to the subterranean scene*".

Verve promotional copy for *The Velvet Underground and Nico*

All Tomorrow's Parties: The Warhol Years
1965–1967

In meeting Andy Warhol, the Velvets acquired what few fledgling bands have been lucky enough to achieve: a wealthy patron. In addition, Warhol's Factory, populated by an enormous range of people of varying talents, provided a fertile cross-pollination of ideas and personalities, whilst also constituting a powerful PR machine.

Enter Nico

For John Cale, Andy Warhol's Factory was like entering a fountain of ideas, with "new things happening every day"; for Lou Reed it was "like landing in heaven". Everywhere they turned there were odd characters and odd situations, and Reed would write down in a notebook fragments of what he heard and overheard. Many of these fragments would end up in song; others would suggest a title or a story situation. The Factory crowd also noticed Reed as well. "Everyone was certainly in love with him – me, Edie, Andy, everyone," confessed Factory regular **Danny Fields**. "He was so sexy. Everyone just had this raging crush … he was the sexiest thing going".

Warhol and Morrissey had recently been approached to get involved with setting up a new discotheque in Long Island; the plans would come to nothing (after seeing the Velvets, the club owner hired **The Young Rascals** instead), but at this point Warhol was actively looking for a rock band to play there. Bizarrely (according to Victor Bockris), Warhol had actually contemplated forming his own rock band three years earlier, with LaMonte Young and Walter De Maria.

Seeing The Velvet Underground at Café Bizarre, Warhol liked the fact that Lou Reed looked "pubescent", and that the audience left the gig looking "dazed and damaged" – according to Reed, Warhol saw them the night they were fired. Paul Morrissey claims that it was his idea to marry underground films to rock'n'roll, but that it was a purely commercial decision to work with the Velvets, rather than an artistic one. At the time, Morrissey also thought that Reed and Cale lacked presence, and that what the Velvets needed was a

The Factory

At the end of 1963 Andy Warhol rented a former hat factory on New York's East 47th Street to use as his studio. The 50 x 100 foot loft space was originally known as the Silver Dream Factory (doubtless because of its all-silver decor, created by Billy Name), its title soon shortened to simply the Factory. It would have four different homes over the next two decades.

Here Warhol worked on his silkscreens and paintings, and also made his movies. Billy Name lived there (as did Gerard Malanga, briefly), and many of the initial visitors came specifically to visit Billy – a crowd that was mainly homosexual, and mainly amphetamine users ("fags on speed", as one catty observer put it).

Through the Factory's doors also came Warhol's "superstars": Baby Jane Holzer, Edie Sedgwick, Candy Darling, Ultra Violet, Viva, Ingrid Superstar and many more, all of them desperate to be in Warhol's movies or simply just to hang around. Doubtless they were attracted by Warhol's fame, but the fact that he was totally non-judgmental about others' lifestyles meant that he was genuinely loved. According to Warhol, the crowd came not to see him, but to see each other: "They came to see who came". They also came to see what would happen, in the certainty that something would, even if it was only dinner.

Despite the sign that read "DO NOT ENTER UNLESS YOU ARE EXPECTED", the Factory also had pretty much an open house policy, and attracted more than its fair share of those with alternative lifestyles: drag queens, hustlers and all-purpose exhibitionists all rubbed shoulders with the celebrities and European aristocrats visiting Andy. "Nobody normal would go near the Factory", Cale would later comment. "It was a protective environment for kooks – quite dangerous for your sanity".

In the mornings Warhol worked; in the afternoon

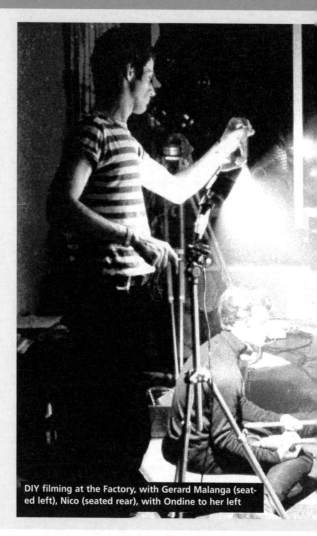

DIY filming at the Factory, with Gerard Malanga (seated left), Nico (seated rear), with Ondine to her left

visitors began to show up and, to quote Henry Geldzahler, the Factory became "a sort of glamorous clubhouse with everyone trying to get Andy's attention". The soundtrack was generally operatic arias, played loud.

It seems strange that the workaholic Warhol surrounded himself with so many people who seemed to lack a sense of purpose. As Mary Woronov noted: "Andy thought if people didn't work they were broken, something was wrong with them". But Warhol the filmmaker preferred to work with people who weren't professional actors. Talent was not a prerequisite for admission; indeed, it sometimes seems pure accident that artists of the stature of the Velvets showed up in the throng as well. Sex was casual among the Factory crowd, as was hard drug use – and with so many drugs and so many people with serious problems, casualties were inevitable. There was violence and paranoia and more than a few overdoses and suicides among them. Photographer Nat Finkelstein somewhat harshly summed the Factory scene up: "Andy bestrode his world like a bleached blond colossus. I witnessed the birth of a monster: a silver sprayed black widow spider: fucking them over, sucking them dry and spitting them out".

That's not a unique view. But how much Andy Warhol ever really knew about what was going on at this non-stop party is debatable. The explanation for Warhol's open-door approach was simple: he liked company to the point of apparently being terrified of being alone, and he was interested in what would come of all this energy, hoping to serendipitously capture it on film or tape.

singer with "a bit of charisma". He suggested someone who was already a part of the Warhol camp: **Nico**.

The suggestion that Nico should join the band didn't go down too well with the Velvets, to put it mildly. Morrissey played them her single on the Immediate label, and according to him Reed was "hostile to Nico from the start". What changed Reed's mind was the fact that Warhol was offering them an enticing management and recording deal. There was of course the recognition that his patronage would bring. In the end, it was too good a deal for the Velvets to turn down. According

Nico (1938–1988)

At the time she "joined" the Velvet Underground, Nico had only recently come under Warhol's wing. She was a German model, actress and singer – or, as Warhol preferred to put it, *"chanteuse"* – born Christa Päffgen in Cologne, six months before the outbreak of World War II. Despite claims of more exotic parentage, both her parents were German. In 1940, she moved to Lübbenau near Berlin with her mother Grete, a tailor; in 1945, they moved into the rubble of bomb-ravaged Berlin. Christa spent the rest of her childhood there; she called it "a desert of bricks", and the image of "the fallen empire" was one she would return to often in her work. Much of Christa's background is hazy, since she was a self-confessed (and inventive) liar, inventing fantastic credentials for her father: he was alternately an archaeologist, Turkish, a friend of Gandhi, a Sufi, or a spy. In reality, Christa was an illegitimate child, and her father Wilhelm was a soldier who was shot in the head by a French sniper in 1943, and then killed by his commanding officer (a standard Nazi treatment for wounded troops).

Life was hard for Christa and her mother, and they were often hungry. There are no existing records to confirm it, but Nico has said that at the age of thirteen, she was raped by an American sergeant. When her mother reported the crime, Christa was forced to testify at the sergeant's trial on multiple rape charges. The

sergeant was convicted and executed. When she was 15, the six-foot tall Christa began an extremely successful career as a fashion model, which took her to Berlin, Paris, Ibiza (where she lived the beatnik life) and Rome. There she had a role in Fellini's *La Dolce Vita* (1959) which would have been larger than it was if Christa

to Nico, Reed agreed simply because he lacked the confidence to refuse – or perhaps, lacked enough confidence in himself as a vocalist. Still, at his insistence the billing would distance Nico from the group, making it crystal clear that she was not a band member. They would be The Velvet Underground and Nico. So Aronowitz was ousted (he'd only had a "handshake deal" – something he subsequently regretted) and Morrissey and Warhol officially became joint managers of The Velvet Underground. In return for 25%, Warhol would invest in new equipment, get them gigs and a recording contract. In fact, after buying

had not been so unreliable about timekeeping. En route she dyed her dark hair blonde, which she claims was at the suggestion of Ernest Hemingway. In 1957, or thereabouts, Christa adopted the name Nico. She later gave many versions of how she came by the name, but the most likely account seems to be that she named herself after Nico Papatakis, a Parisian nightclub owner with whom one of her gay friends was in love; Christa/Nico lived with Papatakis for several years. He took her to New York, where she took singing lessons and attended acting classes with Lee Strasberg (where she claimed to have been in the same class as Marilyn Monroe).

She made another (unremarkable) film in 1963, Jacques Poitrenaud's *Strip-Tease*. She had an affair with the actress Jeanne Moreau, and another with Alain Delon, who she said was the father of her son, Christian Aaron Päffgen (born 19 August 1962), better known as Ari. Although Delon has always denied paternity, others have commented on the resemblance between himself and the grown-up Ari. Although Ari spent some of his childhood with her (including the Factory years), for the most part he was raised by Nico's mother and aunt, and then by his alleged paternal grandmother (Edith Boulogne) and aunt (Didi Soubrier). Meanwhile, Nico went to London, where she dated Brian Jones of The Rolling Stones.

Impeccable credentials, thought Gerard Malanga when he and Andy Warhol met her in Paris in spring 1965. Malanga told Nico to come and visit the Factory if she was ever in New York. Returning to London, Nico recorded a single for Andrew Loog Oldham's Immediate Records: a cover of Gordon Lightfoot's 'I'm Not Saying' b/w 'The Last Mile', written by Andrew Loog Oldham and Jimmy Page. She has also demoed a version of 'I'll Keep It With Mine' with Bob Dylan on piano (he'd written the song for her several years earlier, when they'd had an affair).

But her musical career failed to ignite, and so Nico travelled to Manhattan with the three-year-old Ari that November. She gave Warhol a copy of her Immediate single, which gave Paul Morrissey the idea of wedding her to the Velvets. Meanwhile, Warhol immediately cast Nico in one of his films, *The Closet* (1966). She'd go on to make five more films with him, including *Chelsea Girls* later that year.

Personality-wise, Nico was what was known as "difficult". Dour and brooding, and a confirmed nihilist, she was often depressed (and depressing). Strange and untalkative, she might take five minutes to answer a question. Yet she could also be, as Warhol observed, oddly fascinating: "mysterious and European, a real moon goddess type". Morrissey thought her "the most beautiful creature that ever lived".

two instruments from **Vox**, Warhol got them to supply further equipment for free, having arranged an endorsement deal (the band would later endorse Acoustic, and then Sunn).

But a problem remained: Nico wanted to sing all the songs, which Reed refused point blank to allow. But since her presence meant that some gentler songs were now needed, Reed wrote three ballads for her, which suited her unique, breathy singing style ("like an IBM computer with a German accent", as Warhol put it): 'Femme Fatale', 'All Tomorrow's Parties' and 'I'll Be Your Mirror'. The gentler songs contrasted interestingly with John Cale's experiments in drone-like repetition.

According to Cale, Nico was deaf in one ear (from a perforated eardrum), which caused her to go off-pitch from time to time, much to the band's amusement. "Lou never really liked me" Nico later complained – though that's hard to believe when you listen to 'I'll Be Your Mirror'. She and Reed were lovers early on, and even lived together for a while. Recalling this period, Nico described Reed as "very soft and lovely. Not aggressive at all", and even that "you could just cuddle him like a sweet person". Sterling Morrison was more cynical: "You could say Lou was in love with her, but Lou Reed in love is a kind of abstract concept". The relationship lasted eight weeks, and was supposedly ended by Nico. Cale, meanwhile, had been seduced by **Edie Sedgwick** within 48 hours of arriving at the Factory, and moved in with her for the duration (six weeks) of their relationship. Edie had also had a brief affair with Nico. John Cale has described the material Reed wrote for Nico as "psychological love songs", and even Reed acknowledged her strengths as a performer. Yet after Nico left the Velvets, Reed would write no more songs for her – despite being asked to by both Cale and Nico herself.

Nico had little to do on stage when she wasn't singing except stand stock-still and play tambourine (usually out of time), and at times things could get a little tense between her and the band. Even so, she was a striking vision: dressed all in white in contrast to the Velvets' black attire. Her modelling days had certainly taught her how to strike a dramatic pose. She was also taller than all the men surrounding her and, inevitably, she captured most of the media attention. As Maureen Tucker said: "She was this gorgeous apparition, you know. I mean, she really was beautiful". Critic **Richard Goldstein** described Nico's stage presence as "half goddess, half icicle".

Singing For 'Drella

However little Andy Warhol knew about music (and he never expressed any noted preferences), even he must have sensed that in The Velvet Underground he'd found more than just another rock band. "Andy told me that what we were doing with music was the same thing he was doing with painting and movies i.e. not kidding around" Lou Reed recalled. He was bowled over by Andy's way of looking at the world and once remarked that sometimes he would spend days thinking about something Andy said. Reed was also impressed by Warhol's work ethic: "I'd ask him why he was working so hard and he'd say, 'Somebody's got to bring home the bacon'". Warhol would ask Reed how many songs he'd written that day; Reed would lie and say two. Lou also remarked on Andy's generosity, pointing out that though Andy was the first to arrive for work at the Factory and the last to leave he'd still take them all to dinner: "He gave everyone a chance".

But the exact nature of the group's relationship to their new manager remains vague. As Sterling Morrison pondered: "Was The Velvet Underground some happy accident for him, something that he could work into his grandiose schemes for the show? Would another band have done just as well? I don't think another band would have done just as well. At that time we seemed uniquely suited for each other".

John Cale described Warhol as **"a catalyst"** for the Velvets, that he understood exactly what they were about, how best to bring that out. "I doubt that Lou would have continued investigating song subjects like he did without having some kind of outside support for that approach other than myself" he elaborated. "I think it was just basically Andy and I who really encouraged that side of a literary endeavour". Morrison echoes the fact that Warhol gave them "the confidence to keep doing what [they] were doing".

It's probable that Reed and Warhol each saw echoes of themselves in the other. But Warhol had earned the nickname of 'Drella (a combination of Dracula and Cinderella) that Ondine, another of the Factory crowd, had given him. Warhol had an acid wit that Reed could seldom match, and his jibes were less malevolent than Reed's – they could be bitchy and funny at the same time, whereas Lou was often just bitchy. But as Malanga states, Warhol also had his dark side: "he could slice a person with a glance". In fact, Lou actually came in a poor third to Nico when it came to put-downs. Meeting again shortly after their break-up, there was a moment of frosty awkwardness between the two, followed by a long pause after which Nico came out with the charmless "I cannot make love to Jews any more".

In the end, the Velvets' relationship with Warhol is best summed up by **Mary Woronov**, artist and collaborator: "They were with Andy and Andy was with them and they backed him absolutely. They would have walked to the end of the earth for him". All of the Velvets spoke highly of Warhol ever after, Cale perhaps most succinctly of all: "He was magic".

At this point the Velvets had been ordered by police to stop rehearsing in their West 3rd Street apartment (above a firehouse), and told to rehearse in the country if they were going to make that kind of noise. Cale was experimenting with an electronic "thunder machine" at the time. The same cop had also accused them of throwing human excreta out of their window. So they began to rehearse at the Factory every day, accompanying Warhol in the eve-

The Story

Factory people

Gerard Malanga

A poet and photographer in his own right, Gerard Malanga (b.1943) met Andy Warhol while still a student at Wagner College on Staten Island. He soon became Warhol's assistant in silk-screening (where he probably did most of the actual physical work, and originated at least some of the ideas), also introducing him to New York's literary, theatrical and movie crowds. Malanga also eventually assisted Warhol in his own movie-making. His habit of carrying a leather bullwhip everywhere led to his "whipdance"

routine on stage with the Velvets during 'Venus In Furs' (Malanga had earlier been a dancer on DJ Alan Freed's *Big Beat* TV show). He went on to found *Interview* magazine with Warhol. In 1983, Malanga co-wrote (with Victor Bockris) *Up-tight: The Velvet Underground Story*, the first book to appear on the Velvets.

Billy Name

A photographer and lighting designer who subsidized his artistic work with hairdressing, Billy Name (real name Billy Linich) once decorated his entire apartment

Factory people in party mode: Henry Geldzehler (left) Edie Sedgwick (front), Warhol (in black) and Gerard Malanga (drinking)

with silver foil. Warhol liked the look so much ("Silver makes everything disappear") that he asked Linich to decorate his new studio – the original Factory – in the same way. Billy also worked with Gerard Malanga as an assistant on Warhol's silk screens, designed the cover for *White Light/White Heat*, and claims to have been one of Reed's lovers. Also a musician, Linich was in LaMonte Young's group for a year, leaving them just before the arrival of John Cale. A genuinely eccentric character, Name was effectively the Factory's caretaker, living in one of its black-painted toilets (which he used as a photographic darkroom) for years, studying astrological charts and books on the occult given him by Reed; when the Factory moved home, Billy simply moved into the equivalent space in the new one. In 1968, he sealed himself into this room, and was seldom seen at all between then and the time he finally left the Factory (in the middle of the night) at some point in Spring 1970, leaving a note behind telling Warhol not to worry. Linich subsequently gave up amphetamines, moved back home to Poughkeepsie and pursued his own individualistic spirituality. Today, his photographs of the Factory era are much in demand.

Edie Sedgwick

A Californian debutante from a rich but troubled Bostonian socialite background, Edith Minturn Sedgwick (b.1943) had spent her late teens in a mental institution (as had several of her brothers, two of whom committed suicide). In 1964, at the age of 21, she moved to New York and met Andy Warhol in early 65; for the following year, they were virtually inseparable. She dyed her hair silver to match Warhol's wig and became a kind of mirror image of him, escorting him to society parties and appearing in a dozen of his movies. "She had more problems than anybody I'd ever met", Warhol later said. Perhaps that was the appeal of their relationship, which was certainly not sexual (Truman Capote thought that Andy wanted to *be* Edie).

She became the face of young Manhattan; *Vogue* magazine dubbed her a "youthquaker", and she seemed the archetypal poor little rich go-go girl. Reed wrote 'Femme Fatale' about her (at Warhol's request) and, according to some, Bob Dylan's 'Just Like A Woman' and 'Leopard Skin Pillbox Hat' are both about her. But though undeniably beautiful and pursued by innumerable suitors (including John Cale), Edie was not so much a *femme fatale* as a *femme catastrophique*. She might have been a mainstay of Warhol's movies and danced on stage with the Velvets during their first couple of gigs, but most of the time she was out of her head on a cocktail of drugs of every description, many prescribed by the legendary "speed-doctor" Dr Roberts (immortalized by the Beatles as "Dr Robert"). She later blamed Warhol for her condition. "Warhol really fucked up a great many people's – young people's – lives", she once complained. "My introduction to heavy drugs came through the Factory. I liked the introduction to drugs I received. I was a good target for the scene. I bloomed into a healthy young drug addict". "Edie never grew up", Warhol responded, probably accurately. However, comments of his such as "a girl always looks more beautiful and fragile when she's about to have a nervous breakdown" don't show him in too sympathetic a light. When Edie left him in 1966, Warhol joked bleakly to playwright Robert Heide: "When do you think Edie will commit suicide? I hope she lets us know so we can film it". After Warhol,

Factory people *continued*

Edie attempted to carve a career as an actress (but didn't really have the talent) and a model (but her reputation as an unreliable druggie preceded her), without much success. She died in 1971 of an overdose of barbiturates, at the age of 28.

Paul Morrissey

Underground filmmaker Morrissey (b.1938) had made his own movies ever since his teenage years. As well as managing Warhol's business affairs for many years, from 1966 Morrissey worked closely on numerous movies with him, eventually making several of his own movies under the Warhol banner. The best known of these are the trilogy of *Flesh* (1968), *Trash* (1970) and *Heat* (1972), all of which starred hustler Joe Dallesandro. Morrissey parted company with Warhol in the mid-1970s, after two final exploitation films, *Flesh For Frankenstein* (1973) and *Blood For Dracula* (1974), made with Warhol's backing. He continued to make movies into the late 1980s.

Ondine

Real name Bob Olivo (b.1939) he was also nicknamed "the Pope". Ondine was a manic and charismatic actor and writer, the hub of the amphetamine-driven "Mole People" gay crowd at the Factory. He had nothing to do with the fashionable New York nightclub Ondine's – Olivo had adopted the name of the lead character in Jean Giraudoux's 1939 play *Ondine*, which had been played on Broadway by the iconic Audrey Hepburn. He appeared in numerous Warhol movies, beginning with *Batman Dracula* (1964), and Warhol's

Morrissey filming *Women In Revolt*, with Superstar Jackie Curtis; Warhol dynamically directs

A: A Novel was simply a transcription of tape-recordings of Ondine's speed-fuelled rantings over a 24-hour period. He toured the college lecture circuit during the 1970s, talking about Warhol and screening his performances in Warhol's S&M movie *Vinyl* (1965) and *Chelsea Girls* (1966). In the 1980s, he appeared in numerous off-off-Broadway plays, until ill health forced him to retire. After Ondine's death from liver failure in April 1989, his mother burnt all his writings.

Brigid Polk (Berlin)

Brigid Berlin (b.1939) and her sister Richie, who also hung out at the Factory, were heirs to the Hearst pub-

The Story

lishing empire. Brigid created montage "trip books" – scrapbooks of anything that took her fancy, the most extraordinary containing the impressions of the scars, genitalia, breasts or navels of anyone willing to contribute. She appeared in *Chelsea Girls* (1966), and also with Edie Sedgwick in the film based on the Factory crowd *Ciao! Manhattan* (1972) She tape-recorded pretty much everything she encountered, from phone calls to orgies. This led to her taping Lou Reed's last concert with The Velvet Underground in 1970 – eventually released commercially as *Live At Max's Kansas City* in 1972. Her "Polk" nickname evolved from Factory slang – "taking a poke" meant shooting up with a needle. Berlin gave up amphetamines and alcohol in the 1980s.

Mary Woronov

Mary Woronov (b.1943) was an art student at Cornell University when she met Andy Warhol and became involved with the Factory. She was one of the principal dancers with The Exploding Plastic Inevitable, accompanying Gerard Malanga's whipdance to 'Venus In Furs'. Having appeared in Warhol's movies *Hedy The Shoplifter* and *Chelsea Girls*, Woronov moved to Los Angeles and acted in a zillion B-movies, of which the most notable is probably Roger Corman's *Death Race 2000* (1975). She revealed herself as a talented comedy actress in *Rock And Roll High School* (1979), and Paul Bartel's black comedies *Eating Raoul* (1982) and *Scenes From The Class Struggle In Beverley Hills*

Andy and entourage, left to right, Candy Darling, Ultra Violet and Brigid Polk

(1989), as well as making cameos in mainstream Hollywood movies. Liver damage caused her to give up all drugs and alcohol in the 1980s. She has been a writer-director for the TV show *The Women's Series* and is the author of four volumes of fiction: *Snake*, *Niagara*, *Blind Love* and *Wake For Angels*, which also contains some of her paintings, and *Swimming Underground* (a memoir of her time with the Factory).

The Story

nings to art openings, cocktail parties, dinners and nightclubs, as part of his permanent 10–20-strong retinue. It's doubtful whether the drug-free Tucker tagged along, and she must have been somewhat bemused by the Factory's denizens. (They in turn liked the fact that she looked boyish, which fitted right in with all the blurring of gender going on there.) Later on, Moe worked at the Factory briefly, transcribing tapes of Ondine's rantings for Warhol's book *A: A Novel*. However, she refused to type any of the swear words, substituting asterisks instead. Meanwhile, Ondine had turned Lou Reed on to methedrine, which became his main indulgence for years to come.

The Exploding Plastic Inevitable

Reed relished the idea of the mayhem the Velvets might create in a large venue, and spoke of using hundreds of car horns and playing in the dark, and persuading Morrison to play the trumpet. But it never happened. The Velvet Underground would play their first gig with Nico – while Warhol's movies played behind them and Gerard Malanga and Edie Sedgwick danced on stage – in early Spring, at the **New York Society of Clinical Psychiatrists**' annual banquet at the Delmonico Hotel. "It seemed like a whole prison ward had escaped", one of the nation's top 100 psychiatrists commented, while another described the event as "decadent Dada". A week or so later, the Velvets played at the Cinémathèque (now on 41st Street), again providing a soundtrack to Warhol movies, including one of themselves. That month the Velvets also recorded improvisational soundtracks for two of Warhol's short movies, *Hedy The Shoplifter* and *More Milk Yvette*.

These live events were the prototype for Warhol's touring "total environment" show, of which The Velvet Underground were the core. Between February and April 1966 the ensemble went through a succession of names: Andy Warhol's Up Discotheque soon became Andy Warhol's Uptight (a word with positive connotations at this point – as in the Stevie Wonder song). This was finally renamed **The Exploding Plastic Inevitable** or simply **EPI** by Paul Morrissey (it was very nearly The Erupting Plastic Inevitable, which sounds a lot more painful). Apart from the Velvets, the show also featured projections of Warhol's films by Morrissey (including footage of Nico and the Velvets), "interpretive dance" by Gerard Malanga with **Ingrid Superstar** and/or Ronnie Cutrone and Mary Woronov. For 'Venus In Furs' Malanga and Woronov – dressed in matching black leather trousers – would play out a mock S&M scenario, with Malanga grovelling at his partner's feet, kissing the whip she held and her leather boots. For 'Heroin', Malanga would do mock injections with a huge pink plastic syringe (as used for icing cakes).

A key ingredient of the EPI was its light show – a mixture of liquid slides and strobe lights. In all there were five movie projectors (to show Warhol's movies), five carousel slide projectors, and various spotlights and coloured strobes. Added to this was a silver mirrored ball brought from the Factory, which had once hung in a speakeasy and had been bought in an antique shop; when the EPI played the Dom (see below), the ball hung over the Velvets' heads, and when spun it caught and fragmented the strobe lighting. Within a month, every discotheque in New York had one like it, and the disco glitterball was born.

According to Reed, all this was Warhol's idea.

He has also claimed that both he and Cale started wearing dark glasses on stage simply to defend themselves against the effects of the strobes (which can induce epilepsy in some and have also been known to cause heart attacks). **Danny Williams**, who ran the EPI light show, would subject himself to watching strobes for hours on end, as an experiment. He later committed suicide, though whether the strobes had anything to do with his mental state remains a

The EPI in full swing, with light show, projectors and glitterball

The Story

matter for speculation. Whatever money the EPI earned from a gig was always divided equally – you got the same amount whether you were a guitarist, a dancer or the projectionist.

According to Morrison, "we just played and everything raged about us, without any control on our part". The effect of all this mixed media many found overwhelming – though it might well look tame by today's standards. Back then audiences had never seen anything like it. "At the Plastic Inevitables it is all Here and Now and the Future", wrote underground filmmaker **Jonas Mekas** in *Village Voice*. **Marshall McLuhan** included a photo of the EPI in his book *The Medium Is The Message* (1967) as an example of the evolving world.

The show took to the road in March (with Nico driving them all in a microbus, much to everyone's general terror) to play two more "rehearsal" gigs at Rutgers College (where the Velvets all wore white, while Malanga danced while twirling flashlights) and the University of Michigan (where Warhol discovered the strobe lights). That month, fashion designer **Betsey Johnson** asked Warhol to come up with something for the opening of her hip clothes boutique Paraphernalia. Warhol provided floating (helium-filled) silver pillows, with music provided by the Velvets.

The Exploding Plastic Inevitable made their "official" debut in April 1966 at a club called The Polsky Dom Narodny (or simply "**The Dom**" – "home" in Polish), in the old Polish National Social Hall on St. Mark's Place in the East Village. At the time, this was a very unfashionable neigh-

bourhood, nicknamed "Babushkaville" on account of its largely East European population. Warhol took a month's lease on the club and had the place completely repainted and hung with screens for the movies and light show. "Do you want to dance and blow your mind with The Exploding Plastic Inevitable?" asked the ad in *Village Voice*. 750 people came the first night; while he was on stage, Lou Reed's collection of 1950s doo-wop singles was stolen from his apartment. Within days, Maureen Tucker's tom-toms were also stolen from the Dom, so she miked up two garbage cans and played those for a week. Tucker was still holding down a day job, and living with her parents.

At this time Warhol was riding high. His film *My Hustler*, made the previous year, was showing uptown, and his exhibition of floating silver pillows and yellow and pink cow wallpaper was showing at the Castelli Gallery – this being supposedly his "farewell" to Fine Art. Additionally, Nico was attracting a lot of media coverage. So all of New York's celebrities – from **Jackie Kennedy** on down – came to the Dom to check out what Warhol and this chic new singer were up to. On most nights the place was packed, and the Warhol coffers accordingly swelled with cash. For four performances the avant-garde hillbilly violinist **Henry Flynt** substituted for Cale while the latter was sick. **Salvador Dalí** apparently joined the EPI on stage several times. One night Lou Reed was almost electrocuted by a live microphone (and would have been, if not for a shouted warning from Morrison). On another occasion **Allen Ginsberg** joined the Velvets on stage and chanted Hare Krishna mantras. All this countercultural activity at the Dom was a catalyst for change around St. Mark's Place and the East Village, transforming it in the process from cultural wasteland to hip hangout.

As Andy Warhol later commented: "We all knew something revolutionary was happening. We just felt it. Things couldn't look this strange and new without some barrier being broken". But many were appalled by the Velvets' flirtation with decadence. Critic **Richard Goldstein** described their sound as "the product of a secret marriage between Bob Dylan and the Marquis de Sade". Reviews of the shows were almost uniformly negative (some were included on the inner sleeve of the first Velvets album, which is indicative of the fact that the band were perversely proud of them), and the following month the EPI experience went down like a lead balloon when they played a month-long stint in Los Angeles. At their first night at The Trip on Sunset Strip they were supported by **Frank Zappa's Mothers of Invention** and attracted a celebrity crowd (including Sonny & Cher, Mama Cass, several Byrds and **Jim Morrison** – whom Gerard Malanga would later accuse of stealing his leather-trousered image), but by the second night the crowd had dwindled greatly. The club was closed down by police on the third night for disturbing the peace with the Velvets' "pornographic exhibition". It stayed closed because of a lawsuit between the owners and in order to get paid at all Warhol and the whole EPI had to fulfil

Chanteuse Nico, with Malanga's whip to the fore

Musicians Union conditions and wait out the rest of the month in LA. As it was, it took them three years to get the money.

The EPI then played two nights at **San Francisco's Fillmore**, which confirmed that the East Coast crowd had nothing in common with the Haight-Ashbury scene, and where Malanga was arrested for carrying his whip in public. It was also in San Francisco that Reed injected himself with the drug that caused him to be wrongly diagnosed with terminal lupus (it turned out to be hepatitis).

Returning to New York Warhol discovered that they'd missed the chance to buy the lease

The Story

of the Dom, which had been snapped up instead by Bob Dylan's manager, **Albert Grossman**. The Dom was renamed the Balloon Farm (later becoming the Electric Circus), and went on to make a fortune. The Velvets played there once, grudgingly, resenting the fact that the Dom had been swiped from under their noses. The financial loss involved for the Warhol/Velvets camp would have a dire impact on the marketing of the band's first album.

Into Vinyl

By this point the Velvets had already recorded their debut album. In April 1966, Andy Warhol approached a 27-year-old Columbia sales executive named **Norman Dolph**, whom he'd met when the latter acted as DJ at a Warhol exhibition in Philadelphia. Warhol asked Dolph to find a studio for the Velvets, produce a session and help get them a record deal. Dolph rented

Hold it right there!
Reed directing Nico
whilst recording the
first album

the 4-track studio belonging to the small independent New York label **Scepter Records** for three nights during the week of 18–23 April. The engineer at Scepter was **John Licata**, a seasoned professional. Dolph claims to have overseen the session, but has given credit for most musical decisions made there to John Cale and Sterling Morrison.

According to Moe Tucker, the sessions lasted for a total of eight hours, which was all they could afford, pooling their money with Andy. According to Norman Dolph, they had four working days, which included playback time and mixing. It was a total of probably fewer than sixteen hours, of which the actual recording time was more like ten. Dolph also invested money of his own for the sessions (and was repaid with a Warhol painting). Total studio costs have been estimated at between $1,500 and $3,000. Whatever the amount, it seemed scandalously high to Warhol, according to Morrissey – but then Warhol was accustomed to making movies that only cost a couple of hundred dollars apiece. In fact, in 1966 the average cost of making an album was $5,000, and many other "masterpieces" of the era cost considerably more.

According to Cale, the studio was not Scepter, but **Cameo-Parkway** on Broadway, which he claims was practically a building site. One explanation for this discrepancy in memory is that the group may have tried Cameo-Parkway before moving to Scepter, having found the former unacceptable. Then again, Cale thought Dolph was a shoe salesman, so he's not that reliable a witness.

Nominally, the album was produced by Andy Warhol, but in reality there was no producer – just Dolph, Licata and the band. So, why is Warhol credited? "The advantage of having Andy Warhol as a producer was that because he was Andy Warhol they left everything in its pure state" said Reed. "And so, right at the very beginning we discovered what it was like to be in the studio and record things our way, and have essentially total freedom". Given Reed's controversial lyrics, this freedom was necessary. "Andy made a point of trying to make sure that the language remained intact" Lou explained. "I think Andy was interested in shocking, in giving people a jolt and not to let them talk us into taking that stuff out in the interest of popularity or easy airplay. He said, 'Oh, you've got to make sure you leave the dirty words in'. He was adamant about that. He didn't want it to be cleaned up, and because he was there it wasn't". According to Dolph, Warhol sat quietly in the back of the control room, "observing, making the occasional wry comment … he was more of a presence, really".

Warhol's initial idea had been to get a manufacturing and distribution deal and market the record himself. But in 1966 this approach was virtually unheard of (and certainly when adopted by fine artists without any music biz experience), so instead he attempted to interest an established label in the album. But Reed's lyrics and the band's image were too daunting for both **Atlantic** and **Elektra**, and no deals were forthcoming. Then **Tom Wilson**, a young black producer at Columbia, heard the record. He'd worked with many old jazz artists and young folkies, producing groundbreaking tracks like 'Sounds Of Silence' for Simon & Garfunkel and 'Like A Rolling Stone' for Bob Dylan. Wilson was leaving Columbia to set up a rock division for the jazz label **Verve** (whose only other rock signing was **The Mothers Of Invention**) and he offered the Velvets a deal, buying the tape outright. At Reed's insistence, all money went directly to the Velvets, who would pay Warhol his percentage later on (which upset Warhol, who saw it as a betrayal – he also always claimed he never earned a penny from the record).

But Wilson wanted some changes. After the group eventually signed to Verve, they re-recorded three or four songs at **TTG Studios** in California, where producer Wilson was assisted by engineer Omi Haden (sometimes credited as Ami Hadani). Wilson also felt there was "not enough Nico". For him, she was the star attraction, and probably the reason why he signed the band in the first place. So a third session took place in New York, which Wilson produced and MGM paid for, which yielded one more track: 'Sunday Morning'. The song was written after one all-night Saturday party, with Cale tinkering about on a small pump-organ while Reed improvised the lyrics. Though Wilson wanted Nico to sing the song, once in the studio, Reed insisted that he sung it instead.

The Power Of Negative Promotion

Although Wilson would go on to produce her first solo album, *Chelsea Girl*, Nico and the Velvets would part company long before the first Velvets album's release – which was delayed and delayed until the following Spring. This was due in part to Verve's nervousness about the subject matter, to the almost inevitable production problems with the cover's peelable banana sticker (see p.139) and lastly to the fact that **Herb Cohen**, manager of The Mothers of Invention, made sure their album was the first rock album to come out on Verve. At one point Verve even claimed to have lost the master tapes. In 1966, the year they were "hot", the only Velvet Underground products actually made available to the public would be 'Noise' and 'Loop' (one live and one improvisational feedback-based piece given away free with – respectively – *East Village Other* and *Aspen* magazine) and two edited singles taken from the forthcoming album ('All Tomorrow's Parties' b/w 'I'll Be Your Mirror' and 'Sunday Morning' b/w 'Femme Fatale') which Verve failed to promote at all. If they'd had a more aggressive manager, who would have pressured Verve for results, things might have been different – but Warhol wasn't that kind of businessman, and he had no experience of how the music industry worked. He did, however, create one of the best album covers of all time for them.

When the album was finally released, Verve

Frank Zappa's band were the Velvets' only rock stablemates in the early days at Verve. Zappa's first album was arguably just as subversive, original and ultimately influential as the Velvets' debut would be.

spent very little on promotion, and what promotion there was touted the album as a Warhol artefact. One Verve ad read: "What happens when the Daddy of Pop Art goes Pop Music? The most underground album of all! It's Andy Warhol's new hip trip to the subterranean scene". Another featured a large photo of Warhol and ran "So far underground … you'll get the bends!" Far from giving them credibility, their association with Warhol meant that many critics refused to take the band seriously at the time, assuming the whole thing was just a camp put-on. As Sterling Morrison put it: "We gained all his enemies – the people who thought he was a faker thought we were fakers".

It was also widely assumed that all the Velvets were gay, or else S&M sex maniacs. Or both. What few reviews they got were bad, regarding the band's songs about drugs and sex as proof of true evil; the fact that Reed had used a first-person narrative prompted many listeners to assume the songs were autobiographical, rather than simply using a literary perspective.

Then came what Morrison has called "the crowning moment of doom". **Eric Emerson**, one of the Factory crowd, sued Verve for using a photo of him without his permission on the album sleeve (he was part of a crowd scene). Emerson had been arrested for possessing a large amount of LSD and needed money for legal costs – suing Verve seemed an easy way of getting it. Instead, Verve responded by recalling some copies of the album, stickering others, and reprinting the cover with Emerson's face airbrushed out – all of which caused a further delay in distribution. Eric Emerson died of a drug overdose shortly afterwards.

What with one thing and another, the record (comparatively speaking) sank without trace, though its time would eventually come. Between the recording of the first album and its release, the Velvets continued to tour, while growing increasingly frustrated. In June 1966, they played a series of dates at a club in Chicago called **Poor Richards** while Lou Reed was laid up with that bout of hepatitis. Angus MacLise was briefly re-recruited on drums, with Moe Tucker switching to bass and guitar, freeing Cale for keyboards and viola. He also took all the lead vocals – the first time he'd ever sung in front of an audience, and it built up his confidence. For obvious reasons, Reed wasn't too happy with this line-up (captured on film by **Ron Nameth**), though Sterling Morrison felt it had real potential. The gig itself took place in 106 degree heat, and the lack of Reed and Warhol (who was busy elsewhere) infuriated the local media. Despite this, the band were asked to stay on for an extra week, much

The Story

to Reed's annoyance.

The most bizarre gig of the EPI came in November 1966, when they took part in the highlight of Detroit's "Carnaby Street Fun Festival": the "Mod Wedding" of Gary Norris (an artist) and Randi Rossi (an "unemployed go-go dancer"). Warhol gave the bride away, while the Velvets improvised (though Tucker denies the rumour that they actually played 'Here Comes The Bride'). The couple also won a screen test at the Factory. But Warhol rapidly lost interest in touring with the EPI, and a distance grew between them and the band. When Warhol went to Cannes to promote his *Chelsea Girls* film, he didn't even consider taking the Velvets along for the ride; instead, they were left to play to confused (and occasionally hostile) teenage audiences in Middle America.

An improvisational piece conceived during this period called 'Searchin' would eventually metamorphose into 'Sister Ray' (sometimes performed live with an improvised prelude titled 'Sweet Sister Ray', both parts being of indeterminate length). In April 1967, the Velvets played a new New York club on the Upper East Side called **The Gymnasium**, where they were supported by a group that included future Blondie guitarist **Chris Stein**. But hopes that The Gymnasium could become another Dom fell flat, and the following month the EPI played their last gig at the Scene club. In fact, the Velvets didn't play New York again until 1970 – local radio stations had ignored the first album, so Reed decided to withdraw their presence from the city.

In this period their world also went through some major changes. Firstly, Nico was elbowed out. She'd gone to Ibiza (to model), then Paris

Nico stoned with a Stone at the Monterey Festival in 1967

(to visit Ari) and then London (where she outstayed her welcome as Paul McCartney's houseguest). Returning to the States, she travelled to Boston to rejoin the Velvets – but when she arrived late for the gig, the band simply refused to let her on stage. According to some accounts, the band had already played all the songs Nico might have sung, and had only a couple of numbers left in their set. It's also been claimed the gig in question was in Cincinatti. Regardless, this was basically the end of Nico's involvement with the band, and Warhol for one felt she had been treated badly.

Nico then travelled briefly to California, where she attended the Monterey Pop Festival with **Brian Jones** (and had a fling with **Jimi Hendrix**). In Los Angeles she resumed an affair with Jim Morrison she'd begun in New York earlier in the year. Nico and Morrison were together for about a month. They took peyote together in the desert, and fought loudly when they were both drunk. Morrison showed her how he wrote lyrics, and encouraged her to write her own songs; she dyed her hair red to please him. In San Francisco she bought herself an Indian harmonium, and began to teach herself how to play (after a fashion). Supposedly **Ornette Coleman** gave her her first lessons.

Returning to New York, Nico played a series of gigs downstairs at the Dom. At the earliest of these gigs Nico sang along to a backing tape of Reed playing, until someone finally took pity on her and pulled out a guitar; she was subsequently accompanied by various guitar players including Cale, Reed, Morrison, Tim Hardin, Tim Buckley, Ramblin' Jack Elliott and the 18-year-old **Jackson Browne** (with whom she had an affair). According to some accounts, Warhol films were also shown, and the gigs had the umbrella title of "Andy Warhol's Mod Dom". According to Morrison, these gigs coincided with a period of Velvets inactivity; when they resumed touring, Nico was still booked for three more weeks at the Dom, and chose to go solo rather than rejoin the band. Relations seemed to remain good, however, and just after the first Velvets album was released Nico was recording her first solo album *Chelsea Girls* with the aid of Browne and producer Tom Wilson... plus, perhaps surprisingly, Lou Reed, John Cale and Stirling Morrison. But with Nico's departure, the band felt less musically compromised, and Tucker for one was glad to see her go. "To me she was just a pain in the ass" she admitted.

More painfully, in late Summer 1967 the Velvets parted company with Andy Warhol. He had taken the band a long way but he had no experience of the wider rock world, and Reed decided he could take them no further. "When he told me I should start making decisions about the future, and what could be a career, I decided to leave him" Reed described. "He did not try to stop me, legally or otherwise. He did, however, tell me that I was a rat. I think it was the worst word he could think of". Until the writing sessions for *Songs For Drella*, more than two decades later, John Cale wasn't even aware that it was Reed who had instigated this parting of the ways: "I thought Andy quit".

I Can't Stand It:
Falling Apart

"You can't walk around with anger in your heart. It causes very negative things."

Lou Reed

I Can't Stand It: Falling Apart
1967–1970

The year or so working with Warhol had been a rollercoaster ride and an extraordinary launch for a new – and very different – band. It also provided some hard lessons in music biz pragmatism, lessons which, despite Nico's departure, would place new strains on the band, and create new tensions within it.

Replacing Andy

The Velvet Underground now needed someone to assume Andy Warhol's role as manager (and hopefully improve upon it). Recognizing that they needed a businessman – rather than a creative artist – to talk to the music business, in the summer of 1967 they appointed **Steve Sesnick**, a fast-talking Boston club owner, to look after their affairs. He had already worked on the band's behalf in California, and was thus a known quantity. One of Sesnick's first moves was to contact The Beatles's manager, **Brian Epstein**, in the hopes of landing a deal for the Velvets' songs with Epstein's publishing company – but despite Epstein liking the Velvets' album, nothing resulted from it. Epstein did supposedly set up a European tour for the Velvets later on in 1967, but he died just before the contracts were signed and so the tour fell through.

But Sesnick did produce some immediate results. He persuaded Verve/MGM to underwrite the Velvets' tour expenses by paying for transportation and hotels, which meant that the band were able to keep more of the cash they earned by playing live – a vast improvement on their situation with Warhol, where they subsisted on *per diem* allowances. As a result of Sesnick's Boston connections, they frequently played his club, **The Boston Tea Party**, over the next few years, where they acquired a fanatical local devotee in one Jonathan Richman. The most bizarre gig they played in Boston came in October 1967, when they spent one entire weekend as the opening act for each screening of the notorious Roger Corman LSD movie *The Trip*, starring Peter Fonda, and conceived by Jack Nicholson.

Touring provided the Velvets' only income, since they were receiving no record royalties at all. Even if they had been, their album wasn't

Jonathan Richman

Jonathan Richman (b.1951) was an avid Velvets fan, who saw them on their every visit to his native Boston. He claims to have attended over 100 live shows, as well as watching the group rehearse, and both photographed the band and made a short colour home movie. In fact, it was said that he had been to more Velvets gigs than they had. Richman would later form his own group, the proto-punk

Modern Lovers, whose first album was partly produced by Cale. Richman's first pro music gig would be supporting the Velvets (while using Morrison's guitar), and during his first sojourn in New York he slept on Steve Sesnick's couch. He later recorded with Moe Tucker, and penned the tribute song 'Velvet Underground' on his album *I, Jonathan* (1992).

selling brilliantly (and certainly wasn't getting any airplay – 'Heroin' was widely banned, and so the rest of the album was ignored by DJs). So, they had to tour almost constantly – and would do so for the rest of their brief career – but this touring was confined to the USA. Plans to go to Europe the previous year with the EPI had come to nothing, and another chance fell through when the Italian arthouse director **Michelangelo Antonioni** decided that flying The Velvet Underground to London to appear in his film *Blow-Up* would be too expensive, and memorably, if only briefly, used The Yardbirds instead.

Though the Velvets were all happy with the choice of Sesnick at the time, that was something that would change – drastically. Suffice to say that John Cale later called Sesnick "a snake", and Lou Reed subsequently placed the blame for "destroying" The Velvet Underground squarely on Sesnick's shoulders. Cale claims that Sesnick drove a wedge between Reed and the rest of the band, by inflating Reed's position as "the song-writer", and thus the most important member of the group. Morrison claimed that he had his doubts about Sesnick's handling of the band's finances, while Tucker thinks Sesnick simply had unrealistic goals for the Velvets, wanting them to be the next **Beatles** and so turning down offers that he should have accepted.

Reed and Cale also drifted further apart as Cale became involved with the successful fashion designer Betsey Johnson, whom he met again in May 1967. Johnson was a successful woman who spoke her own mind – which may well have not gone down well with Lou Reed. Then again, Reed's coolness may have been simple jealousy – and he had no serious relationship of his own.

Betsey Johnson

Betsey Johnson (b. 1942) had been at Syracuse University with Lou Reed and Sterling Morrison (whom she had also dated in 1966 – though not seriously, according to Cale). She became the fashion designer for the "youthquake" hip clothes boutique Paraphernalia (left), at the opening of which the Velvets played in early 1966, with a scaled-down version of the EPI. She eventually designed suits for all four Velvets (grey suede for Lou, dark green and maroon velvets for Sterling and Moe, sober black for Cale), but after she and Cale became involved she designed numerous clothes for him, with the result that Cale now cut a much more stylish figure than the other Velvets – which may also not have gone down well with Reed. She and Cale married in 1968 but divorced within three years. In 1969, she opened her own boutique, Betsey Bunki Nini, on the Upper East Side, where Edie Sedgwick was her house model. She went on to build a fashion retail empire with over 45 stores around the world.

Sonic War

The Velvets had written very few (if any) new songs during their time with the EPI, and the material they eventually came up with for their second album is certainly not as immediately user-friendly as their debut. Cale was keen to keep the Velvets' edge sharp ("I had no intention of letting the music be anything other than troublesome to people"), and later admitted that – creatively speaking – he and Reed were "at each other's throats" during this period, something he blames largely on the stress of

the touring life. The band were virtually under siege: no Warhol patronage, no radio airplay and pretty much directionless, watching bands who'd once supported them overtake them on the road to success. Amazingly, although touring gave them little time for rehearsal (let alone experimentation), they still managed to write enough material for their second album – though as Cale admits, "the incoherence of [their] thinking about where the band should go started laying claim to a lot of [their] time". On another occasion he complained that they "lost [their] patience and diligence. [They] couldn't even remember what [their] original precepts were".

Quarrels about musical direction would lead to Cale's departure within the year. They were protracted, and loud, and occasionally turned into **fist fights** between Cale and Reed. Tucker, according to Morrison, "always said there was no reasoning with any of [them], that [they] were all crazy, and there was no sense in arguing". He thought that "basically the band had three uncontrollable personalities" and that when you "throw drugs into the confusion, then you really have problems". One of these problems, Morrison explained, was that the others never knew how Lou Reed was going to react. His mood could range unpredictably from "boyishly charming" to "vicious", depending on what drugs or diet he on. "He was always trying to move mentally and spiritually to some place where no one had ever gotten before", Morrison ventured. Reed was deeply interested in **astrology** during this period, under the influence of Billy Name (an occasional partner of Reed's, with whom he would go to gay bars).

In September 1967, the group began recording *White Light/White Heat*, their second album. Out of all their energetic antagonism was born a record that M.C. Kostek accurately described as sounding like "sonic war", with Cale, Reed and Morrison challenging each other at every turn. Though it stays in the same urban reality that Reed had been exploring for years, that reality now sounded a lot more menacing. The record is distinctly

uneasy listening, delivered at loud volume and high speed, like heavy metal with brains (and a lot of problems). As John Cale later admitted, "It was a very rabid record. The first one had some gentility, some beauty. The second one was consciously anti-beauty". Cale also admitted that the album had been fuelled by "a great deal" of drugs, including heroin.

That month also saw the completion of Andy Warhol's film ****, in which John Cale made a cameo appearance. John and Betsey spent the Christmas period travelling – first to the Virgin Islands and Spain (where Cale bought a sword-stick and his first gun), then on to Wales so that Betsey could meet his parents. The couple were due to marry in February 1968, but the wedding had to be delayed until April, as Cale was quarantined in hospital for four weeks with suspected hepatitis. After John's liver was finally pronounced healthy, the Cales' wedding was attended by Reed, Nico, Billy Name, Andy Warhol and most of the Factory crowd.

Shortly before his illness, Cale played a one-off gig in January 1968 with LaMonte Young's group, and also made some recordings with Tony Conrad a few weeks later. Cale had created a home studio of sorts, stocking it with not only his bass, viola and organ, but also more exotic instruments like a sarinda, a serongi and a dilruba. Some of the home recordings he'd made the previous October (eventually released as *Sun Blindness Music* in 2000) seem to move further along in the same direction as *White Light/White Heat*. Cale spoke of creating music that **could control the weather**, and thought that albums should come with free colouring books (a favourite pastime of speed-freaks) and toys.

As for Reed, Warhol claims that Lou had told him in early 1968 that he was concerned about his speed habit, and was trying to stop using the drug. The reason may have been **Shelley Albin** (see p.7), who had moved to New York that Spring with her new husband. She and Reed had begun seeing each other again – platonically at first, but their relationship would soon turn into an on-and-off affair.

Beyond the Pale: although the band thought it was great, almost everyone delse had problems with the Velvets' second album

The Velvet Underground spent most of 1968 on the road, promoting *White Light/White Heat*; but its lyrical content (and the lack of ballads) ensured that it received zero radio airplay. This time there was no Warhol angle to attract the media, and the album got virtually no reviews – and was once again not distributed properly, stalling on the *Billboard* chart at Number 200. But live, the band were in their element, as Sterling Morrison recalled: "Our touring was successful and our playing was excellent. Perhaps the possibility of real success suddenly became so tangible that we pursued it into megalomania and ruin". The group's energy turned inwards again, with destructive force.

The basic problem was that Cale wanted the band to go further in the same direction as *White Light/White Heat*, while Reed wanted to do something radically different. Probably at the prompting of Steve Sesnick – and inspired, perhaps, by his relationship with Albin – Reed was now writing gentle love songs. Cale was "trying to develop these really grand orchestral bass parts". He was "trying to get something big and grand" but "Lou was fighting against that. He wanted pretty songs". Reed maintained that he didn't want to repeat the *White Light/White Heat* formula: "I thought it would be a terrible mistake, and I really believed that. I thought we had to demonstrate the other side of us. Otherwise, we would become this one-dimensional thing, and that had to be avoided at all costs". Morrison tended to side with Cale: "Lou placed heavy emphasis on lyrics. Cale and I were more interested in blasting the

house down". Cale would later state that Reed "wanted to keep it pure" whereas he "wanted to push the envelope and fuck the songs up", and that that was why they split. "He wanted me to be a sideman in my own fucking group", Cale charged.

Matters worsened because Reed and Cale were barely talking to each other. Much of their communication was routed through Steve Sesnick, who may well not have passed messages on – or not passed them on accurately. Intrigue and machinations now became the order of the day – and would eventually cause Reed as much angst as they now did for Cale. Two recording sessions took place in February and May, with an eye to a possible single (resulting in 'Mr. Rain', 'Stephanie Says' and 'Temptation Inside Your Heart', which would finally become available on *VU* and *Another View*) but ended up not being released – probably because of these tensions between Reed and Cale. They were unable to reconcile their differences, Cale subsequently blaming Reed's drug intake.

While the Velvets were busy touring and scrapping over musical direction, their former manager was lying in hospital. On 3 June 1968, Andy Warhol was the victim of a near-successful **assassination attempt** by Valerie Solanas. Though deeply shocked when he heard of the incident, for some reason Lou Reed did not go to visit Warhol in hospital – something which would cause him guilt pangs for years to come. Reed later wrote a song inspired by the shooting, 'Andy's Chest' (the Velvets' version would finally be released on the *VU* album).

Valerie Solanas: I Shot Andy Warhol

The Story

A wannabe playwright and a radical lesbian feminist, Valerie Solanas had written a manifesto for a proposed extremist feminist group called SCUM (the Society for Cutting Up Men, of which Solanas was the only member). Solanas was dangerously psychotic – Andy Warhol later recalled that she "would talk constantly about the complete elimination of the male sex". Pretty much homeless, Solanas survived by begging, prostitution and selling copies of her SCUM manifesto on the street. In late 1966, she met Warhol, and saw in him a chance for recognition of her work. She demanded that he produce one of her plays, titled *Up Your Ass*; but Warhol wasn't interested. When she continued to pester him for money, Warhol gave her a small role in his film *I, A Man* to shut her up.

On 3 June 1968 Solanas decided to take drastic action against the central figures of her paranoid delusions. Her initial target was avant-garde and pornographic publisher Maurice Girodias, but he was out of town, so instead Solanas switched her attentions to Warhol. She made half-a-dozen visits that day to the new Factory offices at 33 Union Square West, only to be told that Warhol was not present. When the artist arrived at four o'clock that afternoon, Solanas followed Warhol into the Factory, waited until he had finished a phone conversation, before pulling out an automatic pistol and firing three .32 calibre bullets into his chest and abdomen at point-blank range. She also shot art dealer Mario Amaya in the leg before leaving.

Warhol was rushed to Columbus Mother Cabrini Hospital, and was pronounced clinically dead six minutes after his arrival there – he was "dead" for ninety seconds before a doctor cut his chest open and massaged his heart back into action. Four doctors spent the next five hours operating on Warhol's lungs, liver, gall bladder, spleen, intestines and pulmonary artery. Amazingly, Andy survived – though his chest was crisscrossed with scars and he would suffer problems with digestion and sleeping for years to come. He also wore a corset (to keep his stomach muscles in place) for the rest of his life.

Earlier that year Warhol had made his most famous remark: "In the future everybody will be world famous for 15 minutes". Ironically, his own shooting garnered not much more press attention, as Presidential candidate Robert Kennedy was assassinated the next day, pushing Warhol out of the headlines. Though Andy was forgiving towards his attacker, most observers agreed with Nico that he was visibly altered: "He was never Andy again. He was like a silkscreen of himself". There had been two earlier gun incidents at the Factory; no one had been hurt, and Warhol had not made any security precautions. Not any more: security cameras were installed at the Factory, and the "open house" policy ended.

As for Solanas, she surrendered to police several hours after the shooting, and was remanded to mental hospital. Released on bail in December 1968, she made several threatening phonecalls, including one to the Factory. A mandatory pre-trial psychiatric evaluation diagnosed her as a chronic schizophrenic, and recommended she be placed in closed-ward psychiatric care. But the court sentenced her to three years in state prison for "reckless assault" in January 1969 ("You get more for stealing a car", Reed observed). She was released in September 1971, and remained homeless or in mental hospitals. She died of bronchial pneumonia in a welfare hostel in San Francisco on 25 April 1988, 14 months after Andy.

In 1996, Mary Harron's acclaimed film about the events, *I Shot Andy Warhol*, was released, with Lili Taylor as Solanas and Stephen Dorff as Warhol, featuring music by John Cale.

Ousting Cale

In September 1968, the Reed/Cale crisis finally came to a head. Reed convened a meeting in a Greenwich Village café with Morrison and Tucker, and informed them that he wanted Cale out of the group, for good. This didn't go down too well, especially with Morrison, who found the idea "unthinkable". But Reed told them he'd rather dissolve the Velvets completely than continue with Cale, and so – because they both wanted the band to continue – the others eventually acquiesced. Reed left it to Morrison to break the news to Cale, who later observed that "Lou always got other people to do his dirty work for him".

John Cale went quietly, and with as much dignity as he could muster, playing his last gig with the group that month. He would subsequently state his opinion that The Velvet Underground had never really fulfilled their potential. "Drugs, and the fact that no one gave a damn about us, meant we gave up on it too soon" he claimed. In the late 1980s Lou Reed more or less conceded. In the process of ousting Cale, Reed had seriously **alienated** Sterling Morrison, who remained angry at him for years (and possibly decades). The fact that Morrison continued to socialize with Cale only increased Reed's paranoia. Maureen Tucker reluctantly accepted Cale's departure, though she wasn't happy about it – she later stated that she wished the band had done at least one more album with Cale, and that without him the constructive "lunacy" that had fuelled their first two albums was lost.

As Cale's replacement, the band brought in **Doug Yule**, a 21-year-old bass player from Boston. Born 25 February 1947, Yule had been in several local cover bands, including The Argonauts and The Argo, before joining a professional outfit called **Grass Menagerie**. Later on, his organ-playing would go some way to becoming a worthy substitute for Cale's viola drone-effects. He made his live debut with the band in October, after less than a week's rehearsal with them.

Yule had been discovered by Morrison via the Velvets' road manager **Hans Onsager**, but Lou Reed was thrilled with the choice, finding the new bass player's "innocence" a refreshing change. The astrology-obsessed Reed was also delighted to discover that Yule was a Pisces, like himself. With Morrison and Tucker both Virgos, the band was now astrologically balanced.

But the other two had reservations. Morrison liked Yule and thought him a good bass player,

A publicity shot for the new line up, Doug Yule on the right.

but missed the sparks that flew from Cale: "Bands that fight together make better music". When Reed began flattering and praising Yule at length, Tucker feared that all the attention would go to Yule's head and cause yet more problems. It appears that the gift of prophecy was another of Moe's many talents: Yule soon became so influenced by Reed that he began to dress and sound like him.

"Gray" And "Lost"

The time was fast approaching for the Velvets to record again, but this time the group ran into a technical hitch en route to the studio in California. According to Sterling Morrison, all the band's effects boxes were stolen at the airport: "We saw that all our tricks had vanished, and instead of trying to replace them, we just thought what we could do without them". Doug Yule has since poured scorn on this story, pointing out that if it were true these boxes could easily have been replaced in LA. Yule thinks that Reed simply wanted a gentler sound, and a new direction. Regardless, Morrison and Reed kitted themselves out with twin Fender 12-string guitars. The new album would be as quiet as its predecessor was loud, and be comprised of totally new material, most of which had never been performed live.

In fact, much of it hadn't even been written. According to Yule, at this point Sesnick was still managing to get MGM to foot the bill for first-class travel and accommodation. So, in November 1968 the group stayed at the **Chateau Marmont** in LA, where they wrote and rehearsed during the afternoons; they would then record the songs at night. Maureen Tucker was so shy about performing the vocals for 'Afterhours' that she made all the others leave the studio before she would sing it.

Inevitably, without Cale the mania and the menace were gone, and the music was much more orthodox. All the new songs were by Lou Reed, many of them were personal-sounding, and all of them dealt with love – from the adulterous to the religious – and sex. Many were clearly about Shelley Albin, and Reed later stated that the songs can be seen as one large story cycle. But his voice was shot from playing live, and so Doug Yule took the vocals on several tracks. This may well have planted a seed for the future in Steve Sesnick's mind. Yule was good-looking, had the kind of teen appeal that Reed never would or could have – and he could sing. In short, Lou Reed might not be as

essential to the band's survival as he seemed.

Sterling Morrison has described his attitude on the third album as one of "acquiescence", but he was nevertheless pleased with the finished product: "The songs are all very quiet and it's kind of insane. I like the album". But both he and Tucker were annoyed by the fact that – after the album was mixed – Reed went back into the studio and did his own mix. He'd gone behind their backs, and they resented it. Once again, once released the album received little promotion and was badly distributed.

On various dates between May and October 1969, the group were in the studio again, this time recording what would come to be regarded as their **"lost"** MGM/Verve album at the Record Plant in New York. But whether the tracks were ever actually intended for an album is a little unclear, and Doug Yule was under the impression that these recordings were nothing more than "work tapes", in preparation for more polished recordings that were never made. Still, the group were trying to get free from MGM, who were no longer giving them much support – financial or otherwise, and they did contractually owe the label one more album. It seems unlikely they were recording just for the hell of it, but on the other hand their first three albums had been badly promoted and ineffectively distributed. As Maureen Tucker points out, "[The band] weren't that interested in giving them another one to just let it die".

The material they recorded then would subsequently surface on **bootlegs** and – much later

– on the albums *VU* and *Another View*. In the end – and quite probably before they had finished what they set out to do in the studio – MGM dropped them from their roster. At the time MGM President **Mike Curb** issued a statement, part of which read: "Groups that are associated with hard drugs ... are very undependable. They're difficult to work with, and they're hard on your sales and marketing people". This new company policy not only explains why MGM dropped the Velvets from the label, but also why they chose not to release the "lost" album.

Loaded

Surprisingly, it took the group several months to find a new record deal. They eventually signed a two-album contract with Atlantic's Ahmet Ertegun, on the strict condition that there would be no drugs songs. So The Velvet Underground returned to New York, to record at Atlantic Studios. Recording took about ten weeks (between April and July 1970), mainly in the evenings after the group had finished playing live at **Max's Kansas City,** where they had a residency that summer, playing five nights a week. Originally a two-week booking, it was extended to ten weeks.

Mysteriously, with the exception of 'Rock & Roll', the Velvets chose not to re-record the songs from the "lost" album; instead, the finished *Loaded* album would include an additional nine new songs. This may have been because they believed that MGM might still release the

earlier recordings (which the label refused to return to the band), or perhaps because they were legally prevented from re-recording that material. The latter seems unlikely – quite apart from 'Rock & Roll', they did also re-record 'Ocean' (though it wouldn't surface until 1995's *Peel Slowly And See*), and Reed was certainly free to re-record much of the material for his first solo album in 1972. It seems more likely that the group were just disenchanted with the "lost" songs, or found them tainted by the move from MGM, and wanted a fresh start. Whatever the reasons, the songs on *Loaded* were intentionally designed to be as commercial as possible (and despite the ban on drugs songs, they managed a punning reference in the album's title).

But from the start, the Velvets were beset with problems. Sterling Morrison seems to have been largely unaware of the arguments that would soon boil over. He had taken a step back from band politics: having dropped out of college in 1966, he'd taken advantage of the group's prolonged stay in New York to take some academic courses at **City College**, and had his head stuck in Victorian novels for most of that summer. Consequently, as he later noted, "it wasn't really apparent to [him] that we were falling apart".

The band had been touring fairly constantly and, during the course of recording, their gruelling summer residency at Max's Kansas City took its toll on Lou's voice. As a result, the group were forced to let Doug Yule sing lead once again on several tracks. Morrison explained: "We either had to stop the production, or let Doug take over. But no one preferred to have Doug sing". The result, according to Reed, was that "the sense that the songs were handled and interpreted in got changed", because Yule didn't understand Reed's sense of humour on songs like 'New Age' and 'Sweet Nuthin''.

Worst of all, the group lost Moe Tucker. Though she gets a credit on the sleeve of *Loaded*, she was actually absent throughout recording from March onwards, because of her first pregnancy (her daughter Kerry was born in June). Sesnick insisted that the band not wait for Moe's return, but go ahead and record without her – something Yule now admits the band should have vetoed. Tucker was replaced on drums for the sessions by Yule's younger brother **Billy**, who was still at school and who had never heard the Velvets play live until he actually joined them on stage at Max's (his conventional playing style was dismissed by Tucker as "too normal"). The album sleeve credits "percussion assistance" to session drummer Tommy Castanaro and engineer Adrian Barber, and Doug Yule also claims to have played some of the drums.

To this day, Tucker is annoyed that she didn't get to play on the record. Had she been there, she might have been a calming influence. One had certainly been needed, because of their fourth major problem: manager Steve Sesnick. Sesnick had been pushing Reed to become more of a showman, and Morrison later complained that Reed had started to adopt clichéd rock posturing in his live performances. At the same time Sesnick had also been encouraging Doug Yule to take a more prominent role in the group. Whether he intended it or not, the result was that Sesnick drove a wedge between the two. As a result – with Tucker elsewhere and Morrison seemingly uninterested – Reed felt not only betrayed by the people he had relied on as allies (who appeared to be conspiring against him), but totally isolated as well.

Lou himself was in rougher shape than his voice. Apart from his paranoia about the band situation, his relationship with Shelley Albin had finally come to an end in the spring of that year. She'd become pregnant by her husband, and had consequently broken up with Lou – this time for good. Most witnesses blamed Lou's obviously distraught mental state on drugs, but according to Morrison, Reed was drug-free at this point; he was, however, experimenting with strange diets and sleeping hardly at all, which may well have exacerbated the paranoia. Reed told Tucker that he'd been levitating several feet above his bed while trying to get to sleep. According to **Geoff Haslam**, everyone in the studio was aware of Reed's frailty. Lou later squarely blamed Sesnick for what was to follow, claiming the manager had "destroyed the group". Lou averred that Sesnick "took two or three years, but he destroyed it and made it so it wasn't fun any more".

Moe Tucker later placed more blame on Doug Yule than on Sesnick, recalling that when Doug had joined the band, they "all thought

Who's the pretty boy now? Tensions emerged between Reed and Yule almost immediately

he was great – a great guitar player, bass player, singer". But "within a year he'd become an asshole". Yule had a tendency to put himself forward, creating guitar parts for songs (to the annoyance of Morrison) without being asked to. Tucker couldn't understand why Reed put up with this, and thinks Yule was the main reason for Reed's eventual departure, not Sesnick. "Steve clearly picked out Doug as the next 'star'. He took over the vocals and started writing some songs. There seemed to be a lot of ego-petting. Maybe he felt Doug would simply be a lot easier to manipulate".

The atmosphere in the studio must have been pretty terrible. Sesnick even briefly brought in John Cale, in an attempt to reignite former glories, a fact which didn't even surface until 1995 (see *Peel Slowly And See*). This would probably only have increased Reed's paranoia, but Yule thinks it entirely possible that Cale's part might even have been recorded without Reed's knowledge. The situation grated upon Reed, particularly towards the end of their residency at Max's Kansas City: "I never in my life thought I would not do what I believed in, and there I was, not doing what I believed in, that's all, and it made me sick".

Reed Ousts Himself

On 23 August – the same night that **Brigid Polk** (another Factory person) made the cassette recording of the Velvets that would appear as *Live At Max's Kansas City* in 1972 – Lou Reed quit the band. Moe Tucker had come to see her old band in action several nights before. "I didn't hate it", she later said, "but it wasn't the Velvets. To me, there were only two Velvets there, Lou and Sterling. And it didn't work. It was a nice, tight little band. But it wasn't the Velvets". After the show, Lou told her of his intention to quit the group: "I was heartbroken. But I knew something had gone terribly wrong, that he had to leave in order to survive the thing". She tried to persuade him to reconsider, but Lou's mind was made up.

After his final gig, Reed called his long-estranged parents and asked them to come and get him. When he introduced them to Sterling Morrison, the guitarist was baffled, and knew something very strange was occurring – but he would officially hear the news later from Steve Sesnick: "He said, 'Lou's gone home and quit the band.' We finished the week at Max's without him". And that was that.

Reed's later comments seem to indicate that Sesnick had smelled impending success with the new record, and was greedily pushing the group places Reed wasn't too sure he wanted to go. Shortly afterwards Reed boasted: "I gave them an album loaded with hits, and it was loaded with hits to the point where the rest of the people showed their colours. So I left them to their album full of hits that I made". Sesnick selected the rear cover photo – of Doug Yule alone, presumably to indicate that he was now of far more importance to the band than Reed.

The following month *Loaded* was released – though Lou Reed had had no say in the running sequence, and was far from pleased with the production and mixing, citing in particular the "severe" editing of 'Sweet Jane' and 'New Age'. To his ears, the finished product was concrete proof of a "conspiracy" against him. But Sterling Morrison later defended the mixing, and the engineers involved: "*Loaded* is incomparably the best mix of any of our albums. Lou had no control over the mix, and if Geoffrey Haslam and Adrian Barber were involved in such a 'conspiracy', why did the work come out sounding better than anything else?"

Ironically, despite all the obstacles stacked against it, *Loaded* is a bright and breezy collection of outright pop songs, and by far the most commercial record The Velvet Underground ever made. And it paid off – the record even got radio airplay, and reviews were uniformly positive. **Lenny Kaye** wrote in *Rolling Stone*: "Easily one of the best albums to show up this or any other year".

All of this Lou Reed must have found bitterly ironic. Worse, the album sleeve credited "song composition" to Yule, Morrison and Reed, and "lyrics" to Yule and Reed, crediting Reed last each time (almost certainly another Sesnick decision – he had asked Yule which songs he'd helped with, in any way). Lou Reed later sued, claiming the songs were entirely his work. He eventually won back the rights to them – and legally freed himself from his management contract with Sesnick – but he was denied control of the "Velvet Underground" name, enabling Sesnick to continue using it long after the event. Doug Yule later stated that Lou "was doing the writing" whilst the "arranger, musical director" was Yule. "I was handling my half, he was handling his" Yule stated. "Many said Lou was The Velvet Underground ... he was the main force behind it, but it was a band, and like any band its totality is made up of all its members, not just one person with side musicians".

Sterling Morrison later complained that, "[Lou] got the rights to all the songs on *Loaded*, so now he's credited for being the absolute and singular genius of the Underground, which is not true". He went on: "there are a lot of songs I should have co-authorship on, and the same holds true for John Cale. The publishing company was called **Three Prongs**, because there were three of us involved. I'm the last person to deny Lou's immense contribution and he's the best songwriter of the three of us. But he wanted all the credit, he wanted it more than we did, and he got it, to keep the peace".

The Story

I'm Set Free
The Solo Years

"*Very few people can leave a group and survive*".

Lou Reed, 1996

I'm Set Free: The Solo Years
1970–1987

While Cale and Nico had little choice but to develop their careers outside the Velvets (while simultaneously digging themselves deeper into the "underground"), Reed left the band on the one hand in frustration, and on the other convinced of his personal strengths. All three built formidable bodies of work, but these would prove of very varying quality, and too often reflected struggles with their personal demons. Meanwhile, the remaining members of the band would linger on, but with little sense of purpose.

The "Velveteen Underground"

Despite Lou Reed's claim that, "It was a process of elimination from the start. First no more Andy, then no more Nico, then no more John, then no more Velvet Underground", his departure was not quite the end of the Velvets as a functioning (if dysfunctional) band. The remaining trio played out the rest of their residency at **Max's Kansas City**, adding **Walter Powers** on bass (from Yule's old band Grass Menagerie), before continuing to tour. Sterling Morrison stayed on for another year, during which period Moe Tucker also returned to the Velvets' drumstool. Morrison quit in August 1971 after landing a teaching position at the University of Texas – he learned he got the job during a gig in the Lone Star state, and announced at the airport that he wouldn't be getting on the flight to New York with the rest of the band.

With Morrison gone, Doug Yule attempted to keep the Velvets in motion by adding **Willie Alexander** (also from Grass Menagerie) and pushing forward with their tour. Moe Tucker stayed on board, basically because she "didn't feel like getting a job". Journalist **Danny Fields** nicknamed this version of the band the "Velveteen Underground".

The line-up toured Europe, Tucker tagging along because she thought it might be her only chance to see England. She took her baby

By the end of the road it was only Tucker and Yule who were carrying the banner

daughter Kerry with her on the road, and quit the band at the tour's end at least partly because she felt that they were "cheating the people" by using the "Velvet Underground" name. She was replaced by Doug's brother, Billy. **George Kay**, Billy's bandmate from Red Rockets (a group put together by Sesnick) also joined on bass. This line-up toured and made studio recordings of at least two tracks – 'Friends' and 'She'll Make You Cry' – but these were never released. Instead, Steve Sesnick supposedly persuaded Yule to break up the band and record an album entirely by himself, though still using the Velvet Underground name. Yule has since been criticized for this, but has subsequently

pointed out that he was still very young at the time (24), and that he simply went along with whatever his manager suggested. The album, titled *Squeeze*, was recorded in London in the Summer of 1972 and featured only Yule, plus session drummer **Ian Paice** (of Deep Purple) and an unidentified female vocalist (thought to be Yule's girlfriend).

Squeeze was due to be released in October 1972, but was delayed until February 1973 – likely due to legal action by Lou Reed over the use of the "Velvet Underground" name. No singles were released from the album, and it was never released in the United States. Yule did play some American gigs with a band consisting of some of the other "Velveteens" in 1973 but, according to him, they were never supposed to be billed as The Velvet Underground. Soon after, Yule decided to call it a day, and the last performance took place in Vermont early that year.

Both Yules subsequently quit the music business. Doug was dragged out of retirement by – of all people – Lou Reed, who recruited him to play on his 1974 album *Sally Can't Dance*, and also to tour Europe with him the following year. In 1975 he played on **Eliott Murphy**'s album *Night Flights*, before joining a country-ish band called **American Flyer**, with whom he recorded two solo albums in the late 70s. Soon after, he officially retired, busying himself with fatherhood and his own cabinet-making business. On occasion he still played music for fun, jamming with friends, and with his brother Billy (about whom nothing else is known).

Maureen Tucker got married to her boyfriend Steve, moved to Phoenix and had another four children after Kerry: Keith, Kate, Richard and Austen. She also worked for decades as a computer operator, resurfacing musically in 1980 with a single, a version of 'I'm Sticking With You" she'd recorded with **Jonathan Richman** six years earlier. She followed this with a cover of Chuck Berry's "Around and Around", and then the solo album, *Playin' Possum* in 1981 (on which she played all the instruments), with occasionaly live performaces following the release.

In 1985, Moe travelled to New York to be interviewed for *The South Bank Show*, in the course of which she was reunited with Morrison, Cale and Reed for the first time in over a decade. That year she released another EP, *Another View*, and she continued to perform live in concert over the next few years.

After Sterling Morrison finally left the group in 1971, he returned to full-time academia, teaching English Literature at the University of Texas in Austin while studying for his doctorate in Medieval Literature. In 1972 he declined an invitation from Lou Reed to hitch up in a new band ("Maybe I should have done it", he admitted years later). Instead, after gaining his PhD in 1976, Morrison commenced an improbable-but-true new career as a **tugboat pilot** in the Houston Ship Channel. Since the channel was extremely polluted – to the point that it once actually caught fire – John Cale suspects that exposure to it may have been the cause of Morrison's eventual cancer.

After the Velvets, Morrison stopped playing music outside of his own house. "I didn't want to play with anybody else. So I didn't", he explained in 1990. However, he did join John Cale on stage for some encores when the latter played Austin – and in the late 1980s Moe Tucker persuaded him to join her on stage with her band for the occasional gig. Morrison evidently enjoyed it, and began to tour with her.

Morrison and his wife Martha – whom both he and Moe Tucker had known since childhood – had two children, Tommy and Mary Anne. At some point in the 1990s they moved from Texas to Poughkeepsie.

Nico

Chelsea Girl had largely been ignored by the critics, and so the blonde who always wore white reinvented herself in black, dressing "like a Russian" in the heavy leather boots that became a permanent part of her wardrobe. She dyed her hair with henna, became a vegetarian and surrounded herself with candles and (Warhol maintained that a candle shop on Nico's block would be a good business proposition). In short, she became a prototype **Goth**, but according to her sometime roommate Viva, not the cleanliest of people – Viva accused her of smelling "like a pig farmer".

But although Nico was weary of her own beauty and the way others reacted to it, the changes she initiated were more than just cosmetic. Much to everyone's amazement, she proved herself to be an inventive and intriguing songwriter, creating on her Indian harmonium what critic **John Rockwell** called "dirge-like songs themselves full of girlish Gothic imagery and a spacey romanticism". Nico's poetry – and her life – would from now on follow what John Cale defined as "a solitary dream".

She managed to get a record deal with Elektra, recording *The Marble Index* in October 1968. The label suggested that John Cale be brought in as an arranger; and in fact, although Elektra house producer Frazier Mohawk was nominally the album's producer with John Cale as mere arranger, Cale did the bulk of the actual work. He and Nico had had a very brief affair in early 1967, and perhaps because of this were able to transcend the problems posed by Nico's impossible timekeeping and general unreliability, and forged a solid working partnership. According to Cale, Nico's harmonium was "not exactly in tune with itself or with anything else", so he recorded her performing the songs solo first. He then carefully chose instruments that would fit in alongside, and used vari-speed tape effects to make it all hang together. Cale spent four days arranging, recording and mixing the album, and when Nico heard it she cried, because of the beauty of what they had made together. The crying/ fighting cycle would repeat itself with every album they made together from then on, and sometimes the fights were physical – yet Cale would consistently praise Nico's "professional attitude" to her work.

1968 was also the year in which Nico first used heroin. She began by smoking it, but by 1970 had switched to injecting. In 1969 she met the French underground film director **Philippe Garrel** in Paris. The couple's relationship would last for nine years, with Nico appearing in many of his films. She also hooked Garrel on heroin (according to him), while he in turn influenced her sense of fashion and gave her a truly bizarre concept of the state an artist should embody. Their initial involvement was brief, as Nico returned to New York to join John Cale, who was producing **Iggy Pop and the Stooges**' first album. Nico promptly became involved with Iggy, a relationship which lasted for several months.

In 1970, Nico's mother – whom she had virtually abandoned when she developed Alzheimer's – died in Berlin. Now, riddled with guilt, Nico refused to attend the funeral, saying "If I go to my mother's grave, I will never leave it". Nico's remark proved prophetic, as her ashes were eventually interred there (see The Reunion Years). She would attempt to exorcize her guilt on her next album.

That year – after playing a few European gigs to mystified reviews – Nico moved in with Philippe Garrel, sharing an apartment with him in Paris. Both were now junkies. She also starred in Garrel's film *La Cicatrice Intérieure* (*The Inner Scar*), for which she wrote the dialogue. Filmed in Egypt (in the middle of the Egyptian-Israeli war, to which the couple were oblivious), the film is ponderous, pretentious and dull. It received terrible reviews, but Garrel announced it would be the first in a trilogy.

Nico again went to New York, briefly, to visit John Cale, who was attempting to get her another record deal – but then she got into a fight in a restaurant and had to leave town in a hurry. As retribution for some remark Nico found offensive she'd smashed a young black woman in the eye with a glass; the girl was a friend of the militant **Black Panthers**, and Nico – scared they'd seek revenge – fled back to Paris. Meanwhile, Cale did succeed in getting Nico a deal with **Warner**, and produced the resulting album *Desertshore*, recorded during Spring and Summer 1970 in New York and London. Cale was impressed by Nico's progress, both lyrically and musically, but the record received largely negative reviews.

Back in Paris, Nico claims she was walking down a street on 3 July 1971, when a black car passed her; on the back seat sat **Jim Morrison**, now bearded and fat. She tried to attract his attention, but without success. Morrison died that night – two years to the day after the death of another of Nico's conquests, **Brian Jones** – and Nico believed that his spirit (or a part of it) entered into her. She also had a premonition that she herself would die in the month of July (as proved to be the case). It would seem that Nico had a breakdown of sorts shortly after her "encounter" with Morrison, as a result of which kleptomania was added to her other shortcomings. Around this time she met a 22-year-old blonde German guitarist named **Lutz "Lüül" Ulbrich** and began an affair with him – though she was still living with Garrel, who didn't seem to mind.

In January 1972, Nico was reunited with both John Cale and Lou Reed for a one-off live performance at Le Bataclan theatre in Paris. Plans to repeat the concert in London fell through, and this was the last occasion Nico and Reed would ever share a concert stage. Over the next few years Nico made two more films with Garrel: *Athanor* (1973) and *Les Hautes solitudes* (1974, the latter co-starring **Jean Seberg**, with whom Nico had also once had an affair).

Island Hopping

By 1974, John Cale was signed to Island Records, and he managed to get Nico a deal there as well. *The End* was recorded back-to-back with Cale's album *Fear*, and featured the same personnel (Brian Eno and Phil Manzanera). The album included not only the title track – Nico's version of Jim Morrison's Freudian melodrama – but also her version of the old German national anthem "Das Lied Der Deutschen" (or "The Song Of The German People"), which had been banned in that country since 1945. Though written in 1922, in the days of the Weimar Republic, the song's associations with the **Third Reich** were so strong that Nico would be accused of having Nazi sympathies from then on. When she performed the song in Berlin (backed by Cale and Eno), it nearly caused a riot. *Melody Maker's* review dismissed the album as being "as miserable as ever".

Island Records promptly dropped Nico from their roster after she allegedly made some racist remarks ("I said to some interviewer that I didn't like negroes"); Island being **Bob Marley**'s record label, her comments hadn't gone down well. According to Lutz Ulbrich, Nico's bias was real and personal, springing from the fact that she had been ripped off many times by black heroin dealers (and if the tale of her teenaged rape is true, that might add another reason). After this, John Cale attempted to get Nico a record deal with another label, but failed. As a result the two argued, and relations were severed for many years. In the meantime, in late 1974, Lou Reed offered to help, even suggesting that he'd write and produce for her. He paid for an airline ticket to New York, and put her up in his apartment. But the promise was empty; Reed constantly belittled and humiliated Nico, and she fled to a hotel after three days, fearful of actual violence. Cale savagely berated Reed over the phone for his behaviour.

Nico spent the next few years dividing her time between Lutz Ulbrich in Berlin (whom she had also talked into becoming a heroin user) and Philippe Garrel in Paris, with side trips to Amsterdam to acquire more heroin. She'd stopped dyeing her now brown hair and dressed totally in black. She made four more films with Garrel in fairly rapid succession (*Un ange passe*, *Le Berceau de cristal*, *Voyage au jardin des morts*, *Le Bleu des ongines*) as their relationship slowly ground to an end, but she recorded no music. In 1976 she finally lost all legal claim to her son Ari, as **Edith Boulogne** (Delon's mother) formally adopted him as her own son. This was necessary simply to provide Ari with French citizenship; he was actually stateless up until this point, since Nico had never bothered to register his birth.

In the late 1970s Nico returned to live performance, as she began to land bookings in England on the burgeoning punk circuit, supporting bands like The Adverts and The Banshees, many of whom considered her a heroine and a pioneer (when Nico's harmonium was stolen in 1978, **Patti Smith** insisted on buying her a new one). Sadly, the punk audiences often felt very differently, and Nico was chased from the stage by a rain of spit and beer cans on countless occasions.

In Paris, post-Garrel, Nico took up with a group of Corsicans: photographer Philippe

Quilichini, his fiancée Nadett Duget and Antoine Giacomoni. They persuaded her to return to the studio to record an album with a proper rock band – at which point the story becomes very confusing. Giacomoni claims that **Aaron Sixx** of Aura Records effectively stole the session tapes by bribing Nico and the studio engineer, while Sixx claims that he had an agreement to release the album but was double-crossed by Duget (who was a drug dealer), and had a legal right to the tapes. Nico then re-recorded the whole album. The upshot is that there are two versions of the album *Drama of Exile*, one released in France and one in Holland, each featuring different recordings of exactly the same songs. Quilichini and Duget died shortly afterwards in a car crash, and Nico was informed of their deaths while in hospital, recovering from heroin-related septicaemia.

On *Drama of Exile* Nico covered Reed's "Waiting For The Man", the subject of buying heroin being one she now understood only too well, "I find it something to occupy yourself with, running up and down the city". The search for a reliable and steady supply of the drug led her to finally settle in Britain, where imported Iranian heroin was readily available. Nico ended up in Manchester, where she was discovered by local rock entrepreneur **Alan Wise**. She was homeless, alone and generally messed up; Wise undertook the lengthy, difficult and somewhat unrewarding task of rejuvenating her career as her new manager. He sent her to New York, where she played two

shows in 1979 (at CBGB) with Lutz and John Cale before returning to Manchester, where Wise had put together the first of her many touring bands. These were mainly comprised of young and impoverished Mancunian musicians. Line-ups changed frequently, but over the coming years included keyboard player **James Young** (who wrote a riveting memoir of his time with her), trumpet player **Andy Diagram** (later of James) and **Henry Laycock** (later of Primal Scream).

The biggest problem Wise faced was Nico's addiction. It is estimated that between 1980-1988 Nico performed over 1,200 gigs – a harsh pace, but Nico was by no means a high-earning act, and even with her record royalties, Nico still spent more than she earned on heroin. Plus, there were the problems and expenses of acquiring the drug while on the road. On numerous occasions she was cheated (with sugar, salt or scouring powder) and had to endure withdrawal symptoms – and as Wise points out, "If Nico suffered, everyone suffered".

Wise badgered Nico for years to downgrade her habit to methadone before she finally did, in 1983. She became a registered methadone addict at Manchester's Prestwich Hospital – but methadone alone was not enough, and she took to drinking beer heavily (which tended to make her violent). She also still did heroin when she could surreptitiously acquire it, but it does appear that she was genuinely trying to quit. She rode her bike, played pool in the local pub, watched TV and slept. She was frequently bored. She was also constantly poor, and didn't

Nico, hennaed hair and the dreaded harmonium in later years

even own copies of her own albums. And heroin had caused most of her teeth to rot away.

Then Ari returned to her life, tracking her down when he was 22. There was blame and reconciliation, and an uncomfortable intimacy that was surprising given their history, though the pair also fought frequently. As might have been predicted, Nico gave her son his first heroin, though she made sure it was of the finest quality. Ari became a roadie for her – or, to put it another way, her errand boy for drugs. He left, and returned, frequently. In 1984 she went to visit him in New York, and attempted to use this break to write some songs. But nothing would come.

The following year she moved down to London, sharing a house in Brixton with fellow junkie and punk poet **John Cooper Clarke** (also managed by Wise). Clarke had just been through expensive rehab, but in Nico's company quickly started using heroin again. Meanwhile, Wise had managed to get her a record deal with **Beggar's Banquet**, and somehow persuaded John Cale to produce her once again. Nico managed to scrape together a handful of songs, plus a couple of cover versions, and the resulting *Camera Obscura* album was far better than might have been predicted.

In 1987 Ari suffered a nervous breakdown, and was committed to a psychiatric hospital. Over the next few years he would return to hospital many times, enduring electroshock, a brain lesion and a coma. As with her mother, Nico felt responsible and guilty. No one argued with her.

Her talent aside, it's hard to know what to make of Nico. "Socially difficult", was how someone who knew her in Brixton put it. Viva called her "a helpless, adult kid". Yet most of those who knew her remained fond of her, despite the fact that she was a nightmarish junkie. **Iggy Pop** perhaps summed her up most memorably: "I never would call her responsible. Nobody ever said, 'Here comes Nico. Everything's gonna be alright now!' She didn't inspire confidence, but she was a great sport. She was very cute, charming, and a hell of a lot of fun. She was a little crazy, too".

Ari Boulogne

Ari Päffgen spent most of his childhood being raised by Alain Delon's mother (which caused the charmless Delon to sever relations with her, never to be restored). At the age of four Ari had contracted jaundice – the result, some said, of being allowed to drink the dregs of wine glasses downstairs at the Dom while his mother sang on stage. It was also rumoured that in those days she'd rub his gums with heroin to keep him quiet. After dumping her son on relatives, Nico rarely visited him – and there was a period of four years when she didn't even write or call him at all. As with her Alzheimer's-ridden mother, she simply abandoned him.

After his mother's death (see page 110), Ari spent her royalty payments on heroin, travelled the planet and ended up homeless in New York. Stints in psychiatric hospital followed. His current whereabouts are unknown.

John Cale

John Cale's first paid work after leaving The Velvet Underground came in October 1968, when he acted as arranger for Nico's *Marble Index* album at the invitation of Elektra's **Jac Holzman**. Over the coming decades Cale would be in steady demand as an arranger and record producer, often helping new artists make memorable debuts. In June 1969 Cale produced Iggy Pop and the Stooges' first album, recorded at New York's **Hit Factory** in two days flat. Nico turned up for a visit during the recording, and Iggy remembers her and Cale sitting in the recording booth, "looking like they were in the Addams Family".

Meanwhile, encouraged by his wife Betsey, Cale had been attempting to write songs of his own, and at the end of 1968 five of his poems were published in *Aspen* magazine. In February 1969, Cale recorded "Dream Interpretations" with Tony Conrad, and the duo reunited very briefly with LaMonte Young. In early 1970 Cale signed a two-album deal with **CBS** producer **John McClure**, under the condition that one of these records be a collaboration with the minimalist composer **Terry Riley**. *Church Of Anthrax* was recorded before (but released after) Cale's first solo collection of songs, *Vintage Violence*. In the end, the songs that would make up that album were written quite quickly, and displayed a real talent for epic pop. But CBS failed to market the album – its title and cover photograph both suggested that the record was in the same general vein as *White Light/White Heat*, and CBS did nothing to alter that perception. Cale's refusal to tour in support of the record probably didn't help matters.

In the summer of 1970, Cale moved to London to finish production work on Nico's *Desertshore* album (begun in New York that spring) and there resumed a friendship with producer **Joe Boyd**, the man who had persuaded Warner to sign Nico in the first place (on the condition that Cale produce). Through Boyd, Cale met engineer **John Wood**, with whom he would often work; he also played on numerous sessions for Boyd's regular acts alongside **Mike Heron** and **Nick Drake**. By late 1970, Cale had separated from Betsey. Reasons for the break-up seem to have been her wealth and success, and their differing lifestyles – she claims to have been completely drug-free, and worked by day, while Cale still used and had become increasingly nocturnal. He was working through the night for Sony, remixing tapes from the CBS back catalogue into quadraphonic sound (then thought to be a musical development to rival/replace stereo). Pressure and boredom drove Cale's occasional heroin use upwards until he forced himself to go cold turkey.

In early 1971 Cale moved to Los Angeles to work as an in-house producer for Warner Brothers at the invitation of Joe Boyd, then head of Warner's film and music department. Cale was part producer, part A&R man, listening to tapes of new bands and going to their gigs. Newly-divorced from Betsey, Cale soon became involved with **Cindy Wells**, a.k.a. "Miss

Cale working with long-time engineer and collaborator John Wood on his first Island album, *Fear*

classical *The Academy In Peril*, and the song-oriented *Paris 1919*. Despite the fact that *Paris 1919* was loaded with memorable tunes, neither album fared well commercially. Cale also produced some promising demos for Jonathan Richman's group The Modern Lovers (which included future Talking Head **Jerry Harrison**). In March 1973, he took The Modern Lovers to Bermuda to record a proper album, with Warner offering them not only a recording contract but a management deal as well. But Richman announced he no longer liked those songs and wanted to record something else instead, and the whole deal fell through. Cale did produce two albums for **Reprise**, one by Jennifer Warren and one by "Chunky, Novi and Ernie" (a.k.a. songwriter Ilene Rappaport).

Cindy" of the Frank Zappa-sponsored group the **GTOs**, who had broken up the year before. Wells was evidently unstable – a former groupie, she'd had an illegitimate child by Jimmy Page in her teens. The couple were married soon after, and the union was a disaster almost from the start – Cale later described it as "the most destructive relationship I ever had". After her bandmate Miss Christine died from a drug overdose in 1972, Cindy plunged into serious depression and hysteria – to the point that Cale had her committed on the recommendation of a psychiatrist. Meanwhile, he'd developed new substance problems himself, this time with alcohol and cocaine.

While at Warner, Cale recorded two albums for the subsidiary label Reprise: the semi-

...Island Discs

In late 1973, Cale signed a deal with Island Records to record six albums (in three years), and decided to move to London in the following spring. Just before leaving LA he recorded a soundtrack for **Roger Corman**'s girls-in-prison romp *Caged Heat*, improvising the

ACNE: If looks could kill – Cale trying not to attack his cuckold, Kevin Ayers (bottom left). Eno and Nico look on bemused

music on viola as he watched the movie. Cale took Cindy to London with him, but she never forgave him for having had her institutionalized, and her behaviour became increasingly erratic. Cale's drink and cocaine problems also spiralled upwards, and he was now occasionally using heroin again (one bout prompted by a visit from Lou Reed, accompanied by his transsexual lover Rachel).

Island asked Roxy Music guitarist **Phil Manzanera** to produce Cale's first album for the label, and Manzanera recruited his former cohort **Brian Eno** to add special electronic effects, thus beginning the long-standing relationship between Eno and Cale. The resulting album *Fear* (the title track perhaps inspired by the agoraphobia Cale was suffering while trying to quit heroin again) earned rave reviews from both *Melody Maker* and the *NME*. Several members of former Soft Machine bassist **Kevin Ayers**' band also played on *Fear*, which led to a one-off gig on 1 June 1974 at London's Rainbow Theatre by ACNE (Ayers, Cale, Nico and Eno). Ayers took the second half of the evening (with a band that included Mike Oldfield and Robert Wyatt), the other three the first half. Cale performed "Buffalo Ballet", "Gun" and a radical reworking of **Elvis Presley**'s "Heartbreak Hotel". On the downside, Cale was suffering the humiliation of knowing that Ayers slept with Cindy the night before the concert; on the upside, performing in public did a lot for his confidence, and soon afterwards he began making plans for an elaborate solo live show in London. It

was to feature St. Paul's Cathedral Boys Choir performing the Beach Boys' "Surf's Up"… but the plans all came to nothing. Supposedly the Choir and Cale did record a reggae version of "God Only Knows" as part of a planned album of cover versions (shortlisted were "Eight Miles High", "I Can See For Miles" and the hymn "Jerusalem"), but the track was never finished and the proposed album was abandoned.

Since Manzanera had returned to active duty with Roxy Music, Cale recruited session guitarist **Chris Spedding** for his follow-up album *Slow Dazzle* (released April 1975) and once again garnered good reviews. Most of the album was written in the studio; although Cale had a half dozen songs up his sleeve prior to then, he'd become bored with them by the time the studio date came around – a recurrent and problematic trend. Spedding and the other musicians on the album became Cale's new backing band as he embarked on major tours of Britain and France. Touring would become increasingly important to Cale – he thrived on the uncertainty of it all, and the income was vital. Live, he adopted a range of costume disguises that included ski goggles and a hockey mask (which may well have influenced the look of the villain in the *Friday The 13th* movies). Some nights he appeared swathed in bandages, looking like The Invisible Man. His performances became more theatrical and improvised, conjuring up an atmosphere of seething violence and paranoia. One night Cale broke some fake blood capsules concealed in the crotch of a human dummy, and played the remainder of the gig covered in bloodstains. Cale had always been fascinated by gore, and even in his youth had paid visits to the local abattoir. The fascination reached a peak at a gig in Croydon in early 1977, when Cale hacked the head off a chicken he'd killed earlier and tossed its carcass into the audience. Half his band quit in protest.

Much of this was genuine mania, fuelled by Cale's collapsing marriage to the increasingly promiscuous Cindy, as well as by his own booze and cocaine intake. The couple finally parted in late 1975, after Cindy was arrested for shoplifting. Cale bailed her out of jail, said goodbye, and sent her back to Los Angeles for good. Cale himself went to New York, to produce **Patti Smith**'s first album, *Horses* (when she'd first approached him about the project, Cale was unsure whether he was being offered work or asked out on a date). The first thing Cale did was to replace the entire band's instruments, since they wouldn't hold their tune. Cale worked on the record for six weeks, which he later described as "a battle". Sometimes the fights with Smith got physical.

Cale had taken on the Smith project at least partially for money (he was spending vast amounts on cocaine), but **Island** were annoyed that he seemed to be neglecting his own career. Cale went straight from working with Smith into the studio to mix his own *Helen Of Troy* album. After several days there he had to leave to go off on tour again, and while on the road he discovered that Island were planning to release the album as it was. Cale hit the roof, and although the label allowed him to finish mixing the record to his satisfaction, his relationship with them was fatally soured by the incident. *Helen Of Troy* came out in November 1975, and Island released Cale from his contract the following year even though he still owed them three albums (Cale would not record for anyone until 1979). Several unreleased tracks from the Island years remain in their vaults, including a cover version of "Willow Weep For Me".

In 1976, Cale returned to New York, where he became romantically involved with Patti Smith's manager **Jane Friedman**, who would also manage his business affairs. As a result, Cale missed out on the explosion of punk energy that was about to erupt in London, something he'd surely have been a part of – if only as a producer – if he'd stayed in England (both Spedding and Chris Thomas would work with the Sex Pistols). Cale toured with Patti Smith as a solo support act, and in July played several solo shows at New York's Ocean Club, where he was visited one night by Andy Warhol. On another night, he was joined on stage by Patti, Lou Reed and **David Byrne** of Talking Heads. He was given to increasingly bizarre drunken/drugged behaviour on the road, much of it self-destructive. Cale subsequently toured France supporting Patti Smith, and also played at London's Roundhouse – though his new American band had long hair and beards which failed to resonate with image-conscious, leather-clad punk Britain.

Cale in sandals, with Tom Verlaine (centre) and Mick Ronson (rear),working with Patti Smith (right) on her *Horses* album

From Spy To Ze And Back Again

Cale remained in London through the rest of 1976 and 1977, recording his *Animal Justice* EP and doing production work for Miles Copeland's Illegal Records, working with (among others) **Squeeze** and **Sham 69**. He also recorded two tracks for a single, "Jack The Ripper (In The Moulin Rouge)" and "Ton Ton Macoute'", but decided not to release it as he was already bored with the songs (the first song would surface on the *Seducing Down The Door* anthology, but the second never did). 1978 was spent in more production work and also in founding a record label, **Spy**, with Jane Friedman and Michael Zilkha in New York.

Throughout 1979 Cale toured the States almost constantly, resulting in a live album for Spy, *Sabotage Live*. One of the many guitarists Cale worked with during this time was **Davey O'List**, formerly of The Nice and Roxy Music. **Judy Nylon** also joined the band for a while, adding her ad-lib scat poetry to the proceedings. On two different tours, Cale was joined onstage in Austin, Texas, by Sterling Morrison. Cale's songs from this era displayed an obsession with war, terrorism and global politics, and he'd also developed a passionate interest in the workings of the CIA. Cocaine-induced paranoia would eventually lead Cale to believe the agency was following him.

Spy released very few other records, but among them was a single by rock critic Lester Bangs. Cale and Friedman eventually gave up their interest in the label to Michael Zilkha, who re-christened it **Ze**. In late 1979, Cale broke up with Friedman after four years together, having accused her of mismanaging his affairs, something he later learned was untrue. In October he demoed two new songs with David Bowie, which remain unreleased, and later that month Bowie joined him on stage at a benefit concert in Carnegie Hall, playing violin on a version of "Sabotage".

Early in 1980, Cale became involved with **Risé Irushaimi**, an actress and ballerina he'd met at CBGB. The couple were soon living together, and married in October 1981. Through Risé's sister Judy (who was involved with Chris Spedding), Cale met **Sylvia Morales**, and had a one-night stand with her – which probably didn't help his relations with Lou Reed in years to come. Professionally, things weren't going that well. Cale's next album *Honi Soit* attracted mixed reviews, and the one after that, *Music For A New Society*, got great reviews but zero sales. By now Cale's drink and drugs problems had become extremely serious, and though Risé stayed with him she was undoubtedly worried about his welfare – especially after witnessing the occasion when Cale swapped his guitar for cocaine. In 1983 Cale's father died, and he was deeply affected; now, his father would always remain a stranger.

The following year Cale released a below-par studio album, *Caribbean Sunset* and a weak live album, *John Cale Comes Alive*. On a European tour in February 1984, he collapsed in Berlin and the doctor who treated him (with a massive injection of vitamins) warned Cale that if he persisted in his substance-abuse lifestyle it would soon kill him. Between 1984 and 1986 the Cales were also victimized by a deranged female stalker who physically attacked Risé and made countless nuisance calls. Eventually, Cale was able to have her successfully prosecuted.

Travelling to London in Spring 1985 to produce Nico's *Camera Obscura* album, Cale found himself surrounded by numerous junkies, and was soon using heroin again himself. He next recorded an album of his own at the same studio, *Artificial Intelligence*, which was co-written with cult journalist **Larry "Ratso" Sloman**. The record didn't go down that well with the critics or the public, but Cale still liked it. Even so, the process of recording it had left him "physically and emotionally exhausted".

Although Cale received a fair amount of critical acclaim throughout his solo career, commercial success eluded him, and he remained determinedly maverick. As critic **Mary Harron** once observed, throughout Cale's solo career he had "not simply avoided success, but tried to throttle it with both hands". This was at least partly due to Cale's drink and drug problems, but the birth of his daughter Eden in July 1985 planted the seed for a realization that the time had finally come to sober up. It would take many months to bear fruit – during which Cale

recorded another album, *Even Cowgirls Get The Blues* – but he eventually gave up drugs and alcohol for good in early 1986. He began playing squash regularly, underwent a course of Interferon injections to combat liver damage (as Lou Reed had also done several years earlier) and began to repair his damaged system.

Cale took a year off work to be a full-time father, and decided to avoid touring for a while. Instead, he worked on classical pieces on his home computer, many of which would later appear on record from the French label **Crépuscule**. Some were soundtracks for films (including a contribution to the soundtrack of **Jonathan Demme**'s 1986 film *Something Wild*), others commissions from dance companies.

Cale's film-score work ranged from the obscure to the mainstream, including Jonathan Demme's hit comedy

After decades of chaos, John Cale was busily putting his house in order.

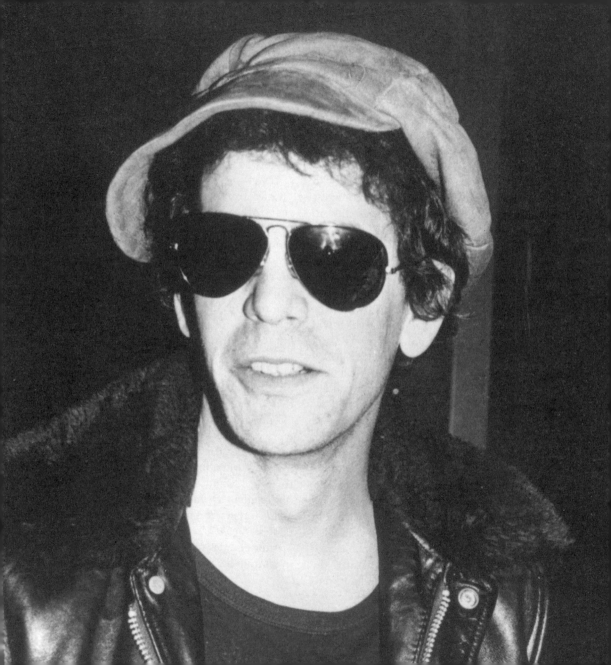

The Story

Lou Reed

After Lou Reed quit The Velvet Underground in August 1970, he went to live with his parents in New Jersey and spent the next year "realigning" himself. He was broke and depressed, and when he suggested to Sterling Morrison that they reform the Velvets without Yule, Morrison turned him down. To many, Reed seemed confused, and possibly on the brink of a nervous breakdown. He did, however, successfully sue to establish copyright ownership of some of the Velvets' songs (but failed to acquire the rights to the name "The Velvet Underground"). He was working as a typist in his father's accountancy firm for $40 a week, and had seemingly given up on music completely. Instead, he wrote poetry for *Fusion* magazine, and even gave a poetry reading at St. Marks Church on the Bowery (where he was joined in the pulpit by John Cale). Reed also started dating **Bettye Kronstadt**, a waitress with acting ambitions who would soon become his first wife. He wasn't drinking heavily, and didn't seem to be using drugs. As he'd describe it shortly after, it was a time of "exile and great pondering".

He was, however, still writing songs and taping acoustic demos at home. Having heard these tapes, Lou's friends **Lisa Robinson** (the rock critic) and her husband, record producer **Richard Robinson** (who had worked with the Flamin' Groovies, among others), persuaded Reed that he should start making records again. They introduced him to RCA's A&R man **Dennis Katz** (who had signed David Bowie to the label), who duly came up with a record contract: Lou Reed was signed to make two albums, the first with Richard Robinson on board as producer. Within a year, Katz would leave the label to become Reed's manager. Reed described his new material as being "all love songs".

The album would be recorded in London, since at the time British studios and engineers were thought to be not only more adventurous and technically advanced than their American counterparts, but also cheaper. In December 1971, an enthusiastic Lou arrived in London accompanied by Bettye and the Robinsons. Recording commenced at **Morgan Studios** a few weeks later with a motley collection of session musicians – partly because Reed was having to settle for whoever he could get. No one could have expected Reed to come up with his best work in those circumstances – and the Velvets' stunning *Loaded* was a particularly hard act to follow – but even making these allowances, Reed's first solo album was a huge let-down for performer and audience alike, and RCA Records were allegedly horrified when they heard it.

After completing the album, Reed flew to Paris to reunite with John Cale and Nico for a gig at Le Bataclan theatre in Paris, rehearsing for several days beforehand. Afterwards, he supposedly suggested to the others that they form a new band, but they turned him down. It was, perhaps, an indication of how desperate he'd become that he'd even asked them. When

Melody Maker asked about the chances of a Velvets reunion, Reed replied, "you couldn't recreate what went on then. It's dead". Plans to repeat the Le Bataclan concert in London came to nothing.

Working With The Star Man

Lou was aware that something drastic had to be done. *Lou Reed* was released in May 1972 and bombed commercially, so fantastically so that there was serious talk at RCA of dropping Reed from the label. Then **David Bowie** entered the picture. Another RCA artist, at this point Bowie was the hottest rock act on the planet, riding high on the success of his *The Rise And Fall Of Ziggy Stardust* album. It was his offer to act as Reed's next producer which undoubtedly persuaded RCA to give Reed another chance.

In an interview given in 1997, Bowie praised Reed's generosity towards him, and admitted to being a little awed by Reed's back catalogue and his talent for lyrical economy when they first met. The admiration was seemingly mutual: Reed later spoke of their creative *simpatico*, and said that their collaboration "reminded me of when I was with Warhol". High praise indeed, since Reed has always given Andy Warhol due credit for his input on the Velvets' early career (and beyond). But it wasn't all smooth sailing, with both parties given to moods and tantrums in the studio.

Still, most people would agree that the results more than achieved Bowie's stated ambition for *Transformer*: that it should be "a memorable album, that people wouldn't forget".

Marrying Reed to the English **glam-rock** scene seemed to make a lot of sense, although Reed was tougher than the English glam dandies, and possessed New York grit and streetsmarts. But Reed was obviously aware of the enormous amount of press coverage Bowie had gained with his admission of bisexuality, and was willing to play the controversy card for all it was worth. Since alternative sexuality was now fashionable, this was the time to exploit his own.

Much of the work of arranging the album was done by **Mick Ronson**, to whom Reed would first play the songs on an acoustic guitar – though Reed himself played very little guitar on the actual album (in fact, he'd play very little guitar on any of his solo records until 1975's *Coney Island Baby*). But Reed found Ronson's Hull accent impenetrable; he was thus somewhat bemused the first time Ronson removed Reed's out-of-tune guitar and started tuning it. Ronson in turn later admitted that some of Reed's more artistic explanations of his lyrics went straight over his head.

When the finished *Transformer* was released, in August 1972, Lou was seemingly overjoyed with the results, and showered praise on his collaborators, saying of Bowie simply: "The kid's got everything … everything". But later on, he'd be deeply resentful that David Bowie received much of the credit for the commercial

David Bowie

David Bowie (b. David Robert Jones, 1947) had been a Velvet Underground fan ever since his manager Ken Pitt had visited the Factory in 1966 and had returned to Britain with an acetate copy of the Velvets' first album ("I'd never heard anything quite like it – it was a revelation to me"). The influence showed on Bowie's 1970 album *The Man Who Sold The World*, and the following year's *Hunky Dory* had contained

not only a song about Andy Warhol, but also a Velvetish pastiche song, 'Queen Bitch', dedicated to the "VU". In 1972, Bowie leapt from being a cult figure to being a superstar, as his *The Rise And Fall Of Ziggy Stardust* album propelled him into the pop stratosphere overnight, and gained him an enormous teen following.

Bowie decided to expand into record production, and who better to start with than one of his heroes? He and Reed had already met several times, and had got on well (it probably didn't hurt that Bowie had publicly called Reed "the most important writer in rock and roll in the world"), so when Bowie offered to produce Reed's second solo album, both Lou and RCA readily agreed.

This might not have been an entirely selfless act on Bowie's part. According to his ex-wife Angie, "David was very smart. He'd been evaluating the market for his work, calculating his moves and monitoring his competition. And the only really serious competition in his market niche, he'd concluded, consisted of Lou Reed and – maybe – Iggy Pop. So what did David do? He co-opted them. He brought them into his circle. He talked them up in interviews, spreading their legend in Britain".

The strategy worked as, deploying some inventive shape-shifting, Bowie remained ahead of the field by some lengths for the next three decades, consistently outselling his competitors, even sometimes with decidedly sub-standard material.

The night Ziggy died: Reed with Mick Jagger, Lulu and Bowie celebrating after Ziggy's farewell concert at the Hammersmith Odeon, July 1973

and artistic success of *Transformer*, and would bitchily dismiss Bowie's input. The Reed/Bowie relationship would have its ups and downs, but this wouldn't be the end of it. Amazingly, the album became a hit, even more amazingly because "Walk On The Wild Side" with its overt trans-sexual, drug and sex-act references became a Top Ten hit. In less than a year, Reed had gone from abject failure to having the biggest success of his career.

Since his position with RCA was now much stronger, Reed flexed his muscles, refusing to work with Bowie again, or to simply repeat the *Transformer* formula for his next album. Instead, he supposedly reached an agreement with RCA over his next project: *Berlin*, which was originally conceived as a double-album. In return for complete artistic control over this "serious" album, Reed would subsequently deliver two further "hit" albums. One was to be a live album, the other a studio album in the *Transformer* mould, as consciously commercial as he could make it. But with *Berlin* he would make no compromises.

Berlin was to tell the story of the disintegrating relationship of Jim and Caroline, two American junkies living in Berlin. The fact that the story ended in suicide meant that everyone knew in advance that this wouldn't exactly be cheery. Many thought the character of Caroline was modelled on **Nico** (and there are certainly some biographical elements that match), but Reed wasn't saying…though Nico would later claim Reed "wrote me letters saying *Berlin* was me". For his producer,

Lou chose **Bob Ezrin**, a 24-year-old Canadian who'd masterminded Alice Cooper's successful career turnaround. Though Reed would later claim that the album was already mapped out, according to Ezrin, Reed only had a few fragments ready when they first met. Ezrin suggested Reed strengthen the storyline and approach the project as if it were a film – there was even talk of making the album the basis for an actual movie at some point (Reed wanted Roman Polanski to direct), but it came to nothing. Once the songs were written, Ezrin worked on orchestral arrangements with the help of fellow Canadian **Allan Macmillan**. Unusually, no violins were to be used; instead, Ezrin substituted violas and cellos, in order to evoke "a Kurt Weill/Bertolt Brecht atmosphere which would suit the lyric".

While recording the album in June 1973, Reed's relationship with Bettye Kronstadt – whom he'd married that Spring – was falling apart. There were stormy scenes of domestic violence, and Bettye was frequently seen sporting a black eye. And according to Reed, Bettye attempted suicide by cutting her wrists in the bathtub. The Reeds seemed to mirror the fictional Jim and Caroline, which probably made it fairly difficult for Reed to deal with recording at all (Bettye finally left Lou shortly after the album's release. She has since remarried and has had several children). Apart from his personal upheavals, Reed was going through creative pains as well, and as Ezrin confessed, "all of us were messing around with things we shouldn't have been messing around with". Specifically, Lou was drinking heavily ("constantly", by his own admission) and also using Valium and methedrine, while Ezrin himself was using heroin (which he'd discovered in London). Reed and Ezrin were also putting in 14- to 20-hour-long days while working on the record, and came close to psychological meltdown as a result.

When the tapes were finally delivered, **RCA** were appalled by what they heard. While Reed was holidaying in Portugal, Ezrin was summoned to a meeting and informed that they would not release the record as a double-album. Ezrin was instructed to cut the hour-long record's length by 15 minutes so that it could be squeezed onto one vinyl disc. Ezrin refused to cut any of the songs – and since the album sleeve and booklet had already been printed, that wasn't really an option anyway. Instead, Ezrin trimmed the tracks, cutting 14 minutes "of endings, solos, interstitial material, digressions inside songs". Soon after making the cuts, Ezrin was hospitalized as the result of "a heroin rebound". The album was mastered in Ezrin's absence by Jack Richardson and Paul King in Nashville.

Understandably, Reed hit the roof over the fact that his work had been mutilated without his even being consulted. When the record finally came out it received almost universally bad reviews. *Rolling Stone* called it "patently offensive". Reed pointed out that adults liked the record, even if younger listeners had trouble relating to it. It didn't matter. Sales were terrible – it stalled at Number 98 in the charts.

"I knew I wasn't writing for a majority", Lou would comment decades later. "I was writing about pain, and I was writing about things that hurt". But if Reed hadn't expected a commercial success, he hadn't expected a flop either; nor did any of this help his relationship with his record label. Years later, Reed stated, "There are people I'll never forgive for the way they fucked me over with *Berlin*. The way that album was overlooked was the biggest disappointment I ever faced". At this point it was as if something fundamental switched off within him, and it would take many years before it switched on again. In 1997, Ezrin proudly spoke of *Berlin* as having been "a seminal work, that digs deeper into the soul of the artist than any other work that had been released, certainly into the American music scene, for fifty years". Perhaps so…but in 1973, the world wasn't ready for it.

Too Fast To Live

Still reeling from the fallout from *Berlin*, Lou Reed returned to **live performance** – the first proper solo tour he'd done, with the huge *Transformer* audience eager to see him. The tour went well, and two New York dates were recorded for a live album, *Rock 'N' Roll Animal*, which proved to be a sound commercial move. Despite the album's musical quality being pretty grim, the heavy quotient of Velvets material included reminded reviewers and Reed's new audience of his pedigree. Reviews were almost all extremely good, as were the sales – the album reached Number 45 on the US charts, and remained in the Top 100 for over six months. Image-wise, Reed now seemed to be exploiting his reputation as a bad boy. He didn't play guitar at all now, and was allegedly injecting vast quantities of speed. He strutted manically round the stage in chains and leather, with a severe crew-cut and facial make-up that made him look like a refugee from *The Rocky Horror Picture Show* (which he'd probably inspired in the first place, to be fair...).

Upholding his image was soon more than he could bear. Reed's next album, *Sally Can't Dance,* was written in the studio during June 1974 by a road-ragged Reed, who was also flat broke and reeling from his divorce the previous Autumn. He was skeletally thin, had shaved Iron Crosses into his bleached-blonde crew-cut, and his use of amphetamine appeared to be out of control. Decisions were largely left to producer **Steve Katz** (brother of Dennis), who produced the album because most of the time Reed "was in the bathroom shooting up". Nevertheless, Reed became involved with **Barbara Hodes**, a successful career woman who worked in the fashion industry, and who he'd known since 1966; inevitably, the relationship didn't last for long.

Recording the album, Reed couldn't even remember the words to 'Ride, Sally, Ride' at all; Katz had to sing the song into a cassette player, then send Reed home with the tape to learn the song. But if Reed trusted Katz to come up with the goods, he hated what Katz actually produced. Though at the time Reed played along

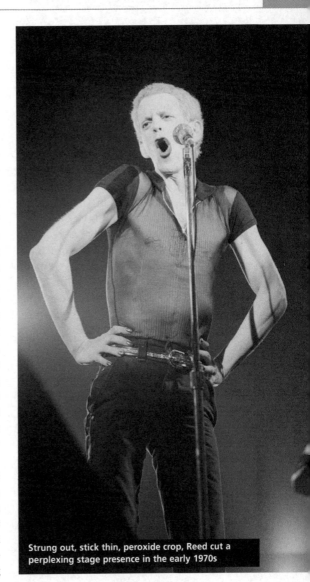

Strung out, stick thin, peroxide crop, Reed cut a perplexing stage presence in the early 1970s

with the publicity machine, later on he got vitriolic, describing *Sally Can't Dance* as "a piece of shit". But ironically, Lou had kept the promise he'd made RCA before making *Berlin*. *Sally Can't Dance* became his biggest commercial success, reaching the Top Ten and staying in the charts for 14 weeks. Lou commented sarcastically, "This is fantastic – the worse I am, the more it sells". To keep the ball rolling, RCA promptly released *Lou Reed Live* the following spring, drawn from the same 1973 concert as *Rock 'N' Roll Animal*. Unremarkable as this album is, it's probably better than any new live material Reed could have recorded during the period. His live act now included him pretending to shoot up on stage, while off stage he was increasingly upping his dose, and was definitely not in good shape. He was hanging out with a crowd of hardcore methedrine users, barely eating or sleeping, and seemingly living on a diet of ice cream and cigarettes.

In the first week of January 1975, Reed went into the studio with **Michael Fonfara** on keyboards, **Bob Meday** on drums and (surprisingly) former Velvet Underground bassist Doug Yule. Steve Katz was nominally the producer for these sessions, but was not actually present in the studio. Five songs were recorded before manager Dennis Katz hit the roof, claiming the songs were far too negative and uncommercial. As Reed later recalled, "a lot of fighting took place. I fired him. Then, typically, there was a money crunch, so I went on tour".

Metal Machine Revenge

When he returned from touring a few months later, Reed discovered that he was knee-deep in legal problems with Katz, and also both broke and homeless. RCA paid for him to stay at the Gramercy Hotel while he put his life back together, giving added urgency to their demand that Reed should deliver a new album. So he gave them one, called *Metal Machine Music*. Reed was contractually obliged to deliver an album, but wasn't yet ready to record one. Instead, according to Michael Fonfara, Reed "went and hooked up all these amplifiers with his guitar in his loft and got it feeding back and made that record. They were so horrified when they heard it. They said, 'Oh my God'. He said, 'This is it, you asked for product, you got it. I've lived up to my part, now you've got to release it'". A double album of **electronic music** created with guitar feedback was not exactly what RCA had been expecting.

Having made the record, Reed sold it – to RCA and the world – as a serious piece of art. This involved a great deal of hyperbole, with Reed listing all the (completely fictional) equipment he'd used on the back of the album. He also claimed that it contained "frequencies that are dangerous…they're illegal to put on a record", and that within it there were also "symphonic rip-offs" from the likes of Beethoven and Mozart. Reed also later claimed that the head of RCA had wanted to put the album out under the label's classical division, but that he'd refused on the grounds that it would be pretentious. In fact, the record caused RCA some problems on the classification front, and Reed claimed, "They don't know how to copyright it. How do you take musical notation on it? I said, 'Look, don't worry. Nobody's gonna cover it.' I can't see The Carpenters doing their version of it". Quite.

Was Reed really serious about this? Either way, critics were divided. **Lester Bangs** said, "Just because it's an amphetamine-head playing around with electronics and tape record-

ers doesn't mean it isn't valid", going on to call it "the greatest album of all time". But the majority of reviews were extremely negative. John Rockwell dismissed it as "sheer self-destructive indulgence". Reed was unrepentant. He told *Creem* magazine, "They should be grateful I put that fucking thing out, and if they don't like it, they can go and eat ratshit. I make records for me". Today the record is generally regarded as having been years ahead of its time, and a major influence on everyone from **Philip Glass** to **Sonic Youth**, and there now seems little doubt that Reed did intend the

Reed with Patti Smith. By the mid-1970s the baton of radical pop music was passing to the next generation

Rachel

Rachel (originally Tommy, last name unknown) was a sultry and inscrutable drag queen that Reed met in a bar. According to him she was "completely disinterested in who I was and what I did. Nothing could impress her. He'd hardly heard my music and didn't like it all that much when he did". Rachel was half Mexican and/or Indian, and though she often appears extremely glamorous in photographs, those who met him/her speak of the illusion dissolving into heavy stubble at close quarters.

Though Reed's relationship with Rachel was occasionally stormy, the couple were clearly devoted to each other, and she provided him with some badly needed stability. They moved in together almost immediately; she toured the world with him, and they were virtually inseparable for the four-year duration of their relationship. When it ended, Reed missed her terribly, then seldom mentioned her ever again. Rachel's current whereabouts are unknown, but many think she may now be dead and that she was the model for the dying character "Rita" on Reed's 1992 album *Magic And Loss*.

work to be taken seriously (whatever his other motives might have been). Mastering engineer **Bob Ludwig** confirmed in 1997 that "Lou was extremely interested in every detail of it, and that it be just right. There was never a hint that this was anything that he wasn't one hundred per cent serious about". But as Reed admitted with refreshing honesty in 1997, "I *was* serious about it, y'know? I was also really stoned".

Regardless of the work's musical merit, there's no doubt at all that it was also Reed's revenge on the executives who'd insisted on cutting the length of *Berlin* and made *Sally* his biggest hit. It certainly wasn't the kind of Lou Reed record people were expecting, though amazingly it sold nearly 100,000 copies. Even so, RCA issued a statement in which Lou Reed seemingly apologized for *Metal Machine Music*, though he later denied he'd been involved in the apology at all, and claimed that the album had achieved "what it was supposed to do".

In October, Reed finally felt ready to re-enter the studio and give RCA the album of songs they'd been waiting for. Strangely, given Lou's legal problems with his brother, Steve Katz was re-enlisted as Reed's co-producer, but the arrangement didn't last. Katz later claimed that by this time Reed's drug problem was markedly worse, to the point that he simply had to quit the project: "I felt that Lou was, at the time, out of his mind. So I had to stop the sessions. I had someone in authority from RCA come to the studio and verify that I could not make an album with the artist – that was that". As Katz's replacement, Reed brought in **Godfrey Diamond**, an engineer in his early twenties. The relationship worked out well, probably because Lou largely got his own way. At the time he stressed the importance of spontaneity, writing most of the songs for *Coney Island Baby* on the spot in the studio.

But Dennis Katz attempted to halt the album even while it was being recorded, and Reed was served three times with three separate subpoenas, as the lawsuits and counter-lawsuits flew back and forth. Some of them took eleven years to settle. But at least Lou's emotional life had reached calmer waters. He'd been involved since late 1974 in a steady relationship with a transsexual named **Rachel**. (Responding to a journalist's query as to whether his boss was "bi", one of Reed's roadies once gave the quotable answer: "Bi? The fucker's quad!")

The relationship is a recurring motif on *Coney Island Baby*. In Rachel, Reed had obviously found a muse, and his happiness and confidence were clearly evident. The record is a minor artistic triumph given Reed's circumstances at the time. Sadly, the critics didn't agree, and it garnered largely bad reviews...though ironically it sold comparatively well, hitting Number 41 on the *Billboard* chart. Still, Reed had finally had it with his record company. In the Summer of 1976 he switched record labels, moving from RCA to **Arista**. Lisa Robinson asked Lou what Arista could do for him that RCA couldn't. "Sell records", Reed quipped. Two other projects from this era never saw the light of day: a book of Reed's collected poetry, to be titled *All The Pretty People*, and a musical based on the book *The Philosophy Of Andy Warhol*, for which Reed apparently wrote all the songs.

Street Hassles

The first album for Arista was recorded almost immediately. Most of the songs were written in the studio, and the entire album took 27 days to record and mix. Sadly, *Rock And Roll Heart* was as awful (in its own way) as *Sally Can't* *Dance* – and this time around it didn't even sell. Reed was almost constantly broke during this period, and most of his earnings went to speed. The following year Reed recorded his next album, *Street Hassle*, using a "revolutionary" technique for stereo sound called binaural, and Reed was evangelistic about the system's 360-degree sound, "There is no stereo, there's no left and right, it's total. You've never heard anything like it in your life. And it is spectacular". The system had been invented by a German, **Manfred Schünke**. Reed was so enamoured of binaural recording that he would also use it for his next two albums, recording the next one, *The Bells*, in Germany with Schünke himself. Though it never caught on with the music industry, Reed still believed in the system's merits in 1990, "I do believe that binaural or virtual reality sound will eventually become the standard for recordings, replacing stereo in the same way that stereo replaced mono. While various technical problems mitigated the success of the effect, I believed then and believe now that I'd heard the sound of the future".

But *Street Hassle* was beset by problems. Amazingly, Reed had recruited Richard Robinson to produce it – but Robinson soon walked out. At the album's end Reed complained about having been "betrayed by all the evil people around me", and he included Arista boss **Clive Davis** (who had originally been encouraging about the project) among them. The album detailed Reed's crumbling relationship with Rachel (they were tempo-

The Story

rarily separated, but would part for good the following year), so he wasn't in great emotional shape. Though the innovative title track showed Reed was still capable of breaking new ground, both lyrically and musically at this point his creative flow was very limited. Lou was as proud as usual, but had an unrealistic view of his position, saying, "I'm right in step with the market. The album is enormously commercial". Actually, it wasn't, and reviews and sales were both grim. It was definitely an improvement on the previous album, but that was never going to be a difficult task.

Reed bought time with a pretty dreadful live album, *Take No Prisoners*, and used the breathing room to produce something a little more interesting in the studio. 1979's *The Bells* showed more experimentation, but nothing that remarkable or melodic – but Reed was obviously enthusiastic, and pleased with his band. However, Arista hated *The Bells*, and Clive Davis thought it only half-finished. Once again, Reed dug his heels in and refused to alter the record at all – his stubbornness resulting in the most minimal promotion from his label. Reed later complained that *The Bells* had been "dropped into a dark well" by Arista. Hardly anybody else liked it either, except **Lester Bangs**, who called it "the only true jazz-rock fusion anybody's come up with since Miles Davis' *On The Corner* period". In 1996, asked which of his albums was the most underrated, Lou replied: "*The Bells*. I really like that album. I think it sold two copies, and probably both to me". After Rachel disappeared from his life for

good, Lou started playing the field. He was living in an apartment on Christopher Street, the hub of Greenwich Village's gay community, and was now outspoken about his homosexuality, and the fact that his love songs were homosexual ones: "I just wouldn't want listeners to be under a false impression".

In April 1979, Reed had a legendary fistfight with **David Bowie** in a London restaurant, witnessed by journalists Allan Jones and Giovanni Dadomo. It started after Reed had supposedly asked Bowie to produce his next album, and had been turned down. Bowie had allegedly told Reed, "clean up your act", and had promptly been biffed by Lou. In fact, Reed was all too aware that he had problems. A shortage of speed in New York had forced him to quit using it, and he'd become overweight as a result; he had also stepped up his already serious alcohol intake to compensate, simply replacing one addiction with another. In addition, he was having financial problems. "I need money to live!" he'd yelled at Arista's Clive Davis during a gig at The Bottom Line in June 1979. In January 1980, Reed and his band flew to Montserrat, to record Lou's final album for the label. They were, according to Lou, thoroughly rehearsed and knew exactly what they were about. But Lou's new muse alcohol created a certain amount of mayhem in the studio, as he later admitted, "*Growing Up In Public* is one of the drinking records of all time…Me and Fonfara were ridiculous. We almost drowned in the pools that they've got there. It's not a good way to make a record. We were animals".

On a more positive note, Reed began seeing a psychotherapist and was delighted with the early results. He also acquired another stabilizing influence in his life when he began dating **Sylvia Morales**. The couple began dividing their time between Manhattan and a house Lou had bought in Blairstown, New Jersey. They would marry the following year.

Growing Up

Regardless of Lou's drinking problem, *Growing Up In Public* was still the best album he'd made in nearly a decade, and a sign of real hope. As

it turned out, that hope was not misplaced. At the start of 1981 Reed joined both Alcoholics Anonymous and Narcotics Anonymous and generally cleaned up his act. He'd badly needed help – asked in the early 1990s how bad his addictions had got, he replied simply, "As bad as it gets". Both as a person and as an artist, Reed had painted himself into a corner; now he was "starting at square one again". Eventually Reed would give up cigarettes and caffeine as well, and he soon discovered health foods and Taoism, and new forms of physical release like Tai Chi, motorbikes, pinball, snorkelling and basketball. He also found time to play a cameo role (as a record executive) in **Paul Simon's**

Bridging troubled waters? Pop godfather Paul Simon offers Reed some words of wisdom

Sylvia Reed

Sylvia Morales was half-Mexican, an artist and designer, and part of the CBGB punk crowd. She was also studying writing and – according to Victor Bockris – funding herself by stripping and working as an S&M dominatrix. She met Lou in a club in 1978, and from then on the couple were inseparable. They married on Valentine's Day 1980. He was nearly 38, she was 24. The relationship was described by some as a punk version of a traditional 1950s marriage, and Reed seemed to confirm that, "I like to look at centuries past, when knighthood was in flower, I'm still a great one for that. I think I've found my flower, so it makes me feel more like a knight". Sylvia Reed would also become Lou's manager, some of her decisions greatly increasing his commercial worth.

movie *One Trick Pony*.

Speaking of his drink and drug problems in 1990 Reed admitted, "It got very out of control. So, it was just obvious it had to stop. To really get a grip on my career and be true to the talent and everything I have to have control". He had no problems in talking about the recovery process, or about drugs in general. The man who had been one of rock's most celebrated drug-users evidently now held very different views, "I think drugs are the single most terrible thing, and if I thought there was anything I could do which I thought might be effective in stopping people dealing in drugs and taking them, I would do it". All these life changes resulted in Lou taking the

next two years off from music. He ceased to tour, and said goodbye to his band of over five years' standing; though Reed had been happy to explore jazz and funk, he now felt he'd "carried this experiment far enough. It's not working". When he re-emerged, he'd switched record labels and had re-signed with – of all people – RCA, and his band was stripped down to a four-piece with a completely different approach, and included former Richard Hell sideman **Robert Quine** (whom Reed had admired for years) on guitar.

Lou's recording technique for *The Blue Mask* was also brand new, and largely improvised. Reed gave each of the musicians a cassette of his demos of the songs, and left them to come up with arrangements. When it came to recording, Quine later reported that they'd entered the studio "with no rehearsals. None of us had ever played together before, but it just clicked immediately. What you hear on the record is totally live. There are no overdubs, except on one track…any mistakes that happen are on the record. If I take a solo, I stop playing rhythm. There is no rhythm guitar fill going underneath. It's the way they used to do things in the 50s. I'm especially proud of that record". The two guitarists were especially *simpatico*. Quine was already a fan of Reed's, and had been since the days of the Velvets (his live recordings of the band would eventually be released as *The Bootleg Tapes Volume I*). The two became close friends (drummer **Lenny Ferrari** described them as being like "the Odd Couple"), though the relationship would eventually sour.

Released just before Reed's fortieth birthday, the album's cover (designed by Sylvia Reed) was a clever pastiche of the image on *Transformer*. The album itself is variable – sometimes meandering and ragged, sometimes genuinely exciting – but mercifully the music is a lot more bluesy, accessible and exciting than anything Reed had done for years, and lyrically he'd obviously matured an enormous amount. His songs were far more confessional than any prior release, many of them seeming to fall under the general heading of therapy (the working title of the album was *Heaven & Hell*).

Reviews were largely ecstatic, which certainly helped restore Reed's artistic confidence – though when critic Robert Palmer complimented Reed on the album, he was generous in sharing the credit, "It's mostly working with the right musicians". As Reed commented years later, "I was playing guitar with a sympathetic guitar player. A monumental bass player, **Fernando Saunders**. And Doane Perry on drums. Plus a good engineer. And I'd made some strides in the improvement of the production". This time around, his pride seemed genuine, "This is my best album to date. This one was pretty much perfect – it came out the way it was supposed to". But if writing it had been a psychological release, it had also taken its toll, since for Reed writing his low-life characters was comparable creatively to method acting, and "doing those characters long enough – it gets to you. Some of those

lyrics are very rough".

Sadly, with 1983's follow-up *Legendary Hearts*, things ran a lot less smoothly – according to Robert Quine, the working title for the album was *The Argument*, reflecting the atmosphere inside the studio. Lou no longer wished to collaborate freely, but this time wanted things done his way. He took the sole production credit, and Robert Quine's guitar parts ended up being buried way down in the mix (and at times were missing altogether). Quine was angry when he heard the results, and though he remained with Reed for another two years, "things were never the same after that". *Legendary Hearts* didn't gain the immediate attention of its predecessor (because this time there wasn't the same "back from the grave" angle), and reviews ranged from indifferent to bad while sales were slim. Next, Reed finally released his first decent live album, *Live In Italy*, recorded during the Autumn 1983 tour, and quickly followed it with another studio album. Reed later stated that he'd "wanted to have fun" with *New Sensations*, and had rediscovered the joys of guitar playing. Perhaps that was why he fired Robert Quine just two days before the recording sessions were due to start.

Thanks largely to the single "I Love You, Suzanne" getting lots of airplay, *New Sensations* became Reed's most successful record in years, artistically as well as commercially. Typically, the next album, 1986's *Mistrial*, was another step backwards – a messy experiment with synthesizers and drum machines that just didn't work. Reviews were terrible, and Reed

Reed, the lean, clean, politically-active machine lends his *gravitas* to an Amnesty International press conference in 1986

was touchy enough to dredge up his previous credentials, "It's very easy to see that the person who wrote The Velvet Underground stuff wrote *Mistrial*. It's not all that different, it's just a little older".

The previous year had seen Reed doing ads for American Express, and using "Walk On The Wild Side" to advertise scooters for Honda, but in 1985 he reunited with his less commercial self, taking part in **Steve Van Zandt**'s anti-apartheid project *Sun City*. Then, in 1986, he toured the world on behalf of **Amnesty International** (in the company of U2 and Peter Gabriel, among others). That year he also delivered an anti-drug TV commercial on behalf of **Rock Against Drugs**; since the spot was aimed at 8-year-olds, Lou kept it simple, "I did drugs … Don't you". Regarding all this political activity he said, "Just because I write about what I write about doesn't mean I don't care about what's going on around me. The days of me being aloof about certain things are over". More proof would come with his very next album.

Whither The Velvet Underground?

As the years passed, the ex-Velvets found themselves increasingly unable to escape the shadow of their former career. The Velvet Underground's critical reputation grew inexorably, as did the recognition of their influence and the size of their audience – all of which was fuelled further by the 'posthumous' record releases.

The first of these, *Live At Max's Kansas City* was released in 1972, without the knowledge or approval of any of the band – though Reed would later acknowledge that he was happy it had come out. Atlantic's **Ahmet Ertegun** – realizing he'd never get the Velvets' second contracted-for album (or at any rate, not one featuring Reed) – had bought the cassette recording of the gig made by Factory stalwart Brigid Polk.

Another live album, *1969: Velvet Underground Live*, followed two years later. The tapes which comprised this had come into the possession of the Velvets' old manager Steve Sesnick … but before he could release them commercially, he needed the permission of the whole band. Amazingly, Lou Reed agreed (the fact that his solo career was at a low point at the time may well have had something to do with it), and when Sterling Morrison refused to play along with Steve Sesnick's plans, Reed called him as well, to try and change his mind.

Morrison still didn't want the album released – partly because of the musical quality (he thought *Live At Max's* had much more energy) and partly because he didn't want the hassle of trying to collect royalties from people he didn't particularly trust. With no current musical career to promote, Morrison saw little reason to co-operate and threatened legal action if they proceeded without his approval. Eventually, Sesnick convinced him to sign a legal release "because he told me he needed the money".

Meanwhile, Mercury records, paying no mind to potential litigation, had gone ahead with production, which is why Morrison wasn't credited on the album sleeve. According to Maureen Tucker, she and Morrison were originally offered the princely sum of $200 each to sign a release form so that the album could come out. They eventually agreed to $1,500 apiece.

1985 saw the release of *VU*, a collection of unreleased studio material mainly drawn from the "lost" album. This was so successful that the next year it was followed by a further collection, *Another View*. Maureen Tucker preferred the first album, Sterling Morrison the second (which Tucker thought had a poor mix – "too clean" – possibly because the original four-track tapes weren't used). Reed and Morrison apparently disliked the fact that so many instrumentals were included, but conceded that fans would want to hear even unfinished material.

The posthumous live albums stirred up speculation about the possibility of a reunion. "It'll never happen", Reed stated flatly. But one obstacle was removed in 1986, when **Christopher Whent**, a lawyer Cale had hired to untangle the Velvet Underground's financial affairs, began to get results. Whent had worked on the problem for nearly four years, and at the end was acting on behalf of all four original Velvets. The group had signed three different record contracts with MGM (partly because of line-up changes), each with a different royalty rate – which meant a headache for everybody. Lou Reed agreed that some of the royalties had been weighted too heavily in his favour, and agreed to a redistribution – an act of good faith that opened communications between himself and Morrison. Whent suggested that the Velvets form a company, which could then divide the money between them however they pleased. As a result they all started to receive the royalty cheques, they'd waited on for such a long time.

But no matter how much interest there may have been in a Velvets reunion, at this point no one seriously expected that it would ever happen. There were just too many disagreements, too much history, too much bad blood.

And then Andy died.

The death of Andy Warhol

Andy Warhol had been ill for a long time. His gall bladder was badly infected, but he had steadfastly procrastinated about having the operation he knew was necessary (following his post-assassination experiences, Warhol had developed an – understandable – terror of hospitals). But the pain eventually became so bad that Warhol could put it off no longer. After a three-hour operation on 21 February 1987, his gall bladder was removed and found to be gangrenous.

Afterwards, Warhol seemed to be recovering well, but he died, alone, early the following morning, seemingly of heart failure. There were rumours of AIDS (which seems unlikely – sexually-speaking, Warhol was reportedly more voyeur than participant), and accusations of hospital incompetence or neglect (the subject of a malpractice lawsuit). Some thought Warhol must have awoken in the night and – not knowing where he was – simply died of fright.

Forever Changed:
The Reunion Years

"There were always conflicts, and presumably always will be."

John Cale, 1974

Forever Changed: The Reunion Years
1987–1993

Signs of a reunion were a long time coming. For those who were aware of the often difficult relationship between Reed and the other former Velvets, the possibility seemed more an impossibility. Nevertheless, as increasingly collaborative projects emerged, not least on *Songs For Drella* and the preparation of authoritative retrospective albums, glimmers of hope emerged.

Singing For 'Drella (II)

Although Lou Reed's friendship with Andy Warhol had continued long beyond the managerial split, relations between them worsened during the 1980s. Warhol was hurt that Reed didn't invite him to his wedding, and the two had not even spoken for years. But Reed was still deeply saddened by Warhol's death, and commented that the artist's way of looking at things still influenced him greatly. With almost poetic symmetry, it was Warhol's death that reunited Reed with John Cale once again, when **Billy Name** brought them together after Warhol's memorial service at St. Patrick's Cathedral on 1 April 1987. It was the first time the pair had met since Cale sobered up, Reed having conspicuously avoided Cale on several occasions during the latter years of his drinking. Cale had also been fairly scathing in his public comments about Reed's post-Velvets career (as had Sterling Morrison), but the two evidently managed to put that behind them, and discovered that the core of their friendship was still intact.

Later that year, Cale began working on a musical tribute to Warhol – an instrumental piece, which Reed would later call "a Mass, of sorts". Cale also toured Japan with Nico as his support act, playing together for the last time at the Palais des Beaux-Arts in Brussels. During this period Cale also became interested in becoming an actor, taking acting lessons from **F. Murray Abraham** and discussing a possible horror movie role with director **George A. Romero**. Cale would eventually make cameo appearances in several low-budget independent films, and played a villain in

The Story

a 1989 episode of television's *The Equalizer*.

In May 1988, Cale contacted Reed, and asked him to listen to the work-in-progress on his Warhol piece. The two started discussing Andy and his impact upon their own lives, and, as Reed would later put it, "the opportunity arose to do the bigger thing". After hours of discussion, the two both agreed that there was a need to correct the public perception of the artist, because of what Reed called, "these evil books presenting Andy Warhol as just a piece of fluff. I wanted to show the Andy I knew".

It was also, as he later said, "a great chance to play together. Here was a subject that we both felt passionately and positively about". And so Cale's Mass began to slowly metamorphose into what would become the *Songs For Drella* song-cycle, titled after Andy's nickname – a composite of Cinderella and Dracula. Reed later described the work as "a brief musical look at the life of Andy Warhol" and also "entirely fictitious". (Interestingly, there's film footage of Warhol and Reed in conversation circa 1975, with Reed suggesting the possibility of a musical biography of Andy).

Over Christmas 1988, Reed and Cale worked on the piece in a small rehearsal studio and at Reed's house. Both men had had remarkable solo careers since parting company twenty years earlier; both had survived battles with drink and drugs and were now happily clean and sober. Cale admitted they were "bringing a lot of baggage to the project", but this time – though creative arguments would inevitably rear up – they were mature enough to work around them. While working on the project, added poignancy came with the news of another death in the "family". now Nico was gone as well.

The death of Nico

After the death of Andy Warhol, Nico seemed to become conscious of her mortality and the need to take care of both her mind and body. She exchanged heroin for methadone, adopted a healthier diet, and took up bicycle riding. She talked of the future, and of writing her autobiography. In March 1988 she performed her last tour – of Japan and Europe – as a support act for John Cale.

She died while on holiday in Ibiza on 18 July 1988, having collapsed by the roadside a few hours after riding off on her bicycle. The song lyric she was working on that morning was titled 'The Last Days Of A Singer'. What caused Nico's fainting fit is unknown: possibly heatstroke, since she was wearing heavy woollen clothing on an extremely hot day; possibly a heart attack – but what killed her was the fact that she'd hit her head on the ground. A taxi driver found her, but three hospitals refused to take her (because she was a foreigner, and one bearing needle marks). At the fourth hospital she was diagnosed with sunstroke, and she died that night, from the after-effects of a cerebral haemorrhage (apparently not drug-related). She was 49 years old. Her body was flown to Berlin, where it was cremated, and her ashes were buried in the grave of her mother, in the Grünewald-Forst cemetery on the outskirts of Berlin. None of The Velvet Underground nor anyone from the Factory attended her funeral.

Working on *Drella,* John Cale was "really excited by the amount of power just two people could do without needing drums, because what we have there is such a strong core idea that the simpler the better...Although I think (Lou) did most of the work, he has allowed me to keep a position of dignity in the process". The entire work is **co-credited**. Cale claims that they both wrote lyrics, but Reed evidently had the final say, and described the album as being "an excruciating son-of-a-bitch to write", at least partly because it involved dealing with his own feelings about Warhol. The results were, as John Cale observed, "an elegant piece of reporting, really. Reporting how misfits get together and create art". The instrumentation itself was kept sparse and tight – Reed on guitar, Cale on keyboards and viola, both sharing the vocals.

Drella remains one of Reed's most satisfying and mature works. Few people have ever received such a touching and intelligent eulogy as Warhol is given here, though in the course of it Reed spares neither Warhol nor himself. Throughout, Andy's own talent and humour shine through, as does Reed's evident affection for his mentor. Afterwards, Cale stated that he felt they had captured the man, but not his art.

Returning To Form

Meanwhile, Reed was recording his first solo album in nearly three years for new record label, **Sire** – and in Sire's head, **Seymour Stein,** Reed found the most sympathetic executive he'd ever dealt with. Reed also acquired a new guitarist, Mike Rathke, who would become a long-term collaborator (he was also married to Sylvia Reed's sister). The album was *New York*, a cycle of songs celebrating Reed's adopted city, warts and all. The year before, Reed had written an article for *New York* magazine that listed the things he liked (and disliked) about the city, which included the freedom and opportunities the city offered – "films, Chinese culture, people, places, things" – its energy and cultural cross-pollination. In contrast, he cited crime, the subways, the traffic, the out-of-date criminal justice system, old-fashioned civil service and unions, regulations, poor public education and an uncaring administration among the things he hated. The city was a subject that he felt passionately about, but despite its shortcomings he loved the town, "I can't do anything outside of New York. It's death".

Reed as protest singer was something new, but he seemed genuinely driven by anger at the city's (and the country's) decline, writing searing attacks on homelessness, pollution and racism. Reed rewrote and polished the songs on *New York* countless times, and the result is a (slightly flawed) masterpiece, an extremely mature work and the album Reed's fans had been hoping he'd pull out of his sleeve for decades. It re-established him as a major player in the eyes of both the critics and the public, and sales were strong enough to crack the *Billboard* Top 50. But Reed's plans for a world tour to promote the album fell apart after a few dates, when he fell off stage and broke his leg. The remainder of the tour was cancelled.

Cale, meanwhile, had been bringing to fruition a project he'd started many years before: *Words For The Dying*. Cale's original intention had been to write an opera about the life of **Dylan Thomas**, but this had developed into an adaptation of Thomas's poetry. In the end, Cale found only nine poems suitable for musical interpretation. Four of these became known as the "Falklands Suite", since they were completed during that conflict. The work premiered in 1987 at the Paradiso in Amsterdam and at St. Ann's Church in Brooklyn, and might not have gone any further had not **Brian Eno** become involved. Eno signed the project for his own record label, and offered to produce the album. However, the cost of a full orchestral backing proved a stumbling block until Eno's wife Anthea suggested they record in Russia, where orchestras and studios were much cheaper. In Spring 1989, Cale and Eno duly decamped to Moscow, where the sober Cale felt somewhat isolated among all the vodka drinkers.

Lou Reed later stated that *Songs For Drella* had been "written for the stage", and that's where the work was honed. An incomplete version was first performed in January 1989 at St. Ann's Church in Brooklyn, and when the duo were reunited later in the year Reed had refined the lyrics, and also added the pivotal number "A Dream", which echoed lines from Warhol's *Diaries*. In December 1989, the completed *Drella* premiered with a four-night run at the **Brooklyn Academy of Music**. On the last night Maureen Tucker joined her ex-cohorts on stage for an encore rendition of

New York revealed a revived and refocussed Reed

"Pale Blue Eyes". In 1989, Tucker had quit her job as a computer operator in a Wal-Mart shipping warehouse based in Tucson, Arizona, and moved to a small town in Georgia. She'd also released another album, the splendidly-titled *Life In Exile After Abdication* (with Lou Reed guesting on a version of "Pale Blue Eyes", which he considered the best recording of the song). That year she'd also supported Reed in concert for a few dates, and played on his *New York* album.

The day after the last Brooklyn concert, Cale and Reed performed the song cycle once again, this time in front of the video cameras for a planned commercial release. On film the duo are professional, confident, assured, with a rapport that verges on the telepathic, and where each nod speaks volumes. They would perform the entire piece only once more in front of an audience, in Japan in 1992. Meanwhile, recording the album version of *Drella* had become stressful. Having decided not to use an outside producer, the duo argued about every little detail, and Reed – who had earlier described the project as a "hundred per cent collaboration" – later implied to others that Cale had not pulled his weight, and even went so far as to try and remove Cale's name from the project. Of Warhol, the inspiration of it all, Reed said simply and eloquently, "We miss him very much". Still, he insisted there would be no further collaborations. Cale (despite saying shortly after the album's completion, "working with Lou is never dull, but I wouldn't want to go through it again") was

more optimistic, "I think we could do anything. I don't think there's a limit". Sadly, there would be, as time would prove. And, tragically, *Drella* never really received the attention it so clearly deserved. Reed stated that he'd hoped the album, "would open up a whole new genre of musical biography on CD. There are so many people it would be interesting to learn about through music".

In the spring of 1990, Reed sang in a benefit concert at London's Wembley Stadium for the recently released **Nelson Mandela**. He then flew to Prague to interview **Václav Havel** for *Rolling Stone* magazine, discovering in the process that journalism was a lot harder than it looked (the finished article was rejected, but Reed later included it in his first collection of lyrics).

Cale went straight from *Drella* into another difficult collaboration, this time with Brian Eno. He moved into Eno's house in Suffolk (where the pair had mixed *Words For The Dying* in 1989) and the two began work on a joint rock album which would appear in late 1990 as *Wrong Way Up* – the first work Eno had done on his own behalf that wasn't strictly ambient over a decade. There were fights and misunderstandings from the start, with Eno making arbitrary decisions to erase musical ingredients, and obviously regarding himself as the sole producer. When the album was done, Eno refused to tour with Cale to support the release. Worse, he issued a press statement announcing he'd never work with Cale again. That year Cale indulged his love of extraordinary clothing by becoming a fashion model for Yohji Yamamoto and Comme Des Garçons, making catwalk appearances in Paris and Tokyo.

Although *Drella* had certainly augured well for future collaborations, few (including any of the band) would have bet money that it might lead to a full-scale Velvet Underground reunion. Reed and Morrison hadn't talked to each other in years (royalties and songwriting credits being the principal bones of contention, along with Morrison's anger at Reed for making him tell Cale he was out of the band in 1968).

The reunion was preceded by an (almost) impromptu gathering of the four Velvets for a performance of *Songs for Drella*

Then, in June 1990, Reed, Cale, Tucker and Morrison all agreed to attend the opening of the Cartier Foundation's **Andy Warhol Exposition** in the small town of Jouy-en-Josas, 20 miles outside Paris. Right up until the last minute Reed was still insistent that, "you'll never get the four of us together on one stage again...ever", and no one could predict how Sterling Morrison would react upon meeting Reed again. Even so, Morrison stated that he wanted a reunion to happen, if at all possible. On the opening day Billy Name defused the tension with humour and Reed mellowed, inviting Morrison, Cale and Tucker to have lunch with him. Fences were mended, and that afternoon (15 June) Cale and Reed performed five songs from *Drella* in front of the audience of 300 invited guests who were mainly journalists ("a nightmare come true", in Reed's words)...and then Tucker and Morrison joined them on stage for a 15-minute version of "Heroin". No rehearsal, no sound check, just straight in at the deep end: The Velvet Underground together again, against all expectations. Naturally, the crowd went nuts.

Afterwards, Reed was noticeably tearful. "That was extraordinary", he later said. "To have those drums behind me, that viola on one side, and that guitar on the other again – you have no idea how powerful that felt". An exhilarated Cale stated, "Three hours ago this was not possible. Now, I'm overcome with emotion". Maureen Tucker was similarly exultant, while Morrison commented simply, "Not bad. Was I in tune?"

Reviewing the event, Nick Kent wrote, "It was ample enough demonstration of a musical chemistry that still smoulders after 22 dank, mostly bitter years apart". Now the ice had thawed, and the four of them spent the next few days together, meeting again several times over the course of the following two years. But still no one suggested a more formal reunion, and meanwhile there were solo careers to concentrate on.

Magic And Loss

Reed's next project tackled subjects hitherto almost completely ignored in rock: death and mortality. Specifically, the *Magic And Loss* album was inspired by the passing of two people that Reed described as "two of the most important people in my life", a woman named **Rita**, and the songwriter **"Doc" Pomus**, both of whom died of cancer. Reed read a lesson at the memorial service for Pomus in March 1991, recalling him as "a wonderful writer, a wonderful man...I grew up listening to so many songs written by 'Doc' Pomus, it was a pleasure to know him, he was a great spirit". Rita was mysteriously undefined. The album was dedicated "especially" to her, but her last name was omitted, and Reed wasn't saying. Some thought Rita might even have been Rachel (whose current whereabouts remain unknown). Others have suggested that it could have been the Factory-era speed-dealer known as Rotten Rita (real name Kenneth Rapp), but this seems somewhat unlikely in the context of the lyrics.

The Story

But death isn't exactly MTV-friendly, although Reed insisted that the record wasn't morbid or gloomy, "This isn't a bleak record. I'm not the only person in the world who's experienced loss – especially these days, with what AIDS and other diseases are doing. These are complex emotions... The record is like a friend talking to you. It's cleansing for the soul. That's why I think it's such a positive record, because it gives you something you can really grasp onto. The record gives the listener something more than music. When loss enters your life, what do you do? Do you go out and get drunk? In the end you wake up, the person's still gone. You can't stay drunk forever – you've still got to deal with it". On a more personal note, he stated simply, "I just wrote it – I didn't have any choice about it, that's why I wrote. That's all I could do at the time". He also railed against those critics who thought illness wasn't a fit subject for rock music, "You don't have anything of any depth in rock". As he pointed out, a writer has to deal with life in all its aspects, "What is there? Birth, life, death and the conflict in between". On its release, *Newsweek* called the album "the most grown-up rock record ever". Reed toured the world in support of the *Magic And Loss* album, requesting that audiences not eat, smoke, drink or talk during his performances.

Although *Magic And Loss* was completed by April 1991, its release was delayed until January 1992, so as not to harm sales of a 3-CD retrospective of Reed's solo career released that spring. Reed simultaneously celebrated his past by issuing his first published collection of lyrics, and both items bore the same title: *Between Thought And Expression* (a quote from "Some Kinda Love"). That summer, Reed gave two public readings of his lyrics in New York.

In 1991, Cale released *Paris S'Éveille* on the French label Crépuscule. Comprised of mainly instrumental music written for movies and ballet, the album also contained an unreleased Velvets track, a live instrumental of "Booker T." from 1968. The following year, Cale's beloved mother died, which affected him greatly. His financial affairs were still in disarray, and having moved into an expensive Greenwich Village house as well as renting a summer home in the Hamptons he soon found himself in trouble with the taxman. Cale buried himself in work, producing more music for ballet (including one called *Iphigenia In Taurus*), and also working on several multi-media pieces. One was *Life On Earth*, a collaboration with the musician and artist **Bob Neuwirth**, which would be released in album form several years later. The other (in 1993) was *Life Underwater*, a reworking of the Orpheus myth that featured a string quartet, a barbershop quartet and slides and films by independent director **Zoe Beloff**.

Moe Tucker made another album in 1991, *I Spent A Week There The Other Night*, which featured her playing with John Cale and Sterling Morrison on several tracks, with Lou Reed on another, and with all of them on one track, "I'm Not". Having managed to coax Morrison back into playing guitar again, she persuaded him to join her band in 1992 for several tours of Europe and one of the States. A live album, *Oh No, They're Recording This Show* came out in 1992. When Reed's *Magic And Loss* tour hit Paris, he crossed paths with Morrison and Tucker, who were also playing a gig in town,

for which Reed joined them on stage. Reed had been made a Knight of the French Order of Arts and Letters that year, and while in Paris received his investiture from the French minister for culture, **Jacques Lang**.

Meanwhile, Lou and Sylvia Reed had begun to drift apart. Though he'd publicly debated the issue of having children with her on "Beginning Of A Great Adventure", he'd finally decided against it, and stopped sleeping with her. They continued to live together,

Jerome "Doc" Pomus 1925–1991

"Doc" Pomus (real name Jerome Solon Felder) began his musical career as a blues singer. With his partner Mort Shuman, Pomus had an incredibly successful run of hits in the 1960s, working in the Brill Building, and probably comparable only to Lieber and Stoller, with whom they variously collaborated at times. Their first major hit was "A Teenager In Love" for Dion and The Belmonts, and they also wrote songs for (amongst others) the Coasters, the Drifters, Fabian, Andy Williams and Elvis Presley (including "Surrender", "Viva Las Vegas", and "Suspicion"). In later life Pomus worked with Mink Deville, and co-wrote B.B. King's 1981 award-winning album *There Must Be A Better World Somewhere* with Mac Rebennack (Dr. John). As a result of childhood polio, Pomus spent the last 30 years of his life in a wheelchair.

Reed's relationship with Pomus had its roots not only in his own song-writing aspirations, but also in his astonishing musical eclecticism – from Broadway to doo-wop – alongside an affection for his early days writing jukebox pop at Pickwick International.

and she continued to manage his affairs, but relations were severely strained as Reed tried to decide if he wanted a divorce or not. He also seemed to be in denial about his past, and allowed no one to make any references to his previous drug use or his past sexual relations with men.

Together, Again

During 1992, all four members of The Velvet Underground got together on several occasions to discuss a couple of pending projects (Sterling Morrison's proposed history of the band – provisionally titled *The Velvet Underground Diet* – and a retrospective boxed set intended to stem a tide of bootlegs). They also started informally rehearsing to see if they could still play together with any degree of enjoyment and enthusiasm. When Reed joked that they ought to play Madison Square Garden for a million dollars, it opened the door for discussions about the possibility of a proper, full-scale reunion. Since Lou Reed's schedule was clear for 1993, things began to roll, with Sylvia Reed setting up concert dates in Europe with plans to make a live album and a video. Morrison and Reed joined Cale on stage during a solo gig at New York University, and Cale announced the Velvets' reunion in November 1992 on *The Tonight Show*. Within two months the four were rehearsing for a European tour. As Sterling Morrison later told *Rolling Stone* editor **David Fricke**, "It was pride that kept us apart. But it was also pride

that made us do well. Nobody cares more about our legacy than we do".

That the motive for the reunion may have been largely financial scarcely mattered to their expectant audience. And Morrison and Tucker both truly needed the money – Moe didn't even own a car, let alone a house, confessing to journalist **Max Bell**, "The money aspect is like winning the lottery to me". Sterling Morrison had to take six weeks off work as a tugboat pilot in order to tour, but he still didn't quit the day job. Morrison was laconically philosophical about the band's turbulent history, "It is odd the way the band just sort of dissolved, without any seeming reason. There were no big blow-ups, no angry fights – people just … fell off as it went along. Lou just dropped off. It was very strange … and since there never was any great apocalyptic moment where we said, 'Screw it, enough is enough, no more of this', that's made it possible for us to come back, just as casually". Cale was "cautiously optimistic" that the tour would lead on to other things, hopefully including new studio recordings – but it was Lou Reed who had the best one-liner about the fact that they were reforming, "Does that mean 'reformed' as in: now we're good?"

So, in the summer of 1993, thousands of Velvets aficionados of all ages (and this was a band who had never been unfashionable) were finally able to see them live in concert. Needless to say, the gigs sold out in seconds, leaving thousands more out in the cold. After another brief rehearsal period in London, the June 1993 tour took in Edinburgh, London, Amsterdam, Rotterdam, Hamburg, Basle and Prague, where the group and their entourage (including Tucker's mother and five kids, who'd flown in to see her play) were the honoured guests of Czech President **Václav Havel**.

After Prague, the tour resumed in Paris, and moved on to Berlin. The Velvets then played five stadium dates in Italy, supporting U2; they also played a brief and fairly shambolic set at Britain's **Glastonbury Festival**. And then it was all over. But at least the three Paris shows (at L'Olympia) had been taped and filmed,

The Story

The live reunion act in 1993 toured the States and Europe

resulting in a live double CD (produced by Mike Rathke) and a video. For fans who might not otherwise be tempted to buy yet another live Velvets album, incentive lay in the inclusion of the first new Velvets song for decades, "Coyote". The song had emerged from their first week of rehearsals together. Cale hoped they'd create others, but Tucker and Morrison were content to simply rely on their back catalogue. As it was, they still argued with Reed about the music publishing – but Cale was still optimistic that the reunion would last and that they'd produce more work, "I hope we do. That was really the premise under which I really participated in this, and I hope it's borne out".

Václav Havel

Václav Havel was born into a wealthy and influential Czech family in Prague in 1936. As a result, he was prevented from finishing his formal studies under the Communist regime and became a laboratory assistant, though he eventually studied drama, writing and producing plays. As a student, Havel had smuggled a copy of *White Light/White Heat* into Czechoslovakia. Taped copies of the album and hand-produced lyric books subsequently became symbols of free speech and artistic expression amongst those opposing the oppressive yoke of the USSR. Even the possession of such a book could lead to arrest, and when a Velvets-influenced Czech rock band, **Plastic People of the Universe** was arrested for playing their music, the impetus for the beginnings of the Charter 77 human rights movement was created. Whether any of these happenings had any bearing on the fact that Czechoslovakia's eventual peaceful move from Communism to democracy was nicknamed the "Velvet Revolution" is a matter for historians to debate.

Nevertheless, despite political harassment, Havel emerged as the leading political figure in the Czech transition from Communism to democracy, becoming the last President of Czechoslovakia, and the first President of the Czech Republic. His understanding of the importance of cultural activities led him to invite many theatrical and musical performers to his country, and he even offered Frank Zappa an honorary post in his government.

But behind the scenes, all was not well. Throughout the tour, Lou Reed had distanced himself from the others, travelling alone and seeming to regard his colleagues as nothing more than just the latest in a long series of backing bands. Unfortunately, tour manager **Sylvia Reed** was treating them the same way, considering them all second-rate compared to Lou and insulting them to their faces. Reed's guitar effects had caused innumerable sound problems live, and Lou's guitar technician also treated the band with disdain. Morrison in particular was furious about their treatment – and Morrison was also a sick man, though nobody knew yet just how ill he was.

Hopes that there would be more concerts to satisfy the thousands who didn't get to see the European dates, perhaps even a new studio album, were dashed in November 1993 when plans for a proposed US tour fell apart in a flurry of "fax fights" between Reed and the others. Though Cale, who had learnt how to pacify Reed during their work on *Drella*, had played peacemaker during the tour, Reed's attitude to a proposed MTV *Unplugged* show had the duo clashing yet again, this time because Reed was adamant that he would only record with the Velvets if he got to produce the resulting album. Cale pointed out the advantages of working with an outside producer, emphasizing the fact that all the top producers in the industry would be overjoyed to work with the Velvets, but Reed wouldn't budge. When Tucker tried to soothe the troubled waters, Reed sent her faxes that Cale thought were both patronizing and insulting, and the Welshman finally lost the last of his patience. He sent Reed a nine-page fax telling him exactly what he thought of him.

And that was that, again. The official statement from Sylvia Reed stated that, "Lou feels he accomplished what he set out to do with the European shows…That being done, he intends to return to his solo work". More sadly, Cale would later describe the state of play as "the end of a very fruitful relationship".

After Hours

"The Velvet Underground will never play again – not that Velvet Underground, which is the only Velvet Underground."

Lou Reed

After Hours
1993–2007

Once again, the creative tensions that made the Velvets such an impressive band turned out to be the very reasons why the reunion could not last. And soon, a key member of the band, Sterling Morrisson, was to become fatally ill, leading all the other founding members to declare that, without him, they could never again perform as The Velvet Underground.

As The Velvet Underground broke up once again, it seemed ironic that their public profile had never been higher. In December 1993 Britain's Channel 4 TV station screened an eight-hour-long tribute to the Velvets and Andy Warhol. Official viewing figures showed an audience of 400,000 – fairly impressive, considering that the show was broadcast in the wee small hours of a Sunday morning.

In March 1994, Lou fired Sylvia Reed as his manager, cancelling her credit cards and other accounts, and leaving her with no choice but to find a divorce lawyer. Reed was also not on good terms with his record company, Sire, who were unhappy that he had blown the chance to create more Velvet Underground albums; when Reed approached them with the idea of recording an album of cover versions, they turned him down. Tellingly, around this time Lou's lawyer told him that he would no longer represent him.

Late the previous year Lou had become romantically involved with the musician and performance-artist **Laurie Anderson,** who some said resembled the young Shelley Albin. Reed would dedicate his next solo album, *Set The Twilight Reeling*, to Anderson, whom he had met at an arts festival in Munich. He spoke publicly about his joy at being involved with another artist, and of the benefits that resulted of being with someone who understood his work and his world: "It's a great relief to have that kind of compassion and back-up available, to have someone who understands what's happening and can actually help you get through it". Reed also claimed to be working on a novel, but Anderson was obviously his main priority. She moved into his new apartment on **Christopher Street,** and the pair duetted on 'In Our Sleep', a track they had co-written for Anderson's album *Bright Red*. There was talk of them making a whole album in this vein, but it never materialized.

In 1994 Tucker released *Dogs Under Stress*, which featured Sterling Morrison playing on

The Story

Sterling Morrison had not seemed well on his last appearances, and the reunion tour proved a timely swan song

five tracks. Later that year, Morrison and Tucker reunited with Cale, performing live as a trio at Pittsburgh's **Andy Warhol Museum**, improvising soundtracks for Andy Warhol's films *Eat* and *Kiss*. They'd earlier recorded demos for a possible album project, plus a cover version of Jim Carroll's 'People Who Died' for Cale's *Antardida* album (with Chris Spedding on guitar). There was talk of the three of them taking the Warhol soundtrack show on a European tour in late 1995, but it wasn't to be. During the week's rehearsal and the actual performance it became apparent that Morrison was seriously ill, and soon afterwards he was diagnosed with cancer (non-Hodgkin's lymphoma). On 30 August 1995, the day after his 53rd birthday, Sterling Morrison died. How long he'd actually been ill is unknown (though he doesn't look that well in the *Velvet Redux* video, and in the sleeve notes to the live album Reed refers to Morrison's "courage"). Morrison chose to spend his last weeks at home in Poughkeepsie, New York with his family, and was visited there by Cale, Tucker and Reed (who would later write a moving account of his visit for *The New York Times* magazine, titled "Velvet Warrior"). Morrison was completely bald, and told Reed that he had watched – and counted – as seven layers of skin had peeled from his body.

Understandably, the others were devastated by Morrison's death, perhaps none more so than Moe Tucker, who had known him since she was eleven. Lou Reed was also stunned, finding the loss very hard to accept: "Jesus, how is it possible? Guy worked out, never

sick a day in his life. Literally. He fucking jogged". He talked at length to the press about Morrison, describing his fellow guitarist's musicianship in glowing terms: "It was hard for other people to appreciate him because he wasn't flashy. But he was holding down our version of the groove. If Cale and I took off, we always had some place to come back to. Because Sterling was there". He also stated that: "No one will ever hear the four of us play again. That's really sunk in: The Velvet Underground cannot exist".

But in a sense they still did. On 16 January 1996, The Velvet Underground were officially inducted into the **Rock And Roll Hall Of Fame**. Reed, Cale and Tucker all attended the award ceremony, along with Sterling's widow Martha, and performed a new song about Morrison written only two days previously: 'Last Night I Said Goodbye To My Friend'. They had written the song together, and each sung one of its three verses. Reed's eyes were visibly moist when he walked onstage. Even so, he hadn't bothered to attend Morrison's memorial service some months before – something Cale found hard to forgive. With timely irony, the Velvets retrospective boxed set *Peel Slowly And See* had finally been released just weeks after Sterling Morrison's death.

Reed's 1996 solo album *Set The Twilight Reeling* would contain an intimations-of-mortality song, 'Finish Line' dedicated "for Sterl". The album had taken him two and a half years to complete, and many of the songs seemed to concern his relationship with Laurie Anderson.

Moe Tucker, Martha Morrison, John Cale and an awkward-looking Lou Reed at the Velvets' belated inauguration to the Rock And Roll Hall Of Fame in 1996

In 1996 Reed also worked with designer/director **Robert Wilson** – who had worked with Philip Glass on *Einstein On The Beach* – on a stage musical (Wilson called it an opera) titled *Timerocker*, which was performed in New York and Amsterdam. Reed claimed the play was "more or less" based on H.G. Wells's novel *The Time Machine*. According to Mike Rathke, when he was writing these songs "Lou would go in and see a scene Robert Wilson was working on, and they'd talk about it a little bit,

he'd watch it, and he'd sit down with his guitar and a pen, then he'd write the song". Plans for an album of the cast recording came to nothing, but clips of the play which surfaced in the *Rock And Roll Heart* video documentary looked truly imaginative in terms of sets, staging and costumes, and one can only hope the entire work will surface on DVD eventually.

Meanwhile, Cale had been commissioned by the city of Vienna in Austria to write an opera about the *femme fatale* and World War I spy

Mata Hari (20 years earlier Cale had turned down a request from the reclusive **Thomas Pynchon** to write an opera based on Pynchon's 1973 novel *Gravity's Rainbow*; playwright **Sam Shepherd** had also unsuccessfully tried to get Cale to turn his story 'The Sad Lament Of Pecos Bill On The Eve Of Killing His Wife' into an operetta). Cale premiered an unfinished version of the Mata Hari work in Vienna in October 1995, and the performance was filmed. Cale's solo performances now increasingly featured a literary component, with readings from numerous writers including Oscar Wilde, Michael Ondaatje, Tennessee Williams, Edgar Allan Poe, T.S. Eliot and Ezra Pound. He also talked of setting some of Pound's *Cantos* to music. Cale also returned to rock in 1996 with his well-received solo album *Walking On Locusts*, which featured a song about Sterling Morrison titled 'Some Friends'. He also composed the music for a 90-minute ballet inspired by the life of Nico, for the Scapino Ballet of Rotterdam, which premiered in October 1997. Choreographer **Ed Wubbe** discussed the singer at length with Cale while preparing the piece.

Laurie Anderson was the guest organizer of 1997's Meltdown arts/music festival in London. She invited Lou Reed to participate, and the

Laurie Anderson

Laurie Anderson was born on 5 June 1947, and taught Art History before launching herself as a performance artist in the late 1970s, at which point she was involved with the late comedian Andy Kaufman. Anderson's pieces incorporated music, poetry and the visual arts, but she might well have remained a figure known only to the *avant-garde* had she not scored a crossover pop hit with 1981's 'O Superman (For Massenet)' single, taken from her lengthy *United States* piece. The record tipped its hat to Jules Massenet's 1885 aria 'O Souverain' while critiquing American foreign policy through a vocoder, and sold enormous quantities in Britain – with the result that Anderson was promptly signed up by Warner Brothers. She performed and toured extensively, notably with, among others, William Burroughs and John Giorno. The best introduction to her work is probably the 2-CD anthology *Talk Normal*. Since 2003, Anderson has been NASA's first artist-in-residence.

Well into his sixties, Cale continues to work incredibly hard recording, touring and promoting his material (as here in 2003 at Borders in London's Oxford St)

result was an acoustic concert, captured on the *Perfect Night: Live In London* album.

In late 1997, Cale and his wife Risé separated, though he remained close to his daughter Eden. Cale then moved into the same apartment building in Christopher Street in which Lou Reed lived; when their paths occasionally crossed, conversation was said to be strained. A year or so later Cale moved downtown, to near the World Trade Center. He was now obsessed with electronic gadgets and with the Internet, tracking the paths of diseases and exploring the intricacies of Chinese politics. He also found a new girlfriend, **Claudia Gould** of the Institute of Contemporary Arts at the University of Pennsylvania.

In 1999, four CDs of recordings of Cale's experimental music from the 1960s began to surface, the tapes having been compiled by Tony Conrad. One of these, *Day Of Niagara*, featured the entire LaMonte Young ensemble; Young threatened legal action over the ownership of the copyright, with Cale and Conrad seeking credit for their co-authorship of the music. The situation seems unresolved, but the discs remain available. That year Cale contributed soundtrack music to **Mary Harron**'s film adaptation of *American Psycho*; he would also contribute an instrumental piece to her following film about Valerie Solanas, *I Shot Andy Warhol*. In May 1999, Cale received an honorary doctorate from the University of Antwerp and in the Autumn he also published his autobiography, *What's Welsh For Zen?*, to general critical acclaim. The following year

Lou Reed joined him on the bookshelves with *Pass Through Fire*, an anthology of his collected lyrics.

April 2000 saw the release of Lou Reed's *Ecstasy* album, his first new work in four years. Many of the songs described relationships in trouble, though it would seem that Reed was recalling his marriage to Sylvia, rather than describing a rocky patch with Anderson. Though lyrically interesting, memorable tunes were largely absent – as they had been since *Magic And Loss*. At the Jubilee 2000 Concert in Italy, organized by Bono to focus attention on world debt, Reed performed before **Pope John Paul II**.

2000 also saw the return of **Doug Yule** to live performance – his first gigs since the mid-1970s. He played a couple of sets for charity in his hometown of Seattle (a recording of which was released two years later as *Live In Seattle*), featuring three Velvets songs and eight new compositions from a "song cycle" he'd been working on for several years about a couple's relationship, set around 8000 BC. Three songs from this story had been recorded by Yule in Boston in 1999, and one – 'Beginning To Get It' – had appeared on a benefit album for adopted children, *A Place To Call Home*. The second Yule gig also featured a set by Moe Tucker's band, and she and Yule duetted on an unrehearsed version of 'I'm Sticking With You', much to the delight of the crowd (the performance is included on Tucker's album *Moe Rocks Terrastock*). According to Lou Reed, the surviving Velvets had debated inviting Yule to join them for their Rock and Roll Hall of Fame appearance, but had decided against it.

Meanwhile, Reed had been working for several years on another theatrical collaboration with Robert Wilson. *Poe-try* was based on the works of **Edgar Allan Poe** and opened first at the Thalia Theatre in Hamburg, Germany, in February 2001. By the end of 2002 the piece had developed into what would become a double-CD titled *The Raven*. Featuring contributions from various actors including Willem Dafoe, Amanda Plummer and Steve Buscemi, and musical guests including David Bowie, Ornette Coleman, Laurie Anderson and the Blind Boys Of Alabama. Reed called the work "the culmination of everything I've ever done", and admitted that artistically it would be hard for him to top. Critics thought otherwise, largely finding it worthy but dull. The work was once again dedicated to Laurie Anderson, "a constant source of inspiration".

In 2001, Cale was living just a few blocks from the **World Trade Center**, and that September had a grandstand view of the events of 9/11, e-mailing friends with a running commentary on the events outside. When the area was evacuated, Cale moved in for a while with Claudia Gould, and was in a state of deep shock. At the end of 2002 Cale mended fences with **Brian Eno**, when the two played together at the opening of a major Warhol retrospective at London's Tate Modern; Eno (and his daughters) subsequently made a guest appearance on Cale's 2003 rock album, *Hobo Sapiens*, which was generally well received. Cale also continued to record soundtracks for movies, including 2003's *Otherworld*, a cartoon adaptation of Welsh myths from *The Mabinogion*.

In 2004, Lou Reed had a surprise single hit with Dab Hands' remixed version of 'Satellite Of Love', which charted in the UK. Interviewing Reed in his apartment in Spring 2005, journalist **Sylvie Simmons** noted the presence of a well-thumbed copy of a book on Prozac and mood swings; whether or not Reed was using that medication, he was visibly smoking cigarettes again. He announced the news that the German group **Zeitkratzer** planned to perform an orchestral version of *Metal Machine Music* at the Berlin Philharmonic Hall (they claimed to have actually transcribed the piece), and that he would play guitar at the event. He also talked of his interest in meditation and Buddhism, and his love for macrobiotic food and Tibetan music.

Seemingly between new musical projects, Reed promoted his range of his specially designed eyewear, a book of his photographs entitled *Emotion In Action* and recordings of his meditation music. During 2006 he toured Europe and the USA, and in December of that year he launched a theatrical presentation of his *Berlin* album at St. Ann's Warehouse in Brooklyn. The show was directed by Julian Schnabel, with musical direction by Hal Willner and Bob Ezrin, *Berlin*'s original producer. Featured personnel included (among others) Reed, Sharon Jones, Antony, Rupert Christie, Steve Hunter, Fernando Saunders, Tony Smith and Rob Wasserman.

Reed guesting with Jack White's sideband, The Raconteurs, in 2006

After Hours

The show played in Sydney, Australia, in January 2007 and dates were announced for a performance at the London Barbican in May and a string of European appearances.

In 2005, Cale released *Black Acetate*, a new rock album heavily influenced by hip-hop, a genre Cale called "the new jazz" because it was constantly evolving (much like Cale himself); he followed it in early 2007 with a triple live album, *Circus*.

Moe Tucker has been quiet in recent years, with 2002's *Moe Rocks Terrastock* her last CD release. Judging by her appearance in 2006's *Velvet Underground Under Review* DVD, it would seem that Moe may have experienced a bout of ill health; she is now a grandmother, and remains undoubtedly the sanest person in this entire story.

It seems extremely unlikely that the surviving members of The Velvet Underground will ever reunite again, though far stranger things have already happened in the course of their career. After Sterling Morrison's death Reed commented: "The Velvet Underground will never play again – not that Velvet Underground, which is the only Velvet Underground". These sentiments were echoed by Tucker: "None of us would want to perform as the Velvets without Sterl". And even if that aspect could be overcome, it seems unlikely that Cale and Reed could ever repair their friendship. In 1995 Cale was asked about Lou in an interview and pondered aloud: "I can't understand how somebody who wrote such intelligent and beautiful songs could be the exact opposite as a person". Regardless, even after the boxed set and the *Fully Loaded* CD, some Velvet Underground material from the 1960s still remains unreleased (see Rarities: page 166), but whether it ever will be is another matter. Whether Morrison's history of the band was ever finished, and whether Reed will ever complete the book of short stories he's been promising for years are more questions that only time will answer. Whatever may happen, it's a safe bet that both **Lou Reed** and **John Cale** will continue to produce music, and probably more besides – and whatever that work may be like, it will at the very least be extremely interesting.

Part Two:
The Music

"I always thought we were the best ... and I still do."

Lou Reed, 2001

The Albums

This section provides a review of the core Velvet Underground albums recorded and released between 1966 and 1972, and includes later releases and compilations of original material from the period, whilst also covering a variety of reunion recordings over the next three decades.

THE VELVET UNDERGROUND & NICO

Verve; recorded April, May and November 1966; released March 1967; available on CD.

SUNDAY MORNING/I'M WAITING FOR THE MAN/FEMME FATALE/VENUS IN FURS/RUN RUN RUN/ALL TOMORROW'S PARTIES/HEROIN/THERE SHE GOES AGAIN/I'LL BE YOUR MIRROR/THE BLACK ANGEL'S DEATH SONG/EUROPEAN SON

Personnel: John Cale (electric viola, bass, piano); Sterling Morrison (rhythm guitar, bass); Lou Reed (lead guitar, ostrich guitar, vocals); Maureen Tucker (drums); Nico (*chanteuse*).

In April 1966 The Velvet Underground recorded the bulk of their debut album at Scepter Records' 4-track recording studio in New York; the following month they re-recorded 'European Son', 'Heroin', 'Waiting For The Man' and 'Venus In Furs' at TTG's Sunset-Highland studio in Hollywood. Cale claims these re-recordings were far superior to those from the Scepter sessions ("we really didn't do anything great in New York"). In November 1966 'Sunday Morning' was recorded as a last-minute addition at New York's Mayfair Sound studios.

The engineers at Scepter were Norman Dolph and John Licata; in California, the engineer was Omi Haden. Tom Wilson produced the 'Sunday Morning' session, and also converted the group's original mono mix of the earlier tapes into reprocessed stereo (though Sterling Morrison always insisted that the mono version of the album is superior). None of the above are credited on the album sleeve, with the sole production credit going to Andy Warhol – which seems somewhat churlish considering that it was the others who did the actual work.

For a debut album, *The Velvet Underground & Nico* is absolutely stunning, as much so today as in 1967 – perhaps because it sounded like nothing else that was being produced at the time. Much as one may love psychedelia, it's very much a product of its era (and sounds it), whereas the Velvets' first album could have been recorded yesterday. It doesn't even matter that it displays so many different musical styles, since the songs themselves are all so good.

The delicate and pretty opener 'Sunday Morning' doesn't sound that revolutionary, being recognizably akin to much of the electric folk-rock then being produced – but there's a paranoia to the lyrics and Cale's droning viola to prove this is by no means run-of-the-mill. The driving rock beat of 'I'm Waiting For The Man' shifts proceedings up a gear. The lyrics are clearly about buying drugs – and the Harlem references make it obvious that it's hard drugs under discussion here, since the drugs that were deemed more socially acceptable at the time (marijuana and LSD) were a lot more easily available in downtown Manhattan.

'Femme Fatale' introduces the world to Nico with a sleepy ballad in which she uses both of her singing voices: the wispy, whispery one, and the more strident one that Sterling Morrison called her "*Götterdämmerung* voice". At first hearing, it's immediately obvious that Nico is one of the most arresting female singers in rock; there had certainly never been anything like her before. One could say the same about 'Venus In Furs', a song which makes the listener sit up from its opening chords onwards. Not only does Cale's viola cut like a razor, but the tambourine, bass and drums make it sound like the soundtrack to some depraved ritual – which is of course all heightened by the lyrics. In an era that found the Rolling Stones' 'Let's Spend The Night Together' controversial, outright paeans to sado-masochism was totally beyond the pale. The "ostrich" guitar used by Reed on this track (and indeed on 'All Tomorrow's

Parties') was a semi-hollow bodied Gretsch with its frets removed, and all its strings tuned to the same note. It made what Cale called "an horrendous noise", and was unfortunately stolen from Reed's apartment.

For a throwaway song written in a hurry, 'Run Run Run' isn't at all bad, if a little obviously influenced by the Dylan of *Highway 61 Revisited*. Once again it's about buying drugs on the street, compounding the Velvets' already depraved image. 'All Tomorrow's Parties' is more accessible. However, for all its folk-rock trimmings, the drums alone make it sound more sinister – and the sadness of the lyric is transfigured into real tragedy by Nico's voice, which sounds like a dark angel heralding inevitable doom. 'Heroin' is awesome by any standards, and its tendency to speed up and slow down again is utterly compelling: once you've started listening to this, you have to hear how it ends. Unfortunately, since the song doesn't take an obvious stance against the drug, many listeners at the time assumed it must be advocating it.

'There She Goes Again' returns to fast-paced folk-rock territory, with jangly Byrds-style guitar and high-pitched backing harmonies. The implicit misogyny might even pass the listener by on a first hearing. 'I'll Be Your Mirror' is back to the world of the gentle ballad, with an ethereally moving love song that entirely ignores the realm of the sentimental, describing real emotions instead. 'The Black Angel's Death Song' kicks off with Cale's screeching viola, with Reed spitting

The Banana Man

The one area of the Velvets' debut where Andy Warhol did undeniably make an important contribution was the Velvet's first album cover, which he designed. This wasn't his first venture into record sleeve design; in 1958, he'd produced a cover for jazz guitarist Kenny Burrell's Blue Note album *Blue Lights: Volume I*, for which Warhol had done an illustration in the style of the French Surrealist poet, painter and film-maker, Jean Cocteau.

For the Velvets' album Warhol had originally planned to use one of his "plastic surgery" series of images of "nose jobs, breast jobs and ass-jobs". Fortunately for posterity, Andy came up with something else instead. With its famous yellow silk-screened banana sticker which – when you peeled slowly – revealed a pink banana underneath, the cover became a memorable and elegant icon. Warhol had explored the banana as sexual metaphor several times prior to this, most notably in his film *Mario Montez Eating Banana*. In 1966, bananas also had a drug culture significance, since smoking dried banana skins was at that time rumoured to get

An immediate Pop Art icon, Warhol's sleeve design, with its phallic peelable banana, remains a masterpiece

you high (it didn't, and it doesn't). However, the cover also created problems, since printing difficulties with the sticker contributed to the album's delayed release. Also, nowhere on the front of the record was The Velvet Undergound's name even mentioned – just the legend 'Andy Warhol', which led many to assume that the artist had now made a rock album. As such, it probably didn't make The Velvet Underground any easier to market – this was several years before Led Zeppelin refused to even have their name, let alone the record label, appear on the sleeve of "*Led Zeppelin IV*", and two decades before Prince turned himself into a mere symbol.

Warhol designed several other rock album covers over the years: for John Cale's The *Academy In Peril*, for the Rolling Stones' notorious *Sticky Fingers* and the appalling *Love You Live*, and for the posthumous John Lennon album *Menlove Ave.* (1986). The cover for the Velvets' second album, *White Light/White Heat*, was executed by Factory-person Billy Name, from a "concept" by Warhol.

The sleeve also featured colour photography by Billy Name

out a Dylanesque stream of nonsense verse; musically it's interesting, but veers towards the annoying and pretentious. 'European Son' wraps up the album with a driving urban blues (punctuated by noise), turning into a raucous extended guitar jam that rattles on for nearly eight minutes. At the time rock songs of this

length were still very rare (though as Sterling Morrison pointed out, "all the songs on the first album are longish compared to the standards of the time"), and the ones that did exist usually made more of an effort to please the listener than this one, which sounds like a giant fuck you to the world. The Velvet

The Albums

Underground had arrived, and they weren't messing around.

Had this album come out in 1966, it would surely have attracted more attention than it did. As it was, in the year of "peace and love", it was deemed both sick and unfashionable, and was generally lost in a deluge of more psychedelic, and extended, debut albums. But for those who heard it, it was instantly unforgettable – it was obvious from the off that Reed was one of the most talented songwriters in rock, and that he had a band that complemented that talent perfectly. For an estimate of the album's eventual impact – which took decades to emerge – one can't better the verdict of contemporary journalist John Wilcock, reviewing the Velvets live in *The East Village Other*: "Art has come to the discotheque, and it will never be the same again".

The standard CD release of the album replaces the original version of 'All Tomorrow's Parties' with a "previously unreleased" one. Both feature the same backing track, but whereas the original featured Nico's vocals double-tracked, the CD has only one vocal track. It's not an improvement, but the situation was rectified with the restored version of the album included in the *Peel Slowly And See* boxed set (see pages 156–160). A deluxe double-CD version of the album also exists, which is recommended. This contains both mono and stereo mixes of the whole album, all of the edited singles released, plus the five Velvets-related tracks from Nico's *Chelsea Girl* album. It also restores the complete cover artwork.

WHITE LIGHT/WHITE HEAT

Verve; recorded September 1967; released January 1968. Available on CD.

WHITE LIGHT WHITE HEAT/ THE GIFT/ LADY GODIVA'S OPERATION/ HERE SHE COMES NOW/ I HEARD HER CALL MY NAME/ SISTER RAY

Personnel: John Cale (vocals, electric viola, organ, bass); Sterling Morrison (vocals, guitar, bass); Lou Reed (vocals, guitar, piano); Maureen Tucker (drums).

Factory resident Billy Name provided the original tattoo design. Later versions included a negative image from a WWI battlefield, or simply a plain black sleeve

White Light/White Heat was recorded at Mayfair Sound Studios in New York, and produced by Tom Wilson with Gary Kellgren as engineer.

It has been claimed that The Velvet Underground recorded their second album in its entirety in under three (some say two) days. According to Moe Tucker it took "approximately seven sessions over a period of two weeks"; even so, that was fast work. John Cale has implied that the time factor was a deliberate artistic choice, rather than a limitation imposed by poverty. "We decided to make that album as live as possible" he claims. We told Tom Wilson we were gonna do it as we do it on stage". In fact, how much Tom Wilson had to do with the record is debatable, and the bulk of the work was done by Kellgren, since Wilson was constantly making phone calls. Moe Tucker complains to this day that Wilson

THE ROUGH GUIDE TO THE VELVET UNDERGROUND

didn't turn on one of her drum mikes for 'Sister Ray' because he was "more interested in the blondes running through the studio".

The Velvets' attempt to create a "live" sound resulted in an album that was murky in the mix, with a ridiculous amount of distortion and feedback (The Yardbirds and The Who were big influences on the group at this point). "There was fantastic leakage because everyone was playing so loud", Sterling Morrison later explained. "We had so much electronic junk with us in the studio – all the se fuzzers and compressors. Gary Kellgren the engineer, who is ultra-competent, told us repeatedly: 'You can't do it – all the needles are on red'". The group simply told Kellgren that they didn't care, and that he should just do the best he could. The distortion and white noise were the inevitable result. "We wanted to do something electronic and energetic", Morrison stated. "We had the energy and the electronics, but we didn't know that it couldn't be recorded ... What we were trying to do was to really fry the tracks". Tucker was more candid: "We didn't know what we were doing".

The record was a release of emotion and energy for the band, as all the anger and frustration and resentment they felt at their lack of commercial success boiled over onto the tape. "Our lives were chaos", Morrison has said. "That's what's reflected in the record". Any listeners expecting more ballads in the vein of 'I'll Be Your Mirror' were going to be sorely disappointed – *White Light/White Heat* was all-out guitar-based mayhem, with lyrics

that were as much of a full-frontal assault as the music. The title track concerns the joys of amphetamine, but – apart from the distortion – it is quite jaunty, dominated by Cale's pounding piano. 'The Gift' is truly macabre: a short story of Reed's, recited by Cale over backing music which was basically a piece they'd performed live, an R&B instrumental titled 'Booker T'. As well as reciting the narrative for 'The Gift', Cale also took lead vocals for 'Lady Godiva's Operation', which starts as a prettily psychedelic ballad before turning into something disturbing, with lyrics to match. 'Here She Comes Now' is the only song on the record that might have fitted on the previous album, and even that has lyrics that imply sexual problems. 'I Heard Her Call My Name' is bluesy garage thrash laced with feedback (and very poor guitar solos from Reed), with lyrics that concern love after death. Tucker and Morrison were both disgusted when Reed remixed this track to bring his own part up in the mix, drowning all the others out; Morrison actually claims to have quit the band for several days over this incident. The album closes with 'Sister Ray', a distortion-heavy blues strut with lyrics that were blatantly about sexual activity and hard drug use (not to mention a murder). For this one the entire band turned all their amps up to ten and just played variations on the riff until they ran out of steam 17 minutes later, the two guitars duelling with Cale's organ throughout.

All in all, not exactly easy listening – but it was also unlike anything else coming out that year, and added greatly to the band's word-of-mouth reputation. Though largely ignored by the media, a review of the album by Wayne McGuire in *Crawdaddy* magazine called the Velvets "the most vital and significant group in the world today".

The album's original black-on-black cover included a photograph by Billy Name of a skull and crossbones tattoo; this was chosen by Reed from Name's portfolio, and was originally a small detail from a still taken from Warhol's movie *Bike Boy*, the tattoo in question belonging to "actor" Joe Spencer. Name greatly enlarged the detail, which is why the image is so grainy. The album design is credited to Billy Name from a "concept" by Andy Warhol. The album has also appeared with several other cover designs, including an enigmatic World War I negative white-out image.

THE VELVET UNDERGROUND

MGM/Verve; recorded November–December 1968; released March 1969; available on CD.

CANDY SAYS/WHAT GOES ON/SOME KINDA LOVE/PALE BLUE EYES/JESUS/BEGINNING TO SEE THE LIGHT/I'M SET FREE/THAT'S THE STORY OF MY LIFE/THE MURDER MYSTERY/ AFTER HOURS

Personnel: Sterling Morrison (guitar); Lou Reed (vocals, guitar); Maureen Tucker (drums); Doug Yule (vocals, bass, organ, piano).

The imaginatively titled *The Velvet Underground* is sometimes known as "The Gray Album", on account of the colour of the cover, featuring a photograph by Factory manager and archivist Billy Name (Billy Linich). It was recorded just over two months after the departure of John Cale at TTG Studios in Hollywood. Credits state that it was "arranged and conducted" by the Velvet Underground,

Tom Wilson (1931-1978)

One of the most extraordinary producers of his generation, Wilson had started his career as virtually the only Afro-American producer working in mainstream popular music. Born in Waco, Texas, he attended Harvard, and was involved with the Harvard New Jazz Society. Recruited by John Hammond, he became a stalwart of Columbia Records before moving on to the fledgling Verve label in 1965, where he was brought in to establish a rock division for the jazz label. His first signing was Frank Zappa. Wilson worked on a remarkable number of milestone albums by a legion of innovative musicians: Sun Ra, Cecil Taylor, Simon & Garfunkel ('The Sound of Silence'), Bob Dylan (*Bringing It All Back Home* and 'Like A Rolling Stone' – he was notoriously dismissed from the *Highway 61 Revisited* sessions), Frank Zappa (*Freak Out!*), The Blues Project and Soft Machine's first album. In taking on the Velvets, pitching himself against strong artistic personas in the shape of of Reed and Cale, his production work proved seminal. His honing of the hard edge of Reed and Cale's aspirations for a new sort of rock culture towards something that the public (although they might not know it themselves) would find palatable – if not wholly acceptable – was critical.

The "gray" album used a black and white image from a series of colour shots by Billy Name of the new band at the Factory

assisted by engineer Val Valentin.

Confusingly, there are two different versions of this album: a mix done by Lou Reed, which was used for the original vinyl release, and a mix done by Valentin (used for the CD re-release). Valentin's mix was done first, after which Reed returned to the studio with the tapes and did his version, christened the "Closet Mix" by Sterling Morrison, who thought it sounded like it had been recorded in a closet. Reed's "Closet Mix" brought his vocals to the fore, while Valentin's approach was more orthodox (and reveals instrumentation inaudible on the "Closet Mix", like the bass on 'After Hours'). The Valentin mix remains available as the standard CD release, but at Reed's insistence the "Closet Mix" – which is admittedly a lot cleaner and clearer – was the one chosen for inclusion in the *Peel Slowly And See* boxed set (see pages 156–160).

The album is another radical change of pace: there are no electronic effects, distortion or feedback this time around – just a collection of songs that were far more straightforward, lyrically as well as musically, than anything the Velvets had done before. Most concerned love, in one form or another, and the individual songs could be seen as comprising parts of a larger whole. Doug Yule takes lead vocal on several tracks, as Reed had strained his voice singing live – but since Yule's voice was quite similar in tone to Reed's, the change isn't too jarring. Reed's vocal problems may also be the reason why Maureen Tucker stepped into the vocal spotlight for 'After Hours'... though Reed has since claimed this was a deliberate choice, because Moe's voice suited the lyric better than his own.

The album kicks off with 'Candy Says', a ballad gentler even than 'I'll Be Your Mirror', with Yule's backing vocals making it evident from the start that this was a somewhat different band to the one that had made the previous album. 'What Goes On' is, for the Velvets, a comparatively straightforward rocker, 'Some Kinda Love' a more straightforward blues (the Valentin mix of the album features a completely different take of this song to the "Closet Mix"). 'Pale Blue Eyes' is a gentle but incredibly powerful love song fairly obviously inspired by Reed's on/off relationship with Shelley Albin. Sterling Morrison – already upset about Cale's departure – was unhappy about the fact that Reed was now writing love songs about his girlfriend, considering it a step backwards in terms of subject matter. However, he allowed Reed to have his way. "My position on the album was one of acquiescence" Morrison said.

'Jesus' comes as a real shock, coming from a band known for songs about hard drugs. The song is, very simply, a prayer – and undoubtedly genuine, though it betokened no conversion. 'Beginning To See The Light' is a joyfully upbeat rocker, 'I'm Set Free' is an epic ballad of loss and resignation, while 'That's The Story Of My Life' is practically vaudeville, with fairly nonsensical lyrics. 'The Murder Mystery' is the most experimental track here, with two sets of vocals performing two different sets of lyrics over a R&B instrumental dominated by Yule's organ. It doesn't really work, but at least provides proof that Reed hadn't totally given himself over to orthodox song structures. The album closes with 'After Hours', a fragile exploration of loneliness and the refuge of alcohol. After this, a solid commercial outing for an already fragmented band, it was impossible to predict where the Velvets might head next.

LOADED

Cotillion/Atlantic; recorded April–July 1970; released September 1970; available on CD.

WHO LOVES THE SUN/SWEET JANE/ROCK & ROLL/COOL IT DOWN/NEW AGE/HEAD HELD HIGH/LONESOME COWBOY BILL/I FOUND A REASON/TRAIN ROUND THE BEND/OH! SWEET NUTHIN'

Personnel: Sterling Morrison (guitar); Lou Reed (guitar, piano, vocals); Billy Yule (drums); Doug Yule (organ, piano, bass, drums, lead guitar, guitar, vocals).

Recorded at Atlantic Studios, New York, *Loaded*'s production would eventually be credited to Geoffrey Haslam, Shel Kagan and The Velvet Underground; Atlantic staff producer Adrian Barber acted as engineer and originally oversaw the proceedings until Kagan and then Haslam were brought in to hurry things along.

Given how beset with problems the band was while recording this album – lacking Moe Tucker, and with Lou Reed suffering from not only a strained voice but also a fragile mental state – it's amazing that it turned out as well as it did. Once again, Doug Yule had to take over lead

A change of place and colour, moving more mainstream with an Art Deco illustration by Stanislaw Zagorski

vocals for several tracks – though Reed later attacked Yule's interpretations of the songs (he claimed Yule "didn't understand" the lyrics to 'New Age'). Reed would also subsequently criticize all the work that was done after he quit the band (ie the mixing and production of the album, the running order the songs had been given, and what he called the "severe" editing of several of the tracks). Reed's carping was understandable and inevitable, given his wounded pride – but the production is in fact excellent. Yule's vocals sounded just fine to everyone but Reed, and the edits actually improved the songs in question, tightening them up. If this wasn't quite the album "loaded with hits" that Reed claimed it was, it was nevertheless loaded with extremely commercial material that not only echoed Reed's doo-wop roots, but also investigated the borders between rock and country (territory being simultaneously explored by many of the Velvets' contemporaries), and did so in an extremely fresh and interesting way. Plus it boasted a couple of *bona fide* classic guitar-based rockers in 'Sweet Jane' and 'Rock & Roll', both exultant celebrations of life and music that would become staples in the sets of indie guitar groups from then on, with innumerable cover versions being recorded.

The album opens with the countryish pop of 'Who Loves The Sun' before moving on to the double-whammy of 'Sweet Jane' and 'Rock & Roll'. 'Cool It Down' is almost bluesy, while 'New Age' is an epic romantic ballad that's literate, funny *and* moving. 'Head Held High' and 'Lonesome Cowboy Bill' are both throwaways, but enjoyable; 'I Found A Reason' is a gentle and sincere love song that's almost doo-wop, thanks to the multi-layered vocal arrangement; 'Train Round The Bend' is bluesy and rather routine; 'Oh! Sweet Nuthin' is another epic ballad, closing the album with its almost gospel-style lament. All of which earned *Loaded* a rave review from *Rolling Stone*, but the irony was tragic; in a sense, The Velvet Underground's story was already over before this record even came out.

The album cover illustration was by Polish designer Stanislaw Zagorski, who had been doing covers for Atlantic's jazz artists for many years. Zagorski rendered a somewhat literal interpretation of the term 'underground', showing a subway entrance with pink smoke emanating from it. Some find the cover charming; others think it a bit of a plunge into tackiness, especially for a band who'd once had Andy Warhol on side for art direction.

LIVE AT MAX'S KANSAS CITY

Cotillion/Atlantic; recorded August 1970; released May 1972; available on CD.

I'M WAITING FOR THE MAN/SWEET JANE/LONESOME COWBOY BILL/BEGINNING TO SEE THE LIGHT/I'LL BE YOUR MIRROR/PALE BLUE EYES/SUNDAY MORNING/NEW AGE/ FEMME FATALE/AFTER HOURS

2-CD version released on Atlantic/Rhino; released 2004; available on CD.

DISC ONE: I'M WAITING FOR THE MAN/WHITE LIGHT-WHITE HEAT/I'M SET FREE/ SWEET JANE (VERSION # 1)/LONESOME COWBOY BILL (VERSION # 1)/NEW AGE/ BEGINNING TO SEE THE LIGHT
DISC TWO: WHO LOVES THE SUN/ SWEET JANE (VERSION # 2)/ I'LL BE YOUR MIRROR/PALE BLUE EYES/CANDY SAYS/ SUNDAY MORNING/AFTER HOURS/FEMME FATALE/SOME KINDA LOVE/LONESOME COWBOY BILL (VERSION # 2)

During the Summer of 1970, the Velvets played a ten-week residency at Max's Kansas City, towards the end of which run Lou Reed quit the band. Although an official Atlantic release, *Live At Max's* is effectively a bootleg, the Velvets knew nothing about it: it was recorded on a very basic Sony TC120 cassette player belonging to Factory stalwart Brigit Polk on 23 August 1970, which turned out to be Lou Reed's last night with the band.

The tape is in mono, and pretty poor in terms of technical quality, since Polk's tape recorder had just been lying on a table; the audience, particularly those seated at Polk's table, is frequently louder than the group. According to Jim Carroll, who was seated with Polk, the club was packed that night – although for much of the Velvets' run at Max's the place had been half-empty (hard as that may be to believe today).

After Reed had left the group, Danny Fields persuaded Polk that the recording might be of value as the group's last recording; they sold the tape to Atlantic for $10,000 outright, which they split between them. Atlantic released an edited version of the concert despite the band's objections, claiming it as the second album the Velvets had contracted for. It was originally released at a budget price, probably because the label was self-conscious about the appalling sound quality.

But despite the sound, *Live At Max's Kansas City* has some things going for it. Although the group (especially Reed) are obviously fairly weary and ragged, what's amazing is how poppy and commercial they sound – especially on the *Loaded* material – as if they might be on the verge of great things. There's certainly no faulting their enthusiasm, backing up Morrison's assertion that they "were ten times better live than on our records". Even Reed seems to be enjoying himself; one can't help but wonder how successful they might have

Max's Kansas City

Andy Warhol described Max's Kansas City as "the exact place where Pop Art and Pop Life came together in the Sixties". From the start, Mickey Ruskin's two-storey bar/restaurant at Park Avenue South and 16th/17th Street attracted a large number of celebrities and artists among its clientele – partly because Ruskin happily gave many artists, Warhol included, credit in return for their paintings. Max's soon became the regular late-night hangout for the Factory crowd, with Warhol holding court (and picking up the tab) after midnight in the back-room dining area. "At Max's the heavyweights of the art world hang around the long bar", wrote Warhol "Superstar" Ultra Violet, "and in the back room, kids, groupies, dropouts, beautiful little girls of fourteen who've already had abortions, get noisy or stoned". Not to mention drag queens, speed-freaks, the occasional celebrity and the whole Factory crowd.

"Everybody went to Max's, and everything got homogenized there".

Andy Warhol

Doug Yule later recalled that "Walking into Max's the first time was like walking into the bar scene in *Star Wars*; a slow pan across alien beings engaged in unfathomable activity". The back room was called "Siberia" by Max's waitresses, since most of its inhabitants were so addled on drugs that they never tipped. Upstairs was originally a disco (the DJ was Wayne County, later Jayne County), which later became a small club where bands played. Max's Kansas City closed its doors forever in December 1974.

The cover of the live album featured a straight monochrome shot of Max's with weird colour plasma emanating from the upper windows

become if he'd only stuck around a while longer. Reed claimed afterwards that his last night at Max's was the only night he really enjoyed himself. "I did all the songs I wanted – a lot of them were ballads", he said. Even if you hate the rest of the album, it's worth the price of admission to hear Lou Reed singing 'After Hours' in a joyously cynical way. "He sings better than I do" was Tucker's comment. On the downside, the 17-year-old Billy Yule is certainly no replacement for Moe Tucker, though he's competent enough.

The group objected to the album's release at the time, but Reed would later acknowledge its worth. "The Max's live set, now that's another album I really love", he confided. "If you want to know what Max's was really like ... it's there, for real, because Brigid was just sitting there with her little Sony recorder. It's in mono, you can't hear us, but you can hear just enough. We're out of tune, per usual ... but it's Sunday night, and all the regulars are there, and Jim Carroll's trying to get Tuirinols, and they're talking about the war ... we were the house band. There it is".

The original release contained only a part of Polk's tape. 'Some Kinda Love' was included on *Peel Slowly And See*, and the complete tape – consisting of both the Velvets' sets in their entirety – was finally released in 2004. If you like the album at all, it's worthwhile getting the expanded version, which contains a nicely put together booklet about Max's and the concert.

SQUEEZE

Polydor/Loaded; recorded summer 1972; released February 1973; vinyl only; out of print.

LITTLE JACK/CRASH/CAROLINE/MEAN OLD MAN/DOPEY JOE/WORDLESS/SHE'LL MAKE YOU CRY/FRIENDS/SEND NO LETTER/JACK AND JANE/LOUISE

More Art Deco, featuring 1930s NY icon the Empire State Building

All titles are credited to Doug Yule, who is thought to have played all the instruments here except the drums (provided by Deep Purple's Ian Paice, though he doesn't get a sleeve credit); there are also some female backing vocals (thought to be by Yule's girlfriend, but again uncredited). The sleeve also states that the album was "arranged and produced by the Velvets", (ie Yule again, since he was the only one left). Yule has subsequently stated that the lyrics to both 'She'll Make You Cry' and 'Mean Old Man' were actually written by Steve Sesnick, to which Yule put music. Sesnick also came up with the album title and oversaw its sleeve design, both chosen to seem like a thematic continuation on from *Loaded*.

Compared to *Loaded*, this sounds pretty poor. What you get on *Squeeze* are so-so pop songs – by no means unpleasant, but also a fairly unremarkable mixture of ragtime, folk-rock, blues and country influences. The best of the songs (such as the Beatlesish 'She'll Make You Cry' and the semi-psychedelic 'Louise') are actually pretty good, in a third-division kind of way; but the worst of them ('Send No Letter', which sounds like a very bad Lou Reed pastiche) prove that whatever it may say on the sleeve, this definitely *isn't* The Velvet Underground.

The song 'Caroline' was inspired by the legendary groupie Christine Frka, aka Miss Christine of the "groupie group" G.T.O.s (who appears on the cover of Frank Zappa's *Hot Rats* album, and who had also inspired The Flying Burrito Brothers' 'Christine's Tune'). Yule had evidently been one of her innumerable conquests; when The Velvet Underground played a Los Angeles gig, Frka and another G.T.O. girl had sent the band a dozen roses with their pictures. "You can't be too subtle", she had pointed out. She died of a drug overdose in 1972. Coincidentally, G.T.O. member Cindy (Miss Cynderella) was at this time married to John Cale.

For curiosity value alone, *Squeeze* deserves a CD release, but it still isn't available – and Reed, Cale and Tucker would presumably be opposed to the idea of the album being reissued under the Velvet Underground name. However, there's no reason why it couldn't be marketed as a Doug Yule solo album instead – after all, that's exactly what this record is. Meanwhile, original vinyl copies are quite hard to find, since *Squeeze* was only pressed in England, and the album was also deleted quite quickly. Some copies were apparently pressed in France during the 1980s, but it's unknown whether

these were legitimate or pirate copies. Expect to pay between £35/$70 and £100/$200 for the real thing, depending on condition. Bootleg copies are usually of poor quality.

1969: VELVET UNDERGROUND LIVE

Mercury double LP; recorded 1969; released April 1974; available on CD.

VOLUME ONE: WAITING FOR MY MAN/LISA SAYS/WHAT GOES ON/SWEET JANE/WE'RE GONNA HAVE A REAL GOOD TIME TOGETHER/FEMME FATALE/NEW AGE/ROCK & ROLL/ BEGINNING TO SEE THE LIGHT/HEROIN
VOLUME TWO: OCEAN/PALE BLUE EYES/HEROIN/SOME KINDA LOVE/OVER YOU/SWEET BONNIE BROWN/IT'S JUST TOO MUCH/WHITE LIGHT WHITE HEAT/I CAN'T STAND IT/ I'LL BE YOUR MIRROR

(The second version of 'Heroin' and 'I Can't Stand It' were added for the CD release).

This is supposedly drawn from over eight hours of tapes, but zero recording details were given on the sleeve. 'Rock & Roll' was recorded by Robert Quine at The Matrix in San Francisco on 25 November 1969; most (if not all) of the rest of this album is supposedly drawn from a gig at the End Of Cole Avenue club in Dallas, Texas on 28 October 1969. At least one other Texas show was taped during this period – at the Vulcan Gas Company in Austin – but that tape is missing, presumed lost.

Despite Sterling Morrison's assertion that "other performances on that tour are ten times better", the record is actually fairly stunning (despite having one of the tackiest covers of all time). The sound quality is almost infi-

Provocatively and unnecessarily sleazy, the front said Volume 1, the back – surprise – Volume 2

nitely superior to the *Max's Kansas City* album, and the band seem in good shape and humour – Reed even chats with the audience, asking them what kind of gig they want. Listening to this – and to the *Quine Tapes* (see pages 162–163) from the same era – it's hard to believe that this is a band on the verge of disintegration; and yet by the time the *Max's* album was recorded (less than a year later), Reed was barely able to complete a sentence.

But here, they're playing well, and Reed in particular sounds relaxed and assured. For most listeners, this was the first chance to hear the Velvets really stretching out, and playing lengthier versions of their album tracks (most of which were quite long to start with). The general approach is slower and more laid-back than on the studio albums – even 'White Light/White Heat' is slowed to a crawl. Doug Yule's extended organ forays (reminiscent of The Band's Garth Hudson) give songs like 'What Goes On' an added dimension, with the others laying down a solid groove as the organ soars above them, the twin guitars constantly jockeying for position. The results are bluesy and energetic, and often surprising. The other really striking component of the album is Sterling Morrison's guitar fills, which are delicately graceful throughout.

'Lisa Says' segues into another, more vaude-villian song (possibly titled 'Why Am I So Shy') before turning back into 'Lisa Says' again. 'Sweet Jane' is a radically different version to that on *Loaded* – slower and bluesier, with completely different words, it sounds a lot like The Cowboy Junkies' later arrangement of the song. According to Reed, the version here has "the original lyrics, even recorded the day I wrote it". 'New Age' also has very different lyrics, namedropping "Frank and Nancy" (Sinatra, presumably) and generally sounding a lot more cynical and world-weary.

As well as previewing tracks from *Loaded* and running through a smattering of their greatest hits – including an exquisite version of 'Pale Blue Eyes' – they also play several songs from the "lost" album. In 1974, these songs were new to most listeners, though Reed had already re-recorded three of them as a solo artist for his first, eponymous, solo album: 'Lisa Says', 'Ocean' and 'I Can't Stand It' (this track was only released in the late 1980s, when it was added as a bonus track for the CD release). Reed would also re-record 'We're Gonna Have A Real Good Time Together' a few years later. The Velvets' studio versions of all these tracks would also surface in the 1980s, but two songs remain available only on this recording (though neither are that remarkable): 'Over You' is a gentle, double-edged love song that could have easily fitted on the third album; 'Sweet Bonnie Brown/ It's Too Much' is fast-paced R&B, but goes nowhere interesting.

Critically, the album went down extremely well. For some reason, it took another five years before the record was released in the UK; when it finally appeared in 1979, British critical response was just as enthusiastic. Post-punk, the Velvets still looked pretty good.

VU

Verve/Polygram; recorded 1968–69; released February 1985; available on CD.

I CAN'T STAND IT/STEPHANIE SAYS/SHE'S MY BEST FRIEND/ LISA SAYS/OCEAN/FOGGY NOTION/TEMPTATION INSIDE YOUR HEART/ONE OF THESE DAYS/ANDY'S CHEST/I'M STICKING WITH YOU

Back to self-conscious minimalism in imagery and title

Subtitled "a collection of previously unreleased recordings", this album was compiled from tapes discovered in the Verve vaults during the process of reissuing the first three Velvets albums on CD. Most of these were unmixed master tapes (only 'Ocean' had been properly mixed at the time of recording); utilizing state-of-the art technology, the tapes were cleaned up and properly mixed in June 1984 by engineer Michael Barbiero at MediaSound in New York. The executive producer for the project was Bill Levenson.

'Stephanie Says' and 'Temptation Inside Your Heart' were both recorded in February 1968 at A&R Studios, New York, and feature John Cale in the line-up; all of the other songs here are taken from the sessions for the "lost" fourth Verve album, which was recorded at the Record Plant in New York between May and October 1969 and engineered by Gary Kellgren. All songs are presumably credited to Lou Reed (no songwriting credits are given on the sleeve) and were produced and arranged by The Velvet Underground. The version of 'Foggy Notion' which appears on the CD is slightly shorter than the one on the vinyl version – a situation that would be rectified when the track was included on *Peel Slowly And See*.

When *VU* was released, critical reaction was near-ecstatic – and not simply because ageing rock critics had been given a chance to indulge their nostalgia, but because the contents of the album were actually extremely good. Kicking off with the irresistible, riff-driven 'I Can't Stand It', the album gives way to the delicate ballad 'Stephanie Says', which features Cale and proves that he had much to offer Reed's new, softer direction, if the two could only have reconciled. 'She's My Best Friend' is poppier than anyone might have expected from the Velvets, and the bluesy 'Lisa Says' is infinitely superior to the version on Reed's debut solo album. The same can – but only just – be said of 'Ocean', which remains a dull song in its every incarnation. 'Foggy Notion' is back-to-basics riff-driven rock, and utterly wonderful. 'Temptation Inside Your Heart' is a mess, but a really interesting one, with a great, Motown-inspired tune. 'One Of These Days'

The "Lost" Album

14 of the tracks on *VU* and *Another View* comprise what would have been the Velvet Underground's "lost" fourth album (which even had a catalogue number, MGM SE-4641). The songs are listed here in the order in which they were recorded (which is almost certainly not the running order the actual album might have had):

FOGGY NOTION
CONEY ISLAND STEEPLECHASE
ANDY'S CHEST
I'M STICKING WITH YOU
SHE'S MY BEST FRIEND
I CAN'T STAND IT
OCEAN
FERRYBOAT BILL
ROCK & ROLL
RIDE INTO THE SUN
ONE OF THESE DAYS
I'M GONNA MOVE RIGHT IN
REAL GOOD TIME TOGETHER
LISA SAYS

ly unexpected proof of just how good this band really was. In some ways, the album is actually more accessible than *Loaded*, supposedly the Velvets' most openly commercial work, and one can't help but wonder what impact the "lost" album might have had, had it been released back in 1969. As Allan Jones noted in *Melody Maker*: "Twenty years on, listening to The Velvet Underground is still like dancing with lightning ... They remain, arguably, the most influential group in the history of rock".

ANOTHER VIEW

Verve/Polygram; recorded 1967–69; released July 1986; available on CD.

WE'RE GONNA HAVE A REAL GOOD TIME TOGETHER/I'M GONNA MOVE RIGHT IN/HEY MR. RAIN (VERSION 1)/RIDE INTO THE SUN/CONEY ISLAND STEEPLECHASE/GUESS I'M FALLING IN LOVE/ HEY MR. RAIN (VERSION 2)/FERRYBOAT BILL/ROCK & ROLL

Personnel: Lou Reed, John Cale, Sterling Morrison, Maureen Tucker, Doug Yule.

is slow country-blues, but not that remarkable. 'Andy's Chest' is Reed's tribute to Warhol following his near-assassination – and also a rarity, in that his solo version (on *Transformer*) is actually far superior to this, which sounds thrashy in comparison. The album closes with Moe Tucker's second vocal outing (accompanied by Lou), 'I'm Sticking With You' – which is either fey and embarrassing or an utter delight, depending on your taste and point of you. Either way, it has one of those tunes that stick in the brain forever.

As a collection, *VU* was additional and total-

Following the critical and commercial success of *VU* in 1985, the following year saw the release of a second batch of unreleased material from the Verve vaults. Again, most of the material was drawn from the "lost" album – but inevitably the second scoop was not quite as sweet as the first, and there was the distinct impression of a barrel being scraped. Utterly minimal sleeve notes are provided, the only clues as to the personnel involved being the recording dates. 'Guess I'm Falling In Love' dates from December 1967, and is thus an out-take from *White Light/White Heat*.

The Music

Another unimaginative – and gray – title and concept to confuse discophiles

The two versions of 'Hey Mr. Rain' were recorded in May 1968 at TTG Studios in Hollywood, while everything else here was recorded in May–September 1969 during sessions for the "lost" album. All songs are credited to The Velvet Underground. 'I'm Gonna Move Right In', 'Ferryboat Bill' and 'Rock & Roll' were all mixed at the time of recording; all other tracks were mixed during March 1986 by J.C. Convertino at Sigma Sound. As with *VU*, Bill Levenson was executive producer of the project.

'We're Gonna Have A Real Good Time Together' is a straightforward rocker, minor but enjoyable, while 'I'm Gonna Move Right In' is a lengthy but unremarkable blues/soul instrumental. The first version of 'Hey Mr. Rain' is a folk/blues ballad, launched into another league by Cale's soaring viola; the second version is slightly more upbeat, but less successful in terms of effect. The version of 'Ride Into The Sun' here is an instrumental, but a lot more powerful and likeable than the version with words which appears on *Peel Slowly And See*; as it stands, it's probably the Velvets' finest instrumental. 'Coney Island Steeplechase' is a vaudevillian throwaway. 'Guess I'm Falling In Love' is a thrashy instrumental version of a song that would also appear (in a live version)

on the *Peel Slowly* boxed set – it has some nice guitar work, but is otherwise unremarkable. 'Ferryboat Bill' is simply nonsensical novelty, and also utterly dispensable. The album closes with the "original version" of 'Rock & Roll', which is both fascinating and likeable – and in some ways preferable to the finished article.

Though not as immediately impressive as the first collection, *Another View* still contains three absolute gems – more than enough to make the album an essential purchase.

LOU REED/JOHN CALE: SONGS FOR DRELLA – A Fiction

Sire/Warner Brothers; recorded winter 1989/90; released April 1990; available on CD.

SMALLTOWN/OPEN HOUSE/STYLE IT TAKES/WORK/TROUBLE WITH CLASSICISTS/STARLIGHT/FACES AND NAMES/IMAGES/ SLIP AWAY (A WARNING)/IT WASN'T ME/I BELIEVE/NOBODY BUT YOU/A DREAM/FOREVER CHANGED/HELLO IT'S ME

Personnel: Lou Reed (vocals and guitars); John Cale (vocals, keyboards and viola). Produced and written by Lou Reed and John Cale.

Since this record is such a key part of the Velvet Underground story, it's being considered here rather than under solo recordings. Reed and Cale's first collaboration after a 20-year gap can arguably hold its head up proudly alongside their early work, and is certainly in the top rank of solo output for both of them. Their inspiration here comes from the passing of their mentor Andy Warhol, and the album provides an overview of the artist's life and work, beginning with his childhood in 'Smalltown' – except that, although Warhol

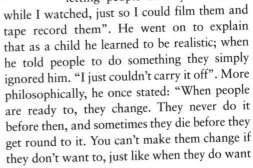

sometimes claimed to come from the small town of McKeesport, Pennsylvania, in reality he'd grown up in Pittsburgh. Still, even Pittsburgh is small compared to New York (and Reed is also clearly drawing on his own upbringing in New Jersey). As with most of the songs here, Reed sings in the first person, as Warhol.

'Open House' explores Warhol's enduring love of (and need for) company, as well as his early career in New York. John Cale takes over the vocals (and the role of Andy) for 'Style It Takes', an exploration of some of Warhol's most famous work, and a depiction of how the artist could sweet-talk and flatter whatever (money, space, a performance) was required out of whoever was being asked. 'Work' sees Reed abandoning the Warhol persona and recounting some of his own memories of Warhol – including his firing of Andy as the Velvets' manager – and exploring the workaholic nature of the man who once asked, "Why do people

The artists reach middle age and a sense of maturity – and mortality

think artists are special?" protesting that "It's just another job".

Cale returns for 'Trouble With Classicists', a comparative analysis of artistic methods and their failings, before Reed returns to examine Warhol's films in 'Starlight' – and also Andy's approach and attitudes to the medium, and to "stardom". Back to Cale for 'Faces And Names', which illustrates that although Warhol was seemingly incessantly drawn to

fame and beauty, many claim he treated everybody alike. The fact that Warhol had a terrible memory for names might explain his view that life would be a lot simpler if we were all interchangeable, though he also pointed out that: "If everybody's not a beauty, then nobody is".

A viola-drone riff dominates in 'Images', as Reed (as Warhol once again) defends the artist's most famous stylistic trademark: multiple images of the same thing, each subtly different from the others. In 'Slip Away (A Warning)', Reed-as-Warhol is warned that the Factory is getting out of hand, but refuses to listen.

In 'It Wasn't Me', Reed-as-Warhol denies responsibility for the high mortality rate (via suicides and drug-related deaths) in the social world which revolved around him – a subject about which many accusations have been hurled at Warhol, prompting several responses from him. Here's one of them: "Now and then someone would accuse me of being evil – of letting people destroy themselves while I watched, just so I could film them and tape record them". He went on to explain that as a child he learned to be realistic; when he told people to do something they simply ignored him. "I just couldn't carry it off". More philosophically, he once stated: "When people are ready to, they change. They never do it before then, and sometimes they die before they get round to it. You can't make them change if they don't want to, just like when they do want to, you can't stop them".

Reed abandons the Warhol persona for 'I Believe', personally entering the fray to describe Valerie Solanas' assassination attempt, Warhol's injuries and recuperation, and his own feelings of a need for retribution – that Solanas got off way too lightly – and the feeling of guilt that he never visited Warhol in hospital. He also states outright that it was "the hospital" that eventually killed Warhol.

"There is nothing like getting shot to kill a party", Factory photographer Nat Finkelstein once bitchily observed, and 'Nobody But You' examines the aftermath of the Solanas incident. Most observers agree that the artist was a completely different person afterwards: an Andy Warhol who went to endless parties and night-clubs and dinners but produced, by his standards, very little worthwhile work. Reed's lyric (as Warhol) explores the artist's own reactions to his new life ... and the mood is one of utter, crippling, isolation. 'A Dream' resulted from Cale's suggestion that Lou write a short story about Warhol, and that they set it to music the way they had with 'The Gift'. Reed decided to make it a dream, rather that something event-based ("That way we can have Andy do anything we want"), and the result is a reverie in Warhol's mind shortly before his death. When the lyrics were published in his *Between Thought And Expression* collection, Reed wrote: "This is not an excerpt from Andy's diaries". Reed had been appalled by the shallow inanity and bitchiness of Warhol's published *Diaries*, (something he'd emphasize further on 'Hello, It's Me') and wove verbatim quotes from the book (including Warhol's remarks about himself and Cale) into a monologue that reveals much (both good and bad) about what Warhol was actually like as a person. Though Reed has performed this live in concert, here it's Cale who takes the vocal, his Welsh lilt heightening the dreamlike atmosphere. Added in its later stages, this became the album's centrepiece and undisputed gem.

In 'Forever Changed', Cale-as-Warhol muses on the different changes his life passed through – including, presumably, the final one. (There is, of course, an album by Love entitled *Forever Changes* – but the use of the past tense here underlines the sense of finality.) The album closes with its most personal (and moving) song in 'Hello It's Me', in which Lou Reed bids Warhol a final farewell. Few people have ever received a tribute on a par with this album; it's far more important than most critics gave it credit for, and was obviously made with both care and love.

LIVE MCMXCIII

Sire/Warner Bros; recorded June 1993; released October 1993; available on CD.

DISC ONE: WE'RE GONNA HAVE A REAL GOOD TIME TOGETHER/VENUS IN FURS/GUESS I'M FALLING IN LOVE/ AFTERHOURS/ALL TOMORROW'S PARTIES/SOME KINDA LOVE/I'LL BE YOUR MIRROR/BEGINNING TO SEE THE LIGHT/ THE GIFT/I HEARD HER CALL MY NAME/FEMME FATALE

DISC TWO: HEY MR. RAIN/SWEET JANE/VELVET NURSERY RHYME/WHITE LIGHT WHITE HEAT/I'M STICKING WITH YOU/BLACK ANGEL'S DEATH SONG/ROCK & ROLL/I CAN'T STAND IT/I'M WAITING FOR THE MAN/HEROIN/PALE BLUE EYES/COYOTE

Recorded at the three 1993 Paris shows at l'Olympia music hall, and produced by Reed's guitarist Mike Rathke.

An abbreviated, single-CD version was also released at the same time (and with the same title, confusingly).

TRACK LISTING: VENUS IN FURS/SWEET JANE/ AFTER HOURS/ALL TOMORROW'S PARTIES/SOME KINDA LOVE/THE GIFT/ROCK & ROLL/I'M WAITING FOR THE MAN/HEROIN/PALE BLUE EYES

It's that banana again, this time in a non-peelable metallic sheen

Reviews of the reunited Velvet Underground's live shows were mixed (and reviews of the album and video would be equally divided); once the emotional impact of seeing the four of them together on stage again (against all expectations) had subsided, many critics leveled accusations that the whole thing was just too "showbiz" for comfort. The fault isn't with the music particularly – which veers from the amateurish ('We're Gonna Have A Real Good Time Together') to the epic ('Hey Mr. Rain'), but with enough truly stunning ingredients to make it worth hearing. The main problem lies with Reed, whose vocals aren't invested with any real feeling much of the time, to the point that they approach self-parody. On much of the record he sounds like a lounge singer in a cheesy rock cabaret, and everything suffers accordingly. Cale and Reed had divided Nico's vocal role between them, Reed taking 'I'll Be Your Mirror' while Cale took the rest (to much better effect). Also on the downside, there's the 'Velvet Nursery Rhyme', Reed's introduction to the band in verse, which only just avoids making the listener wince with embarassment.

There are however plus points: Morrison's tasteful guitar fills, Tucker's drumming and her show-stealing solo spots, Cale's searing viola, great versions of 'All Tomorrow's Parties', 'I Can't Stand It' and 'I'm Waiting For The Man'. You also finally get to hear the words to 'Guess I'm Falling In Love' (which features the line "I've got the fever in my pocket", a quote from Bob Dylan's 'Absolutely Sweet Marie'). And 'Pale Blue Eyes' sounds as if it was always meant to feature Cale's mesmeric viola-playing. And for once Reed's world-weary vocal approach fits perfectly; this is the definitive version, and worth the price of admission on its own.

Though the band are sometimes ragged, most of the time they're in great form, their rapport often uncanny, and their playing occasionally approaching the sublime. The real stars of the show are John Cale and Moe Tucker, the sheer solidity of whose drumming is astonishing (and a stunning visual spectacle, as the video proves). And, of course, state-of-the-art recording technology makes this a lot more accessible than their previous live albums – though it does make you wish someone had made a decent live recording of them back in 1966. As to the one new song, 'Coyote' ... Reed's laconic tale of desert dogs could be an allegory for the Velvets' own troubled history; it could also easily have fitted on *Loaded*. With its thunderous bass/ drum combination, Morrison's delicate guitar-work and the dry observations of Reed's lyric – if it proves to be their swan song, it'll do.

The Music

The Music

WHAT GOES ON

Raven; recorded 1966–1970; released 1993; available on CD.

DISC ONE: "ANDY WARHOL PRESENTS"/MELODY LAUGHTER/ HEROIN/I'M WAITING FOR THE MAN/SUNDAY MORNING/ I'LL BE YOUR MIRROR/RUN RUN RUN/ALL TOMORROW'S PARTIES/VENUS IN FURS/FEMME FATALE/IT WAS A PLEASURE THEN/FROM THE MUSIC FACTORY/WHITE LIGHT WHITE HEAT/LADY GODIVA'S OPERATION/I HEARD HER CALL MY NAME/UNTITLED

DISC TWO: SISTER RAY/HERE SHE COMES NOW/GUESS I'M FALLING IN LOVE/STEPHANIE SAYS/HEY MR. RAIN # 2/CANDY SAYS/SOME KINDA LOVE/PALE BLUE EYES/BEGINNING TO SEE THE LIGHT/I'M SET FREE/THE MURDER MYSTERY/FOGGY NOTION/I CAN'T STAND IT

DISC THREE: OCEAN/ONE OF THESE DAYS/INTRODUCTIONS/ TOO MUCH/SWEET JANE/NEW AGE/OVER YOU/WHAT GOES ON/AFTER HOURS/I'M STICKING WITH YOU/TRAIN ROUND THE BEND/HEAD HELD HIGH/WHO LOVES THE SUN/ROCK & ROLL/RIDE INTO THE SUN/AFTER HOURS/"NO MORE REUNIONS"/THANKS ANDY WARHOL

An Australian compilation, which was of note at the time for containing several then-unreleased tracks (and the then-unavailable "Closet Mix" of six tracks from the third album, see above), all of which have since been collected on either *Peel Slowly And See* or *Fully Loaded*.

The only material left on this set which is still unavailable elsewhere (or at any rate, very hard to find) are the spoken word track: a brief interview with Warhol promoting the gigs at the Dom; a conversation between Reed and Tom Wilson circa *White Light/White Heat*, with Reed trotting out some great fine art ideas; a 1966 conversation between Nico, Cale, Reed and others (from *Andy Warhol's Index Book*, discussing the book); a snatched quote from Reed on the street in 1985, denying the pos-

sibility of reunions; and eight minutes' worth of fascinating interviews with all four Velvets and M.C. Kostek at the opening of the Cartier Warhol retrospective at Jouy-en-Josas in June 1990. The live version of 'Heroin' performed that day can be heard running underneath the interviews. This track first appeared on a free flexidisc inserted into issue # four of the Velvets fanzine *What Goes On.*

No banana, no grey band shot, in fact nothing but the name

Leaving aside the spoken material, this is also an excellent compilation, and one which takes in a slightly broader sweep of the Velvets' career than *Peel Slowly And See*. Its appearance also doubtless galvanized the Velvets into putting together their own official retrospective boxed set.

PEEL SLOWLY AND SEE

Polydor; recorded 1965–1970; released September 1995; available on CD.

The Velvets' official boxed retrospective is a lavish affair, containing five CDs. On these could be found the band's first four albums (re-edited/mixed where necessary), plus a wealth of unreleased material – including a whole disc full of early demos. The set's packaging echoed that of the Velvets' first album, complete with (peelable) banana, and the box also contained a well-designed booklet containing an excellent career overview by David Fricke. Released shortly after Sterling Morrison's death, the set amply fulfilled its purposes – to set a seal on the band's history, and to stem the tide of bootlegs. Much of the unreleased material had been supplied by Morrison from his archives, and *Peel Slowly And See* stands as a worthy epitaph for him.

DISC ONE

This consists of previously unreleased demo material from John Cale's archives, recorded at his Ludlow Street apartment in New York during July 1965. Reed and Morrison play guitars, while Cale plays viola and sarinda (an Afghani stringed instrument). There is no drummer, since Angus MacLise had forgotten to turn up for the session. John Cale: "Angus was really living on the Angus calendar. If you told Angus that there was a rehearsal at two o'clock on Friday, he wouldn't understand what you were talking about. He would just come and go, whenever and wherever he pleased". Though the material here is definitely interesting, one listening is sufficient for most people. For one thing, there are multiple takes of most of the songs; for another, most are delivered in an acoustic, folky style that gives little hint of where they'd end up eventually. According to Cale, their months of experimentation during rehearsal were what paid off in the long term: "We started detuning instruments, playing with gadgets, puttering about in general until we landed with something".

'Venus In Furs' is sung by Cale almost as a folk ballad, in medieval minstrel mode, and sounding somewhere between 'Scarborough Fair' and 'Greensleeves'. Very surprising, considering how much Cale hated folk music – it sounds almost like parody. Several takes of the song pretty much all run together without a break (lasting over 15 minutes). 'Prominent Men' (written by Cale/Reed and sung by Reed) is a Dylanesque protest song (complete with harmonica) that rails against the high and mighty. It's fairly unremarkable, and doesn't really fit with the other material, which probably explains why the Velvets dropped it from their repertoire. 'Heroin' gets five different takes, not all of which make it all the way through (over 13 minutes' worth). The lyrics are slightly different (see page 243), but otherwise the bones of the finished version are all present here, from the arrangement to the pacing – though Reed's wavering vocals sound ultra-nasal and Dylanish once again. 'I'm Waiting For The Man' rates three takes (just under ten minutes' worth, which feature some painfully messy harmonica and viola). The song is done as a ragtime country-blues, complete with slide guitar and a bizarre vocal interjection from Cale. Reed's 'Wrap Your Troubles In Dreams' is sung by Cale as a mournful dirge. The metronomic percussion here is provided by Sterling Morrison rapping his knuckles against the back of Cale's sarinda. The song would later be recorded by Nico on her *Chelsea Girl* album (a version that is infinitely better than this). There are several takes of this – nearly 16 minutes' worth – and one features a brief argument which is a lot more interesting than the music. 'All Tomorrow's Parties' is also given the folk ballad treatment, with Cale and Reed harmonizing (but still sounding like Dylan). The first version is really fast, but collapses in a shower of Anglo-Saxon. Eight more (mainly incomplete) takes follow, with varying degrees of success making up over 18 minutes of the disc. The most interesting aspect here is that this was recorded nearly six months before they met Warhol, which gives the lie to the theory that Reed had written it to please Andy's sensibilities.

DISC TWO

Consists of *The Velvet Underground & Nico* in its entirety, plus the following four extra tracks:

• A mono single version of 'All Tomorrow's Parties', originally released in July 1966. It's a drastically edited version of the album track (cut from 5 min. 58 secs. down to 2 min. 49 secs.).

• 'Melody Laughter', which was previously unreleased. A drone-like improvisation piece that could last anywhere from two minutes to forty-two and feature almost any combination of their instruments, this version was recorded live at the Valleydale Ballroom, Columbus, Ohio on 4 November 1966, and was edited down to just under eleven minutes from thirty. The writing is credited to all four Velvets plus Nico, who sings wordlessly – as Tucker put it, "just warbles". It veers between being interest-

The "boxed set" format made for an awkward crop of Warhol's original composition. Good title though

ing and just plain self-indulgent and at times it's pretty painful.

• 'It Was A Pleasure Then' was first released on Nico's 1969 solo album *Chelsea Girl*, and written by Nico, Cale and Reed – though it sounds like it almost certainly developed out of 'Melody Laughter'. Dirge-like and Gothic, it was the first hint of the template that Nico would echo for most her future career. Recorded at Mayfair Sound Studios in New York, April/May 1967, it was produced by Tom Wilson, and engineered by Gary Kellgren.

• 'Chelsea Girls' was written by Reed/Morrison, and also included on Nico's *Chelsea Girl* album. Commissioned for the Warhol movie of the same name, but completed too late for inclusion in the film, the song is a very folky ballad that lists various characters that haunted the Factory and the Chelsea Hotel. It was recorded during the same 1967 sessions as 'It Was A Pleasure Then', at Mayfair Sound Studios in New York, produced by Tom Wilson, and engineered by Gary Kellgren. Nico hated Larry Fallon's orchestral arrangement for the song, as did Reed: "Everything on it, those strings, that flute, should have defeated it. But the lyrics, Nico's voice ... It managed somehow to survive".

DISC THREE

Consists of *White Light/White Heat* in its

entirety, plus 'Stephanie Says' and 'Temptation Inside Your Heart' from *VU*, and 'Hey Mr. Rain (Version 1)' from *Another View*, and includes five previously unreleased tracks from a demo acetate recorded early in 1967 at John Cale's Ludlow Street apartment:

• 'There Is No Reason' is an acoustic folk ballad and a lover's complaint – fairly unremarkable, and also fairly amateurish. Written by Reed/Cale, sung by Reed.

• 'Sheltered Life' is written, and sung, by Reed. It's really enjoyable psychedelic ragtime-folk, with downright funny nonsense lyrics and a kazoo solo, sounding like something The Purple Gang (of 'Granny Takes A Trip' fame) might have come up with. Reed would later re-record the song for his 1976 album *Rock And Roll Heart*.

• 'It's All Right (The Way That You Live)' is again fairly ordinary, a mixture of folk and R&B, with a great booming bass line. Written by Reed/Cale, sung by Reed.

• 'I'm Not Too Sorry (Now That You're Gone)' is Beatlesish pop, overlaid with a lot of psychedelic guitar work. Another minor work, but enjoyable. Written by Reed/Cale, sung by Reed.

• 'Here She Comes Now' has different lyrics to the version later recorded for *White Light/White Heat*, with some very weird echoing viola that makes it sound much more psychedelic. Written by Reed/Cale/Morrison, it is sung by Reed in Dylan mode.

Additionally, there are two good quality live tracks recorded at The Gymnasium in New York, April 1967, both of which are credited to all four Velvets: 'Guess I'm Falling In Love' is a high-energy performance of the song that pisses all over both the version on the 1993 live album, and the instrumental one on *Another View*; 'Booker T.' is an R&B instrumental, inspired by Booker T. & The MGs' 'Green Onions'. The track would later evolve into the backing music for 'The Gift'. A three-minute extract from this (fairly sloppy) six-and-a-half-minute performance had previously been released in 1992, on John Cale's solo album *Paris S'Eveille* (see below).

DISC FOUR

Kicking off with the "Closet Mix" of *The Velvet Underground* album in its entirety, the disc also includes 'Foggy Notion', 'I Can't Stand It', 'I'm Sticking With You', 'One Of These Days' and 'Lisa Says' (all from *VU*) and the following three previously unreleased tracks:

• 'What Goes On', recorded live 2 November 1968 at La Cave, Cleveland, Ohio. A fairly undistinguished live version, with pretty rough sound quality. The point of interest here lies in the fact that this gig was supposedly Doug Yule's concert debut with the band.

• 'It's Just Too Much' comes from the same era as the version on *1969: Velvet Underground Live*, but this one was recorded live on 28 November 1969 at The End of Cole Avenue club, Dallas, Texas. It's country blues, and pretty dull.

• 'Countess From Hong Kong' is a demo version of a song co-written by Cale and Reed, but not recorded until late 1969 (i.e. long after Cale's departure). No other recording details are given. Reed plays harmonica, which sounds incongruous given that the general treatment here is more like bossa nova than folk. The song takes its title from Charlie Chaplin's last film as a director, a romantic comedy starring Sophia Loren and Marlon Brando, which was released in 1967. Lou Reed is evidently a big Chaplin fan – check out 'City Lights' on his solo album *The Bells*.

DISC FIVE

Here we are presented with 1970's *Loaded* in its entirety, but with full-length versions of 'Sweet Jane' and 'New Age' replacing the edited ones from the original release. 'Sweet Jane' gains Reed's intended ending; 'New Age' has an extended closing refrain – and it has to be said that neither of the restored versions is actually an improvement on the edited ones. Also included here are a live version of 'I'll Be Your Mirror' (from *Live At Max's Kansas City*), a laconically bluesy live version of 'Some Kinda Love' (an out-take from the same album) and seven previously unreleased out-takes from *Loaded*:

• 'Satellite Of Love' would be revived by Reed in 1972 (with slightly different lyrics) for his *Transformer* solo album. Here it's still overtly a pop song, but nowhere near as hummable and commercial as it would become with the Bowie/Ronson arrangement. The subject matter is the painfully promiscuous infidelity of one's partner, and the resultant jealousy of the singer.

• 'Walk And Talk' is an undistinguished folk/blues sung by Reed (with harmonies by Yule), who would re-record it in 1972 for his first solo album, *Lou Reed*. Some think the song was influenced by Hubert Selby's controversial novel *Last Exit To Brooklyn*, but it's hard to see how.

• 'Oh Gin' is another minor blues, which Reed would re-work (to even lesser effect) as 'Oh Jim' for his 1973 solo album *Berlin*.

• 'Sad Song' is an achingly beautiful ballad about a rocky relationship. By the time Reed re-recorded it for *Berlin* three years later it had become a fairly bitter song about divorce.

• 'Ocean' was originally thought to be a version that featured John Cale. When *Peel Slowly And See* was released few were aware of the fact that Cale had briefly returned to the Velvets fold in 1970. "I was brought in by Steve Sesnick in a half-hearted attempt at reuniting old comrades". he explained to David Fricke. However, it subsequently turned out that this wasn't the version with Cale after all, which would eventually surface on *Fully Loaded*. This cut actually features Doug Yule on an organ part that swells like a tide, includes some great guitar work, and is more moodily melodramatic and vocally atmospheric than the version on *VU*. Reed would re-record the song yet again for his eponymous debut album in 1972.

• 'Ride Into The Sun' had already appeared on *Another View* as an instrumental; this time it has words about wishing for an escape from the city, but it still sounds very Beatles-influenced. It was another song in re-recorded in 1972 by Reed for his first solo album.

- 'I Love You' is, as its title implies, a straight-forward love song from Reed; sadly, it isn't a very good one.

All seven songs are credited solely to Reed except 'Ride Into The Sun', which is credited to Reed/Cale/Tucker/Morrison.

FULLY LOADED

Rhino; recorded 1970; released February 1997; available on CD.

DISC ONE: WHO LOVES THE SUN/SWEET JANE/ROCK & ROLL/ COOL IT DOWN/NEW AGE/HEAD HELD HIGH/LONESOME COWBOY BILL/ I FOUND A REASON/TRAIN ROUND THE BEND/OH! SWEET NUTHIN'/RIDE INTO THE SUN/OCEAN/I'M STICKING WITH YOU/I LOVE YOU/ROCK & ROLL/HEAD HELD HIGH
DISC TWO: WHO LOVES THE SUN/SWEET JANE/ROCK & ROLL/COOL IT DOWN/NEW AGE/HEAD HELD HIGH/ LONESOME COWBOY BILL/ I FOUND A REASON/TRAIN ROUND THE BEND/OH! SWEET NUTHIN'/OCEAN/I LOVE YOU/ SATELLITE OF LOVE/OH GIN/WALK AND TALK/SAD SONG/ LOVE MAKES YOU FEEL TEN FEET TALL

After *Peel Slowly And See*, most people assumed that the well of unreleased Velvets studio material was now exhausted. Then several boxes of tapes were discovered in Atlantic's vaults, some of them apparently labelled "garbage", and these formed the core of this double-CD set. 17 of the 33 tracks had never been available before, and though a few are simply alternate mixes, the rest are a revelation. Remastered by engineer Bob Ludwig, *Fully Loaded* was thoughtfully packaged, with a lenticular sleeve that echoed the original *Loaded* album cover. The booklet liner notes were once again by

David Fricke.

DISC ONE

This opens with a "restored" version of the original *Loaded* album, including "full-length" versions of 'Sweet Jane' and 'Rock & Roll', and a "long version" of 'New Age'. Of the remaining six tracks

Marketing inspiration reached rock bottom with a recycled cover design, and recycled title – although this time the smoke was pink

on the disc, three had already appeared on *Peel Slowly And See*, while the remainder included previously unreleased alternate mixes of 'Rock & Roll' (with grotesque backing vocals) and 'Head Held High', plus an outtake of 'I'm Sticking With You' that simply isn't as good as the one on *VU*.

DISC TWO

Now we come to another alternate version of *Loaded*, made up of demos, early versions and alternate mixes (though, of the latter –'Who Loves The Sun' and 'Train Round The Bend' – neither is an improvement). There's an incredibly slow early version of 'Sweet Jane' with slightly different lyrics and highly erratic percussion, which is fascinating without actually being much good; a wonderful demo of 'Rock & Roll' which features some incredibly delicate guitar work; an equally fine piano-driven early version of 'Cool It Down'; the "full-length" version of 'New Age' (which fades on a very nice guitar solo); early (and unimpressive) versions of 'Head Held High' and 'Lonesome Cowboy Bill'; a great country-folk demo of 'I Found A Reason' (with Dylanesque harmonica); and a bluesy early version of 'Oh! Sweet Nuthin' that features a very wheezy organ, but isn't that good.

In addition to this, Disc Two also contains seven more tracks. Three of these had been included on *Peel Slowly And See*, while the other four had not appeared before: an early (and rather tentative) demo of 'Ocean' featuring John Cale on organ; an outtake of 'I Love You' which has a much more interesting arrangement than the version on the boxed set (though it's still not that impressive a song); a different (and very stripped-down) demo of 'Satellite Of Love' to the one included on the boxed set, which is still nowhere near as good as the *Transformer* version; and finally the demo for a hitherto unknown song called 'Love Makes You Feel Ten Feet Tall', which is Reed in pure Dylan mode – but the backing is a lot better than the song.

All in all, a very interesting compilation. Worth the price of admission if you already own a copy of *Loaded*? Definitely.

BOOTLEG SERIES VOLUME I: THE QUINE TAPES

Polydor; recorded 1969; released 2001; available on CD.

DISC ONE: I'M WAITING FOR THE MAN/IT'S JUST TOO MUCH/ WHAT GOES ON/I CAN'T STAND IT/SOME KINDA LOVE/ FOGGY NOTION/FEMME FATALE/AFTER HOURS/I'M STICKING WITH YOU/SUNDAY MORNING/SISTER RAY
DISC TWO: FOLLOW THE LEADER/WHITE LIGHT WHITE HEAT/VENUS IN FURS/HEROIN/SISTER RAY
DISC THREE: ROCK & ROLL/NEW AGE/OVER YOU/BLACK ANGEL'S DEATH SONG/I'M WAITING FOR THE MAN/RIDE INTO THE SUN/SISTER RAY/FOGGY NOTION

Recorded at: The Family Dog, San Francisco (7–9 November 1969); The Matrix, San Francisco (23–25 November, 27 November, 1 December, 3 December 1969); Washington University, St Louis (11 May 1969). Personnel: Lou Reed, Sterling Morrison, Doug Yule, Maureen Tucker.

More artful minimalism, reproducing Quine's own homemade tape cover

All tracks were recorded by Robert Quine on a portable Sony cassette recorder with a hand-held microphone. 'Rock & Roll' had appeared on the *1969 Live* album, but everything else was previously unreleased.

The sound quality is pretty good on the Family Dog tapes, less so on the ones from the Matrix, and the material is generally comparable to that on the *1969 Live* album.

If anything, the band are tighter and more energetic, delivering driving versions of 'I Can't Stand It', 'Some Kinda Love' and 'Foggy

Notion', and wonderfully ragged versions of 'I'm Sticking With You' and 'Ride Into The Sun'. On the downside, Yule is really no substitute for Cale on tracks like 'Venus In Furs' or 'The Black Angel's Death Song'. Worse, there's a general tendency towards extended improvisation, including a 17-minute meandering mess entitled 'Follow The Leader' and no less than three extremely long versions of 'Sister Ray', which feature as much lyrical improvisation as musical. The longest of these lasts for 38 minutes, and they're either fascinating or self-indulgent, depending on your point of view; such lengthy jamming was *de rigueur* for the times, but didn't really last beyond them (punk rock happened for a reason).

Nothing in this collection is truly essential, but there's more than enough good material included to make it well worth checking out … and the 'Volume I' part of the title at least holds out some hope for future releases in the series.

Robert Quine (1942–2004)

Robert Quine was a law student from Akron, Ohio, who moved to San Francisco in the Autumn of 1969 after passing his bar exams in Missouri. Quine was already a devoted Velvet Underground fan, and when the group came to California Quine attended – and taped – every gig. Noticing his presence, the Velvets invited him backstage for conversation, and also to soundchecks and rehearsals. Fortunately, Quine had the foresight to transfer four hours' worth of the best of the material onto reel-to-reel tapes, from which these CDs were mastered; his original cassettes subsequently suffered damage and were eventually lost.

Quine never practised law. After two years in San Francisco, he moved to New York, where he wrote textbooks on tax law for three years and became friends with Tom Verlaine and Richard Hell. Quine had played guitar in various amateur bands since his teens, and in 1975 decided to finally abandon his textbooks and form a serious band, The Voidoids, with Hell. Lou Reed became a fan early on, eventually hiring Quine for his new post-rehab band in the early 1980s, beginning with *The Blue Mask*. Quine remained in Reed's band for nearly four years, subsequently playing with numerous other artists including Tom Waits, Brian Eno, Lloyd Cole, Marianne Faithfull, Matthew Sweet and John Zorn. After Quine's wife Alice died of heart failure in August 2003, he became severely depressed, and is believed to have made at least one suicide attempt during that Winter. He died of a heroin overdose – which was almost certainly intentional – on or about 31 May 2004; his body was discovered approximately five days later.

FINAL V.U.: 1971–1973

Captain Trip Records; recorded 1971–1973; released 2002;
available on Japanese import CD.

*DISC ONE: CHAPEL OF LOVE/ I'M WAITING FOR THE MAN/
SPARE CHANGE/SOME KINDA LOVE/TURN ON YOUR LOVE
LIGHT/WHITE LIGHT WHITE HEAT/PRETTY TREE CLIMBER/
ROCK & ROLL/BACK ON THE FARM/DOPEY JOE/SISTER RAY/
NEVER GOING BACK TO GEORGIA/AFTER HOURS*

Recorded at The School Of Oriental And African Studies
(S.O.A.S.), London, England, 5 November 1971.
Personnel: Doug Yule (guitar and vocals); Walter Powers
(bass); Willie Alexander (piano and vocals); Maureen
Tucker (drums and vocals).

*DISC TWO: I'M WAITING FOR THE MAN/SPARE CHANGE/
SOME KINDA LOVE/WHITE LIGHT WHITE HEAT/HOLD ON/
WHAT GOES ON/COOL IT DOWN/BACK ON THE FARM/OH
SWEET NUTHIN'/SISTER RAY/AFTER HOURS/DOPEY JOE/ROCK
& ROLL*

Recorded at Concertgebouw, Amsterdam, Netherlands,
19 November 1971.
Personnel: Doug Yule, guitar and vocals; Walter Powers,
bass; Willie Alexander, piano and vocals; Maureen Tucker,
drums and vocals.

*DISC THREE: I'M WAITING FOR THE MAN/WHITE LIGHT
WHITE HEAT/SOME KINDA LOVE/LITTLE JACK/SWEET JANE/
MEAN OLD MAN/RUN RUN RUN/CAROLINE/DOPEY JOE/
WHAT GOES ON/SISTER RAY/TRAIN ROUND THE BEND/ROCK
& ROLL/ I'M WAITING FOR THE MAN*

Recorded at St. David's University, Lampeter, Wales,
6 December 1972.
Personnel: Doug Yule (guitar and vocals); Rob Norris
(guitar); George Kay (bass); Mark Nauseef (drums).

*DISC FOUR: I'M WAITING FOR THE MAN/LITTLE JACK/ WHITE
LIGHT WHITE HEAT/CAROLINE/SWEET JANE/MEAN OLD
MAN/WHO'S THAT MAN/LET IT SHINE/MAMA'S LITTLE GIRL/
TRAIN ROUND THE BEND*

Recorded at Oliver's, Boston, Massachusetts, 27 May 1973
Personnel: Doug Yule (guitar and vocals); Billy Yule
(drums); George Kay (bass); Don Silverman (guitar).

The "bonus tracks" on Disc Four are radio broadcast versions of four tracks from Disc Two.

These bootleg-quality recordings were licensed
from Doug Yule, who also provided an essay in
the illustrated book-
let. The set is lavishly
packaged in a box,
which makes it seem
far more important
than it is, since what's
included here is nei-
ther representative of
any of the other Velvet
Underground records
or very good. The
recording quality veers
from poor to atro-
cious, and the musi-
cal content is proof
positive that anyone
who paid money to
see the "Velveteens"
live would have been
sorely disappointed.

The "Velveteens" grace the
cover which otherwise might
have proved misleading

They're simply a ramshackle bar band trotting out a lot of blues clichés (though the bass
and guitar solos are actually of slightly more
interest than the songs that surround them),
albeit one that happens to know a lot of Velvet
Underground songs. Hearing Moe Tucker sing
'After Hours' with this group sounds bizarrely
out of place, and more than a little sad. Save
your money.

LOU REED, JOHN CALE & NICO: LE BATACLAN '72

Alchemy Entertainment; recorded 29 January 1972; released 2003; available on CD.

WAITING FOR THE MAN/BERLIN/BLACK ANGEL'S DEATH SONG/WILD CHILD/HEROIN/GHOST STORY/THE BIGGEST, LOUDEST, HAIRIEST GROUP OF ALL/EMPTY BOTTLES/FEMME FATALE/NO ONE IS THERE/FROZEN WARNINGS/JANITOR OF LUNACY/I'LL BE YOUR MIRROR/ALL TOMORROW'S PARTIES/ BONUS REHEARSAL TRACKS: PALE BLUE EYES/CANDY SAYS

Lou Reed (vocals, acoustic guitar); John Cale (vocals, guitar, viola and piano); Nico (vocals and harmonium).

Since this CD captures another key moment in the Velvet Underground story, it's being considered here rather than under solo recordings. After over 30 years, anyone who was unable to attend the actual concert can now hear the results of the unexpected reunion of three of the Velvets' core personnel in January 1972. Paris's Bataclan Theatre was filled to its capacity of 1,000 people for the event (with an estimated 2,000 more disappointed fans turned away at the door).

What it actually sounds like is "The Velvet Underground Unplugged" – acoustic, often bluesy treatments of half-a-dozen Velvets' classics, plus a small selection from the trio's solo songbooks. 'Waiting For The Man' and 'Heroin' might well have sounded like this back when Reed and Cale were performing it as buskers. 'The Black Angel's Death Song' here resembles something Leonard Cohen might have come up with, while 'Wild Child' sounds like Bob Dylan on a bad day (though it's far better than the studio version). Cale contributes a lacklus-

tre 'Ghost Story', plus 'The Biggest, Loudest, Hairiest Group Of All', a throwaway ballad about a rock band on the road (if it's intended to be about the Velvets, it doesn't do them justice). Cale's on firmer ground with 'Empty Bottles', but

Very evocative of the era and the on stage presence of the ensemble

it's not as strong as many of the songs on his first solo outing, 1969's *Vintage Violence*, that he could have picked in its stead.

Nico weighs in with 'Femme Fatale' (with great harmonies from Cale and Reed), before heading for the harmonium and a selection of her solo material – all of which is great, but of a completely different mood to what's gone before. It's as if the audience has been suddenly transported to a Gothic cathedral, then transported back again for the finale of 'I'll Be Your Mirror', followed by a somewhat ragged encore of 'All Tomorrow's Parties'. (The rehearsal tape of 'Pale Blue Eyes' and 'Candy Says' consists of Reed actually teaching Cale the songs, and is thus very tentative and generally a bit of a mess – which is obviously why these songs didn't get included in the actual concert).

Given that Reed's solo career was in sorry shape at this point, he sounds both confident and in good voice – while Cale, who was then very inexperienced at singing before an audience, sounds pretty shaky. One can't help but wonder what might have happened at this point if the other two had agreed to Reed's suggestion of making this a more permanent reunion – which would have resulted in a Velvet Underground with three songwriters instead of just one. Sadly, we'll never know.

When an interviewer asked Reed about this album in 2003, Lou expressed surprise at the news that it had been released, and talked of getting an injunction to stop it being distributed. However, the sleeve clearly states that the record has been licensed from Sister Ray Enterprises and is thus legitimate (and definitely had the approval of Cale), so perhaps Reed was just living up to his image. The album sleeve states that the project was "co-ordinated" by one Carlton P. Sandercock, which certainly sounds like a pseudonym for somebody!

Regardless of its flaws, a great live album.

Compilations

There have been numerous "best of" The Velvet Underground compilations released over the decades, usually drawing their material mainly from two albums: *The Velvet Underground and Nico* and *Loaded*. There seems little point in listing any of them here, since anyone buying this book will presumably already own much of the Velvets' output – failing which, the reader is advised to invest in a copy of the *Peel Slowly And See* boxed set as the best starting point.

However, completists may care to note that the recent 2-CD compilation *The Velvet Underground Gold* includes previously unreleased mixes of both 'Temptation Inside Your Heart' and 'Stephanie Says'.

RARITIES

There are numerous pressings of all Velvet Underground albums, and of the singles taken from those albums. The rarer the pressing, the more its financial worth – and copies of the first album with its cover banana unpeeled tend to be scarce (though pirate versions abound). However, there is actually very little material that was released on vinyl that has not been now released on CD ...

THE VELVET UNDERGROUND & NICO – ACETATE

Undoubtedly the rarest Velvets record, this was bought in a yard sale in Manhattan for 75 cents by Canadian record collector Warren Hill. The record had no sleeve, and only the words "The Velvet Underground" and "Mr. N. Dolph" scrawled on the label. It turned out to be a mono acetate copy of the first Velvet Underground album – or rather of the version recorded at Scepter Studios, before later re-recording of some of the songs at T.T.G. in Los Angeles. After the sessions, Norman Dolph had had the acetate cut through his contacts at Columbia Records, and had then given it to either Andy Warhol or Paul Morrissey. He has no idea how it ended up for sale.

The mixes of all tracks on it differ from the released version. In addition, there are completely different takes of 'European Son', 'Heroin', 'Venus In Furs' and 'I'm Waiting For The Man'. Since the master tapes for the album have been lost, this may well be the only copy in existence of those recordings. In late 2006 the acetate was sold for $155,000 through e-Bay. Norman Dolph thinks that it's possible that the original tape from which the acetate was made may still be lurking in Columbia's long-term storage vaults; if so, then a commercial release of the material may eventually become possible.

NOISE

Contained on *The East Village Other Electric Newspaper* LP, released August 1966. This is a fragment (about a minute) of the Velvets playing live, but is almost inaudible since the radio broadcast of President Johnson's daughter Lucy's wedding which runs through the whole record virtually drowns out the band.

LOOP

A feedback-based improvisational piece, given away as a flexidisc with *Aspen* magazine in December 1966. Tucker doesn't play on this.

Both 'Noise' and 'Loop' usually fetch an asking price of around £100/$200 each (or a great deal more – probably a minimum of £600/$1200 – if you want the *Aspen* magazine as well). Before parting with your cash, it's worth noting that the Velvets themselves chose to include neither of these items in the *Peel Slowly And See* boxed set.

CONVERSATION

Contained on a flexidisc (printed with a photograph of Reed) given away free with *Andy Warhol's Index* book (published February 1967). Consists of Reed, Cale Nico and vari-ous other people discussing Warhol's book while their first album plays in the background. The book usually sells for at least £700/$1,200 (hardback) or £500/$1,000 (paperback). The track itself can also be found on the *What Goes On* boxed set (see page 156).

There are also a couple of MGM radio promo items from 1968 and 1969 (featuring an interview with Cale and Reed) which sell for around £500/$1,200 apiece.

Of far more interest is…

THE UNRELEASED VELVET UNDERGROUND

In addition to the material listed above, there are still some unreleased Velvets' songs from the 1960s:

• 'Get It On Time': rehearsal tape recorded at the Factory, 1966.

• 'If I Tell You': details unknown.

• 'I'm Not A Young Man Any More': performed live, 1967.

• 'Kill Your Sons': Reed re-recorded this in 1974 for *Sally Can't Dance*. A version by the Velvets is thought to exist.

• 'Lonely Saturday Night': performed live, 1969.

• 'Lonesome Cowboys': recorded for the "lost" album, according to Moe Tucker, and apparently a different song to 'Lonesome Cowboy Bill'. This was written for Andy Warhol's movie of the same name. Since the movie opened in May 1969, the song may have been recorded even earlier; then again, Reed may have been as behind schedule as he was for Warhol's *Chelsea Girls*.

- 'Men Of Good Fortune': rehearsal tape recorded at the Factory, 1966. Reed would re-record this in 1973 for *Berlin*.
- 'Miss Joanie Lee': rehearsal tape recorded at the Factory, 1966. This eleven-minute long extravaganza was due to be released on the "deluxe" double-CD version of *The Velvet Underground & Nico*, but was pulled at the last minute when band members demanded a renegotiation of their record contract.
- 'Never Get Emotionally Involved With Man, Woman, Beast Or Child': a demo tape from 1965 is thought to exist.
- 'The Nothing Song': a lengthy instrumental, performed live with the EPI in 1966.
- 'Passing By': possibly not the correct title, but a song written by Doug Yule in 1969. The Velvets are thought to have recorded a demo.
- 'Sister Ray Part III': improvisational extension of 'Sister Ray', performed as an encore 1967–1968.
- 'Sweet And Twenty': an adaptation (by Reed) of verses by Shakespeare (from *Twelfth Night*), dating from 1969.
- 'Sweet Rock And Roll (Sister Ray Part II)': preamble to 'Sister Ray', performed live in 1968 (with John Cale). According to Sterling Morrison, a version was taped at a post-gig party in California.
- 'Sweet Sister Ray': preamble to 'Sister Ray', which may have been an earlier version of 'Sweet Rock And Roll (Sister Ray Part II)'.
- 'A Symphony Of Sound': rehearsal tape recorded at the Factory, 1966. Warhol also filmed this 26-minute jam session (unfortunately without sound).

Bootlegs

In a sense, the Velvets were their own best boot-leggers, in terms of recycling their back recordings both in the studio and on stage, and in endorsing the Quine Tapes (see above) they scooped up the cream in a manner not dissimilar to the Grateful Dead's Dick's Picks series. Nevertheless, there have been dozens – if not hundreds – of unofficial Velvet Underground bootlegs over the years. None are known to contain unreleased studio material, but there are many live recordings – of extremely variable quality – that are so far only available on bootleg. Unfortunately, the only way to find out if they're worth the asking price is by buying them.

- 'Walk Alone': rehearsal tape recorded at the Factory, 1966. The song was co-written by Reed with Jerry Pellegrino, Terry Phillips and James Smith, while still working for Pickwick.
- 'Wild Child': a demo exists, from 1970.

Some of the above have been bootlegged, others are merely believed to exist, though their whereabouts may be unknown; some may even be alternate titles for songs already released. There is also – judging by the number of bootlegs – a vast amount of live material, including lengthy jam sessions.

Additionally, there are also the Morrison, Cale and Tucker demos from the *Eat/Kiss* period, and the final Rock And Roll Hall Of Fame performance of 'Last Night I Said Goodbye To My Friend'... In short, there should be more than enough material to make *The Bootleg Series Volume II* a viable proposition. Whether it will ever get the green light is another matter.

The Solo Albums

The Velvet Underground remain completely unique in that their influence as a band is well attested, but the influence of the individual performers that constituted the band has, over the last four decades, proved just as important. The very forces that created the powerhouse that was the Velvets, forces which meant that the band couldn't ever stay together, were the same forces that contributed to the persistent creativity of the band's individual members. While Reed, Tucker and Doug Yule sought commercial success in various forms, Cale danced along the borderline attempting to achieve some sort of commercial success whilst retaining at the same time his credibility as a "serious" musician; and Nico remained supremely leftfield in her post-Underground career. Nevertheless, all of them established a body of creative and provocative work, their careers frequently criss-crossing, which has no comparison elsewhere in modern music. And the sheer amount of released work (outstanding in Cale's case) bears testament to this. This section has been assembled in alphabetical order by artist to avoid any suggestion of bias.

Starting Points: Compilation Albums

The list of solo products of the various members of The Velvet Underground is so extensive and varied in quality, that the uninitiated are advised to dip their toes in the water by following this pocket guide to the territory. Full reviews of recommended solo albums are listed later in this chapter under the artist's name.

JOHN CALE

Three compilations are available. The best is the 2-CD Rhino anthology *Seducing Down The Door: A Collection*, which covers the years 1970–1990 and includes three rare tracks: the single 'Dixieland & Dixie', the *Academy In Peril* outtake 'Temper' and the unreleased single 'Jack The Ripper'. However, this may be hard to track down. Also good is the 16-track *Close Watch: An Introduction To John Cale*. The 2-CD *The Island Years* contains the albums *Fear*, *Slow Dazzle* and *Helen Of Troy* in their entirety, plus five rare tracks from that era: 'Mary Lou', 'All I Want Is You', 'Bamboo Floor', 'Sylvia Said' and 'You And Me'. The live *Fragments Of A Rainy Season* also provides a good career overview. Other good starting points would be *Paris 1919* or *Fear*.

NICO

Avoid *Innocent And Vain: An Introduction To Nico* (poor track selection). The best compilation is the US release *Classic Years*. Both compilations draw material from the first Velvets album, which seems unnecessary; a wiser investment might be the best two solo albums, *Chelsea Girl* and *Desertshore*, or indeed *The Frozen Borderline* 1968–70 (see below) the remastered double album comprising *The Marble Index* and *Desertshore*, with plenty of extras.

LOU REED

There have been numerous Lou Reed compilations over the decades. The best currently available are the 3-CD *Between Thought And Expression* (reviewed below) and the 2-CD *NYC Man: The Ultimate Collection* (confusingly, there's also a single CD version with the same title). Otherwise, good starting points would be the solo albums *Transformer* or *New York*.

MOE TUCKER

There are no compilations available. The best of her albums are *Life In Exile After Abdication* and *I Spent A Week There The Other Night* (see pages 235–238).

John Cale

"I'm a classical composer, dishevelling my musical personality by dabbling in rock and roll" – John Cale, 1999

VINTAGE VIOLENCE

Columbia; recorded 1969; released July 1970; currently available on CD.

HELLO, THERE/GIDEON'S BIBLE/ADELAIDE/BIG WHITE CLOUD/CLEO/PLEASE/CHARLEMAGNE/BRING IT ON UP/ AMSTERDAM/GHOST STORY/FAIRWEATHER FRIEND

Produced by John Cale and Lewis Merenstein. Personnel: John Cale (bass, guitar, keyboards, viola); Harvey Brooks (bass); Ernie Coralla (guitar); Garland Jeffreys (guitar and backing vocals); Sandie Konikoff (drums); Stan Szelest (piano).

"I was trying to see if I could write songs", John Cale later said of his solo debut – and the result leaves no doubt that he could. As he'd do throughout his career, Cale peopled his songs with characters – and performing them became akin to method acting for him. *Vintage Violence* was also the public's first proper introduction to Cale's singing voice, which critic Allan Jones memorably termed an "unforgettably moving Eisteddfod tenor, a voice of blasted Welsh beauty". The album was supposedly recorded in ten days, though Cale claims to have taken only three, one of which was spent teaching the band the songs. He also claims this was recorded the week after recording the *Church Of Anthrax* album (which was released some months later, see below).

The musicians on the album (sometimes referred to as "Penguin"), were actually Grinderswitch, Garland Jeffreys' backing band (drummer Konikoff was dating Debbie Harry, who was then working as a waitress at Max's Kansas City). Jeffreys had been a contemporary of Lou Reed's at Syracuse, and he and Cale had become friends; he wrote one song on the album ('Fairweather Friend') and also a poem about Cale for the sleeve notes.

As to the music, it runs the gamut of everything from driving rockers ('Hello, There') to gentle country/soul ballads ('Please') to epic, Spectoresque pop ('Big White Cloud'). Cale's lyrics were literate and memorable without being obvious, often evocative of a mood (or a place, or a person) without necessarily following a linear narrative – "stretching out the verbs and nouns", as he put it on 'Gideon's Bible'. It was clear that he was well read, and had a gift for word games and a vocabulary to match.

A replacement design featuring the first of several Cale mask motifs

Often he'd name a song after a person or a place, yet it would be impossible for the listener to find a lyrical connection to the title, or even to analyse the lyrics closely at all; yet the songs would still succeed on some level. *Vintage Violence* was a stunningly capable and impressive debut – even its throwaway fluff, like 'Adelaide' and 'Cleo', is enjoyable – and proved beyond a doubt that Cale was a major talent in his own right. Ed Ward's review in *Rolling Stone* compared the album to Van Morrison's *Astral Weeks* and Dylan's *Highway 61 Revisited*; decades later, this still seems a fair assessment.

An early CD pressing of the album on Edsel has poor quality reproduction; the later release (on Columbia Legacy) contains two extra tracks: an alternative version of 'Fairweather Friend' and an unreleased instrumental called 'Wall', which is six minutes of viola drone.

CHURCH OF ANTHRAX

Columbia; recorded 1969; released February 1971; a CD was briefly available but is currently out of print. Credited to John Cale and Terry Riley

CHURCH OF ANTHRAX/THE HALL OF MIRRORS IN THE PALACE OF VERSAILLES/THE SOUL OF PATRICK LEE/IDES OF MARCH/THE PROTÉGÉ

Apparently recorded before *Vintage Violence*, this collaboration between Cale and minimalist

A doll's house interior similar to the disturbing assemblages of Joseph Cornell

composer Riley was mainly improvised on the spot, and recorded in four days at CBS studios in New York. John McClure of CBS nominally produced it, but Cale did the actual studio work (Cale also mixed the album, though Riley disapproved of the results). Cale played bass, harpsichord, piano, guitar and viola; Riley played piano, organ and soprano saxophone; session players Bobby Columby (of Blood, Sweat & Tears) and Bobby Gregg both played drums. Cale had also asked both Sterling Morrison and Angus MacLise to play on the session, but both were out of town at the time.

The album consists of four instrumental pieces (two lengthy, two short), which marry Riley's repetitive minimalist keyboard parts with a rock/blues backing, with varying degrees of success. At their worst (as on the title track), the results resemble the more annoying kind of jazz-rock fusion that was then fashionable, with flute parts soaring above the proceedings to no real effect. At its best, as on 'The Hall Of Mirrors In The Palace Of Versailles', and despite some awkward changes of pace, it approaches the ambient, and is rather pleasant. The title refers to the location of the signing of the Versailles Peace Treaty in 1919, which divided up the spoils of Europe after World War I (thus sowing the seeds for World War II).

The album also includes one Cale song, 'The Soul Of Patrick Lee'. This is sung by Adam Miller, a songwriter friend of Cale's who mainly worked on commercials, and whose voice is vaguely reminiscent of The Zombies' Colin Blunstone. Cale almost certainly took a back seat here because he lacked confidence in his own vocals – and this was also the first of

Terry Riley

Minimalist composer Terry Riley (b. 1935) came to prominence with his piece *In C*, which was premiered in 1964 and recorded in 1968, and proved influential on other composers working in this field, such as Philip Glass and Steve Reich. Riley played with LaMonte Young around 1966–68, and recorded a more accessible work, *A Rainbow In Curved Air* in 1969 (in fact, he was recording it at the same time as working on *Church Of Anthrax*). This album would be a major influence on Soft Machine and Tangerine Dream, as well as on The Who's Pete Townshend, who acknowledged the debt with 'Baba O'Riley' on *Who's Next* (named after Riley and the spiritual master Meher Baba, who was Townshend's guru). Riley went on to record approximately 40 more albums, including one with the Kronos Quartet. Also recommended is 1972's *Persian Surgery Dervishes*.

his own songs ever to be recorded. The fairly impenetrable lyrics sound somewhat like those for a traditional folk ballad – but the choir of harmony vocals launch it into territory somewhere between epic pop and the theme for a spaghetti Western. Definitely worth tracking down to hear, it could easily have fitted on *Vintage Violence*.

THE ACADEMY IN PERIL

Reprise; recorded early 1972; released July 1972; available on CD.

THE PHILOSOPHER/BRAHMS/LEGS LARRY AT TELEVISION CENTRE/THE ACADEMY IN PERIL/INTRO/DAYS OF STEAM/3 ORCHESTRAL PIECES: (A) FAUST (B) THE BALANCE (C) CAPTAIN MORGAN'S LAMENT/KING HARRY/JOHN MILTON

Produced by John Cale; the mixing engineer, 'Jean Bois', was John Wood.

This record grew out of Cale's desire to do a "straight classical music thing", and was arranged and recorded (at Richard Branson's The Manor, Oxfordshire) in just three weeks, which Cale later realized was not long enough. For the orchestral pieces he used the Royal Philharmonic Orchestra. The album is an odd mixture, kicking off with the instrumental 'The Philosopher' (with Ron Wood on slide guitar), which starts sounding basic and bluesy, then gets complicated and interesting. 'Brahms' is a very dull piano piece – as is the title track – while 'Legs Larry At Television Centre' features the Bonzo Dog Doo Dah Band's 'Legs' Larry Smith doing a 'comedy' TV producer's voice-over while Cale plays an otherwise dull string piece. Short though it is, 'Days Of Steam' is a wonderfully involving tune, and one can see exactly why Andy Warhol wanted to use it for film music the second he heard it. Cale would later dismiss the three orchestral pieces as "wishy-washy Vaughan Williams stuff", and they are pretty unremarkable; but at the time Cale was simply happy to have finally gotten

Warhol and *The Academy In Peril*

The cover for *The Academy In Peril* was designed by Andy Warhol, and featured 25 colour photos of Cale (mainly of his eyes) framed by Kodachrome colour slide mounts. Always one to barter where possible, Warhol's fee for the work was the right to use 'Days Of Steam' as the theme for his film *Heat*. A copy of the album signed by Warhol was recently seen for sale at £500. Warhol was also originally supposed to have provided a cover for *Vintage Violence*, with a similar idea – laying strips of black and white film against a plain white background – which looked "fantastic", according to Cale. The idea wasn't used simply because Cale had cut off his long hair just after the photographs were taken, although the final cover did introduce the mask image, which has cropped up several times in both Cale and Reed's solo careers.

The Music

around to working with an orchestra at all, and it revived his ambition to write a proper symphony one day (which he still hasn't done – though the instrumental music he's produced from the 1990s onwards is much better than most of the tracks here). 'King Harry' is interesting (though one wishes that Cale would burst into actual song, rather than the whispered vocal he delivers), and the closing 'John Milton' is another unimpressive instrumental. In all, the album is disappointing – but it's still worth getting for 'Days Of Steam' alone.

PARIS 1919

Reprise; recorded late 1972; released March 1973; available on CD.

CHILD'S CHRISTMAS IN WALES/HANKY PANKY NOHOW/THE ENDLESS PLAIN OF FORTUNE/ANDALUCIA/MACBETH/PARIS 1919/GRAHAM GREENE/HALF PAST FRANCE/ANTARCTICA STARTS HERE

Produced by Chris Thomas; recorded at Sunwest studios in Los Angeles.
Personnel: John Cale (bass, guitar, keyboards, viola); Wilton Felder (bass); Lowell George (guitar); Richie Hayward (drums); Bill Payne (keyboards); Chris Thomas (tambourine).

This album was a return to the melodic and memorable pop of *Vintage Violence*, this time augmented by a full orchestra. Curiously, despite Cale's assertion that this was the first album of his where the songs had been properly written and arranged in advance, and despite the fact that Chris Thomas had been recommended to Cale as a producer because of his work earlier in the year on Procol Harum's *In Concert With The Edmonton Symphony*

Orchestra, Cale had apparently not originally intended to use any orchestration for this album – it was added as an afterthought, with Thomas providing the arrangements for the UCLA Symphony Orchestra. The engineer was Phil

Art Nouveau feel and lettering in keeping with the title

Sheer, once tour manager for the Velvets. Backing musicians this time included Wilton Felder from The Crusaders on bass, and three members of Little Feat (though guitarist Lowell George left early, having apparently fallen out with a drunken Cale).

Although musically it was possible to see the influence of songwriters that Cale admired (such as Brian Wilson and the brothers Gibb), lyrically the songs were as evocative – and obscure – as on Cale's debut. There was certainly a literary theme, though: the opening 'A Child's Christmas In Wales' was not only autobiographical, but had the same title as a Dylan Thomas prose piece (a writer to whose work Cale would return much later in his career). There were also songs about Macbeth and the author Graham Greene (in probably the only rock song ever to make reference to both Chipping Sodbury and the incendiary British MP Enoch Powell). The amazingly catchy and baroque title track again concerned the location of the peace treaty that concluded World War I (see *Church Of Anthrax*, above), and thus had contemporary resonance with the closing days of the Vietnam War. Paris in 1919 was also the setting for the early days of both Dada and Surrealism, both loves of Cale's (he was very influenced at this time by Guy de Maupassant and various surrealist writers). The album has the occasional weak track ('Macbeth') but is otherwise remarkably tuneful and tasteful throughout, wrapping up with the slow ballad 'Antarctica Starts Here', which – like the Velvets' 'New Age' – concerned an ageing film star. It was supposedly influenced by Billy Wilder's 1950 movie *Sunset Boulevard*, and was a song that Cale would return to several times in the decades to come.

Despite receiving critical acclaim and being a solidly commercial work, *Paris 1919* was deleted after only a year. A 2006 reissue of the album on Reprise/Rhino contains an extra eleven tracks, ten of which are rehearsal tapes, alternate takes and different mixes, plus one unused song from the sessions, 'Burned Out Affair' (a fairly weak song about childhood). While none of these extra tracks are indispensable, as works-in-progress they all provide interesting glimpses into the creative process.

FEAR

Island; recorded Spring 1974; released September 1974; available on CD.

FEAR (IS A MAN'S BEST FRIEND)/BUFFALO BALLET/ BARRACUDA/EMILY/SHIP OF FOOLS/GUN/THE MAN WHO COULDN'T AFFORD TO ORGY/YOU KNOW MORE THAN I KNOW/MOMAMMA SCUBA

Produced by Phil Manzanera, who also played guitar, Manzanera drafted in his former Roxy Music cohort Brian Eno to do electronic treatments, plus the rhythm section of Kevin Ayers' band, a couple of people from Eno's band, and Bryn Haworth on slide guitar; Richard Thompson (who Cale knew through Joe Boyd) also makes a guest appearance. Backing vocals were supplied by Irene and Doreen Chanter and Liza Strike; on 'The Man Who Couldn't Afford To Orgy' the spoken word backing was by Judy Nylon, a friend of Eno's (who would later form the duo Snatch with Patti Paladin, going on to tour with Cale as a backing vocalist in the late 1970s and early 1980s). The album

Stark paranoia in black and white: a proto-punk design

was recorded at Sound Techniques and Olympic studios in London, and once again the engineer was John Wood.

Darker and rockier than *Paris 1919*, the album kicks off with the title track, an insistent rocker about paranoia that eventually dissolves into vocal and instrumental histrionics. 'Buffalo Ballet' is a cinematic piano ballad that could easily have fitted on the previous album; 'Barracuda' was like mutant reggae, odd but irresistible, and the first of several songs here about drowning (which, in terms of his personal life, Cale in a sense was). The epic piano ballad 'Emily' continues the marine motif, while the rockily Dylanesque 'Ship Of Fools' concerns life on the road, name-checking both Tombstone and Swansea. 'Gun' is an eight-minute-long hard-edged, guitar-driven rocker about police detectives that eventually turns into an extended guitar thrash. 'The Man Who Couldn't Afford To Orgy' (in which "orgy" is deliberately mispronounced with a hard "g") is a wonderfully swingalong ode to compassion punctuated by Judy Nylon's breathy verbal improvisation; it's infectious without being the least bit commercial – as is the folky 'You Know More Than I Know'. The album wraps up with 'Momamma Scuba', a song about a man who wants his girlfriend to drown him, delivered in the rock style of 'Gun'.

Throughout, the songs conjured an atmosphere of sex and death, love and dread – and did so to a backing of memorable tunes. Lester Bangs' review of *Fear* compared the album to the kind of music that Lou Reed could have been making "if his imagination had not short-circuited", noting that it "does the Velvet Underground tradition proud". The public, to some extent, agreed, and the record initially sold over 30,000 copies.

Brian Eno

Brian Peter George St John le Baptiste de la Salle Eno was born in Woodbridge, Suffolk, on 15 May 1948. In 1969 he moved to London and, as a result of accidentally bumping into an old friend, Andy MacKay, on a train, he joined him as one of the founder members of Roxy Music, despite the fact that Eno didn't play any orthodox musical instruments. Instead, he applied his electronic synthesizer 'treatments' to the others' instruments – which, coupled, with his flamboyant stage appearance, made him seem more of a novelty figure than he actually was. Leaving Roxy Music after their second album, Eno went on to carve an extraordinary musical career despite having famously described himself as a "non-musician". In 1974 he collaborated with ex-King Crimson guitarist Robert Fripp on the instrumental *No Pussyfootin'*, and also issued his first album of original songs, *Here Come The Warm Jets*. After *Fear* Cale recruited Eno to play on Nico's *The End* album which Cale produced, and the pair also collaborated on the *June 1 1974* concert. Cale played on Eno's 1975 album *Another Green World*, and Eno would also be involved in several further solo projects of Cale's in the decades to come. Particularly noted for his development of ambient music, he also collaborated with David Byrne on the astonishing *My Life in the Bush of Ghosts* (1981), an early example of sampling and remixing "found" tape material. Eno would attain his greatest commercial successes as a record producer working with numerous first division artists, including David Bowie, Talking Heads and U2.

KEVIN AYERS/JOHN CALE/ ENO/NICO: JUNE 1ST 1974

Island; recorded 1/6/74; released Summer 1974; available on CD.

BRIAN ENO: DRIVING ME BACKWARDS/BABY'S ON FIRE/JOHN CALE: HEARTBREAK HOTEL/NICO: THE END/KEVIN AYERS: MAY I?/SHOUTING IN A BUCKET BLUES/STRANGER IN BLUE SUEDE SHOES/EVERYBODY'S SOMETIME AND SOME PEOPLE'S ALL THE TIME BLUES/TWO GOES INTO FOUR

Produced by Richard Willams; engineered by John Wood.

ACNE, with distinct tension between Ayers and Cale

A recording of the one-off concert at London's Rainbow theatre, featuring ACNE (Kevin Ayers/ John Cale/Nico/Eno). It was basically Ayers' gig, with the others as guest stars; backing was provided by Ayers' regular band The Soporifics (Ollie Halsall on guitar and piano, Rabbit on organ, Archie Leggatt on bass and Eddie Sparrow on drums). Also on board are Ayers' former bandmates Robert Wyatt (on percussion) and guitarist Mike Oldfield (then beginning to enjoy phenomenal success with his *Tubular Bells* album). Backing vocals are provided by Liza Strike, Doreen Chanter and Irene Chanter.

Cale's contribution is a cover of something that would become a staple of his live act: a version of Elvis Presley's 'Heartbreak Hotel' that attempts to properly explore the dread and loneliness of the subject matter. The version here is nowhere near as dark as later ones.

Nico (aided by Eno on synthesizer) contributes a doom-laden version of 'The End' (the title track of the album she was then in the process of recording with both Cale and Eno). Cale also plays on both Eno tracks, and contributes some viola to Ayers' 'Two Goes Into Four.' It was probably fun on the night, but there's nothing that remarkable here – for completists (and Kevin Ayers fans) only.

SLOW DAZZLE

Island; recorded Winter 1974; released April 1975; available on CD.

MR. WILSON/TAKING IT ALL AWAY/DIRTY-ASS ROCK 'N' ROLL/ DARLING I NEED YOU/ROLLAROLL/HEARTBREAK HOTEL/SKI PATROL/I'M NOT THE LOVING KIND/GUTS/THE JEWELLER

Personnel: John Cale (piano, organ, clavinet, vocals); Chris Spedding (guitar); Pat Donaldson (bass); Timmy Donald and Gerry Conway (drums); Chris Thomas (violin, electric piano).

Cale's follow-up to *Fear* was the most commercially successful of his Island albums, although his conscious decision to "write singles" for the album doesn't really pay off. Several of the songs on *Slow Dazzle* are very substandard (while several of the tunes on *Fear* are a lot more memorable than anything here). Most of the material was written in the studio. This time Cale produced himself, since Manzanera was busy elsewhere (though both he and Eno made guest appearances). The album was recorded at Sound Techniques, and the backing musicians would go on to become Cale's touring band. Maria Muldaur's husband Geoff provided harmony vocals on two tracks.

The Music

Sunglasses as big as a mask, an unusually literal design

The overall sound is rock that is musically less edgy – still good, but a lot more predictable. The bouncy opener 'Mr. Wilson' was apparently about both Prime Minister Harold Wilson and Brian Wilson (and fades on music comparable to *Smile*-era Beach Boys), but most of the songs here concerned Cale's "misery and pain" (as he sang on 'Taking It All Away') and his collapsing personal life. At times this is almost tuneful, as on the bluesy 'Darling I Need You'; elsewhere it was a scream of sheer agony, as on Cale's dark and ominous studio reworking of 'Heartbreak Hotel'. Several songs concern infidelity and betrayal, with the opening line of the impassioned and memorable 'Guts' ("the bugger in the short sleeves fucked my wife") referring to Kevin Ayers' seduction of Cindy Cale. The song was originally titled simply 'Bugger'. The album closes with the mirror-imagery of 'The Jeweller', a successor to 'The Gift' in that its 'lyrics' are a short prose piece recited over moody organ music, and one which reveals beyond doubt that Cale had some major emotional problems at this point. But although Cale's personal pain is audibly mirrored in *Slow Dazzle*'s music, it sadly doesn't make for great listening – and the album sounds a lot less impressive now than it did then.

Two extra tracks were recorded during these sessions, which would surface on the anthology *The Island Years*: 'All I Want Is You' and 'Bamboo Floor'.

HELEN OF TROY

Island; recorded Summer 1975; released November 1975; available on CD.

MY MARIA/HELEN OF TROY/CHINA SEA/ENGINE/SAVE US/ CABLE HOGUE/I KEEP A CLOSE WATCH/PABLO PICASSO/ CORAL MOON/BABY WHAT YOU WANT ME TO DO/SUDDEN DEATH/LEAVING IT UP TO YOU.

Personnel: John Cale (keyboards, guitar, vocals); Chris Spedding (guitar); Pat Donaldson (bass); Timmy Donald and Phil Collins (drums); Eno (synthesizer).

For reasons unknown, Cale decided to produce this album himself. It was recorded and mixed (at Sound Techniques again) amid traumatic and shambolic circumstances – namely Cale's final split with Cindy, after which he

Baroque vs. minimalism, plus mirror double-take. But not very clever

went to New York to produce Patti Smith's debut album, returning to London to mix *Helen Of Troy* afterwards. It wasn't an ideal way to work.

All songs were Cale originals except for a Dylanesque cover of Jonathan Richman's 'Pablo Picasso' and a slow and dirty treatment of Jimmy Reed's blues 'Baby What You Want Me To Do'. Many of Cale's own songs here are about lust, and/or the rarity of trust – but only 'I Keep A Close Watch', 'Coral Moon' and 'Leaving It Up To You' are strong enough to stay in the memory. Cale "got the title" for 'Cable Hogue' from the 1970 Sam Peckinpah western *The Ballad Of Cable Hogue* (Cale was a big Peckinpah fan), but the song itself isn't as good as the movie. The chorus of 'I Keep A Close Watch' quotes lyrically from Johnny Cash's 'I Walk The Line' and is a song Cale would return to several times during his career; here it's performed as an epic and stately ballad, with a lavish orchestral arrangement (Cale once stated that he'd hoped Frank Sinatra would record a cover version). The US release of the album omitted 'Leaving It Up To You' (apparently because the song mentioned Manson victim Sharon Tate), and replaced it with 'Coral Moon' (which was not included on the UK vinyl release). Both tracks are included on the CD. Also recorded during these sessions were versions of 'Willow Weep For Me' and 'God Only Knows', which remain unreleased. Another out-take, 'Mary Lou' was included on *The Island Years* compilation.

SABOTAGE (LIVE)

Spy; recorded June 1979; released December 1979; available on CD.

MERCENARIES (READY FOR WAR)/BABY YOU KNOW/ EVIDENCE/DR. MUDD/WALKIN' THE DOG/CAPTAIN HOOK/ ONLY TIME WILL TELL/SABOTAGE/CHORALE

Personnel: John Cale (piano, guitar, fretless bass, viola, vocals); Marc Aaron (lead guitar); Joe Bidwell (keyboards, vocals); George Scott (bass, vocals); Doug Bowne (drums, vocals); Deerfrance (backing vocals).

Recorded over three summer nights at CBGBs in New York it was produced by Cale, who later admitted that taping the gigs had "killed the atmosphere". Despite being a live album, there are no old favourites here, all the material being

Cale goes undercover, deploying negative effect, one of hundreds at this time

new (though a studio version of 'Mercenaries' had been released as a single). Apart from a brooding cover of Rufus Thomas's 'Walking The Dog', these songs had been written on the road, most of them growing out of live improvisation; the sound was hard-edged in-your-face guitar rock. Lyrically, the album – particularly the opening 'Mercenaries (Ready For War)', which opened with a quote from Machiavelli – reflected the rise of Reagan and Thatcher, the Russian invasion of Afghanistan and the numerous conflicts in Africa and South America; the more personal songs concerned paranoia and drunkenness ("I can't keep living like this", Cale sings on 'Captain Hook'). The album's title track was both experimental and extreme, and practically a rant. Only the gently pretty ballad 'Only Time Will Tell' (sung by Deerfrance, and featuring some delicate viola work) and the moving, hymn-like 'Chorale' offer relief from the onslaught; as a gig it was probably very impressive, but – apart from the two gentler tracks – the album is not one that one tends to return to.

The Music

The CD release also contains the lethargically menacing 'Rosegarden Funeral Of Sores' (the B-side to the 'Mercenaries' single; the master tape for the studio version of 'Mercenaries' itself is lost, which is why it is not included here), plus the three tracks from Cale's *Animal Justice* EP (recorded in 1976, released in August 1977): 'Chickenshit', 'Memphis' and 'Hedda Gabler'. 'Chickenshit' refers to the incident in Croydon where Cale beheaded a chicken on stage, causing his band to quit; 'Memphis' is a cover of the Chuck Berry song, with added paedophile overtones; the Gothic, doomy 'Hedda Gabler' is "inspired by" Norwegian dramatist Henrik Ibsen's 1891 play – except that Cale seems to be setting his version in the 1930s, judging by the reference to Hitler.

HONI SOIT

A&M; recorded late 1980; released March 1981; available on CD.

DEAD OR ALIVE/STRANGE TIMES IN CASABLANCA/FIGHTER PILOT/WILSON JOLIET/STREETS OF LAREDO/HONI SOIT/ RIVERBANK/RUSSIAN ROULETTE/MAGIC AND LIES

Personnel: John Cale (keyboards, guitar, viola, vocals); Sturgis Nikides (guitar, backing vocals); Jim Goodwin (keyboards, synthesizer, backing vocals); Peter Muny (bass, backing vocals); Robert Medici (drums, backing vocals); John Gatchell (trumpet); The Bomberettes (actually the girl group The Mo-dettes) (backing vocals on 'Fighter Pilot').

Recorded at CBS Studios in New York, where Cale had recorded *Church Of Anthrax*, this was the last album to be recorded at the historic studio, demolished soon afterwards, and was produced by Mike Thorne, whose work

with Wire and Soft Cell Cale had admired. Mixed at Media Sound in New York.

Though more accessible musically than *Sabotage*, many of the songs here were improvised in the studio, Cale free-associating the stream-of-consciousness lyrics. The subject matter included war, global politics, the fate of Vietnam vets and cruelty on both a personal and global scale – or "death, decay, corruption", as critic Allan Jones put it. The one cover – the

Another Warhol concept, surely breaking Crown Copyright?

traditional 'Streets Of Laredo' – slotted perfectly into this mix, played more as an angry complaint than a sad lament (Cale had wanted Nico to cover the song on *The End*, but she refused). Even though Cale was now far happier emotionally, he evidently still had a lot of pain and anger to express; the trouble was that the material was again substandard, the worst of it (the title track) approaching the downright dumb. The only moments of real beauty on the album come with the trumpet part on 'Dead Or Alive' (which is utterly joyous, though the song itself is pretty bleak), the haunting ballad 'Riverbank' (which is still fairly tragic territory) and the impressively epic ode to damaged romanticism, 'Magic And Lies' which is insistently hummable (the title for this presumably inspired Lou Reed's *Magic And Loss* many years later).

The album title refers to the phrase "*Honi Soit Qui Mal Y Pense*", which translates as 'shamed be he who thinks evil of it'. The words appear upon the crest shown on British passports, and it is also the motto of the Order of The Garter. The album was subtitled "*La Première Leçon De Français*". The album was originally to be titled *Russian Roulette*.

The album cover concept – featuring Cale's passport – was suggested by Andy Warhol, who also thought that it should appear in black and white. Cale opted for blue and pink instead, and subsequently realized that he should have listened to Warhol. During cover discussions, Warhol's business manager Fred Hughes came up with a suggestion that both Cale and Warhol liked: that Cale should be photographed with Yoko Ono, so that the album could then be titled *John And Yoko*!

MUSIC FOR A NEW SOCIETY

Ze-Passport; recorded Spring 1982; released July 1982; released on CD but out of print.

TAKING YOUR LIFE IN YOUR HANDS/THOUGHTLESS KIND/ SANITIES/IF YOU WERE STILL AROUND/CLOSE WATCH/ MAMA'S SONG/BROKEN BIRD/CHINESE ENVOY/CHANGES MADE/DAMN LIFE/RISÉ, SAM AND RIMSKY KORSAKOV

An optimistic title for a dark and pessimistic record, the result of a five-day writing session in New York during which Cale wrote and recorded 30 songs which he then edited, adding snippets of Beethoven, Debussy and Rimsky-Korsakov *en route*. Cale claimed the record explored what he termed "the terror of the moment"; he'd wanted to record simply,

improvising with just a piano, but the record company insisted that at least one track feature a band (the mediocre 'Changes Made'). Engineer David Lichtenstein (son of the Pop artist, Roy) ended up playing drums, while assistant engineer David Young played guitar (both would later tour with Cale, and play on his next album; Young would co-write and generally collaborate with Cale for years to come). In addition, there were half-a-dozen guest musicians, including Chris Spedding and Blue Öyster Cult's guitarist Alan Lanier.

Oriental-style calligraphy designed by Betsey Johnson gets the artist's name across

The record is decidedly experimental, with random percussion and bizarre interjections (like laughter and bagpipes) revealing Cale's *avant-garde* roots for the first time in years. Musically and lyrically, it's pretty bleak territory – though Cale's anger had now seemingly been replaced by melancholy; even though he was happily married at this point, there's genuine heartache in 'If You Were Still Around'. Perhaps he was exorcizing old ghosts, or simply dealing with his ongoing substance problems. Other songs concerned self-pity and familial problems, or the general angst of existence; there is hope for the future here, but it's pretty faint. "It was kind of rabid", he said of the album in 2007, admitting that he "wasn't in the most stable frame of mind". The ethereally beautiful 'Taking Your Life In Your Hands' concerned a murderess (who had possibly killed her own children). 'Thoughtless Kind' was supposedly about The Velvet Underground – if true, Cale hadn't forgotten or forgiven. The title of 'Sanities' was the result of someone's accidental misreading of the word "Sanctus", which Cale preferred (though he'd later use 'Sanctus' for a title as well). 'Risé, Sam and Rimsky-Korsakov' adapted a poem about the radio written by Sam Shepard, recited by Risé Cale. Risé also co-wrote 'Damn Life' with Cale (and Beethoven, come to that). While there's no denying that *New Society* was a bold and adventurous step forward, sadly most of its songs were mournful ballads that meandered along without much of a tune – an absence that was thrown into sharp relief by the inclusion of a new version of 'I Keep A Close Watch'. Here, given a statelier and simpler arrangement than on *Helen Of Troy*, it's easily the best thing on the album.

Cale's ex-wife Betsey Johnson provided the cover photo. The CD release adds an extra track, an outtake from the sessions titled 'In The Library Of Force'.

CARIBBEAN SUNSET

Ze-Island; recorded 1983; released January 1984; vinyl only, out of print.

HUNGRY FOR LOVE/EXPERIMENT NUMBER 1/MODEL BEIRUT RECITAL/CARIBBEAN SUNSET/PRAETORIAN UNDERGROUND/ MAGAZINES/WHERE THERE'S A WILL/THE HUNT/VILLA ALBANI

Personnel: John Cale (guitar, keyboards, vocals); Dave Young (guitar, vocals); Andy Heermanns (bass, vocals); Dave Lichtenstein (drums); Brian Eno (AMS pitch changer). Produced by John Cale, recorded at Right Track Recording in New York.

This time Cale avoided improvising material in the studio, many of the songs here having already been honed on the road; most of them Cale had co-written with David Young, with a couple more being co-written with maverick journal-

A self-conscious design for a self-conscious album

ist Larry Sloman. The exception is 'Experiment Number 1', which is obviously improvised – with Cale shouting out chord changes to the band as it goes along. There were some love songs, with other material once again concerning matters military and/or political. 'Model Beirut Recital' obviously focussed on the Middle East ("something must be done about it"), while 'Villa Albani' (which translates as 'White House') was about corruption, and arms-for-oil deals; both are pretty dull, the latter being enlivened somewhat by the presence of Eno. On a more personal level of politics, 'Praetorian Underground' concerned the reassessment (and imitators) of The Velvet Underground.

Cale compared *Caribbean Sunset* to *Fear*, but he was being over-optimistic, and his other comment is far more accurate: it's an album that "lurches along with good intentions". The title track is pleasantly moody with interesting instrumentation (strings, kettle drums, a fairground organ), but no more; several other songs sound like they're going to go somewhere interesting but don't (though wishing for an end to 'Magazines' is a laudable sentiment). Distinctly below average.

JOHN CALE COMES ALIVE

Ze-Island; recorded February 1984; released September 1984; vinyl only, out of print.

OOH LA LA/EVIDENCE/DEAD OR ALIVE/CHINESE ENVOY/ LEAVING IT UP TO YOU/DR. MUDD/WAITING FOR THE MAN/ HEARTBREAK HOTEL/FEAR/NEVER GIVE UP ON YOU

Personnel: John Cale (guitar, piano, vocals); Dave Young (guitar); Andy Heermanns (bass); Dave Lichtenstein (drums).

Punkish high art, or desperation? Of its time

An unremarkable live set recorded at The Lyceum in London and book-ended with two new studio tracks. Of the live material, the only aspect of note is that both 'Dead Or Alive' and 'Chinese Envoy' are revealed as being stronger songs than had previously been apparent. The studio tracks are both mediocre and unimpressive. Though 'Ooh La La' (an ode to lechery co-written with Larry Sloman) has vaguely amusing lyrics, it also has mannered vocals and not much of a tune. The same is true of 'Never Give Up On You' (co-written by the entire band), which also has some truly awful female backing vocals. Even the album's production (by Cale) was weedy; he reportedly seemed uninterested in the project.

ARTIFICIAL INTELLIGENCE

Beggar's Banquet; recorded September 1985; released October 1985; available on CD.

EVERYTIME THE DOGS BARK/DYING ON THE VINE/THE SLEEPER/VIGILANTE LOVER/CHINESE TAKEAWAY (HONG KONG 1997)/SONG OF THE VALLEY/FADEAWAY TOMORROW/ BLACK ROSE/SATELLITE WALK

Personnel: John Cale (keyboards and vocals); David Young (guitars); James Young (keyboards); Graham Dowdall (percussion); Suzie O'List and Gill O'Donovan (backing vocals).

A return to more radical design, in fact a more bookish design

Produced by Cale and recorded at Strongroom Studios in London, where Cale had just finished producing Nico's *Camera Obscura* album (Dowdall and James Young were both members of Nico's backing band). Unfortunately, the drum sound and tinny synthesizers mark this album as a product of its era, and it sounds very dated now.

All the songs here were co-written with Larry 'Ratso' Sloman, sometime editor of *High Times* magazine and author of a very good book about Bob Dylan's *Rolling Thunder* tour. The two used Brion Gysin's "cut-ups" technique on the lyrics (which David Bowie has also been fond of using); 'Everytime The Dogs Bark' and 'Vigilante Lover' were both co-written by Cale, Sloman and David Young. 'Chinese Takeaway (Hong Kong 1997)' is an improvised instrumental incorporating snatches of (amongst other things) Bach, Ennio Morricone and the theme from the BBC's rural soap *The Archers*!

The songs told of damaged romance, reflecting Cale's increasing desperation as he stuggled with cocaine and booze problems. Unfortunately, once again they're distinctly average, with only one real standout track: 'Dying On The Vine' is a superb song about self-destruction, though the arrangement here lets it down.

EVEN COWGIRLS GET THE BLUES

Special Stock; recorded 1978 and 1979; released 1986; vinyl out of print; abridged CD version also out of print.

DANCE OF THE SEVEN VEILS/HELEN OF TROY/CASEY AT THE BAT/EVEN COWGIRLS GET THE BLUES/JACK AND THE MOULIN ROUGE/DEAD OR ALIVE/SOMEBODY SHOULD HAVE TOLD HER/INSTRUMENTAL FOR NEW YEAR'S 1980/MAGIC AND LIES (GUTS)/MEMPHIS

Personnel: John Cale (vocals, guitar, electric piano, viola); Ritchie Fliegler (lead guitar); Ivan Kral (bass); Bruce Brody (keyboards); Jay Dee Dougherty and Robert Medici (drums); Judy Nylon (narration, vocals).

Another live album, originally available only via mail order. Half of this album is taken from a gig at CBGBs in December 1978; the second half is taken from a gig a year later at the same venue, recorded on New Year's Eve 1979/1980. Between these two recordings the *Sabotage (Live)* album had been recorded at the same club.

The sound quality is pretty poor, and the main point of interest with this album is that several of the songs had not appeared before; unfortunately, most of them aren't that remark-

able. 'Dance Of The Seven Veils' features Judy Nylon improvising a version of the tale of Salome, which is interesting but not that great; the title track (named after Tom Robbins' 1976 novel) is good but sounds far from fin-

A completely enigmatic return to high art referencing

ished, and is dominated by Nylon's fairly tuneless scat backing vocal. The one real gem is 'Jack And The Moulin Rouge', a macabre little pop song about Jack the Ripper's adventures in Paris; it's reminiscent of songs by The Who's John Entwistle, and Cale really should have released the studio version at the time.

WORDS FOR THE DYING

Opal/Land; recorded Spring 1989; released October 1989; available on CD.

THE FALKLAND SUITE:
INTRODUCTION/THERE WAS A SAVIOUR/INTERLUDE I/ON A WEDDING ANNIVERSARY/INTERLUDE II/LIE STILL, SLEEP BECALMED/DO NOT GO GENTLE INTO THAT GOOD NIGHT

SONGS WITHOUT WORDS:
SONGS WITHOUT WORDS I/SONGS WITHOUT WORDS II/THE SOUL OF CARMEN MIRANDA

Produced by Brian Eno for his Land label, the core of this album is 'The Falklands Suite', Cale's symphonic adaptation of the poetry of Dylan Thomas, so titled because he'd worked on it during the Falklands/Malvinas war. The orchestra was recorded in Moscow with Gostelradio's Orchestra Of Symphonic And

The serious artist, with a serious haircut

Popular Music, conducted by Alexander G. Mikhailov. Choral parts featuring the Llandaff Cathedral Choir School were recorded in Cardiff. The two 'Songs Without Words' were recorded in New York; 'The Soul Of Carmen Miranda' was a Cale/Eno collaboration, recorded at Wilderness, Eno's studio in Woodbridge, Suffolk.

The work is easily Cale's strongest and most tuneful in over a decade. It had been premiered live in Amsterdam in November 1987; by the time he got around to recording it, Cale's drug and alcohol problems were behind him – as was his initial work on the stunning *Songs For Drella* (see **The Velvet Underground: The Albums**, above) – and the whole project exudes his confidence in the material and his own talent. 'The Falklands Suite' is a moving and epic pastorale; having Dylan Thomas for a lyricist had evidently brought out the best in Cale. The most successful of the adaptations is 'Do Not Go Gentle Into That Good Night', the arrangement for which is irresistible ... though some may find the children's voices cloying and prefer Cale's solo versions of the material on *Fragments Of A Rainy Season* (see below).

The two 'Songs Without Words' pieces are graceful piano instrumentals, but neither are as good or as memorable as some of the piano pieces Cale would later write for film soundtracks. 'The Soul Of Carmen Miranda' is a likeable, haunting and evocative ballad, enhanced by Nell Catchpole's violin and viola. Cale had been lost for a long time; now he had found himself again.

SONGS FOR DRELLA – A FICTION

See pages 152–154.

WRONG WAY UP

Opal/Land; recorded Summer 1990; released November 1990; available on CD.
Credited to John Cale and Brian Eno.

LAY MY LOVE/ONE WORD/IN THE BACKROOM/EMPTY FRAME/CORDOBA/SPINNING AWAY/FOOTSTEPS/BEEN THERE DONE THAT/CRIME IN THE DESERT/THE RIVER

Seemingly a full collaboration, with Cale and Eno sharing the credit for all the songwriting and playing most of the instruments (augmented by half-a-dozen session players). Cale is credited as co-producer, but the final say was

A bit of a mess, reflecting the state of Eno/Cale relations

Eno's as the main producer; in fact, this project seems more weighted in Eno's favour, and the two argued frequently about production issues (presumably other bands that Eno has produced were content to leave him to his own devices).

Halfway through the sessions Cale went off to play at the first Velvet Underground reunion at the Cartier Foundation, and was presumably under a lot of stress; for whatever reason, the two fell out badly and the album cover reflects this, showing the two men separated by a row of naked daggers.

The songs also seem to be predominantly Eno's, with Cale not even appearing on the closing 'The River' at all. This was Eno's first demonstration of his songwriting abilities since *Before And After Science* over ten years earlier, and his last until 2005. In fact, it's a remarkably strong collection, much of the music here incorporating folk and world music influences, as well as approaching the ambient. Cale wrote the lyrics for three songs, and co-wrote lyrics with Eno for three more. The gently seductive 'One Word' is a return to the pop sensibilities of *Vintage Violence* and *Paris 1919*; 'In The Backroom' is a likeable blend of Latin beat and ambient background, but goes on too long. The menacing 'Cordoba', described by Cale as being a "portrait of a terrorist", includes lyrics Eno had found from phrase a book entitled *Spanish In Three Months*; it is reminiscent of 'Dying On The Vine', but not as good. 'Footsteps' is fairly substandard, as is the singalong 'Been There, Done That' and the country rocker 'Crime In The Desert'. By contrast, all the Eno songs are good.

PARIS S'ÉVEILLE

Crépuscule; released 1991; available on CD.

PARIS S'ÉVEILLE/ SANCTUS/ANIMALS AT NIGHT/THE COWBOY LAUGHS AT THE ROUND-UP/PRIMARY MOTIVE/BOOKER T./ ANTARCTICA STARTS HERE

A mixed bag, containing Cale's soundtrack for Olivier Assayas' film *Paris S'Éveille* (or *Paris Wakes Up*) performed by the Soldier String Quartet, plus five other instrumental pieces and one song. Two were music for ballet: 'Sanctus',

A film soundtrack, with a still from the film

or 'Four Études For Electronic Orchestra', was written for the Randy Warshaw dance company, and 'Animals At Night' was written for the Ralph Lemon dance company. 'The Cowboy Laughs At The Round-Up' may have been music abandoned from the soundtrack to Julian Schnabel's film *Basquiat*, while 'Primary Motive' was the soundtrack for a film by Dan Adams. The album closes with a fairly unremarkable reworking of 'Antarctica Starts Here' from *Paris 1919*. The instrumental pieces are all enjoyable enough (some of them verging on the ambient), but for most people the real reason to buy this at the time was the inclusion of 'Booker T.', a live Velvet Underground performance from 1968 which would subsequently be included on *Peel Slowly And See* (see **The Velvet Underground: The Albums**, above).

FRAGMENTS OF A RAINY SEASON

Hannibal; recorded Spring 1992; released 1992; available on CD.

A CHILD'S CHRISTMAS IN WALES/DYING ON THE VINE/ CORDOBA/DARLING I NEED YOU/PARIS 1919/GUTS/FEAR (IS A MAN'S BEST FRIEND)/SHIP OF FOOLS/LEAVING IT UP TO YOU/THE BALLAD OF CABLE HOGUE/THOUGHTLESS KIND/ ON A WEDDING ANNIVERSARY/LIE STILL, SLEEP BECALMED/ DO NOT GO GENTLE INTO THAT GOOD NIGHT/BUFFALO BALLET/CHINESE ENVOY/STYLE IT TAKES/HEARTBREAK HOTEL/(I KEEP A) CLOSE WATCH/HALLELUJAH

Didn't the Stones do this with Beggar's Banquet?

A solo live album that acts as an extremely good career retrospective, with Cale accompanying himself on piano and acoustic guitar. In fact, it's not only a reminder of how many great songs Cale had written, but also a measure of how strong those songs are that they still work with such sparse arrangements; in some cases (as with the Dylan Thomas pieces), these stripped-down versions are better than the earlier studio outings. The encore, Leonard Cohen's epic 'Hallelujah', Cale had first tackled for *I'm Your Fan*, a 1991 Leonard Cohen tribute album (at which point Cohen sent him the lyrics for dozens of unrecorded verses). Cale's version appeared on the movie soundtracks of both *Basquiat* (1996) and *Shrek* (2001), and his arrange-ment of the song was also used by both Jeff Buckley and Rufus Wainwright.

23 SOLO PIECES FOR *LA NAISSANCE DE L'AMOUR*

Crépuscule; recorded 1992; released 1993; available on CD.

LA NAISSANCE DE L'AMOUR I/IF YOU LOVE ME NO MORE/ AND IF I LOVE YOU STILL/JUDITH/CONVERGING THEMES/ OPPOSITES ATTRACT/I WILL DO IT, I WILL DO IT/KEEP IT TO YOURSELF/WALK TOWARDS THE SEA/UNQUIET HEART/ WAKING UP TO LOVE/MYSTERIOUS RELIEF/NEVER BEEN SO HAPPY (IN LONELY STREETS)/BEYOND EXPECTATIONS/ IN THE GARDEN/ LA NAISSANCE DE L'AMOUR II/SECRET DIALOGUE/ROMA/ON THE DARK SIDE/ LA NAISSANCE DE L'AMOUR III/EYE TO EYE/MARIE'S CAR CRASH AND HOTEL ROOMS/ LA NAISSANCE DE L'AMOUR IV

Cale's soundtrack for the French/Swiss feature film *La Naissance de l'Amour* (*The Birth Of Love*), directed by Philippe Garrel (who Cale had first met through Nico in the late 1960s). As its title suggests, it comprises 23 short piano instru-

An uninspired film soundtrack sleeve design

mentals, which are uniformly pleasantly melodic; though not as memorable as his best rock work, it's still well worth a listen if you can track a copy down, the tunes lying somewhere between Erik Satie and Joni Mitchell. Amazingly, all of this was improvised by Cale – at Garrel's insistence – while he watched the film being screened. Cale's motto for the project was "letting the piano breathe". It was produced by Jean-Michel Reusser.

LAST DAY ON EARTH

MCA; recorded 1994; released 1994; available on CD.
Credited to John Cale and Bob Neuwirth.

*OVERTURE/CAFÉ SHABU/PASTORAL ANGST/WHO'S IN
CHARGE?/SHORT OF TIME/ANGEL OF DEATH/PARADISE
NEVADA/OLD CHINA/OCEAN LIFE/INSTRUMENTAL/MODERN
WORLD/STREETS COME ALIVE/SECRETS/MAPS OF THE
WORLD/BROKEN HEARTS/THE HIGH AND MIGHTY ROAD*

**Back to the *avant garde*
approach à la early 1990s**

John Cale and Bob
Neuwirth first
played together live
– and began work-
ing on this project
– in September 1982.
Last Days On Earth
was performed as an
"evolving multimedia
piece" at St. Ann's
Church in Brooklyn in March 1990, and again
in Germany in March 1991. The album version was recorded at Skyline studios in New
York and produced by Cale and Neuwirth; all
songs were co-written by the duo, who were
augmented by half-a-dozen session players and
the Soldier String Quartet.

The ad for the original concert read, in part:
"The meek, if they so want, can inherit the
Earth, and it's time the road maps were re-writ-
ten". The "plot" of the piece concerns travel-
lers meeting at the mysterious Café Shabu and
exploring time, culture and themselves, and
contains spoken passages and instrumentals as
well as songs.

Undoubtedly ambitious, the work as a whole
skirts the edges of pretentiousness, but the

Bob Neuwirth

Bob Neuwirth
(b. 1939) has
been producing
music as a singer-
songwriter since
the days of the
early 1960s folk
scene in Boston
and Cambridge,
though according
to Andy Warhol
Neuwirth initially
only turned to
music to subsi-
dize his painting.
A friend of Bob
Dylan, Neuwirth became the singer's road manager
and confidant (he can be seen, frequently, in D.A.
Pennebaker's 1967 documentary of Dylan's 1996
"Judas" tour, *Don't Look Back*). He probably first
encountered John Cale during the Factory era;
both men had dated Edie Sedgwick (as had Dylan).
Neuwirth also co-wrote the song 'Mercedes Benz'
with Janis Joplin for her *Pearl* album, released
posthumously in 1971, and assembled the backing band for Dylan's 1975 *Rolling Thunder Revue*.
In more recent years, Neuwirth has been active as
a visual artist, as a documentary film and record
producer, and continues to record music.

music is largely both adventurous and interesting, and the actual song content isn't bad
either. Even so, only the countryish 'Old China'
is really impressive, and this is probably not an
album you'd return to that often.

ANTÁRDIDA

Crépuscule; recorded 1994–1995; released 1995; released on CD, now out of print.

FLASHBACK 1 # 1/ANTÁRTIDA/VELASCO'S THEME/MARIA'S APARTMENT/ FLASHBACK 1 # 2/ON THE WATERFRONT/ PASODOBLE MORTAL/ MARIA'S DREAM/BATH/ FLASHBACK 1 # 3/ANTARCTICA STARTS HERE/FLASHBACK # 3/SUNSET/GET AWAY/ FLASHBACK 1 # 4/ANTÁRTIDA STARTS HERE/FRAME UP/ BARN/PEOPLE WHO DIED/FLASHBACK

Another soundtrack, for the film by Catalan director Manuel Herga. It's a real mixture: there are atmospheric, ambient electronics, orchestral passages that sound like variations on folk airs, doomy organ pieces, some tunelessly chaotic meandering and two more versions of 'Antártida/Antarctica Starts Here' (Cale must really like the song), one of them a classical guitar instrumental by Chris Spedding. There's also a rocking cover version of Jim Carroll's 'People Who Died', featuring Spedding, Moe Tucker and Sterling Morrison. About half the album is tuneful and memorable, the other half discordant and dull.

N'OUBLIE PAS QUE TU VAS MOURIR

Crépuscule; released 1995; released on CD; out of print.

WELCOME TO EUROPE/EVERYBODY'S COLD SOMETIMES/A SNAKE IN CHINA/FAST TRAIN TO HEAVEN/MARTYRS AND MADMEN/TAKE A DEEP BREATH/NEVER SEEN ANYTHING SO BEAUTIFUL/ANGELS IN THE CLOUDS/MADONNA'S BLUES/ SUNFLOWER FIELDS/AL DENTE/HADRIAN WAS HERE/KISS ME ONCE MORE MY LOVE/ALIVE AT DAWN/SKIN IN THE MIRROR/WHO SAID LOVE'S SAFE?/100% PURE/DO NOT FORGET/LAST TRAIN TO BOSNIA/COLD AND CRIMSON/SO FAR SO GOOD

Soundtrack to a film by French director Xavier Beauvois, consisting of mock-baroque instrumentals for both solo piano and a string quartet. The tunes aren't as instantly accessible as on some of Cale's other instrumental work, but there are some gorgeous passages.

WALKING ON LOCUSTS

Rykodisc; recorded 1996; released 1996; available on CD.

DANCING UNDERCOVER/SET ME FREE/SO WHAT/CRAZY EGYPT/SO MUCH FOR LOVE/TELL ME WHY/INDISTINCT NOTION OF COOL/SECRET CORRIDA/CIRCUS/GATORVILLE AND POINTS EAST/SOME FRIENDS/ENTRE NOUS

Recorded at Sorcerer Sound studio in New York, with some 18 session players, including slide-guitar player B.J. Cole, Maureen Tucker and David Byrne, who plays guitar on 'Crazy Egypt', a song he co-wrote with Cale. All other songs are written by Cale.

Back to self-portraiture *in extremis*, a recurring theme

Sadly, Cale's first "proper" solo outing since *Artificial Intelligence* isn't much of an improvement; in fact, apart from the gorgeously orchestral 'Circus' and 'Gatorville And Points East' what's on offer here is distinctly average. The gentle 'Set Me Free' started life as another song about the circus, but in the writing process turned into a song about The Velvet Underground, something from which Cale "never wanted to be set free". 'Some Friends' is a slow intimations-of-mortality ballad about the passing of Sterling Morrison.

The Music

EAT/KISS: MUSIC FOR THE FILMS OF ANDY WARHOL

Rykodisc; released 1997; available on CD.

KISS MOVEMENTS 1–11/EAT MOVEMENTS 1–4

The soundtrack for Warhol's films which Cale had put together with Sterling Morrison and Moe Tucker for Pittsburgh's Warhol Museum in 1994 was never recorded. This album is a live recording of part of a subse-

A striking design with a still from Warhol's Kiss

quent performance at the Théâtre Sebastopol in Lille, France. Prior to the concert, sections of the original music were expanded upon during a week's rehearsal. Apart from Cale (who played keyboards) and Tucker, personnel here include a four-piece string section, vocalists Tiyé Giraurd and Jimmy Justice, and pedal-steel guitarist B.J. Cole. The piece contains a so-so version of Nico's 'Frozen Warnings' and a reading/recital by Cale of Emanuel Swedenborg's mystical essay 'Melanathon'. For the rest, there's a certain amount of tuneless meandering, but much of the music is highly atmospheric and enjoyable – and the sound of Tucker's drums playing against Cale's viola can't help but evoke the ghost of something "Velvet".

DANCE MUSIC

Detour; recorded late 1997; released 1998; available on CD.

INTRO/NEW YORK UNDERGROUND/NIGHT CLUB THEME/ MODELLING/OUT OF CHINA/DEATH CAMP/ARI SLEEPY TOO/ ICEBERG I/JIM/ICEBERG II/ESPAÑA/NIBELUNGEN

This contains Cale's music for *Nico, The Ballet*, which was commissioned by the Scapino company of Rotterdam and choreographed by Ed Wubbe. The album was recorded live during the ballet performances, the ballet itself being an interpretation of Nico's

Not immediately clear it's for a ballet, it looks as if it features Nico

life. "Biography is best left to historians, ballet to visionaries", Cale observed in his sleeve notes, a touching account of why he attempted to create what amounts to a musical biography of Nico anyway. The music is mainly performed by the nine-piece orchestral group Ice Nine. 'Ari Sleepy Too' features Nico's spoken words (from the floppy disc in the *Andy Warhol Index* book); 'España' is a solo piano piece performed by Cale (recorded in New York); the album closes with 'Nibelungen' by Nico (from *The Marble Index*). It's hard to judge the music outside of its context, but all of the pieces are evocative and fairly intense, with elements that sound Middle Eastern or oriental. Not as immediately accessible as *Eat/Kiss*.

LA VENT DE LA NUIT

Crépuscule; released 1999; available on CD.

ON THE ROAD TO PORTOFINO/AT THE BOATS/NAPLES/ON THE ROAD TO TURIN/TURIN AT NIGHT/THE SEINE AT NIGHT/ SUICIDE I/TRUCK PARKING LOT AT NIGHT/ON THE ROAD TO GERMANY/WAITING/THINKING AND ACTING/SUICIDE II/PRESIDENT Y. IS STILL STABLE/B. CALLS/DARKNESS ON THE DELTA/WHAT MRS. IVES SAID TO MR. IVES/MY PIANO THANKS YOU FOR VISITING

The soundtrack for the film of the same name, by director Philippe Garrel (starring Catherine Deneuve) was recorded at Dubbing Brothers and Acousti studios in Paris. Piano pieces (occasionally with harpsichord) by

Hopperesque and enigmatic, you might even want to see the movie

Cale, accompanied by slide guitar from Mark Deffenbaugh, are punctuated by the sound of a thunderstorm. It's all pleasant, but none of it that remarkable or memorable. Once they'd finished the soundtrack the duo kept recording more music in a similar vein, and the final five tracks on the album are bracketed together under the subtitle 'Memories Of Paris'.

THE UNKNOWN

Crépuscule; released 1999; available on CD.

THE UNKNOWN PARTS 1 – 8

In late 1993, John Cale was commissioned by the Italian Pordenone Silent Film Festival to write a new electronic score for the 1927 silent film *The*

Unknown. Directed by Tod Browning (of *Freaks* fame) and starring Lon Chaney Sr., the film is a melodramatic and bizarrely horrific tale of love, mutilation and revenge. Cale's new score premiered at a screening of the film in Pordenone in October

A nicely period feel for a silent movie soundtrack

1994, and the soundtrack album was recorded at another screening in Paris two months later. It's a succession of moody keyboard-based instrumentals, most of which sound as doom-laden as the plot, though without seeing the accompanying film it's hard to know how well they work in context. For completists only.

SAINT CYR

Virgin France; released 2000; available on CD.

OPENING THEME/IRONIC TRUMPET/STATELY/ESTHER/ OPENING THEME # 2/PILLAR THEME/ PILLAR THEME # 2/ 2ND THEME/2ND THEME # 2/WAR TIME/WAR TIME # 2

Another soundtrack, this time to an 18th-century period film by Patricia Mazuy, starring Isabelle Huppert. The music is fully orchestral (featuring brass and harpsichord), with a few choral passages and a suitably period feel.

In-your-face marketing: a standard movie soundtrack design

The Music

More accessible than many of Cale's instrumental soundtracks, and if you like baroque classical music, recommended.

INSIDE THE DREAM SYNDICATE VOLUME I: DAY OF NIAGARA

Table Of The Elements; recorded 1965; released 2000; available on CD.
Personnel: John Cale (viola); Tony Conrad (violin); Angus MacLise (percussion); LaMonte Young and Marian Zazeela (vocals).

The medium is the message: you know this is minimalism

Recorded in New York on the 15 April 1965, and exactly what you would expect if you knew anything about the group: a single piece of music, lasting just over 30 minutes, that is basically a drone (and nothing but), varying only slightly in pitch and intensity throughout. While this may have been revolutionary – and we can be thankful for its influence on the Velvets and others – it's not exactly easy listening, being only fractionally more bearable than Reed's *Metal Machine Music* (see below).

SUN BLINDNESS MUSIC

Table Of The Elements; recorded 1965–1968; released 2000; available on CD.

SUN BLINDNESS MUSIC/SUMMER HEAT/THE SECOND FORTRESS

Produced by Tony Conrad, these are three pieces recorded by Cale during his time with The Velvet Underground (in 1967, 1965 and 1968 respectively) at his apartment in LaGuardia Place and elsewhere. The first piece lasts for nearly 43 minutes, for which Cale produces a sequence of sustained chords on a Vox Continental organ. The effect is minimalist music reminiscent of Terry Riley, though somewhat more demanding. Even so, it has tuneful passages as well as jarring sequences, and some moments of extreme beauty. The second piece is just over eleven minutes long, and features Cale strumming away with great precision on a distorting rhythm guitar, barely varying the pace or the key. It's pretty monotonous. Finally, Cale delivers a ten-minute drone piece created with "electronic sounds". For fans of *avant-garde* music only.

A nice series feel for the collectors of Cale's early work

INSIDE THE DREAM SYNDICATE VOLUME II: DREAM INTERPRETATION

Table Of The Elements; recorded 1965–1969; released 2000; available on CD.

DREAM INTERPRETATION/EX-CATHEDRA/UNTITLED, FOR PIANO/CAROUSEL/A MIDNIGHT RAI OF GREEN WRENS AT THE WORLD'S TALLEST BUILDING/HOT SCORIA

More of Cale's experimental music from the 1960s, some of it produced in tandem with Tony Conrad or Angus MacLise. Much of it is drone-based or otherwise experimenting with sustained notes, or else completely random and, frankly, cacophonous. For diehards only.

INSIDE THE DREAM SYNDICATE VOLUME III: STAINLESS GAMELAN

Table Of The Elements; recorded 1965–1968; released 2000; available on CD.

STAINLESS STEEL GAMELAN/AT ABOUT THIS TIME MOZART WAS DEAD AND JOSEPH CONRAD WAS SAILING THE SEVEN SEAS LEARNING ENGLISH/TERRY'S CHA-CHA/AFTER THE LOCUST/BIG APPLE EXPRESS

More of the same, though this time Sterling Morrison joins in for a couple of tracks, along with Conrad, MacLise and saxophonist Terry Jennings. Mildly more listenable than the previous volume, but only mildly – though 'Terry's Cha-Cha' is quite likeable, and actually has a tune (even if it does get a bit monotonous after eight minutes).

5 TRACKS

EMI; recorded 2003; released 200; available on CD.

VERSES/WAITING FOR BLONDE/CHORUS OF DUMPTEY/ IS MISSING/WILDERNESS APPROACHING

Recorded at Media Luna studios, New York and Engine studios, Chicago. Musicians uncredited.

As its title suggests, a slender volume, lasting for just over 19 minutes. These are slow and moody songs composed on the computer, and more interesting and

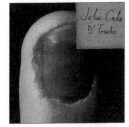

Cale puts the finger on his latest album

likeable than most of the material on *Walking On Locusts*. In 2007, Cale indicated that this record had come closest to satisfying his original ambitions for it. 'Verses' veers from pretty (with wordless female backing vocals, supposedly by Cale's daughter Eden) to ugly (shouting and feedback); the female vocal makes it sound almost like the soundtrack to a romantic French movie. The subtle 'E Is Missing' is a real grower, with Gothic strings, Duane Eddy-style guitar and a snatch of the Christmas carol 'Noel'. The stately and likeable piano ballad 'Wilderness Approaching' is from the soundtrack to the film *Paris*, and boasts a terrific performance by a (sadly uncredited) female backing singer.

HOBO SAPIENS

EMI; recorded 2003; released 2003; available on CD.

ZEN/READING MY MIND/THINGS/LOOK HORIZON/ MAGRITTE/ARCHIMEDES/CARAVAN/BICYCLE/TWILIGHT ZONE/LETTER FROM ABROAD/THINGS X/OVER HER HEAD

Once again Cale establishes a distance between the artist and his audience

Co-produced by Cale and Lemon Jelly's Nick Franglen, and featuring numerous session musicians and backing singers. 'Bicycle' features a drum part by Brian Eno (and giggling by his two daughters). It's a patchy collection, though still far stronger than *Walking On Locusts*. 'Reading My Mind' is infectiously bouncing, as is 'Things' (which lyrically references Brian Eno's *Taking Tiger Mountain By Strategy*, Warren Zevon's 'Things To Do In Denver When You're Dead' and Charles Schultz's *Peanuts* cartoon). The delicate 'Archimedes', 'Caravan' and 'Over Her Head' are slower, but gently impressive; 'Bicycle' could easily be a Lemon Jelly track. Despite its dull moments and some annoyingly contrived experimentation, still a very likeable album. The record also contains a 'hidden' track, 'Set Me Free'. The album title was originally Cale's jocular nickname for Bob Dylan.

LOU REED, JOHN CALE AND NICO: LE BATACLAN '72

Alchemy Entertainment; recorded 29 January 1972; released 2003.

See pages 165–166.

PROCESS

Syntax; released August 2005; available on CD.

THEME INTRO/THEATRE/POST-SEX/MUSEUM/RADIOLOGY/ CANDLES/BEDROOM/CAR BLUE/PACKING BOOKS/READING POEM/BURNING-PAINTING/LA DÉFENSE-METRO/SUICIDE THEME/ASCENSCION

Cale's soundtrack for C.S. Leigh's independent French film of the same name consists of 14 instrumental pieces – mainly solo piano, sometimes organ, and for the most part fairly tuneless. For completists only.

Another film still, another movie soundtrack

BLACK ACETATE

EMI; recorded 2005; released October 2005; available on CD.

OUTTA THE BAG/FOR A RIDE/BROTHERMAN/SATISFIED/IN A FLOOD/HUSH/GRAVEL DRIVE/PERFECT/SOLD-MOTEL/ WOMAN/WASTELAND/TURN THE LIGHTS ON/MAILMAN (THE LYING SONG)

The personnel are basically a trio of Cale, Herb Graham Jr. (on drums and bass) and Dave Levita (on guitars), augmented by other session musicians (though 'Sold-Motel' features a different band and is a rather dull rocker). Herb Graham Jr co-produced the album except for 'Sold-Motel', which was co-produced by Mickey Petralia.

Back to portrait photos, possibly the most disturbing yet

The album is far harder-edged than *Hobo Sapiens*, and right from the start the listener is thrown off balance by the musical approach (basically a mixture of hip-hop and funk influences) and also by Cale's bizarrely falsetto vocal on the likeable 'Outta The Bag', which he claims was done "just for the humour and the charm of it". Some of what's on offer here is dull or irritating (or both), but the record still definitely has its share of good moments: 'Satisfied' is a seductive and charming love song; 'In A Flood' is a good Dylan-style blues; 'Gravel Drive' (with wonderfully atmospheric backing vocals by Jasper Baj) is a sweetly gentle song about leaving home to tour, and was written for Cale's daughter; 'Perfect' is infectiously dumb beatpop; and 'Mailman (The Lying Song)' is wonderfully atmospheric, experimental but accessible. With *Black Acetate* Cale demonstrated that he was still travelling; at least half the time he still arrives somewhere interesting.

CIRCUS

EMI; recorded 2006; released February 2007; available on CD/DVD.

DISC 1
VENUS IN FURS/SAVE US/HELEN OF TROY/WOMAN/BUFFALO BALLET/FEMME FATALE/ROSEGARDEN FUNERAL OF SORES/ HUSH/OUTTA THE BAG/SET ME FREE/THE BALLAD OF CABLE HOGUE/LOOK HORIZON/MAGRITTE/DIRTY ASS/ROCK AND ROLL

DISC 2
WALKING THE DOG/GUN/HANKY PANKY NOHOW/PABLO PICASSO-MARY LOU/DRONE INTRO/ZEN/STYLE IT TAKES/ HEARTBREAK HOTEL/MERCENARIES/OUTRO DRONE

Personnel: John Cale (lead vocals, guitars, keyboards, electric viola, samples); Dustin Boyer (lead guitar, toys, backing vocals); Joseph Karnes (bass, nord 3, samples, backing vocals); Michael Jerome (drums, samples, backing vocals). Personnel on Disc 2, tracks 6–9: John Cale (lead vocals, keyboards, samples); Mark Deffenbaugh (guitars, banjo, harmonica); Deantoni Parks (drums, samples). Personnel on Disc 2, tracks 5 and 10: John Cale (samples); Charlie Campagna (samples).

Disc 2, tracks 6–9 were recorded at the Paradiso, Amsterdam. No venues are listed for the rest of the album, but it would seem to have been recorded at various gigs in Holland.

Produced and arranged by John Cale.

A boxed set of live material, packaged with a lavish colour booklet. It's a truly career-spanning selection – with large chunks taken from *Helen Of Troy* and *Hobo Sapiens* – but also a real mixture quality-wise. Overall, the rockier tracks are the least rewarding – often verging on Gothic thrash – while the more delicate material comes off best, with really good versions of 'Woman', 'Buffalo Ballet', 'Set Me Free', 'Cable Hogue', 'Hanky Panky Nohow'

The Music

Colourful typography, the message is clear

and 'Style It Takes'. 'Femme Fatale' gets a genuinely innovative treatment, as a growling Cale segues into 'Rosegarden Funeral Of Sores', while both 'Gun' and 'Heartbreak Hotel' are slowed to a crawl (which considerably increases the atmosphere of menace). The proceedings close with a brooding, world weary reading of 'Mercenaries', its anti-war message even more relevant than when the song was written.

The set also contains a third disc, this being a DVD that includes black and white footage of the tour rehearsals in Los Angeles, both electric and acoustic sets. These include fragments of (electric set): 'Model Beirut Recital', 'Sold Motel', 'Gun', 'Reading My Mind' and 'Heartbreak Hotel'; (acoustic set) 'Dancing Undercover', 'You Know More Than I Know', 'Gravel Drive', 'Chorale' and 'Ghost Story'. As with the live album, the acoustic material is far more interesting than the electric (with great versions of all those songs), but the footage itself is visually very straightforward. Perhaps that's why Cale chooses to don his old hockey mask for the closing 'Ghost Story', but it seems more than a little excessive! The disc also contains an animated video for 'Jumbo In Tha Modern World' (sadly, a fairly dull song) and two audio tracks: a 'Blathamix' remix of 'GravelDrive' (depressing and doom-laden)

and 'Big White Cloud 2007' (a good version of the *Vintage Violence* track – but not as good as the original).

Possibly not the best of career retrospectives, but there's still more than enough good material here to reward the faithful and to intrigue the newcomer.

Cale As Producer

John Cale has also worked as a record producer and/or arranger for an astonishing number of artists, some quite surprising, including:

Lester Bangs	Maids Of Gravity
Art Bergman	Marie Et Les Garçons
Big Vern	The Mediaeval Babes
Chunky, Novie and	Menace
Ernie	Model Citizens
Julie Covington	Modern Guy
Cristina	The Modern Lovers
Element Of Crime	Necessaries
Louise Feron	Nico
Garageland	Sham 69
Goya Dress	Siouxsie And The
Happy Mondays	Banshees
Jesus Lizard	Patti Smith
David Kubinec	Snatch
Larry and Tommy	Squeeze
Les Nouvelles	Alan Stivell
Polyphonies Corses	The Stooges
Lio	Harry Toledo And The
Los Ronaldos	Rockets
Made For TV	Jennifer Warnes
Anne Magnuson	

Cale has stated that the one artist he'd really like to produce is Captain Beefheart.

Angus MacLise

"Angus was living on the Angus calendar"
– John Cale

MacLise recorded numerous albums, of which the following seem to be the only ones available:

BRAIN DAMAGE IN OKLAHOMA CITY

Quakebasket; recorded 1967–1970; released 2000; available on CD.

ANOTHER DRUID'S NEST/HAIGHT RIOT MIME/EPIPHANY/ LOFT COLLAGE/DRUM SOLO/DREAMWEAPON BENEFIT FOR THE OKLAHOMA CITY POLICE DEPT. PART I/ DREAMWEAPON BENEFIT... PART II/CEMBALUM

As could have been predicted, MacLise's solo output is not exactly tuneful; indeed, there are passages that rival Reed's *Metal Machine Music* (see below) for testing the endurance of the listener. There's a great deal of bongo-playing, vocals that are halfway between moaning and chanting, some minimalist organ pieces spiced up with percussion, a taped conversation that could match a Warhol movie for dullness, a mildly impressive drum solo, some obvious (but unmelodic) oriental influences and a great deal of tuneless noodling. Experimentation is a good thing, but it doesn't always bear fruit.

Quakebasket's intriguing semi-abstract cover art is more exciting...

ASTRAL COLLAPSE

Quakebasket; recording details unknown; released 2003; available on CD.

SMOTHERED UNDER ASTRAL COLLAPSE/6TH FACE OF THE ANGEL/BEELZEBUB/CLOUD WATCHING/DRACULA/DAWN CHORUS

More of the same: MacLise recites poetry over a tape of Tibetan-inspired music, there's a lengthy repetitive ambient electronic piece (like Terry Riley, but not as much fun), a MacLise bongo solo (over tapes that sound like insects buzzing) and lots more tuneless meandering, some of it on an arp synthesizer. The album closes with more poetry, recited over tapes of local noise and music recorded by MacLise in India.

...than what's inside

Sterling Morrison

There are no solo recordings by Sterling Morrison.

Nico

"A true artist must self-destruct"
– Nico, 1984

CHELSEA GIRL

Verve; recorded April/May 1967; released October 1967; currently available on CD.

THE FAIREST OF THE SEASONS/THESE DAYS/LITTLE SISTER/ WINTER SONG/IT WAS A PLEASURE THEN/CHELSEA GIRLS/I'LL KEEP IT WITH MINE/SOMEWHERE THERE'S A FEATHER/WRAP YOUR TROUBLE IN DREAMS/EULOGY TO LENNY BRUCE

Recorded at Mayfair Sound studios, New York, the album was produced by Tom Wilson and arranged and conducted by Larry Fallon. Musicians are uncredited. Five tracks here have Velvets connections, and feature the playing of Reed and/or Cale and/or Morrison. 'Wrap Your Troubles In Dreams' (written by Reed) and 'Little Sister' (written by Reed and Cale) had both been recorded during sessions for the first Velvets album (with the orchestra-

Siren or pensive chanteuse: the cover image makes the most of Nico's astonishing looks

tion added later by Wilson). Three other tracks were recorded specifically for this album: 'Little Sister' (written by Cale), 'Chelsea Girls' (written by Reed and Morrison) and 'It Was A Pleasure Then' (written by Nico, Reed and Cale), the last of which had evolved out of the Velvets' live piece 'Melody Laughter'.

Three tracks were written or co-written by the 18-year-old Jackson Browne: 'The Fairest Of The Seasons', 'These Days' and 'Somewhere There's A Feather', the first two of which are the real highlights of the album (over 20 years later, both songs would appear on the soundtrack of Wes Anderson's quirky 2001 comedy *The Royal Tennenbaums*). Bob Dylan's touching 'I'll Keep It With Mine' was a song he'd written for Nico long before she gained any fame outside of modelling circles, and figures as one of his best (it would be covered by Fairport Convention the following year). Tim Hardin's sombre 'Eulogy For Lenny Bruce' celebrates the late comedian, and is as doom-laden as anything Nico would record later.

Nico hated the orchestration the songs were given ("I asked for drums, they said 'no'"), and claims to have cried with frustration and anger when she heard it. In truth, the arrangement of 'Wrap Your Troubles In Dreams' is a heavy-handed mess, but in the main the results are gorgeous – baroque folk-pop with soaring strings and a psychedelic tinge, which was perfectly suited to the times (although 'It Was A Pleasure Then' sounds like it belongs on a different record).

Chelsea Girl is easily Nico's most commercial album, though it didn't fare well at the time. Had she recorded an album like this a few years earlier, she might have carved out a career in this style. As it was, she faced stiff competition from a new wave of female singers like Judy Collins and Joni Mitchell, whose voices were a lot less idiosyncratic and more radio-friendly – but Nico would choose a different path for her next album and, rather than covering the work of others, she would mine her own unsuspected talents instead.

The Chelsea Hotel

The Chelsea in question is New York's Chelsea Hotel on West 23rd Street, which has been home to many literary and artistic types down through the decades (usually when they were young and struggling). Mark Twain, Tennessee Williams, Dylan Thomas, Arthur Miller, Jackson Pollock, Allen Ginsberg, Edith Piaf, Gore Vidal, Bob Dylan, Leonard Cohen and Janis Joplin have all lived there; Sid Vicious and Nancy Spungen played out the final act of their tawdry tragedy there.

Lou Reed's lyric for 'Chelsea Girls' reads like a roll-call of Warhol's Factory crowd (and their sexual and narcotic proclivities); among those mentioned are Ondine, Bridget (Berlin, a.k.a. Polk), Ingrid (Superstar), Mary (Woronov) and Susan (Bottomley, a.k.a. International Velvet). Nico herself briefly lived at the Chelsea, as did Edie Sedgwick (who nearly burned the place down when a fire started in her room) and John Cale.

THE MARBLE INDEX

Elektra; recorded October 1968; released January 1969; available on CD.

*PRELUDE/LAWNS OF DAWNS/NO ONE IS THERE/ARI'S SONG/
FACING THE WIND/JULIUS CAESAR (MEMENTO HODIE)/
FROZEN WARNINGS/EVENING OF LIGHT*

A somewhat brutal Guy Webster portrait, reminiscent of Cale's *Fear* album in directness

Recorded at Elektra Sound Recorders, Los Angeles, the album was nominally produced by Frazier Mohawk, but all the actual work of arranging and recording was done by John Cale.

The Marble Index couldn't be more different to its predecessor. Nico's voice had become even more otherworldly, her meandering tunes owing a debt to the traditions of German *lieder* and at times becoming almost chant-like. Cale's arrangements for the songs veer from the tunelessly *avant-garde* to the neo-classical, while Nico's harmonium evokes an atmosphere of medieval religious doom, somewhere between the monastery and the madhouse (small wonder she'd be repeatedly described as "Gothic"). It's not exactly easy listening, though it is remarkable – and at this point there'd certainly been nothing like it in rock before. The album title comes from a Wordsworth poem: "the marble index of a mind forever voyaging through strange seas of thought alone"; some of Nico's lyrics show a marked debt to Sylvia Plath and to William Blake, and there is no doubt that she wanted to be taken seriously as an artist herself. As John Cale once remarked: "She was quite clear about it; she wanted to be the female Jim Morrison".

Nico once said that 'No One Is There' is about Richard Nixon; 'Ari's Song' is a lullabye of farewell to her son; 'Frozen Warnings' concerned a hermit (Nico has intimated that the song is about Jim Morrison) and is the album's strongest track, with a comparatively strong tune and a minimal arrangement reminiscent of Terry Riley. Nico played a toy piano on the album's closing track, 'Evening Of Light', which fittingly concerned "the end of time". As John Cale would point out, the album was an artistic endeavour, "not a commercial commodity. You can't sell suicide". One reason for the album's short running time is thought to be the fact that neither Mohawk nor engineer John Haenhy could stand to listen to much more of it.

The CD release contains two extra tracks: 'Roses In The Snow' (which is comparable to 'Frozen Warnings', but not as good) and the acapella 'Nibelungen' (which is certainly striking, but not exactly merry).

DESERTSHORE

Reprise; recorded Spring/Summer 1970; released December 1970; available on CD.

JANITOR OF LUNACY/THE FALCONER/MY ONLY CHILD/LE PETIT CHEVALIER/ABSCHIED/AFRAID/MÜTTERLEIN/ALL THAT IS MY OWN

Recorded at Vanguard studios, New York, with further sessions at Sound Techniques in London. Nico made some changes after Cale

The sleeve featured stills from Garrel's film *La Cicatrice Intérieure*

had flown back to New York: what they were is not known, but Cale was not pleased. Much more tuneful than its predecessor, *Desertshore* is an album that not only convinces the listener that Nico had real talent as a writer and performer, but shows huge promise for her future. The songs it contained were originally written as a soundtrack for Philippe Garrel's 1972 film *La Cicatrice Intérieure*, and Cale gives them a hugely sympathetic arrangement, mainly consisting of delicately tuneful piano fills. He also provided backing vocals, along with Adam Miller (of *Church Of Anthrax* fame). Occasionally Cale allows Nico's harmonium to hold sway, as on the Gothic 'Janitor Of Lunacy' (supposedly written about Brian Jones). 'The Falconer' was about Andy Warhol, while two songs were about Nico's son: 'My Only Son' (which has gorgeous, multi-tracked a capella vocals) and 'Le Petit Chevalier' (sung by young Ari); two more were about her mother: 'Mütterlein' and 'Abschied' ('Farewell Song'), both of which are sung in German and are fairly doomy – the former has some deeply ominous viola from Cale.

The album's remaining tracks are perhaps its best: the deeply moving ballad 'Afraid', and the closing 'All That Is My Own', which sounds as if Brecht and Weill had decided to write a song with *Arabian Nights* overtones (the lyric contains the titular "desertshore" reference). Throughout the album, Nico's voice (and talent) rings clear as a bell, and (with a few exceptions) sounds far more modern than medieval. A truly impressive album.

ACNE JUNE 1ST 1974

See page 177.

THE END

Island; recorded Summer 1974; released November 1974; currently available on CD.

IT HAS NOT TAKEN LONG/SECRET SIDE/YOU FORGOT TO ANSWER/INNOCENT AND VAIN/VALLEY OF THE KINGS/WE'VE GOT THE GOLD/THE END/DAS LIED DER DEUTSCHEN

The follow-up to *Desertshore* was a giant leap backwards. John Cale again produced, drafting in Brian Eno (on synthesizer) and Phil Manzanera (on guitar), with whom he had just worked on his solo album *Fear*.

An arty cover, which pretty much reflects the music inside

Cale himself played twelve different instruments, with backing vocals from Vicki Woo and Annagh Wood. But despite such a distinguished cast, Eno delivers little but irritating noises, Nico's harmonium positively warbles and there's no relief from any other quarter. The songs themselves are plodding, tuneless and exude nothing but doom and angst. The definition that springs immediately to mind is "Goth" ... and there are passages that sound exactly like soundtrack music Danny Elfman might have come up with for a particularly gloomy Tim Burton picture. None of Nico's original songs sticks with the listener (though for the record, 'We've Got The Gold' is supposedly about Andreas Baader), and the album ends with two cover versions that are only mildly better. The first is the title track, the Freudian melodrama by Jim Morrison that was first heard on The Doors' eponymous 1967 debut. Nico's version is not an improvement, and sounds even more pompous and po-faced than the original (though Nico apparently didn't like Cale's arrangement). Nico had also wanted to record another Doors' song, 'You're Lost, Little Girl' but Cale vetoed it; Cale wanted her to record the traditional cowboy ballad 'Streets Of Laredo' instead, but she refused (he'd later record it himself, on the *Honi Soit* album). Either would have been a welcome addition. As it is, the only truly memorable song on this record is the closer, a controversial cover version of 'Das Lied Der Deutschen' (or 'The Song Of The German People'), written by August Heinrich Hoffman von Fallersleben. The song is better known as 'Deutschland Über Alles' which, though written long before the Nazi era, immediately evokes the ghost of Hitler. God only knows what point Nico was trying to make by covering it (her politics were at best an addled form of nihilism), but at least it has a tune, and a clarion-voiced Nico gives it her all.

DRAMA OF EXILE

German version: Aura/Line; recorded 1981; released July 1981; available on CD.
French version: Paris; released 1982; may be available on Czech CD.

GENGHIS KHAN/PURPLE LIPS/ONE MORE CHANCE/HENRY HUDSON/WAITING FOR THE MAN/SIXTY FORTY/THE SPHINX/ ORLY FLIGHT/HEROES

As stated elsewhere, there are two versions of this album. Having sold the tapes to Aura for German release, Nico subsequently re-recorded the same material for the French release, using the same musicians. These included

A Klimt-style artwork which evokes Nico's Germanic background

Corsican guitarist Muhammad Hadi, drummer Steve Cordona, bassist Philippe Quilichini (who also produced the record), keyboard player Andy Clarke (who had played on David Bowie's 'Ashes To Ashes') and Davey Payne (of The Blockheads) on sax. Although the raucous rock arrangements framing Nico's voice here initially come as a bit of shock, they also make this a far more accessible album than *The End*. The songs are also slightly more tuneful this time around, though only slightly. 'Genghis Khan' and 'Henry Hudson' were inspired by the historical personalities (the barbarian and the explorer), while Nico dedicated 'The Sphinx' to terrorist Andreas Baader, "because he had that hypnotic look" and it's given a vaguely Arabic arrangement, as is 'Orly

Flight'. None of the above songs are particularly memorable in any way, but the album does boast one absolutely standout track: the atmospheric 'Sixty Forty', about a doomed relationship in New York, which is worthy to sit alongside the very best of Nico's output (including her work with the Velvets). As to the two cover versions included: 'Waiting For The Man' simply proves that Lou Reed had been right not to let Nico sing it in the first place. It's not only pedestrian, it sounds like self-parody. Her version of David Bowie's 'Heroes' is only mildly better. Nico was convinced that the song had been written about her; she'd supposedly been in Berlin when Bowie had been recording there, and she also claimed he'd long been infatuated with her. The truth was that when she tried to contact him, he refused to see her (probably because he was in the process of giving up drugs, and she was a junkie). Regardless, her cover of the song is second-rate and unnecessary.

CAMERA OBSCURA

Beggars Banquet; recorded 1985; released August 1985; available on CD.

CAMERA OBSCURA/TANANORE/WIN A FEW/MY FUNNY VALENTINE/DAS LIED VON EINSANEN MÄDCHENS/ FEARFULLY IN DANGER/MY HEART IS EMPTY/INTO THE ARENA/KÖNIG

Nico's final studio album was recorded at Strongroom studios in London, and is credited to 'Nico + the faction', who consisted of two members of her regular touring band, James Young on keyboards and Graham Dids (a.k.a. Dowdall) on percussion, plus

Ian Carr on trumpet. She was also reunited with John Cale in the producer's chair, and Cale apparently thought Nico was in better shape than when he had seen her last, and had deepened personally, musically and lyrically in

Possibly Nico's most enigmatic cover, redolent of angst and unseen threat

that time. Unfortunately, Nico had been suffering from writer's block for some time, and had come up with only six new (and fairly unremarkable) songs for the album – and one of these, the title track (credited to Nico, Young, Dowdall and Cale), sounds very much like it was improvised on the spot. Since actual tunes are still thin on the ground, much of the record only works – or rather, half-works – because of Young's arrangements, some of which conjure echoes of John Barry's jazzier theme music. The album also boasts a memorable and genuinely moving cover of the Rodgers and Hart standard 'My Funny Valentine' – a song Nico had sung in cabaret long before she ever heard of Lou Reed – with a great trumpet part from Carr and some lovely piano from Young. The other cover version here is 'Das Lied Von Einsanen Mädchens' ('The Song Of The Lonely Girls'), a traditional German ballad given an atmospheric, lilting treatment. As an epitaph, the album could have been far worse – and for all its faults was still Nico's most interesting record for quite some time.

FEMME FATALE

Castle/Aura; recorded 1980–1985; released 2003; available on CD.

This 2-CD anthology includes the entire *Drama Of Exile* album (the first version), and may actually be easier to find than that album on its

own. Also collected here are six *Drama Of Exile* out-takes, the so-so *Live At Chelsea Town Hall* album and two singles recorded in 1980, 'Saeta' and 'Vegas'. The former is doomy, sub-standard indie-rock; the latter boasts a drum

A full-on colourful pop sleeve, undercut by anxiety

machine and synthesizer backing that sounds vaguely like Duran Duran, against which Nico's vocal sounds somewhat incongruous. That said, it's actually not at all bad.

LOU REED, JOHN CALE AND NICO: LE BATACLAN '72

See pages 165–166.

THE FROZEN BORDERLINE 1968–70

Rhino; recorded 1968–70; released 2007; available on CD.

A two-CD set that includes remastered versions of *The Marble Index* and *Desertshore*, plus a wealth of unreleased material. This includes alternate versions of all the Marble Index tracks, demo versions of all the songs from *Desertshore* and four *Marble Index* out-takes. In addition to 'Roses In The Snow' and 'Nibelungen' (included on the previous CD release) there

Leopoldo Pomés' stunning design, in a stylish cardboard sleeve

are the hitherto unheard 'Sagen Die Gelehrten' and 'Rêve Réveiller', the first of which would have greatly improved the original release, had it been included. Clearly the definitive version of these albums.

The Nico story effectively ends with *Camera Obscura*. There are at least nine live albums (including one *Peel Sessions* album), recorded in every country imaginable and of varying quality (some very poor). *Live Behind The Iron Curtain* was actually recorded in Rotterdam! Most feature versions of the songs Lou Reed had written for her back in 1966 ("Those songs were Lou's gift to me. I sing them because I treasure that gift"). None of these records are particularly worth investing money in.

For the completists: Nico also made guest appearances on Kevin Ayers' *The Confessions Of Doctor Dream* (1974), Marc Almond's *The Stars We Are* (1988), and Bauhaus's version of 'I'm Waitin For The Man'.

Lou Reed

*"I always like my most recent album best,
and that applies to every single one of them"
— Lou Reed, 1985*

LOU REED

RCA; recorded January 1972; released May 1972; currently available on CD.

I CAN'T STAND IT/GOING DOWN/WALK AND TALK IT/LISA SAYS/BERLIN/I LOVE YOU/WILD CHILD/LOVE MAKES YOU FEEL/RIDE INTO THE SUN/OCEAN

Recorded at London's Morgan studios with a curious collection of British musicians, including Elton John's sideman Caleb Quaye, Rick Wakeman and Steve Howe from Yes and drummer Clem Cattini (who had played with Johnny Kidd and The Pirates, and on the Tornados' classic instrumental 'Telstar'). They were all capable musicians, but hardly *simpatico* to Reed's style or subject matter. Strangely, Lou himself did not play any guitar on the record.

The results are disappointing. For one thing, Reed didn't have a strong enough collection of material. Although he seemingly demoed a great many new songs, most of these he eventually rejected, opting instead to fill most of the album with re-recordings of songs he'd previously recorded with The Velvet Underground (although the Velvets' versions remained unreleased until the 1980s). Reed would continue to occasionally plunder the Velvets' unreleased back catalogue for many years to come – and even if his solo versions impressed at the time, in almost every instance the Velvets' versions would eventually be discovered to be far superior. Only four songs here are completely "new": 'Going Down', 'Berlin', 'Wild Child' and 'I Love You' (the latter two both seemingly about Bettye).

The whole album sounds limp and bland, largely because of the arrangements and playing – though the production was also tinny and sterile, something about which Reed later complained to his co-producer Richard Robinson. This was at least partially due to a

The cover painting by Tom Adams was commissioned by Reed. Adams had done covers for paperback editions of Raymond Chandler novels, which Lou had liked

major technical glitch which remained a mystery until certain tracks were remastered for the *Between Thought And Expression* boxed set. The entire album was remastered in 1999.

The Music

In hindsight, the record is of interest mainly for the song 'Berlin', an epic romantic ballad, set in Berlin "by the wall", but the orthodox rock arrangement the song gets here lets it down; Reed would briefly reprise it when he returned to the divided city as the territory for his third solo album song-cycle (*Berlin*, in 1973, see page 208). In reality, he didn't actually visit the place until 1979. Sterling Morrison later called the album "derivative and not very good", but most reviews at the time weren't that bad (except for the *NME's* Nick Kent, who hated it). Sales were another matter – and they were appallingly low –about 7,000 worldwide. If not for David Bowie, the Lou Reed story might very well have ended here.

TRANSFORMER

RCA; recorded August 1972; released November 1972; currently available on CD.

VICIOUS/ANDY'S CHEST/PERFECT DAY/HANGIN' ROUND/ WALK ON THE WILD SIDE/MAKE UP/SATELLITE OF LOVE/ WAGON WHEEL/NEW YORK TELEPHONE CONVERSATION/I'M SO FREE/GOODNIGHT LADIES

Transformer remains one of the real highlights of Reed's long career, and a large part of the credit has to go to David Bowie, who co-produced the album with his regular guitarist Mick Ronson. Ronson also did all the string and brass arrangements, and Bowie and Ronson got a further credit – alongside Lou – for "song arrangements".

The album was recorded at London's Trident studios, using a choice selection of session musicians. Ronson and Lou played guitars; on electric and string bass was Herbie Flowers (with Klaus Voorman also playing on some tracks), who also played tuba; drummers were John Halzey, Barry Desouza and Ritchie Dharma; Ronnie Ross played baritone sax;

The Pierrot look: Mick Rock provided all the *Transformer* photography

and piano and recorder were played by the incredibly versatile Ronson (who probably had more to do with the production than Bowie did). Backing vocals were by Bowie, Ronson, and some unnamed girl singers credited simply as the "Thunder Thighs". Flowers' most notable contribution was the double bass tracking (upright and electric) that was the making of 'Walk On The Wild Side' (for which he received double the session fee).

This time around Reed had a much better selection of material, including at least three absolute classic songs: 'Perfect Day', 'Walk On The Wild Side' and 'Satellite Of Love'. True, the latter was another Velvets leftover (as was 'Andy's Chest'), but nobody knew that at the time – and for once these were actually better than the Velvets' versions, thanks to Ronson's arrangements. In addition, Reed had a clutch of songs he'd written in 1971 for a musical based (very loosely) on Nelson Algren's 1956 novel *A Walk On The Wild Side*, which was to have been produced by Andy Warhol and fashion designer Yves St. Laurent but which never got off the ground. These definitely included 'Vicious', 'Walk On The Wild Side', 'Make Up' and 'New York Telephone Conversation', and possibly some of the others. The line about being "hit with a flower" in 'Vicious' is supposedly a direct quote from Warhol, made to Reed as they were strolling around New York discussing the show.

The whole album could be seen as a tribute to the Factory world. When the Algren project failed to get off the ground, Reed altered the lyrics to 'Walk On The Wild Side', changing the song's protagonists from Algren's characters into real people from Warhol's Factory: Holly (Woodlawn), Candy (Darling), 'Little' Joe (Dallesandro) and the Sugar Plum Fairy (possibly named Joseph Campbell, who was a drug-dealer and "hustler out of San Francisco", according to Reed). Candy Darling (real name James Slattery) had earlier been the protagonist of the song 'Candy Says' on the third Velvet Underground album. Speaking of Holly and Candy, Patti Smith commented: "They were the rag-tag queens of Max's Kansas City, and they've got very little in return for all of the groundbreaking things that they did, and to be heralded by someone like Lou was lovingly compassionate without being syrupy". As Nick Kent noted in the *NME*: "Any song that mentions oral sex, male prostitution, methedrine, valium ... and still gets Radio One airplay, must be truly cool".

The album's second standout track is 'Satellite Of Love', which (with slightly different lyrics), was first recorded by The Velvet Underground during the sessions for *Loaded* (and eventually released on *Peel Slowly And See*, see above). It is also the song closest in character to Bowie's own work. The song is partly about obsessional jealousy brought about by the painfully promiscuous infidelity of the singer's partner, and it's ironic that such a beautiful song (especially as arranged by Mick Ronson) is – if you listen to the words – actually pretty depressing. (This sense of lyrical/musical irony is almost a Lou Reed trademark). "I'm just glad the melody was pretty", commented Reed. The song got a new lease of life in 2004, when a remixed version became a minor hit.

The album's third masterpiece is 'Perfect Day', a gentle love song, beautifully enhanced by Mick Ronson's piano and string arrangement. The relationship here would seem to be that of an illicit affair – almost certainly Shelley Albin – since all the lovers can have are stolen moments, like one "perfect day". As a measure of its timelessness, the song acquired a new lease of life in the 1990s, firstly through its appearance on the soundtrack of the hit 1995 movie *Trainspotting*, and then again in 1997 when an all-star cover version was produced to raise money for the BBC's Children in Need charity.

The subject matter of most of the album – drugs, bisexuality and homosexuality, bitchiness and transvestism – was very much in tune with the glam-rock "divinely decadent" times, and with Bowie's audience, a lot of whom undoubtedly picked up on the album and helped make it a hit. The fact that there were several openly gay songs undoubtedly resonated with the gay community as well; Reed said of 'Make Up' that he'd wanted to write a song which made being gay sound "terrific, something that you'd enjoy". Underlining the sexual ambiguity, the album's back cover photograph featured Lou's tour manager Ernie Thormahlen dolled up in drag (and also in 'straight' guise, with a banana stuck down his trousers). Despite the fact that Ernie looked nothing like Reed, rumours persisted that this was Reed himself. The front cover featured Reed wearing eyeliner and ultra-white make-up, to accentuate his "pale New Yorker" image.

Back sleeve of *Transformer* with Ernie Thormahlen playing both roles, with banana (again)

Amazingly, the album spawned both radio airplay and hit singles. In the US, the Candy Darling verse was cut from the single version of 'Walk On The Wild Side'; in the UK it went out uncensored, since British DJs apparently had no idea what "giving head" meant. Some US stations also bleeped out the references to "coloured girls" and "valium". Extraordinarily, though sales for *Transformer* would be staggeringly good, the record received quite a few bad reviews when it was released – possibly on account of the controversial subject matter. But despite its low spots it remains an extremely impressive pop record, and one which has stood the test of time far better than, say, *Ziggy Stardust*. Later CD versions also include acoustic demos of 'Hangin' Round' and 'Perfect Day', both of which are pretty unremarkable.

BERLIN

RCA; recorded June 1973; released July 1973; available on CD.

BERLIN/LADY DAY/MEN OF GOOD FORTUNE/CAROLINE SAYS I/HOW DO YOU THINK IT FEELS/OH JIM/CAROLINE SAYS II/THE KIDS/THE BED/SAD SONG

A Brechtian operetta about two junkies that includes scenes of domestic violence – and the woman losing custody of her children because of her promiscuity and/or activities as a prostitute – and ends with one of the pair committing suicide was never going to qualify as easy listening. In the wake of an album as determinedly commercial as *Transformer*, it came as a hell of a shock, and so Reed's most ambitious project to date inevitably alienated many of his listeners and critics. The late Lester Bangs dismissed it as "a gargantuan slab of maggotty rancour that may well be the most depressed album ever made". Reed himself called it "an album for adults".

Berlin was recorded at London's Morgan studios (with later sessions taking place at New

York's Record Plant). Orchestral arrangements were by producer Bob Ezrin (aided by Allan Macmillan), and the session musicians were a fairly stellar cast: Steve Winwood on organ and harmonium, Jack Bruce on bass, Aynsley Dunbar on drums (except for 'Lady Day' and 'The Kids', where B.J. Wilson – of Procul Harum – was the drummer), plus session guitarists Richard Wagner and Steve Hunter (both of whom had worked with Ezrin on Alice Cooper sessions). Reed later said that Jack Bruce wasn't supposed to play on the whole thing, but stayed on because he was enjoying himself so much. He also noted that Bruce was the only musician he worked with in the early years of his solo career who actually bothered to read the lyrics, in order to play more empathically. Bruce had replaced an unnamed bass player who didn't work out and some of whose parts were later overdubbed in New York by Tony Levin (on 'The Kids') and Eugene Martynec (on 'Lady Day'). Lou's vocals were also later overdubbed in New York (at the Record Plant). Michael Brecker played tenor sax; Randy Brecker played trumpet; Jon Pierson played bass trombone; Bob Ezrin played mellotron and piano (Allan Macmillan played piano on 'Berlin'; Blue Weaver played piano on 'Men Of Good Fortune'). Backing vocals were by Reed, Ezrin, Dennis Ferrante, Steve Flyden, Elizabeth March and Richard Wagner.

Once again, several songs here were re-recordings of Velvets' material: 'Oh Jim' (originally 'Oh Gin'), 'Caroline Says II' (albeit in a drastically different form, as 'Stephanie Says'), 'Men Of Good Fortune' and 'Sad Song' (supposedly recorded as a Velvets demo). The title track is a fragmentary reprise – dramatically reworked – of the song from Reed's first solo album (it's unknown whether the brevity is intentional, or just one of the edits Ezrin was forced to make). Apparently Reed had hated the way the song was arranged first time around.

A memorable, if recessive, sleeve by Pacific Eye & Ear

Towards the end of the song 'The Kids' one can clearly hear – for over a minute – the sound of children crying in the background. Unsatisfied by tapes available from sound archives, Ezrin supposedly went home and kidnapped his own young children. Informing them their mother had left them, he then locked the by now hysterical children in a cupboard (where a tape recorder had been set up) leaving them to howl their eyes out in the dark. "Even I thought that was going too far", said Reed. "But that's how fucked-up we got on that record". Ezrin later maintained that the anecdote was exaggerated. He'd told his seven-year-old son David that he was doing a play and needed voices of children who sounded scared because their mother was being taken away. The first two takes didn't really work, but on the third Ezrin's two-year-old joined in by screaming; both children screamed so loud that they distorted the tape. Ezrin compressed the recording in the studio, and "the more compressed it got, the more anguished it seemed. Most people can't listen to it". Ezrin claims that the crying heard underneath was simply a pre-bedtime tantrum he'd recorded at home one night, but the compression on it "makes it so unbelievably emotional people accused me of beating my kids".

Berlin is an extremely odd mixture. Some songs (like 'The Kids') sound ponderous and Germanic, while others (like 'Caroline Says I') were so poppy that they could almost have fitted on *Transformer*, despite the unorthodox instrumentation – and 'Sad Song' sounds like something from a Disney movie (except for the lyrics).

Lyrically, it's impossible not to see echoes of the lives of both Nico and Daryl (whose kids were taken into care) here, as well as of Reed's collapsing marriage to Bettye and his own drug experiences.

As a whole, the record is undeniably depressing, but that doesn't make it bad. It's certainly ambitious, and a large chunk of it is very good indeed ... but you probably wouldn't play it that often. Still, the fact that it *is* so powerful is surely a sign of its worth, and it's strange that a restoration of the work at its complete length has yet to appear – if the master tapes still exist, they should surely be worthy of release. At any rate, a recording of the 2006 theatrical version is fairly inevitable. On a purely musical level, *Berlin* is largely superb: while still recognisably rock music, it draws on every other musical strand, from folk to musicals, and blends them into something very interesting indeed. And its influence on popular music has been huge. Four years after *Berlin* was released, David Bowie would set his epic romance 'Heroes' in the shadow of the Berlin Wall.

ROCK 'N' ROLL ANIMAL

RCA; recorded 1973; released February 1974; available on CD.

SWEET JANE/HEROIN/WHITE LIGHT, WHITE HEAT/LADY DAY/ ROCK 'N' ROLL

Reed's touring band in the Autumn of 1973 had been put together by Bob Ezrin, and consisted of guitarists Steve Hunter and Dick Wagner from the *Berlin* sessions, plus Ray Colcord on keyboards, Prakash John on bass and drummer Pentti Glan (from The Black Stone Rangers, a group that included Reed's future sideman Michael Fonfara).

The sleeve reflected the somewhat perplexing Reed stage image of the early 1970s. As did the title...

Both sets from the last night of the tour – 21 December 1973, at New York's Academy of Music – were recorded using a Record Plant mobile studio, and this live album was released six weeks later. It was co-produced by Reed and Steve Katz (brother of Dennis and once the guitarist for Blood Sweat And Tears).

As can be seen from the tracklisting, Reed's solo work barely got a nod here – this was a celebration of his years with The Velvet Underground, reworked as heavy rock, or "heresy of sorts", in the words of critic Nick Kent. Many of Reed's audience may well have been unaware of his prior incarnation, and he admitted he wanted them "to know exactly what preceded 'Walk On The Wild Side'". Sadly, the music is … pretty pedestrian to modern ears. It's not that it's bad, particularly – though plodding and uninspired – it's just that these versions of the songs are nowhere near as good as the Velvets' originals (or even the Velvets' live versions). Reed himself would later dismiss the album as crass and commercial: "It was like a walking time-warp to me … but I had to get popular".

SALLY CAN'T DANCE

RCA; recorded June 1974; released September 1974; available on CD.

RIDE SALLY RIDE/ANIMAL LANGUAGE/BABY FACE/N.Y. STARS/ KILL YOUR SONS/ENNUI/SALLY CAN'T DANCE/BILLY

Ironically, this record – since disowned by both Reed and producer Steve Katz (who called it "a rotten album") – was incredibly successful. Personnel included Danny Weiss on guitar, Prakash John on bass, Michael Fonfara

...and sleeve designs like this don't sell

on keyboards, Richard Dharma and Pentti Glan on drums, Michael Wendroff and Joanna Vent on backing vocals, and an uncredited brass section. Weiss and Fonfara had both previously been in The Black Stone Rangers with Glan. Additionally (and amazingly, given the bad blood that had existed between them), Reed had also dragged his former Velvet Underground colleague Doug Yule out of retirement to play bass on the song 'Billy'. Yule would also join Reed's band for the 1975 European tour.

The results are pretty awful. Steve Katz stated that he'd "take all the blame for this album", and the ball does seem to be in his court. The arrangements are overblown, making it sound like an attempt to recreate *Transformer*, but without the songs, the taste or the commitment from Reed – or a producer/arranger with the talent of David Bowie or Mick Ronson, for that matter.

As to the songs: 'Animal Language' was originally titled 'Mrs O'Riley's Dog', and was possibly influenced by Hubert Selby Jr.'s novel *The Room*, known to be one of Reed's favourites (though once again, it's hard to see how). Lyrically at least, 'Kill Your Sons' supposedly dates back to the days of the Velvets (some think it even pre-dates them). Reed has stated that it's about the electroshock therapy he'd been subjected to at age 17, for which he blamed his father. The title track would seem to be about Edie Sedgwick, who did indeed "ball folksingers" (Bob Dylan, to be specific), though Reed has subsequently said that it was inspired by a murder on the Lower East Side – the reason Sally can't dance is because she's dead, her body now in the trunk of her killers' car. 'Billy' is supposedly the story of one of

Reed's contemporaries at college, who'd been a star student while Reed had been a drop-out. 'Billy' had gone to serve in Vietnam, while Reed had been exempted from the draft, and had returned as a shadow of his former self. 'Billy' is probably the best thing on this album, but it's still not that great. The overall result veers from the saccharine to the raucous, to no real purpose, and Reed often sounds mannered to a point beyond self-parody. For completists only.

LOU REED LIVE

RCA; recorded December 1973; released March 1975; available on CD.

VICIOUS/SATELLITE OF LOVE/WALK ON THE WILD SIDE/I'M WAITING FOR THE MAN/OH JIM/SAD SONG

Released to capitalize on the success of *Sally*, this is the second live album to be taken from the tapes record-ed at New York's Academy of Music in December 1973. (Only two songs from the concert remain unreleased – Reed was

Into shades again, plus bohemian headwear and leathers

unhappy with his vocals on 'Caroline Says' and 'How Do You Think It Feels'). This time the material is drawn more from Reed's solo work than the Velvets' back pages, but other-wise it's of the same standard as *Rock 'N' Roll Animal*, displaying a heavy-handed heavy-rock approach to the material ... and the fact that it's the "second-best" scoop from these tapes

speaks for itself. Uncharacteristically, Reed left the production duties for *Lou Reed Live* entirely to Steve Katz.

METAL MACHINE MUSIC

RCA; recorded Spring 1975; released July 1975; available on CD.

Lou Reed once claimed that this album was not only his revenge on his record company, but also his revenge on his audience – or at any rate, the ones who yelled out requests at concerts. Subtitled "An Electronic

It was always going to be difficult to convey the contents of this album

Instrumental Composition", *Metal Machine Music* was originally released as a double-album, comprising 'Metal Machine Music Parts 1–4', one part per vinyl side, each side exactly 16:01 minutes in length. Reed had bounced tapes of guitar feedback between two recorders, treating them electronically and varying the tape speeds en route. It sounded like all his rage against the music industry unleashed at full volume, but he described it as "Combinations and Permutations built upon constant harmonic Density Increase and Melodic Distractions".

The novelist Neil Gaiman once stated that when he was writing a sequence for his fantasy comic *Sandman* that was set in Hell, he'd lis-tened to *Metal Machine Music* to conjure up

the necessary atmosphere. It's easy to understand why. The record is a strange mixture of cacophony and harmony, in which you seem to hear echoes of a thousand other things: birdsong and whalesong and traffic noise, and what sound like familiar tunes going by so fast that you can never pin them down. It's an assault on the senses on a par with spending hours under a dentist's drill, yet buried deep within it are a few moments of absolutely dazzling beauty. Anyone who's sat all the way through it feels a real sense of achievement … and also never wants to hear the damn thing ever again. Reed claims that the balance on the CD version is off, and that it is not an accurate reproduction of the record: "It's like the Mona Lisa missing a nose or something".

CONEY ISLAND BABY

RCA; recorded October 1975; released December 1975.

CRAZY FEELING/CHARLEY'S GIRL/SHE'S MY BEST FRIEND/ KICKS/A GIFT/OOOHHH BABY/NOBODY'S BUSINESS/CONEY ISLAND BABY

Reed had closed the sleeve notes to *Metal Machine Music* with the boast: "My week beats your year". But he'd had a particularly bad year himself, and this album was put together in the middle of extreme legal and financial problems. It was recorded at New York's Media Sound studios with the Down-Trodden Three: Bob Kulick on guitar, Bruce Yaw on bass and Michael Suchorsky on drums. Steve Katz returned (briefly) as Reed's co-producer, before being replaced by engineer Godfrey Diamond. Backing vocals were

by Reed, Diamond, Michael Wendroff and Joanne Vent.

Throughout, the band's playing is intelligent and sympathetic, rather than *Sally*'s parade of rock clichés – and Lou's vocals sound a lot more sincere. For all

Androgyny and theatrics; also how many different signatures has he got?

of the talk about Reed's drug intake at the time, it doesn't seem to be affecting his game in terms of performance. As to the material, some of it is lacklustre and pointless ('Ooohhh Baby'), some of it is just enjoyably dumb pop ('Charley's Girl' and 'Crazy Feeling'), some of it ('A Gift') is genuinely funny. As a collection it's competent rather than inspired, but at least Lou sounds like he's having fun. The album's worst fault – that of songs that aimlessly meander on forever – is simply par for the course in the pre-punk '70s. 'Kicks' is a prime example of that – a jazzy rap that aims to take you inside the mind of a switchblade-wielding killer. "At the time I was hanging around the criminally-inclined, put it that way", Reed commented in 1990.

But most of the songs here seem inspired by Reed's relationship with his new transsexual lover Rachel. 'She's My Best Friend' was an old Velvets number, but this is one of the few occasions when Reed's re-make almost lives up to the original: the Velvets' version was dumb beat-pop, while this is slower, bluesier, and more self-consciously epic. While in the Velvets, Reed had written a song titled 'Coney Island Steeplechase', so he was obviously fond of New York's old amusement park (which was well past its prime by the time of Reed's childhood). Victor Bockris claims that an early draft of 'Coney Island Baby' even pre-dates the Velvets, and was originally about Reed's college girlfriend Shelley Albin ... but Rachel seems a much more believable inspiration, especially given the song's closing declaration of love. A smoky blues with jazz overtones, the song also bears witness to Reed's long-time love of close-harmony doo-wop. 'Coney Island Baby' was also the title of an obscure 1962 doo-wop song by The Excellents, while the "glory of love" chorus is a tip of the hat to the 1951 song of that name by The Five Keys (or The Harptones, depending which source you believe). Sadly, the song is nowhere near as good as most classic doo-wop.

Even so, the album as a whole is a revelation; at this point in his career, hardly anybody expected Lou Reed to come up with anything this good. Though the actual material is nowhere near as commercial, this is still easily his most accessible album since *Transformer*. A remastered 2006 reissue of the CD overseen by Reed contained six extra tracks from 1975: 'Nowhere At All', 'Downtown Dirt' and 'Leave Me Alone' (all of which had previously appeared on the *Between Thought And Expression* boxed set), plus demos of 'Crazy Feeling', 'She's My Best Friend' and 'Coney Island Baby'. The demos all feature Doug Yule

on guitar, but are really of interest only as sketches of work-in-progress.

ROCK AND ROLL HEART

Arista; recorded Summer 1976; released October 1976; available on CD.

I BELIEVE IN LOVE/BANGING ON MY DRUM/FOLLOW THE LEADER/YOU WEAR IT SO WELL/LADIES PAY/ROCK AND ROLL HEART/CHOOSER AND THE CHOSEN ONE/SENSELESSLY CRUEL/CLAIM TO FAME/VICIOUS CIRCLE/A SHELTERED LIFE/ TEMPORARY THING

Recorded in New York, the musicians included Michael Fonfara on keyboards, Bruce Yaw on bass, Michael Suchorsky on drums and Marty Fogel on saxophone. The majority of the songs were written in the studio, and it

Looking younger than his years, the photo had a blue-TV screen blur to help the effect

shows. *Rock And Roll Heart* was a giant leap backwards. Lou sounds mannered throughout, the lyrics are minimal and substandard and the music is a mixture of blandly jazzy lounge music and nonsensical rock thrash.

'A Sheltered Life' dates back to the Velvets (a demo exists, from 1967). Here it's given a jazzy arrangement that makes it sound like Tom Waits on a very bad day.

'Temporary Thing', a mock-epic rock dirge about the end of a relationship, is bleak and pompous, taking over five minutes to go precisely nowhere. By the time it's over, you want to kill the drummer. The title track is a bouncy, joyously dumb celebration of rock 'n' roll – but it's way too dumb, and thus a real let-down. Clive Davis of Arista wanted to add strings to it, in the belief that with a little more work the song could be a hit single, but Reed refused. 'Ladies Pay' isn't bad – an atmospheric rock ballad about women generally not having an easy time of it in this world. The Velvets-style guitar-part aside, it sounds a bit like the Dylan or Springsteen of this era. Still, it's so depressing that it could have fitted comfortably onto *Berlin*.

'Vicious Circle' is also almost okay – a lyrically minimal and bitter ode to paranoia, with a folky approach. Supposedly Reed had been sent a poem with this title by a British fan, who was subsequently amazed to discover his hero using both the title and the theme for a new song. Originally titled *Nomad*, the album was supposed to have a cover by Andy Warhol, but that fell through. When released, reviewers largely thought it dull and lacklustre (which it is), and sales weren't that great – not surprisingly, since it's one of Reed's most inarticulate records, perhaps indicating that drugs were once again taking their toll.

STREET HASSLE

Arista; recorded Summer/Autumn 1977; released February 1978; available on CD.

GIMMIE SOME GOOD TIMES/DIRT/STREET HASSLE (A) WALTZING MATILDA (B) STREET HASSLE (C) SLIPAWAY/I WANNA BE BLACK/REAL GOOD TIME TOGETHER/SHOOTING STAR/LEAVE ME ALONE/WAIT

Sweat, shades plus shine presumably equals streetsmarts?

Some of *Street Hassle* was recorded live, during dates on Lou's 1977 European tour (at Munich, Wiesbaden and Ludwigshafen in Germany). The rest was recorded that Autumn at New York's Record Plant studios. Co-produced by Reed and Richard Robinson (though Robinson left before the album was completed), musicians included Stuart Heinrich on guitar, Marty Fogel on saxophone and Michael Suchorsky on drums. Michael Fonfara played keyboards on 'I Wanna Be Black'. The album was mixed in the new binaural system that had claimed Lou as a disciple.

Street Hassle is a real mixture, and although a vast improvement on *Rock And Roll Heart*, still contains a heavy proportion of turkeys. Several of the songs dated back to *Coney Island Baby*, when they'd been rejected as substandard – and they hadn't improved with time. But 'Gimmie Some Good Times' is strangely likeable, and quite funny. 'Dirt' is an incredibly slow and vitriolic blues – there's real hate here, and a rambling reference to Bobby Fuller's 'I Fought The Law' seems to imply a legal battle being part of the background to all this venom. Reed later confirmed that the song was aimed at his former manager, described here as "a pig of a person" and "uptown dirt". This was probably valuable as therapy, but the rest of us really didn't need to hear it.

The title track is divided into three sections: 'Waltzing Matilda,' 'Street Hassle' and 'Slipaway'. The middle section at least is several years old – Reed had wanted to record it for *Coney Island Baby*. Reed later claimed that after Arista boss Clive Davis heard the original two-minute version of the song, he told Reed to make it longer. The hypnotic cello riff – echoed on the bass – conjures up memories of Reed's partnership with John Cale. Reed plays the piano, with a guest vocal from Genya Ravan. The first section is about sex with a male prostitute (and is not even remotely connected to the Australian song of the same name); the second section is about a drug-related death. According to Reed, he'd loosely based this on the drug overdose death of Factory associate Eric Emerson, changing only his gender. For the track's last section, Reed drafted a 'neighbour' in for a cameo vocal: Bruce Springsteen, who'd been mixing tracks in the studio below Reed. Reed said Springsteen was "really fabulous. He did the part so well that I had to bury him in the mix". Two years earlier, Reed had publicly described Springsteen to *Punk* magazine as "a shit" and "a has-been". Lyrically, Springsteen's cameo tips its hat to his own song 'Born To Run'.

Although the track is way too long, and definitely flawed, it's still interesting and mesmeric. It's also head and shoulders above everything else here.

"He wants to be black", Nico had once said of Lou, and now he turned it into a boast, but claimed: "Nobody could possibly take 'I Wanna Be Black' seriously". At one point this was going to be the album title as well. It's a mediocre R&B shuffle with girlie backing singers, as Lou extols all the reasons he wishes he was black. It's in seriously bad taste, and would be downright racist if you didn't suspect Reed was doing it just to upset people. 'Real Good Time Together' is a limply mannered version of the Velvets song (from the "lost" album). The album's last track, 'Wait', is a tribute to early Sixties pop harmony groups and quotes both The Shirelles' 'Met Him On A Sunday' and Jan & Dean's 'New Kid In School', while singing the praises of virginity. It's not that great (and gets messy in the middle), but at least it has a sense of fun. The album still maintains Reed's tendency to sink into a quagmire of messy jazz, but at least he seemed to be trying to improve.

LIVE: TAKE NO PRISONERS

RCA; recorded Spring 1978; released November 1978; available on CD.

SWEET JANE/I WANNA BE BLACK/SATELLITE OF LOVE/PALE BLUE EYES/BERLIN/I'M WAITING FOR MY MAN (SIC)/CONEY ISLAND BABY/STREET HASSLE/WALK ON THE WILD SIDE/ LEAVE ME ALONE

Personnel: Lou Reed (guitar, Roland guitar synthesizer and vocals); Mart Fogel (electric saxophone); Michael Fonfara (Yamaha electric piano); Stuart Heinrich (guitar and vocals); Ellard 'Moose' Boles (bass and vocals); Michael Suchorsky (drums); Angela Howell (vocals and tambourine); Chrissy Faith (vocals).

This live double-album was recorded at New York's Bottom Line in the Spring of 1978 on the Record Plant's mobile, and mixed at Manfred

Down and dirty on the mean streets. Rubbish

Schünke's Delta studio in Wilster, Germany, for binaural sound. Reed took the sole production credit. A contractual dispute with Reed's old label RCA resulted in them being given this album to release instead of Arista. Lou had heard the title as a phrase shouted from the audience, and fell in love with it: "It couldn't have been more appropriate. Don't take us prisoners, beat us to death, shoot us, maim us, kill us, but don't settle for less, go all the way. That's what I took it to mean".

And he took the maxim to heart. The set comprises jazzy extended versions that veer from the great ('Satellite Of Love' and 'Coney Island Baby') to the lacklustre ('Street Hassle') to the bombastic ('Berlin' and 'Leave Me Alone') to stuff so ramshackle that it makes you want to hurl bricks at the stage ('I'm Waiting For My Man'). But the music itself is almost irrelevant here – what lingers in the memory afterwards are Reed's improvised and extended 'lyrics', which are virtually a stand-up comedy routine that takes swipes at a wide variety of targets: Barbra Streisand, Patti Smith, Candy Darling, Joe Dallesandro, rock 'n' roll audiences, black people, Jews, Catholics, lesbians, rock critics John Rockwell and Robert Christgau, Jane Fonda, Norman Mailer, politics in general, and – of course – the audience itself. Amusing

as some of it is, you don't want to hear it more than once. Reed himself later admitted that as a songwriter he'd "run out of inspiration" at this point. It should also be pointed out that the album also has one of the worst album sleeves in history.

THE BELLS

Arista; released April 1979; available on CD.

STUPID MAN/DISCO MYSTIC/I WANT TO BOOGIE WITH YOU/ WITH YOU/LOOKING FOR LOVE/CITY LIGHTS/ALL THROUGH THE NIGHT/FAMILIES/THE BELLS

It says it all: Lou with mirror

Recorded at Manfred Schünke's Delta studio in Wilster, Germany, the album was produced by Reed, who played electric guitar and guitar synthesizer (one of the first times this instrument had been used on a record); Michael Fonfara played keyboards; Marty Fogel played saxophone, ocarina and Fender Rhodes (on the title track); Ellard Boles played bass (and electric 12-string on 'Families', which had Reed playing bass synthesizer); Michael Suchorsky played drums. Don Cherry (a former Ornette Coleman sideman, and the father of Neneh) played trumpet and African hunting guitar.

This record was also the first time in a decade that Reed had co-written: three songs here were written with Nils Lofgren (another three would surface on Lofgren's album

Nils), five more were written with various members of the band. The album continues Reed's dalliance with jazz – much of it ponderously meandering and instantly forgettable. Several songs actually sound like incidental music for a bad 1970s TV show. 'I Want To Boogie With You', co-written with Michael Fonfara, isn't bad – a slow, simple R&B love song. Reed had supposedly been enormously impressed by *Born To Be With You*, the album Phil Spector had produced for Dion in 1977, and had deliberately set out to recreate that sound here. 'City Lights', co-written with Nils Lofgren, is also okay – a strong, romantic little ballad about Charlie Chaplin's banishment from America, which takes its title from one of his most famous movies. (Lou is evidently a big Chaplin fan – the Velvets had named one of their songs after another Chaplin film, *Countess From Hong Kong*). This would have been better without the trumpet part, which sounds messy and bizarre.

'All Through The Night', co-written with Don Cherry, is a tuneful ode to nothing much at all, overlaid with studio chatter. A minor work, but quite enjoyable.

'Families', co-written with Ellard Boles, is an uncharacteristically rosy and nostalgic view of family life from Lou; there are certainly autobiographical elements, but Reed describes the family dynamics with sadness, instead of his usual venom. Lou later wrote that he'd never use words like "papa" in real life, so perhaps this should be regarded as fiction. The title track is an atmospheric and jazzy performance piece, co-written with Marty Fogel. Supposedly inspired by the Edgar Allan Poe poem of the same name (though apart from the title they would seem to have nothing in common), and by Ornette Coleman's 'Lonely Woman' (there's arty), it clocks in at over nine minutes in length and ends with the sound of a 15-foot gong Lou had rented for the occasion. Reed had no lyrics prepared; undaunted, he just stepped up to the microphone and improvised the entire thing. Most of it is recited (and inaudible), until he starts singing ("The vocal came to me as I sang, and each year since I wonder at its meaning").

According to Reed the song is about a suicide, a man who's "on the edge of the building, and he looks out and thinks that he sees a brook, and he says, 'There are the bells'. And as he points, he tumbles over a drum roll. It's beautiful". Reed loved the song so much, he chose it to conclude *Between Thought And Expression*, his first published collection of lyrics. As he wrote in 1991: "We had a beautiful instrumental track with no lyric. On mike I found myself singing this lyric. Unchanged it remains my favourite to this day". The album still stays true to Reed's career path during the drug years – a step forward, a step back again. The good tracks aren't all that great, and saying that it manages to stay in the same place as *Street Hassle* would be a mite too generous.

GROWING UP IN PUBLIC

Arista; recorded January 1980; released April 1980; available on CD.

HOW DO YOU SPEAK TO AN ANGEL/MY OLD MAN/KEEP AWAY/GROWING UP IN PUBLIC/STANDING ON CEREMONY/SO ALONE/LOVE IS HERE TO STAY/THE POWER OF POSITIVE DRINKING/SMILES/THINK IT OVER/TEACH THE GIFTED CHILDREN

He's on the front again, but looking sober and serious

Recorded at George Martin's Air studios on the island of Montserrat, the sessions were completed in three weeks flat, and all Reed's vocals were done in one take (an economic decision, rather than an artistic one). Musicians included Stuart Heinrich and Chuck Hammer on guitar, Michael Fonfara on keyboards and guitar, Ellard Boles on bass and Michael Suchorsky on drums. Reed played no guitar at all. Fonfara co-produced the album with Reed, and also co-wrote all the songs with him. Technical difficulties caused Reed to reluctantly and finally give up on binaural sound with this record.

Several songs dealt with family, though Lou declared that they weren't autobiographical – but on another occasion admitted that 'My Old Man' was actually written for his father. Despite this, he claimed that his parents "both like the album".

Several songs here have a confessional feel to them, and several more concern new girlfriend Sylvia Morales, soon to become his second wife and later also his manager. Reed's love songs to her are among the most naked he'd ever written, and 'Think It Over' is virtually a marriage proposal. 'So Alone' is a really good song about an awkward courtship. Driven by bass and piano, it touches on the confusion that arose when sex roles began to change, post-feminism, and is easily the best thing Reed had done in years.

'The Power Of Positive Drinking' is a joyous, reggae-tinged ode to the pleasures of booze, "written by two people who enjoy drinking" (i.e. Reed and Fonfara). Reed not only enjoyed it, he was almost evangelical about it. In 1978 there'd also been a country song with the same title by Mickey Gilley, but it's entirely possible that Reed was totally unaware of this, and that both writers were simply making the same pun on the title of Norman Vincent Peale's 1952 self-help bestseller *The Power Of Positive Thinking*.

'Teach The Gifted Children' is a slow gospel-blues reminiscent of Al Green's 'Take Me To The River' (a song which it actually quotes), about what education ought to be like. Reed's note in his selected lyrics dwells on how much he hated his own schooling. The song came about late at night in a hotel room, when Fonfara was tinkering around with the tune on an acoustic guitar, and Reed improvised the lyric in its entirety. The album showed strong signs that Lou was slowly making his way out of the grave. His vocals were less mannered, his lyrics more articulate than they'd been in years

219

– often downright funny (as in the title track), and often also genuinely touching. Though the music itself remained at times messily jazzy, it was less so than on the previous three albums – and had stronger tunes. There were clear signs that Lou's life was not only changing but improving – but no one could guess at this point just how far-reaching and radical those changes would be.

THE BLUE MASK

RCA; recorded October/November 1981; released February 1982; available on CD.

MY HOUSE/WOMEN/UNDERNEATH THE BOTTLE/THE GUN/ THE BLUE MASK/AVERAGE GUY/THE HEROINE/WAVES OF FEAR/THE DAY JOHN KENNEDY DIED/HEAVENLY ARMS

Personnel: Lou Reed (vocals and guitar); Robert Quine (guitar); Fernando Saunders (bass and backing vocals); Doane Perry (drums).

Recorded at RCA's New York studio, with Sean Fullan as engineer. Fullan was given a credit as Reed's co-producer. According to Reed, he gained the credit simply "to try to get him not to fuck around with the shit". Lou later proudly

Recycling Mick Rock from the transformer shoot, in blue. Original

announced that there were no overdubs on *The Blue Mask*. Robert Quine insists that even the vocals were live (though these may only have been guide vocals): "That's what's really cool about that record. People are really intensely listening to each other, trying to cross barriers; they did that magical jazz thing. Something special is happening and you can hear it on the record. It still amazes me".

Lyrically, Reed was more thoughtful and intelligent than he'd been in a decade – doubtless connected to the fact that he was now clean and sober. The bluesy ballad 'My House' was dedicated to Delmore Schwartz, and details Reed's belief that the ghost of Schwartz was haunting his New Jersey house, after the poet had seemingly contacted Lou and Sylvia via a Ouija board. Regardless, there's beauty, humour and a real sense of contentment here. In 'Underneath The Bottle' Lou recalls his (mis)adventures with booze – powerful lyrics but, sadly, the tune lets them down. 'The Gun' is a painful, slow tale of gun law in the hands of a psycho. Though it seems to detail an armed mugging, Reed disavowed any autobiographical ingredients; he also described the song's armed protagonist as "none of me" – as well he might, for his performance as the character sends a chill to the spine. An even more extreme version of the song was recorded but abandoned.

The title track is a tortuous, frenetic tale of sex (including incest), pain and punishment, S&M; Lou has since described the song as a "self-portrait". Howling guitar and a driving bass make it very powerful, but not particularly easy listening.

'The Heroine' is a song of yearning for an idealized love. It's slow and turgid, and generally just doesn't work. The recording is Reed's original solo demo (deemed to be better than the version the full band recorded). 'Waves Of Fear' is great and really strident despite its oppressive subject (which would appear to be the mental and physical pain of drug withdrawal). 'The Day John Kennedy Died' is a mixture of reportage and idealism: Reed recalling hearing the news of the assassination when he was a college student, and juxtaposed this with an idyllic reverie about just how much also died with Camelot that day. Slow, but evocative and compelling.

'Heavenly Arms' is a touching song of love for Sylvia, that conjures echoes of 'Satellite Of Love.' It's slight, and dumb, and could easily have been mawkish … but it works.

Hailed at the time as showing a real return to form, *The Blue Mask* now seems more like a transitional work; nevertheless, not since John Lennon's first solo album had therapy provided the spur for such interesting rock music, and listening to Reed claw his way back from oblivion is utterly fascinating. The band is also truly great – Saunders' booming bass style is often reminiscent of the late Jaco Pastorius, and Robert Quine's guitar is delicate and tasteful throughout. The guitar on the left-hand channel is Robert Quine, the one on the right is Reed.

LEGENDARY HEARTS

RCA; recorded late 1982; released May 1983; available on CD.

LEGENDARY HEARTS/DON'T TALK TO ME ABOUT WORK/ MAKE UP MY MIND/MARTIAL LAW/THE LAST SHOT/TURN OUT THE LIGHT/POW WOW/BETRAYED/BOTTOMING OUT/ HOME OF THE BRAVE/ROOFTOP GARDEN

Recorded at RCA's New York studios. The musicians were once again Robert Quine on guitar and Fernando Saunders on bass, but this time Fred Maher replaced Doane Perry on drums.

A not very collectable rarity: Reed's not on the front sleeve (but what is?)

The album was dedicated "to Sylvia". It's a patchy work, though it certainly has its moments. The title track is a wonderful pop-rocker about "legendary love", contrasting romantic ideals with human frailty. The band (especially Saunders) is on top form here. 'The Last Shot' is a powerful and honest song about quitting alcohol and drugs, admitting just how hard it is. 'Turn Out The Light' is an enjoyably gentle blues-folk stomp about the joys of soft lighting and a nocturnal lifestyle. 'Pow Wow' is dumb but fun: a potted history of the centuries-long plight of the Native American, performed as a lightweight pop song (Lou announces he wants to dance with them!). 'Home Of The Brave' is a slow and brooding ballad about loneliness and alienation in the modern world; despite its intensity, it's really quite beautiful. One of the characters in the song is clearly Reed's old college room-mate Lincoln Swados. The song concludes by quoting from Arthur Alexander's Sixties soul hit 'Every Day I Have To Cry'. 'Rooftop Garden' is acoustic folk-rock (with wonderful bass), about having your own romantic private world upstairs. Lyrically, it tips a hat to The Drifters' 'Up On The Roof' (which was co-written by Doc Pomus, whom Reed would later befriend). Otherwise, the proceedings meander a lot, but at least do so prettily; however, in some cases, like 'Bottoming Out', the tunes just don't live up to the lyrics. As a whole, *Legendary Hearts* is simply average, and that's being kind.

LIVE IN ITALY

RCA; recorded September 1983; released January 1984; available on CD.

SWEET JANE/I'M WAITING FOR MY MAN/MARTIAL LAW/ SATELLITE OF LOVE/KILL YOUR SONS/BETRAYED/SALLY CAN'T DANCE/WAVES OF FEAR/AVERAGE GUY/WHITE LIGHT WHITE HEAT/SOME KINDA LOVE/SISTER RAY/WALK ON THE WILD SIDE/HEROIN/ROCK & ROLL

Recorded at gigs at the Verona Arena and Rome's Circus Maximus, with the Quine/Maher/ Saunders line-up, this was originally released as a double album in Europe only.

Like the album inside, this sleeve does the business, but little more

Reed's fourth live album and – finally – a good one, due to the presence of a tight and *simpatico* band. Reed sounds confident and assured, and the playing throughout is first-rate. Though the set is heavily slanted towards the Velvets era, there are two tracks apiece from the previous two studio albums and – strangely – two tracks from the dire *Sally Can't Dance*, including the dreadful title song. But here 'Kill Your Sons' has an air of real sadness that transforms it into something far more touching (the same is true of 'Betrayed' here), and even 'Sally Can't Dance' is halfway bearable. Highlights include 'Satellite Of Love' (despite a sparse arrangement, it's truly beautiful), 'White Light' (performed with real joy) and 'Walk On The Wild Side' (with some wonderful basslines). Most of the tracks are too long, but the band is so good you don't really mind. Recommended.

At the Rome performance, the band had been teargassed, as Robert Quine explained: "We were playing Circus Maximus – an outdoor place. Apparently a crowd had gathered outside the fence before the concert, and the police dispersed them using teargas the moment before we came out. When we came on stage, the wind blew the tear gas directly on us. So during the first 45 minutes of the show I could not see a thing. I could not even see the little dots on the neck of my guitar. And there was snot running down my face and they were throwing wine bottles full of piss on the stage. People said we were really brave to stay on stage, but we had to. There would have been a riot. There were God knows how many of them. And it was a pretty emotional performance".

NEW SENSATIONS

RCA; recorded between December 1983 and February 1984; released April 1984; available on CD.

I LOVE YOU, SUZANNE/ENDLESSLY JEALOUS/MY RED JOYSTICK/TURN TO ME/NEW SENSATIONS/DOIN' THE THINGS THAT WE WANT TO/WHAT BECOMES A LEGEND MOST/FLY INTO THE SUN/MY FRIEND GEORGE/HIGH IN THE CITY/DOWN AT THE ARCADE

Recorded at Skyline studios in New York over two months – to date the longest period Lou had ever spent on recording an album. It was co-produced by Reed and engineer John Jansen, about whom Reed was uncharacteristically

More self-worship, maybe dressed up as parody, but he's still playing with himself

complimentary: "I think Jansen did an incredible job. His stereo spread is really awe-inspiring". Typically, Reed also stated the contrary, claiming that he'd had "a relationship with the engineer that was more involved than I would normally like to have".

Reed himself played all the guitars (having just fired Robert Quine), with a little assistance from Fernando Saunders, who played rhythm guitar on two tracks (in addition to also playing both string and electric bass); Fred Maher played drums; L. Shankar played electric violin; Peter Wood played piano, synthesizers and accordion. Backing vocalists were Jocelyn Brown, Fernando Saunders, Connie Harvey, Eric Troyer and Rory Dodd. Also featured was

a horn section that comprised Michael and Randy Brecker, Jon Faddis and Tom Malone (who also did the arrangements).

Throughout, Lou certainly seems to have rediscovered a joy in the guitar. The album kicks off with 'I Love You, Suzanne' – a great single, and deservedly a hit. It kicks off with a quote from 'Do You Love Me (Now That I Can Dance)' before launching into a bouncy and brilliantly dumb love song. The drums now sound a bit dated, but otherwise it's wonderful. 'My Red Joystick' would seem to be an ode to compulsive masturbation – the protagonist would rather deal with his "red joystick" than with women. As if to undermine all this double-entendre, the cover photograph proves Lou is actually referring to his home videogame controls. The tune is very reminiscent of Talking Heads, but marred by irritating backing vocals. 'Turn To Me' sees Reed turning in a passable Keith Richards impression on a bluesy – and very funny – statement of commitment.

The title track kicks off with an insistent soul beat, before turning to Lou's laconic list of things he'd like to do, be and have – which then turns into an account of an idyllic motorbike ride. The arrest Reed refers to is indeed autobiographical – he spent one Christmas in jail for trying to cash someone else's illegal drug prescription (he was subsequently defended by one of Richard Nixon's Watergate lawyers).

'Doin' The Things That We Want To' is more irresistible intelligent pop. "Sam's play" refers to Sam Shepard's *Fool For Love*, and this describes the impact the play had upon Reed.

Supposedly, the song prompted Shepard to enter the rock arena himself with 'Brownsville Girl,' a song he co-wrote with Bob Dylan (for 1986's *Knocked Out Loaded* album), which proved to be one of the few high spots of Dylan's career during the 1980s. By a neat piece of coincidence that closes the circle, Dylan saw Lou performing 'Doin' The Things That We Want To' live, and supposedly told Sylvia Reed afterwards that he wished he'd written it himself. Reed compares Shepard's play with the movies of Martin Scorsese, going on to name-check Travis Bickle (from *Taxi Driver*) and Johnny Boy (from *Mean Streets*), and ending with the assertion that he considers Shepard and Scorsese to be his peers. An oddity, but curiously compelling.

'What Becomes A Legend Most' features an electric violin that conjures up a "Velvets" atmosphere. It's a mock-epic ode to an ageing Nico-esque singer who's living an empty and loveless existence on the road. A totally over-the-top arrangement (including Beatles-style harmonies), but it works and is utterly wonderful – a sort of successor to the Velvets' 'New Age'. The title phrase was a highly successful advertising slogan for the furriers Blackglama during the 1950s. 'Fly Into The Sun' of course echoes the Velvets' 'Ride Into The Sun', and is so unusual – for Reed – that it makes you really sit up and pay attention. It's a joyously optimistic slab of pure mysticism, a hymn to life and love and God, delivered to an upbeat blues that's almost gospel. Great stuff.

'My Friend George' is an odd little number, but insistent and likeable, about friendship gone awry which Victor Bockris thinks is about Lincoln Swados … but though Swados was certainly (from all accounts) odd, there's no evidence to suggest that he was a murderer! 'High In The City' is a joyfully cynical song about survival in New York. Gently catchy pop with a tinge of reggae (and a steel drum), all of which contrasts sharply with the lyrics. 'Down At The Arcade' is a heavy-rock strut about being the reigning champion of the video-game arcade. Dumb but fun, with some genuinely amusing lyrics. In all, *New Sensations* was a vast improvement – easily Lou's most tuneful album since *Transformer*. Even the filler is way above average.

MISTRIAL

RCA; released April 1986; available on CD.

MISTRIAL/NO MONEY DOWN/OUTSIDE/DON'T HURT A WOMAN/VIDEO VIOLENCE/SPIT IT OUT/THE ORIGINAL WRAPPER/MAMA'S GOT A LOVER/I REMEMBER YOU/TELL IT TO YOUR HEART

Reed's final album for RCA marked the end of another era. For one thing, it would be his final collaboration with bassist Fernando Saunders, who co-produced this (though Saunders

Direct, dull and dated: very much a design of its time

would return ten years later for *Set The Twilight Reeling*). Unusually, this album was recorded in reverse of the conventional pattern: vocals and guitars were recorded first, drums and bass last. One reason for this may have been that no other musicians were used, and Reed was relying on computerized percussion and synthesizers (though Reed's old friend Ruben Blades – whose solo album Lou would later co-produce – sings backing vocals on two tracks).

Unfortunately, the era ended badly. The album is a weak one, both in terms of the songs and their execution. The drum machines and synthesizers sounded bad enough at the time; now they sound incredibly dated. Worse, much of the material here is downright dreadful, and sounds as contrived and empty as anything on *Sally Can't Dance*. 'The Original Wrapper' is the one really interesting track, which sees Lou experimenting with rap and commenting on the contemporary moral vacuum and all manner of social concerns: herpes, the Middle East, abortion and much more. *En route* he points an accusing finger at (amongst others) Ronald Reagan, Jerry Falwell and Louis Farrakhan. It's effective stuff (and a precursor of things to come with *New York*, below), but the percussion gets very annoying towards the end. Otherwise, although there's some nice guitar playing throughout the album, only 'Don't Hurt A Woman', 'Mama's Got A Lover' and 'Tell It To Your Heart' are even worth a listen as songs – and then only just.

NEW YORK

Sire; recorded Autumn 1988; released January 1989; available on CD.

ROMEO HAD JULIETTE/HALLOWEEN PARADE/DIRTY BLVD./ ENDLESS CYCLE/THERE IS NO TIME/LAST GREAT AMERICAN WHALE/BEGINNING OF A GREAT ADVENTURE/BUSLOAD OF FAITH/SICK OF YOU/HOLD ON/GOOD EVENING, MR. WALDHEIM/XMAS IN FEBRUARY/STRAW MAN/DIME STORE MYSTERY

A sleeve as elegant, forthright and powerful as the album it contains

Nearly three years after *Mistrial*, Reed returned with one of the finest albums of his career. *New York* was recorded in the city itself (naturally), at Media Sound studios. Reed co-produced the album with Fred Maher, who also played drums on most of the tracks. On 'Last Great American Whale' and 'Dime Store Mystery' the drummer was Moe Tucker. Reed's guitar is on the left-hand channel, with the other guitarist Mike Rathke (Sylvia Reed's brother-in-law) on the right-hand channel; the bassist was Rob Wasserman (except for 'Romeo Had Juliette' and 'Busload Of Faith', where bass was played by Fred Maher).

New York comes as a revelation: at this point, virtually nobody thought Reed was capable of work of this quality. There's scarcely a bad number on it, and it's both melodic and intelligent, with a theme of social comment that was more acutely observed than the work of any other lyricist in rock apart from Bob Dylan. Subject matter included homelessness, AIDS, ecology, racism and more. Reed's sleeve note stated that *New York* was intended to be listened to in a single sitting, "as though it were a book or a movie". He was insistent that there was a definite sequence to the songs, that they built as you went along.

The album kicks off with 'Romeo Had Juliette', a rocking, guitar-driven, literate love story set against a backdrop of streetcrime and drugs (though the idea of updating Shakespeare's teenage romance into a fable of cross-cultural love between New Yorkers had first been done several decades earlier, by Stephen Sondheim and Leonard Bernstein, with *West Side Story*). The Latin inscription Reed refers to which translates as "It's hard to give a shit these days" is (according to Reed): *asperum aestimare fimi alquid hodie.* 'Halloween Parade' is a bouncy, theatrical singalong celebrating the annual (and predominantly gay) Hallowe'en costume parade in Greenwich Village, and mourning the losses in a community that had been decimated by AIDS. It's genuinely moving. 'Dirty Blvd.' is an irresistibly compelling rocker that details a hellish childhood of beatings and poverty, contrasting it with the affluence others enjoy, and also celebrating the magic of the New York streets, and the power of hope. 'Endless Cycle' is a gentle but pessimistic folk-rock about cycles of abuse, and the genetic factor in addiction. 'There Is No Time' sees Reed ranting and railing at … just about everybody,

urging the need for immediate and drastic action on social issues. The tune sounds like 'Bottoming Out' revisited.

'Last Great American Whale' is almost a talking blues, dominated by booming, whale-like bass. It's the mythic account of a totemic whale freeing a Native American chief who'd killed a racist; the whale is then killed by a bazooka-wielding NRA member (this from a man who'd given up drugs, remember); the rest of the song is a diatribe about selfish Americans thoughtlessly polluting the planet. 'Beginning Of A Great Adventure' is a jazzy rap, with Lou deliberating the pros and cons of possible fatherhood. Reed's eventual decision that he didn't want children is thought to have been a major factor in the eventual disintegration of his marriage to Sylvia.

'Busload Of Faith' is a driving, bluesy slow rocker. Lyrically, it's a gloomy catalogue of woes, insisting that we're all on our own; though Reed insists we all need a "busload of faith to get by", he spends the rest of the song pessimistically dismembering the concept of faith in anything. 'Sick Of You' is bouncy, countryish rock – a grimly funny rant that Reed described as a "fantasy newscast", a long list of environmental disasters and political corruption. 'Hold On' is social protest set to driving rock, listing incidents of New York streetcrime and political unrest. On 10 May 1989 the song's lyric was reprinted in the pages of *The New York Times* under the headline "Anarchy In The Streets". 'Good Evening Mr. Waldheim' is more electric protest, about racism and hypocrisy (Kurt Waldheim was the Austrian politician who had denied his Nazi past). The song also targets Jesse Jackson, Louis Farrakhan and the Pope. 'Xmas In February' is an elegant and extremely moving, gently electric talking blues, about the plight of the Vietnam vets who returned home from the war crippled and scarred (and not just physically). 'Strawman' is a searing electric rant against consumerism and greed, with an epic guitar solo. 'Dime Store Mystery' is a moody, brooding talking blues dedicated to Andy Warhol. Reed contemplates Warhol's death, the mysteries of existence, and the memorial Mass for Warhol to be held at St. Patrick's church the following day. Realizing he'd never see his mentor again hit Lou Reed very hard indeed, as *Songs For Drella* would prove.

"You can't beat guitars, bass, drum", stated Lou's final sleeve note, and when they're played at this standard, he's absolutely right.

LOU REED/JOHN CALE: SONGS FOR DRELLA – A FICTION

See pages 152–154.

MAGIC AND LOSS

Sire/Warner Bros; recorded April 1991; released January 1992; available on CD.

DORITA/WHAT'S GOOD/POWER AND GLORY/MAGICIAN/ SWORD OF DAMOCLES/GOODBYE MASS/CREMATION/ DREAMIN'/NO CHANCE/WARRIOR KING/HARRY'S CIRCUMCISION/GASSED AND STOKED/POWER AND GLORY PART II/MAGIC AND LOSS

Recorded at the Magic Shop in New York, the band was once again Mike Rathke on second guitar and Rob Wasserman on bass, with Michael Blair on drums. Backing vocals were by Reed, Michael Blair, Roger Moutenot (on 'What's

A restrained and appropriately sombre modified photographic design

Good') and "the legendary Little Jimmy Scott" (on 'Power And Glory'). The album was co-produced by Reed and Mike Rathke (who also co-wrote four of the songs). For marketing reasons the album's release was delayed until January 1992 – four months before Lou Reed's fiftieth birthday.

"Between two Aprils I lost two friends", reads Lou's cover note, these friends being "Doc" Pomus and "Rita", and most of the album is about watching these friends suffer through terminal illness. Each of the songs here is given a subtitle as well as a title, the overall effect seeming to be that of a journey from grief and loss through to acceptance and growth. The territory explored is not pretty: cancer, radiotherapy and chemotherapy (Reed musing on his own experiences with dexedrine and morphine), funerals and cremation and pain and absence. You thought *Berlin* was hard? This is harder. But Reed maintained that it was "inspiring to see real people facing death".

There's a strange shift of pace with 'Harry's Circumcision', a bizarre little fable about self-mutilation, recited over an exquisitely delicate guitar instrumental. Vaguely reminiscent of 'The Gift' on the second Velvet Underground album (Reed even sounds a little like John Cale here), the song was another inspired by Reed's college room-mate Lincoln Swados: "He was a very talented guy. He was just insane. I always thought he made the people at the Factory pale by comparison. Nothing I saw there was anything compared to what I saw him do".

Elsewhere, Reed touches on alchemy, shamans, philosophy and mysticism, seeking some kind of answers. The title track which closes the album is a powerful and wonderful song about rebirth, be it psychological or literal (the symbolism here is almost Buddhist). After travelling through some of the bleaker passages on this record, it makes the journey worthwhile.

Musically, *Magic And Loss* veers from monotone dirges to sweeping rock epics to folk-blues ballads of farewell; but the tunefulness (when it occurs) doesn't make it any easier to listen to. It's a difficult record – at just under an hour long, quite an ordeal. Although it's undeniably extremely good, it's not something you'd play for fun, or even that often. Nonetheless, it's courageous.

BETWEEN THOUGHT AND EXPRESSION

RCA; recorded 1972–19; released April 1992; available on CD.

A 3-CD retrospective of Reed's solo career prior to *New York*. He'd used the same title for his first collection of lyrics, which

had been published several months previously. This is the only compilation album in which Reed had been personally involved, selecting tracks and remastering them with the aid of engineer Bob Ludwig. Reed stated: "Short of

An unoriginal pose, but an original approach to sleeve design

a manufacturing glitch which I can't control this should stand, for now, as a definitive post-Velvet Underground collection and the only one in which I have had the luxury of technical involvement".

It consists entirely of previously released material:

DISC ONE

I CAN'T STAND IT/LISA SAYS/OCEAN/WALK ON THE WILD SIDE/SATELLITE OF LOVE/VICIOUS/CAROLINE SAYS/HOW DO YOU THINK IT FEELS/OH JIM/CAROLINE SAYS II/THE KIDS/SAD SONG/SWEET JANE (LIVE, FROM ROCK 'N' ROLL ANIMAL)/KILL YOUR SONS/CONEY ISLAND BABY

DISC TWO

NOWHERE AT ALL/KICKS/DOWNTOWN DIRT/ROCK AND ROLL HEART/VICIOUS CIRCLE/TEMPORARY THING/REAL GOOD TIME TOGETHER/LEAVE ME ALONE/HEROIN/HERE COMES THE BRIDE/STREET HASSLE/METAL MACHINE MUSIC/ THE BELLS

• 'Nowhere At All' was first released as the B-side of the single release of 'Charley's Girl'. Recorded during the sessions for *Coney Island Baby*, but left off the album – not that surprising, since it doesn't sound anything like the rest of that record. It's more like glammed-up heavy rock, with Reed in Dylan's world-weary mode. Great stuff.

• 'Downtown Dirt' was previously unreleased. With a line-up of Lou Reed, guitar, Michael Fonfara, keyboards, Doug Yule, bass and Bob Meday, drums it was recorded in January 1975. A slow and bluesy ode to the lowlife and its denizens. The song was later rewritten, and re-recorded for *Street Hassle*.

• 'Leave Me Alone' was also previously unreleased. Line-up: Lou Reed, guitar and vocals; Bob Kulick, guitar; Bruce Yaw, bass; Michael Suchorsky, drums; Michael Wendroff and Joanne Vent, background vocals. Recorded during sessions for *Coney Island Baby*. A choppy Dylanish rocker that sounds like it grew out of a jam session – and nothing special. The song was later re-recorded for *Street Hassle*.

• 'Heroin' is a previously unreleased live version, recorded 1 December 1976 at The Roxy in Los Angeles. Engineered by Ray Thompson for radio broadcast by station KMET. Line-up: Lou Reed, guitar and vocals; Michael Fonfara, keyboards; Bruce Yaw, bass; Michael Suchorsky, drums; Marty Fogel, saxophone; Don Cherry, trumpet. Clocking in at over twelve minutes, this has a distinctly jazzy feel, with Cherry's gently atmospheric trumpet adding a sense of real melancholy. Sadly, Reed's voice sounds ragged and raw, and the jazz aspect gets very messy and annoying before the end.

• 'Here Comes The Bride' is a previously unreleased out-take from *Take No Prisoners*, recorded live at the Bottom Line in NYC on 21 May 1978 (the Late Show). Line-up: Lou Reed, guitar and vocals; Michael Fonfara, keyboards; Ellard 'Moose' Boles, bass; Michael Suchorsky, drums; Marty Fogel, saxophone; Stuart Heinrich, guitar; Angela Howard and Chrissie Faith, background vocals. Reed described it in 1990 as "A fun song". Actually, it sounds like a slowed-down 'Sweet Jane', and though the song itself isn't that bad – a Springsteen-like tale of an interrupted wedding – the band turn it into something truly dull.

• 'Metal Machine Music' is a one-and-a-half-minute extract from the album of the same name. For the version of 'The Bells' on this disc, Reed had problems, since the master tapes no longer existed as a result of record company neglect. In the end, a vinyl copy of the record was taped, then "cleaned" by a special computer programme.

DISC THREE
AMERICA/THINK IT OVER/TEACH THE GIFTED CHILDREN/ THE GUN/THE BLUE MASK/MY HOUSE/WAVES OF FEAR/ LITTLE SISTER/LEGENDARY HEARTS/THE LAST SHOT/NEW SENSATIONS/MY FRIEND GEORGE/DOIN' THE THINGS THAT WE WANT TO/THE ORIGINAL WRAPPER/VIDEO VIOLENCE/ TELL IT TO YOUR HEART/VOICES OF FREEDOM

• 'America' (a.k.a. 'Star Spangled Banner') is an out-take from *Growing Up In Public*, with the same line-up as for that record (it was left off the album simply for reasons of length). Reed's version of Francis Scott Key's anthem owes practically nothing to Jimi Hendrix's famous Woodstock instrumental; this is a vocal version, with Reed making it sound like the rousing climax to a Broadway musical. Interesting (if bizarre), but Fonfara's synthesizer is really annoying. In 1990 Reed pondered: "I don't know why we did it. It would be interesting to know what was going on in the world that would have caused that. It had to be something that set that off. Maybe they were kidnapping Americans, I don't know".

• 'Little Sister' comes from the soundtrack of the movie *Get Crazy*, was recorded during the sessions for *New Sensations* and was written especially for the movie. Reed made a cameo appearance in the film (a black comedy that starred Malcolm McDowell), performing the song at the end of the movie, backed by the Legendary Hearts band. The song itself is a gently touching ballad with a lengthy guitar solo; Reed said his little sister loved it.

• 'Voices Of Freedom' was recorded live in London, March 1987, at a benefit concert for Amnesty International, for which the song was especially written. Line-up: Lou Reed, guitar and vocals; Rick Bell, saxophone; Youssou N'Dour and Peter Gabriel, backing vocals. First released on *The Secret Policeman's Third Ball (The Music)*. A gloriously dumb rocker with gospel overtones and the audience clapping time. Also recorded at this concert (but still unreleased) is a version of 'Tell It To Your Heart'.

SET THE TWILIGHT REELING

Warner Brothers; released March 1996; available on CD.

EGG CREAM/NYC MAN/FINISH LINE/TRADE IN/HANG ONTO YOUR EMOTIONS/SEX WITH YOUR PARENT PART II/ HOOKYWOOKY/THE PROPOSITION/ADVENTURER RIPTIDE/ SET THE TWILIGHT REELING

Personnel: Lou Reed (virtually all the guitars); Fernando Saunders (bass); Tony 'Thunder' Smith (drums – both provided occasional backing vocals).
Produced by Lou Reed and recorded live at The Roof (Reed's own studio in downtown Manhattan) and at The Magic Shop. Released on Warner Brothers (Sire's parent company).

Despite the inclusion of a song about Sterling Morrison's passing, death took a back seat this time around, and *Set The Twilight Reeling* was as different from its predecessor as it could possibly be – there were lots of love songs, for one thing (and

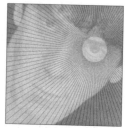

Something of a step back to the trippy days of the '60s, maybe conceived to appeal to a new generation of ravers

Reed's new muse Laurie Anderson herself contributes electronically-treated backing vocals to 'Hang Onto Your Emotions'). But the results are patchy and disappointing, since most of the songs are below par (musically, if not lyrically) and often way too long. 'NYC Man' is a slow and bluesy love song which makes reference to no less than five Shakespearean tragedies (Julius Caesar, Hamlet, Macbeth, King Lear and Othello). Mature and soulful, it's gorgeously enhanced by a gently swelling horn section (Oliver Lake, J.D. Parran and Russell Gunn Jr.) and Fernando Saunders' acoustic guitar. 'Finish Line', dedicated "for Sterl", is Lou's farewell to Sterling Morrison, and comprises gentle musings on mortality, set to a slow rock rhythm, and ending with a quote from 'The

Bells'. It's touching, but not that great musically. 'Hang Onto Your Emotions' is a bizarre-but-pretty love song, with some great bass from Saunders. 'Sex With Your Parents' is a bluesy rap, with Reed scathing in his targeting of a wide range of "right-wing Republican shit", including Republican Presidential candidate Robert Dole. Republicans have all committed incest with their parents, Reed insists – that's why they're so messed up. It's funny, but it doesn't bear repeated listening.

'Hookywooky' is a gentle, humorous rocker about sex and jealousy, with a great guitar solo, released as a single, to zero airplay and terrible reviews (which it didn't deserve). Mildly infectious, it definitely grows on you. The title track is a gentle, subtle song about the rebirth that love can bring. Great bass from Saunders, a blistering guitar conclusion from Reed, and another grower. But even the good stuff is nowhere near as good as one had come to expect from Reed in the '90s, and overall this was his least satisfying album since *Mistrial*.

PERFECT NIGHT: LIVE IN LONDON

Reprise; recorded July 1997; released 1998; available on CD.

I'LL BE YOUR MIRROR/PERFECT DAY/THE KIDS/VICIOUS/ BUSLOAD OF FAITH/KICKS/TALKING BOOK/INTO THE DIVINE/CONEY ISLAND BABY/NEW SENSATIONS/WHY DO YOU TALK/RIPTIDE/ORIGINAL WRAPPER/SEX WITH YOUR PARENTS/DIRTY BLVD.

Recorded on 3 July 1997 at the Royal Festival Hall in London, as part of the arts festival

Meltdown (organized by Laurie Anderson), it was produced by Lou Reed and Mike Rathke. The band line-up is the same as for *Set The Twilight Reeling*, but this time Reed was playing a new acoustic guitar that he'd fallen in love

Mellow, assured, mature and confident. The sleeve matches the contents

with – one "with the sound of diamonds". This caused him to revise his standard live set, to see what would work with the new instrument, the result being that the evening kicks off with four acoustic numbers before the band kicks in. Reed sounds relaxed, mellow and assured throughout (even gently humorous at times), even if his vocals are a tad laconic; the acoustic treatment gives new delicacy and grace to familiar material, and the band is superb. The three new songs from *Timerocker* were at least interesting, if not particularly memorable: 'Talking Book' seems to be about the pros and cons of computers, and is folky, but also tuneful and profound; 'Into The Divine' is a moving rocker about love and conflicting world views; 'Why Do You Talk' is a bluesy complaint about a lover's quest for spiritual answers. In fact, the whole album tends towards the bluesy, with 'Perfect Day' sounding positively doomy and depressed. But there are really nice versions of 'Coney Island Baby' and 'New Sensations', and this was still his best live album to date.

The Music

ECSTASY

Reprise; recorded 1999; released April 2000; available on CD.

*PARANOIA KEY OF E/MYSTIC CHILD/MAD/ECSTASY/MODERN
DANCE/TATTERS/FUTURE FARMERS OF AMERICA/TURNING
TIME AROUND/WHITE PRISM/ROCK MINUET/BATON ROUGE/
LIKE A POSSUM/ROUGE/BIG SKY*

Personnel: Lou Reed (vocals, guitar, percussion); Mike
Rathke (guitar); Fernando Saunders (bass, backing vocals);
Tony 'Thunder' Smith (drums, persussion, backing vocals);
Don Alias (percussion); Laurie Anderson (electric violin);
Steven Bernstein (trumpet, horn arrangements); Jane
Scarpantoni (cello); Doug Wieselman (tenor and baritone
saxophone); Paul Shapiro (tenor saxophone).

**Not sure if we want to know
what's happening here. Is it
pain, is it pleasure?**

Recorded in New
York at Sear Sound
studios, *Ecstasy* is a
thoughtful album,
though not exactly a
cheerful one. Many
of the songs – writ-
ten in the wee small
hours, because Reed
was suffering from
insomnia – deal with
collapsing relationships ("It's not a life, being
a wife", he sings on 'Modern Dance'). Since
Laurie Anderson actually plays on the album
it seems unlikely that Reed was writing about
her (though with Reed, you never know); it
seems more likely that his tales of infidelity
and sleeping apart hark back to the last days
of his marriage to Sylvia Morales, possibly to
exorcize ghosts and guilt.

Unfortunately, most of the songs are over-
long and lack a decent tune. The title track is
good, as is 'Modern Dance' and 'Rock Minuet'
(which Reed called a "light-hearted" look at
oedipal problems). But 'Like A Possum' almost
sums up the album's problems – it runs for
over 18 minutes, without much of a tune, and
doesn't really repay the journey. Reed may well
have been following his muse, but he wasn't
cutting his audience much slack.

AMERICAN POET

Superior; recorded December 1972; released 2002; currently available on CD.

*WHITE LIGHT WHITE HEAT/VICIOUS/I'M WAITING FOR MY
MAN/WALK IT TALK IT/SWEET JANE/INTERVIEW/HEROIN/
SATELLITE OF LOVE/WALK ON THE WILD SIDE/I'M SO FREE/
BERLIN/ROCK & ROLL*

Personnel (apart from Reed) are possibly The Tots (Reed's
backing band in that era). In the interview on this disc
Reed names them as Bobby Riscinio, Vinnie LaPorta, Eddie
Reynolds and Scott Clark (no clues as to who plays what).

Live album recorded
in Hempstead, New
York, the day after
Christmas Day 1972
– or to put it anoth-
er way, one month
after the release of
Transformer. The
concert was evidently
recorded in front of
an audience in a radio

**Another recycling of Mick Rock,
this time in keeping with the
mood and the moment**

recording studio, for broadcast (probably live,
since they plug Reed's gig the following night)
on station WLIR FM. The set is interrupted
halfway through for a five-minute interview, in
which Reed is amenable and funny – although

extremely prickly on the subjects of Doug Yule and *Loaded*. The recording quality is pretty good, and as Reed's live albums go, this is excellent. The set list alternates between Velvets songs and Reed's solo work, and although the proceedings are a mite ramshackle, Reed sounds relaxed and confident throughout (though occasionally singing flat). The band are no more than adequate, with one of those drummers who think cymbals should be virtually continuous, and the lack of decent backing vocals is noticeable; even so, the whole thing has a fair amount of vital energy.

Quite how this album came to be released at all is something of a mystery – perhaps Reed simply had no objections, since the quality is so good. Grab it while you can, just in case. The booklet contains a few really good photos by Mick Rock, from the same photo session as the *Transformer* cover.

THE RAVEN

Reprise; recorded; released 2003; currently available on CD.

DISC ONE/ACT ONE: THE PLAY
THE CONQUEROR WORM/OVERTURE/OLD POE/PROLOGUE (LIGEIA)/EDGAR ALLAN POE/THE VALLEY OF UNREST/CALL ON ME/THE CITY IN THE SEA/SHADOW/A THOUSAND DEPARTED FRIENDS/CHANGE/THE FALL OF THE HOUSE OF USHER/THE BED/PERFECT DAY/THE RAVEN/BALLOON

DISC TWO/ACT TWO
BROADWAY SONG/THE TELL-TALE HEART PART I/BLIND RAGE/ THE TELL-TALE HEART PART II/BURNING EMBERS/ IMP OF THE PERVERSE/VANISHING ACT/THE CASK/GUILTY (SPOKEN)/GUILTY (SONG)/A WILD BEING FROM BIRTH/I WANNA KNOW (THE PIT AND THE PENDULUM)/SCIENCE OF THE MIND/ANNABEL LEE/THE BELLS/HOP FROG/EVERY

FROG HAS HIS DAY/TRIPITENA'S SPEECH/WHO AM I? (TRIPITENA'S SONG)/COURTLY ORANGUTANS/FIRE MUSIC/ GUARDIAN ANGEL

The Raven was released in both one and two-CD versions. The shorter version, Reed explained, was "for those who don't want to listen to two hours of it, or who want to try it out before committing to the two hours. So there's the *grand mal* version or the exquisite but smaller version".

SINGLE CD VERSION:
OVERTURE/EDGAR ALLAN POE/CALL ON ME/THE VALLEY OF UNREST/A THOUSAND DEPARTED FRIENDS/CHANGE/THE BED/PERFECT DAY/THE RAVEN/BALLOON/BROADWAY SONG/ BLIND RAGE/BURNING EMBERS/VANISHING ACT/THE CASK/ GUILTY/I WANNA KNOW (THE PIT AND THE PENDULUM)/ SCIENCE OF THE MIND/HOP FROG/TRIPITENA'S SPEECH/WHO AM I? (TRIPITENA'S SONG)

"He likes Edgar Allan Poe", Reed had written of himself in 'Love Is Here To Stay' back in 1980, and this album is ample proof of a love that's practically obsessional. *The Raven* began life as a theatrical piece (in collaboration Robert

A suitably Gothic and theatrical approach given the subject matter

Wilson) that was performed in Germany in February 2001, which evolved into this two-hour long conceptual work. Reed's regular band of Mike Rathke, Fernando Saunders and Tony Smith are augmented by a horn and string section (the latter largely under the supervision of cellist Jane Scarpantoni, who would later tour with Reed) and half-a-dozen other session musicians. The album was co-produced by Reed and Hal Wilner (who was well-used to working on complicated musical projects involving numerous artists). The work features extracts from Poe's verse and prose performed by actors Willem Dafoe, Elizabeth Ashley, Amanda Plummer, Fisher Stevens and Steve Buscemi, with musical contributions from David Bowie, Antony, Kate and Anna McGarrigle, Ornette Coleman, Laurie Anderson and the Blind Boys Of Alabama (the album was once again dedicated to Anderson, "a constant source of inspiration").

Unfortunately, it's a muddle – the recitals of Poe's work well enough (especially the title track), although it should be pointed out that many of the pieces are Poe rewritten by Reed (and rather well, too). But although it contains some gorgeous instrumental passages, Reed's actual song contributions are almost all both substandard and hackneyed. Possibly this is why he chose to include new (and extremely good) versions of a couple of his 'classics': 'The Bed' (from *Berlin*) and 'Perfect Day' (the latter performed by Antony – Hegarty, he of the Johnsons – a truly extraordinary singer). Both songs are head and shoulders above anything else on the album, and almost worth the price of admission on their own.

Of the guest spots, three get the best new tunes: the MacGarrigles on 'Balloon', Bowie on 'Hop Frog' and the Blind Boys Of Alabama on 'I Wanna Know'. Steve Buscemi sings on 'Broadway Song' – a pastiche of a show num-

ber that's completely unremarkable. There's even some *Metal Machine*-style electronics in 'Fire Music,' which was recorded two days after 9/11, in a studio close to Ground Zero (but it's still unforgiveable noise, frankly). Since Poe's endings tend to be dark and Reed wanted something lighter to finish, the album closes with the more personal 'Guardian Angel'. Both that and 'Vanishing Act' are quite touching and enjoyable, yet without being at all memorable.

As per usual, Reed thought his new album was great, and called it "the culmination of everything I've ever done", saying he thought it would be hard for him to top artistically. Sadly, he may be the only person who feels that way. The whole thing's overly self-conscious, and sorely in need of a few more actual tunes. As it stands, it's the kind of record you play once and then file away forever. Do you really need the longer version? Not really.

LOU REED, JOHN CALE AND NICO: LE BATACLAN '72

See pages 165–166.

ANIMAL SERENADE

Sire/Reprise; recorded 24th June 2003; released 2004.

DISC ONE
ADVICE/SMALLTOWN/TELL IT TO YOUR HEART/MEN OF GOOD FORTUNE/HOW DO YOU THINK IT FEELS/VANISHING ACT/ECSTASY/THE DAY JOHN KENNEDY DIED/STREET HASSLE/THE BED/REVIEN CHÉRIE/VENUS IN FURS
DISC TWO
DIRTY BLVD./SUNDAY MORNING/ALL TOMORROW'S PARTIES/

The Music

CALL ON ME/THE RAVEN/SET THE TWILIGHT REELING/
CANDY SAYS/HEROIN

Produced by Lou Reed and Fernando Saunders.

Yet another live album, this one recorded at LA's Wiltern Theater during a 60-date tour. As well as the regular band of Rathke and Saunders, the line-up includes two of the contributors to *The Raven*: cellist Jane Scarpantoni, and Antony on backing vocals. Curiously, there are no drums

Another collectable: is this the first time we've seen the Man's back?

(except for a couple of tracks where percussion is provided by Saunders). Reed is in good humour and laid-back throughout, but at least his vocals are less throwaway than on previous live recordings, and largely stick to the tune in question. The backing vocals and Scarpantoni's cello add a new dimension to the more minor material, but the rest is very variable – 'Sunday Morning' is great, 'All Tomorrow's Parties' is awful. 'Revien Chérie' is a solo spot for Fernando Saunders (who wrote the song). At its best the album's pleasant, at its worst it's self-indulgent (the world didn't really need a ten-minute version of 'Venus In Furs'), and there's very little here other than 'Set The Twilight Reeling' (with a great vocal from Antony) that isn't better in its studio incarnation.

Maureen 'Moe' Tucker

"One of the greatest drummers in the entire world" – Lou Reed, 1998

PLAYIN' POSSUM

Trash/Rough Trade; released 1981; vinyl only; out of print.

BO DIDDLEY/HEROIN/SLIPPIN' AND SLIDIN'/I'LL BE YOUR
BABY TONIGHT/LOUIE LOUIE/SLIPPIN' AND SLIDIN'/
CONCERTO IN D MAJOR/AROUND AND AROUND/ELLAS

Basically a collection of cover versions, with one new track from Tucker, Moe plays all the instruments here, and proves herself an extremely competent guitarist; that said, the approach is basically punk-rock: garage music that's enthusiastic but fairly primitive (with times when it verges on the inept). Tucker's voice is also not the strongest in the world, though it does possess a certain ragged charm and sounds better when multi-tracked. There's

The Music

Memorabilia and nostalgic snaps litter the sleeve, with Moe looking rural

a creditable version of 'Heroin', and a truly awful one of Dylan's 'I'll Be Your Baby Tonight', with the best of the R&B material being her cover of Chuck Berry's 'Around And Around'. Easily the strongest track here is a multi-tracked guitar instrumental of Vivaldi's 'Concerto In D Major', which is an utter delight. Tucker also contributes another guitar instrumental of her own, 'Ellas', which goes on for too long but is still quite interesting – there are echoes of surf music, of Link Wray, and of Bo Diddley.

LIFE IN EXILE AFTER ABDICATION

50 Skadillion Watts; released March 1989; released on CD; out of print.

HEY MERSH/SPAM AGAIN/GOODNIGHT IRENE/CHASE/ANDY/ WORK/PALE BLUE EYES/BO DIDDLEY/TALK SO MEAN/DO IT RIGHT

The Revola CD adds four tracks from Tucker's *MoeJadKateBarry* EP:

GUESS I'M FALLING IN LOVE/BABY WHAT YOU WANT ME TO DO/WHY DON'T YOU SMILE NOW/HEY MR. RAIN

Somewhat more professional and much more impressive than her debut, and recorded with a full band and some high-profile guest stars, including Steve Shelley, Thurston Moore and Lou Reed (who contributes guitar to 'Hey

Mersh' and 'Pale Blue Eyes'). This was the first time Reed and Tucker had played together since 1970. John Cale was set to produce the album at one point, but other commitments prevented it. Tucker sings and mainly plays guitar (and drums on two tracks), also writing much of the material. The infectious 'Spam Again' and the punk protest 'Work' are both scathing about Tucker's previous employer, Wal-Mart, while 'Andy' is a touching farewell to Warhol. 'Mersh' was Tucker's nickname for her old friend Martha Morrison, Sterling's wife. 'Talk So Mean'

A decidedly indie look to Moe's second solo outing

is bluesy but on the dull side, while 'Chase' is tuneless thrash; 'Goodnight Irene' a very conventional reading of the Leadbelly song, and 'Pale Blue Eyes' quite possibly the best version of the song (Reed thought so). 'Do It Right' is both charming and compelling, and proof that Tucker can write a truly interesting song. The whole album is definitely worth checking out.

The *MoeJadKateBarry* material is more mundane, very thrashy and basic: so-so covers of two Velvets songs and one by Jimmy Reed, plus 'Why Don't You Smile Now', which is interesting – it's a throwaway pop song written by Reed and Cale (with Vance and Phillips) while Reed was still at Pickwick.

I SPENT A WEEK THERE THE OTHER NIGHT

New Rose; recorded 1991; released October 1991;
released on CD, but now out of print.

*FIRED UP/THAT'S B.A.D./LAZY/S.O.S./BLUE, ALL THE WAY TO
CANADA/(AND) THEN HE KISSED ME/TOO SHY/STAYIN' PUT/
BABY, HONEY, SWEETIE/I'M NOT/I'M WAITING FOR THE MAN*

More in the same vein, with a full band and Tucker sticking mainly to guitar, and sounding much more confident vocally. Sterling Morrison appears on several tracks, and on a some-what bizarre cover of Phil Spector's 'And

And a decidedly *outré* punk look to her first album for New Rose

Then He Kissed Me' he and Tucker are joined by John Cale on viola; Lou Reed plays guitar on 'Fired Up', and all of the Velvets appear on the eerily compelling 'I'm Not' (which is worth the price of admission on its own). Keeping it in the family, Martha Morrison also appears as one of the backing singers, and Sylvia Reed was art director for the cover. The mate-rial is still largely fairly thrashy/garage: 'That's B.A.D' is another diatribe against poorly paid work, 'Lazy' a gripe against domestic chores; 'Blue, All The Way To Canada' is folkier, concerns Native Americans and Chrysler auto-mobiles and is vaguely reminiscent of R.E.M.'s 'Belong'; 'Baby, Honey, Sweetie' is irresistible punkabilly, and 'I'm Waiting For The Man' is

actually better than one could have imagined, with a tragically sad vocal from Moe. Worth tracking down.

OH NO, THEY'RE RECORDING THIS SHOW

New Rose; recorded 23 February 1992; released
September 1992; available on CD.

*SPAM AGAIN/HEY, MERSH/STAYIN' PUT/ THAT'S B.A.D./
GOODNIGHT IRENE/TOO SHY/TALK SO MEAN/LAZY/
BABY,HONEY,SWEETIE/S.O.S./FIRED UP/TOO SHY/BO DIDDLEY*

A pretty good live album, recorded live at L'Ubu in Rennes, France. Featuring a five-piece band that includes Sterling Morrison. Good sound quality, and Moe's even more confident vocally; even though the studio versions are

Another interesting graphic approach for Moe's French outing

usually better, still well worth a listen.

DOGS UNDER STRESS

New Rose; recorded 1993; released 1994 on CD; out of print.

*CRACKIN' UP/ME, MYSELF AND I/I'VE SEEN INTO YOUR SOUL/
I DON'T UNDERSTAND/CRAZY HANNAH'S RIDIN' THE TRAIN/
DANNY BOY/LITTLE GIRL/SATURDAY NIGHT/TRAIN/POOR
LITTLE FOOL/I WANNA*

Back to the studio, for a much more profession-al-sounding album – it was recorded at Reeltime in Savannah, Georgia, which was decidedly a step up on the kind of studios Tucker had

A more surreal design approach, which would probably have worked with either title

used to date. Sterling Morrison plays on five tracks. There are great covers of Bo Diddley's 'Crackin' Up' and Ricky Nelson's 'Poor Little Fool', plus a touching reading of 'Danny Boy'; the rest are Tucker originals, though the standard isn't as high as on her previous two studio albums, and none of them are particularly remarkable or memorable. The original title for this album was *Inexplicably Spanked While Leading A Conga Line*.

WAITING FOR MY MEN

Rokarola; recorded 1991 & 1994; released 1998; available on CD.

FIRED UP/I'M WAITING FOR THE MAN/ BLUE, ALL THE WAY TO CANADA/TOO SHY///(AND) THEN HE KISSED ME/I'M NOT/ ME, MYSELF AND I/I DON'T UNDERSTAND/DANNY BOY/ LITTLE GIRL/I WANNA/CRACKIN' UP/ I'VE SEEN INTO YOUR SOUL/ SATURDAY NIGHT/TRAIN

Belgian compilation album comprising six tracks apiece from *I Spent A Week There The Other Night and Dogs Under Stress*, which is probably easier to track down than those two albums.

Moe and the Men

MOE ROCKS TERRASTOCK

Captain Trip Records; recorded 5 November 2000; released 2002; only available on Japanese import CD.

SPAM AGAIN/I WANNA/I'M STICKING WITH YOU/CRACKIN' UP/B.A.D./HEY MERSH/FIRED UP/BO DIDDLEY

Another live album, recorded in Seattle in 2000. It's not bad, though Moe's voice is a shade hoarse. The most notable aspect of this is the appearance of Doug Yule, who plays piano and sings on 'I'm Sticking With You' – though

What is it with live albums and brick walls?

both he and Tucker occasionally lose their way vocally, it only adds to the charm of hearing the two of them reunited again. Yule also plays guitar on 'Crackin' Up'.

There are no Tucker compilations available. The best of her albums are *Life In Exile After Abdication* and *I Spent A Week There The Other Night*.

Doug Yule

"We all thought he was great – a great guitar player, bass player, singer" – Moe Tucker

AMERICAN FLYER

United Artists; released 1976; released on CD; out of print.

AMERICAN FLYER: SPIRIT OF A WOMAN

United Artists; released 1977; released on CD; out of print. Personnel unknown (apart from Yule). Track details largely unknown.

American Flyer produced extremely bland country-tinged AOR – somewhat like The Eagles, except minus the tunes. Yule only takes a songwriting credit for three tracks: 'Lady Blue Eyes' and 'Queen Of All My Days' on the first album, and 'Flyer' on the second.

'Queen Of All My Days' isn't bad – a pleasant enough gentle rocker with a reggae/calypso feel – but the other two are both fairly dull. For one halfway decent track, it's scarcely worth the bother of tracking this down.

The two American Flyer albums have been released as a double bargain basement CD set

LIVE IN SEATTLE

Captain Trip Records; recorded 25 May 2000 and 4 November 2000; released 2002; CD available on Japanese import only.

CANDY SAYS/BEGINNING TO GET IT/WHAT GOES ON/ SWEET JANE/AFTER THE FALL/LOVE SONG/WHITE DEVILS/ TWO MORE HANDS/RULES/PURPLE MOUNTAIN GLORY/ BEGINNING TO GET IT/WHAT GOES ON

Tracks 1–4 recorded at the Crocodile Café, Seattle, WA; tracks 5–12 recorded at the Terrastock 4 Festival, Show Box theater, Seattle, WA. Sound by Jennifer Yule; album produced by *VU* fanzine editor Sal Mercuri.
Personnel: Doug Yule (vocals and guitar); Seth Warren (violin); Steve Stusser (drums); Gigi Catanzariti (flute); Dave Keppel (guitar); Mark Johnson (guitar); Dave Martin (keyboards and guitar); Jason Tally (bass).

Yule's first proper outing for 30 years is a ramshackle but enjoyable live album, which includes creditable versions of three Velvets songs. The remaining tracks are all Yule originals, taken from his unreleased album *Song Cycle One* (an "original, evolving, work-in-progress"). It veers between country, rock and folk, and there are several songs (like 'Beginning

Yule almost resists plugging his VU chops on the cover, although the playlist on the Show Box marquee gives the game away

To Get It' and 'Purple Mountain Glory') that could have fitted comfortably onto *Loaded* – though they're not quite in the same league. It's actually hard to judge, since Yule's vocals sound less comfortable on his own songs than on the crowd-pleasing Velvets material, and once or twice he falters. Still, it would be nice to hear a studio version of *Song Cycle One* but, to date, there's no sign of it.

Solo Rarities And Oddities

Much of the Velvets' solo output is rare by definition, since many albums have been deleted or are out of print and are quite hard to track down. Beyond that, there are numerous collectable 'rarities' whose only claim to fame is the fact that they're on coloured vinyl or have picture sleeves. There are also a few items that are worth a lot of money but aren't actually very good musically, like Lou Reed's 1998 *Live At The White House*, an 8-track CD recorded live at the White House during the Clinton residency. This was never commercially released, but distributed to Reprise staff members and copies currently fetch about £275/$550.

There are also numerous uncollected Lou Reed B-sides and guest appearances, none of which are really essential, with the exception of the following...

September Song

Reed's version of Kurt Weill and Maxwell Anderson's composition, which can be found on the 1985 tribute album compiled by Hal Willner, *Lost In The Stars: The Music Of Kurt Weill*. Reed makes the song his own; it was also released as a single.

One For My Baby...

Reed's sublime take on a song made famous by Frank Sinatra, Arlen and Mercer's 'One For My Baby (And One More For The Road).' This can be found on Rob Wasserman's 1988 album *Duets* (Wasserman was the bass player on Reed's *New York* and *Magic And Loss*).

Perfect Day

The 1997 all-star cover version of 'Perfect Day', which was released only as a single. This featured vocals (and instrumental contributions) by Bono, Morcheeba, David Bowie, Suzanne Vega, Elton John, Boyzone, Lesley Garrett, Burning Spear, Thomas Allen, The Brodsky Quartet, Heather Small, Emmy Lou Harris, Tammy Wynette, Shane McGowan, Sheona White, Dr John, Robert Cray, Huey, Ian Broudie, Gabrielle, Evan Dando, Courtney Pine, Andrew Davis and the BBC Symphony Orchestra, Brett Anderson, the Visual Ministry

Choir, Joan Armatrading, Laurie Anderson, Tom Jones and Reed himself. All profits were donated to the BBC-sponsored charity Children in Need. The record is an utter delight (as was the video) and thoroughly deserved its hit status (it reached Number 1 in the UK). Reed had approval over all the participants, but one of his choices – Curtis Mayfield – was unable to take part because of illness. Still, Reed declared himself pleased with the final result: "It flowed, it sounded like one breathing unit".

I Wanna Be Around

Of all John Cale's many guest appearances on others' records, the only one that is really indispensable is his irresistibly idiosyncratic cover version of Johnny Mercer's 'I Wanna Be Around', which can be found on Jools Holland's 2001 album *Small World Big Band*.

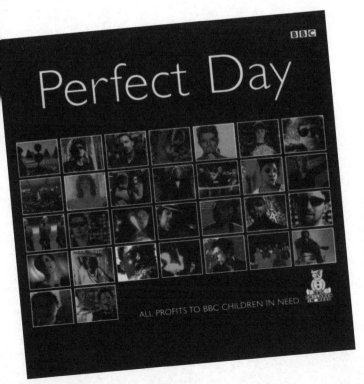

The BBC's Children in Need charity single, masterminded by the Man, featured a star-studded cast of guest musicians who were displayed on the sleeve. It sold phenomenally, bringing Reed to the attention of an altogether different – and younger – audience. Not that he has exactly capitalized on this opportunity

"What is there? Birth, life, death and the conflict in between."

Lou Reed, in writing *Magic & Loss*

30 Vital Velvet Undergound Songs

And The Stories Behind Them ...

This section is an unapologetically subjective review of the best VU songs, in chronological order. It doesn't just stick to the albums recorded between 1966 and 1972 – it takes in later releases and compilations of material from the period, whilst also cherry picking from the variety of reunion recordings that came out over the next three decades.

1. I'm Waiting For The Man

(Reed)

Recorded May 1966; available on *The Velvet Underground & Nico*

This song and its sister, 'Heroin' (see below), proved to be the two highly controversial and attention-grabbing moments on the debut album. A driving urban blues that sounds as desperate as its subject matter – scoring heroin in Harlem – it's also a detailed, well-observed account. Reed wrote the song while still in college, and it provides an early signal not only of Reed's astonishingly mature songwriting, but also of his intention to bring realism, in this case gritty street life (and its argot), into the domain of pop music. He later observed that, while the $26 in the song's protagonist's

hand won't get you much of anything these days, everything else about the song still holds true. "P.R. shoes" refers to Puerto Rican Fence Climbers, an imaginative (if racist) nickname for the pointy-toed shoes known in Britain as "winklepickers". Although it echoes the clipped literary style of Beat writer junkies such as William Burroughs and Herbert Hunke (not to mention their subject matter), to some extent the song can be seen as autobiographical, as Reed was known to acquire at least some of his drugs from Harlem.

2. Heroin **(Reed)**

Recorded May 1966; available on *The Velvet Underground & Nico*

Like 'Waiting For The Man', this was written by Reed while he was still in college, and experimenting with the drug himself. It was a period in which he would later categorize himself as a "rather negative, strung-out, violent, aggressive person". He wrote them in order "to sort of exorcize the darkness, or the self-destructive element" in him. He'd spend a sizeable chunk of his career having to justify this song, since many assumed that he was actually advocating heroin use. As Reed later explained, the song "was about what it's like to take heroin". He claimed that "it wasn't pro or con" and was simply "just about taking heroin, from the

Five great Velvets rockers

The Velvets were never too precious to pump out simple (on the surface at least), good-time rockers. Most of these would have made very respectable singles. Except maybe the last one.

'Beginning To See The Light' (Reed, 1968; available on *The Velvet Underground*)

A bouncy rocker bright-eyed with hope and optimism. Although it sounds almost like a variation on "I'm Waiting For The Man", it is a lot more joyous and genuinely positive. The buoyant lyric and chugging rhythm is underpinned by one of Yule's most naggingly infectious bass lines.

'What Goes On' (Reed, 1968; available on *The Velvet Underground*)

Multiple guitar overdubs bolster a song about being messed about, messed around and messed up by love. The first line echoes the Beatles song of the same title, while the repeated instruction "lady, be good" is the title of a song by George & Ira Gershwin.

'I'm Set Free' (Reed, 1968; available on *The Velvet Underground*)

This might be another driving rocker, but the song's exultant title is misleading – this is about heartbreak and pain, as the mournfully bluesy guitar solo attests. The relationship is now over; the best that can be hoped for is eventually to find another one, but even that will just be another illusion.

'Foggy Notion' (Morrison, Tucker, Yule & Hy Weiss, 1969; available on *VU*)

Dumb beatpop – and there ain't nothin' wrong with that. Its title belies the fact that this is a song positively dripping with lustful anticipation. According to Morrison, it was recorded totally live in the studio.

'I Heard Her Call My Name' (Reed, 1967, available on *White Light/White Heat*)

A piece at a near-manic fast-pace, with Reed going truly berserk on the guitar. It seems to be about love beyond the grave – though whether it's articulating the delusions of someone mentally disturbed or just sorrow for a dead love is left for the listener to decide. Nevertherless, as a crystallization of a bundle of angst, self-loathing, guilt and obsession after things have gone wrong, it remains unparalleled. And the musical setting is a perfect mirror for the muddled aftermath of a young love affair. A classic.

point of view of someone taking it". He also pointed out that if the lyrics had been part of a novel, no one would have considered it shocking. "I'm still not sure what was such a big deal," he commented, years later. "So there's a song called 'Heroin'. So what?"

Throughout the song, Moe Tucker's persistent drumming keeps pace with the increasing tempo of Reed's strumming; coupled with Cale's seesawing viola, they vividly conjure up the desperation implicit in the lyric. The first time you hear it, it's awesome. As Lou Reed has pointed out: "It's just two chords. And when you play it, at a certain point there is a tendency to lean in and play it faster. It's automatic ... Also, if you check out the lyrics, there are more words as you go along. The feeling, naturally, is to speed up". When the song was re-recorded in California (the version included on the first album) Reed changed the opening line from "I know just where I'm going" to "I don't know where I'm going", thus changing the entire meaning of the song. Cale for one thought it was a cop-out. Tucker was also unhappy with the version on the record, but for a different reason: the band recorded it live, but since the others had plugged their instruments directly into the mixing desk, Tucker couldn't properly hear what they were playing. "It just became this mountain of drum noise in front of me. I couldn't hear shit" she revealed. "So I stopped, and being a little whacky, they just kept going, and that's the one we took." Nevertheless, she considered "Heroin" to be the band's "greatest triumph" and furthermore "Lou's greatest triumph too, maybe, songwriting-wise". Incidentally, if you're wondering who or what the nefarious "Jim-Jims" are in the lyrics you are not alone; the derogatory term was a concoction of Reed's, who apparently thought that invented slang was the best kind.

3. All Tomorrow's Parties (Reed)

Recorded April 1966; available on *The Velvet Underground & Nico*

Cale's insistent piano drives this plaintive social lament. Despite rumours that the song was about Edie Sedgwick or Andy Warhol – or even that it was written specifically for Nico to sing – it was actually written sometime early in 1965, long before the Velvets encountered the artist and his retinue. Coming straight out of the psychedelic folk-rock backwoods, it was nevertheless "Andy's favourite song", according to Reed. Which, from one perspective, makes perfect sense: its Cinderella imagery would certainly appeal to a man nicknamed 'Drella; and, as Reed has since pointed out, this is a Cinderella story with no Prince Charming in sight. He also claimed it was "a very apt description of certain people at the Factory at the time", although Cale claims that it was actually written about Daryl, who was also one of the inspirations for Reed's *Berlin* album. The song title has since entered the wider public consciousness, lending knowing cool points to a 1999 novel by cyberpunk high-priest William Gibson, and providing a rather obvious name for an annual alternative British music festival.

4. There She Goes Again (Reed)

Recorded April 1966, available on *The Velvet Underground & Nico*

A re-working of Marvin Gaye's 'Hitchhike', using the same chord sequence, "There She Goes Again" is also a pretty straightforward Buddy Hollyish pop song in the manner of many of the jukebox-targeted songs Reed had been writing at Pickwick International. Except that it messes around with tempo, with the guitar solo intentionally slowing down and speeding up again, while the deceptively pop-oriented approach also conceals a characteristic sting in the tail, as the song appears to be advocating misogynist violence as a solution to relationship problems. Cale thinks it might be about either Electra or Daryl, who were both no strangers to domestic violence.

5. Run Run Run (Reed)

Recorded April 1966; available on *The Velvet Underground & Nico*

More urban drug-related blues – this time about the perils of New York's Union Square, then infamous as a hangout for dealers and junkies. Keening guitar feedback heightens the mood of manic paranoia. The song was written just prior to the group's residency at the Café Bizarre in December 1965, when they realized that they were desperately short of original material. As Morrison later recalled: "I remember we had the Christmas tree up, but no decorations on it. We were sitting around busy writing songs, because we had to – we needed them that night!"

6. The Black Angel's Death Song (Reed, Cale)

Recorded April 1966; available on *The Velvet Underground & Nico*

The song that supposedly got the group fired from their residency at Café Bizarre sounds more like a collision between avant garde classical music and modern jazz than rock. Reed later commented that "the idea here was to string words together for the sheer fun of their sound, not any particular meaning". Over Cale's swooping viola, Reed rapidly intones lyrics rich in imagery; comparisons with Dylan would be inevitable, though today they sound rather pretentious. In fact, the song's lyrics began life as a poem Lou wrote back in his college days.

7. European Son (Reed, Cale, Morrison, Tucker)

Recorded May 1966; available on *The Velvet Underground & Nico*

A song of driving psychedelia, it's dedicated to Reed's creative writing lecturer and college mentor Delmore Schwarz – probably because of its lyrical sparsity, since the poet hated rock music and all songs with lyrics. The vocal part sounds like a boogie version of one of Dylan's "put down" songs, but most of the musical focus is on feedback, guitar soloing and general experimentation which simply keeps going until it expends itself, after about eight minutes. Just after the vocal part you can hear John Cale scraping a chair across the floor, and in doing so dropping a glass – in perfect time to the music.

According to Tucker, the song turned out differently every time they played it. As Cale put it: "we wanted to break the rules, so we broke every fucking rule we could".

8. Femme Fatale (Reed)

Recorded April 1966; available on *The Velvet Underground & Nico*

Lou Reed has occasionally claimed that this song is about Nico, but more often he's admitted that he wrote it at the request of Andy Warhol (who came up with the title) and that it's about Edie Sedgwick. An ethereal ballad sung by Nico, it's also a cautionary tale – as, indeed, was Edie's life story. Cale claims the song was "informed" by the making of Warhol's 1966 film *The Chelsea Girls* (featuring both Nico and Edie Sedgwick), which he described as truly harrowing: "You'd see the girls disintegrating and sliding down walls with tears in their eyes".

9. I'll Be Your Mirror (Reed)

Recorded April 1966, available on *The Velvet Underground & Nico*

A folky love song, it was supposedly written for (and about) Nico. Reed claims the title was something she'd said to him, but according to Victor Bockris he'd started writing the song two years earlier for Shelley Albin. The lyric could just as easily be about deep friendship as romantic love, although Cale has described it as "a song of infinite desire, strangely tender".

Reed later described it as "very compassionate, very loving, very nice". According to Sterling Morrison, the band had to badger Nico to stop singing it too stridently, until she finally burst into tears: the next take was perfect. However, Morrison also claimed that the "haunting" quality in Nico's voice was simply because she "was just really depressed."

10. Venus In Furs (Reed)

Recorded May 1966; available on *The Velvet Underground & Nico*

A celebration of sado-masochism (and fetishist clothing), on which Cale's viola really comes into its own. Written by Reed after reading the 1870 novel of the same title by Leopold von Sacher-Masoch, the song basically recounts the story of the book (Sterling Morrison called it "a musical synopsis"), whose protagonist Severin is whipped by his cruel mistress Wanda while she's dressed in furs. The novel was supposedly at least semi-autobiographical; Sacher-Masoch considered himself the "slave" of his mistress, Baroness Bogdanoff. "I just thought it would be a great idea for a song" Reed later said. "Now everybody thinks I invented masochism." This is slightly disingenuous, as the Factory crowd were busy making a number of S&M movies at the time, the most notorious being *Vinyl*, in which Gerrad Malanga played a masochist and Sedgwick his dominatrix, and which involved a specialist S&M "consultant". The assured, grinding musical setting was quite unlike anything else yet heard in popular music, and bears the hallmarks of Cale's avant garde musical experimentation, while Reed launches us straight into the situation ("Shiny, shiny – shiny boots of leather...") with no preamble. Almost certainly written under the influence of the hedonistic denizens of the Factory, this song, with 'Waiting For The Man' and 'Heroin', squares the circle of themes explored on the debut album. "The closest we ever came in my mind to being exactly what I thought we could be" was Sterling Morrison's summing up of the song.

11. Sunday Morning (Reed, Cale)

Recorded November 1966; available on *The Velvet Underground & Nico*

This song was added after the initial sessions at the request of Verve producer Tom Wilson, who wanted a specific vehicle for Nico. When the time came, Reed refused to let her handle the vocals, and insisted on singing the song himself; Nico did occasionally sing the song with the band in concert, and covered it later in her solo repertoire. Supposedly written by Reed and Cale in a friend's apartment at 6 am one Sunday morning after being up all night, it's a gentle, folky ballad of paranoia and reassurance. Sterling Morrison described it as capturing the particular feeling of "when you've been up all Saturday night and you're crawling home while people are going to church. The sun is up and you're like Dracula, hiding your eyes."

12. White Light/White Heat (Reed)

Recorded September 1967; available on *White Light/White Heat*

A hymn to speed, the house drug of choice of the Factory crowd, which Reed and most of the Velvets inevitably got into at the time. Whilst not sharing the starkness and highs and lows of 'Heroin', it resembles the earlier song in capturing very accurately the physiological and psychological effects of the drug's high, plus the ever-present user's sense of paranoia at the inevitable comedown. And it manages this whilst never diminishing its integrity as a song, or a piece of music. The setting is an insistently pounding fuzz-toned thrash that ends up in a speedball frenzy. It is a song which would influence everybody from The Rolling Stones to *Ziggy*-era Bowie and on to the Ramones, Mötorhead and even the thrash-metallers.

13. The Gift (Reed)

Recorded September 1967; available on *White Light/White Heat*

The "lyrics" to this song were originally a short story written by Reed for his creative writing class at Syracuse University, and were inspired by his first summer-long separation from girlfriend Shelley Albin. The tale of the unfortunate Waldo Jeffers and his love for his girlfriend Marsha plays like a cross between Roald Dahl and Stephen King (with echoes of Reed's avowed hero, Edgar Allan Poe). It was set to music at the suggestion of John Cale, who also narrates the piece in a deadpan manner, his lilting Welsh accent heightening the sense of the bizarre. Cale read the whole thing through in one take. To simulate the sound effect of Waldo being stabbed in the head, Reed recorded the noise of a cantaloupe being hit with a wrench, and was later disappointed that this noise wasn't clearer and louder on the finished track. The backing music (credited to all four Velvets) grew out of a live instrumental piece called 'Booker T.' (see *Peel Slowly And See*), so called because it was inspired by Booker T. & The MGs' 'Green Onions'. The track was mixed so that Cale's voice comes out of one speaker, and the music comes out of the other.

14. Lady Godiva's Operation (Reed)

Recorded September 1967; available on *White Light/ White Heat*

This baroque Gothic horror piece prefigures some of John Cale's later solo work, but was actually written by Lou Reed. Referring to the use of sound effects, John Cale described the piece as "a BBC Radiophonic Workshop idea". Some think this is about a sex-change operation, but the lyrics actually sound like they're describing something even grislier – an operation for a brain tumour, perhaps? As with 'The Gift', it's not one for the squeamish. Reed subsequently blamed the 24 shock treatments he'd had when he was 17 for causing him to write songs like this one. He said the song was about

"fear of sleep" describing it as "the perfect thing for the people [he was] running around with, staying up 15 days at a time".

15.Here She Comes Now (Reed)

Recorded September 1967; available on *White Light/ White Heat*

The words were by Reed, but the music was by all four Velvets. It was probably written with Nico in mind; she had sung it in concert – possibly ironically – but by the time they came to record it she was long gone. Reed sings it in folky/blues mode, but as a man frustrated. It would seem to be about sexual problems: despite the song's title, Reed is actually singing "If she ever comes now". (Which he follows up with "Ooh, it looks so good", followed with "She's made out of wood". And that's about the total sum of the lyrics.) Perhaps the lyric was simply too close to the bone to use as a song title. Nevertheless, this brief song would appear to speak volumes about the equally brief Reed/Nico off-stage relationship, neatly addressing it from both sides of the fence.

16. Sister Ray (Reed)

Recorded September 1967, available on *White Light/ White Heat*

Even to the most casual listener, the lyrics (possibly influenced by Hubert Selby Jr.'s novel *Last Exit To Brooklyn*) are clearly depicting both hard drug use and homosexual activities. Musically, the track is structured mayhem, with Cale's R&B organ vying with the two guitars for your attention while everybody meanders towards and away from the tune; somehow, Tucker's drumming holds it all together. Reed claims to have written the lyrics while driving to a gig, and that it was built around a story he wrote about a scene of total debauchery and decay. "I like to think of Sister Ray as a transvestite smack dealer" he once said. "The situation is a bunch of drag queens taking some sailors home with them and shooting up on smack and having this orgy when the police appear". Admitting that it was "a graphic song", Reed recalls Warhol telling him, "Oh, Lou, make sure that you make them do the sucking-on-my-ding-dong song". The results were, in Reed's words, "seventeen minutes of violence". The music itself is just as uncompromising, with Reed later claiming that, musically he was trying to create the rock'n'roll equivalent of Ornette Coleman; he has also compared it to heavy metal. Unable to agree on an arrangement for the song, the band decided to record it in one take – during which, according to Reed, engineer Gary Kellgren actually left the studio. "He just said, 'Let me know when it's over'" Reed explained.

17. Candy Says (Reed)

Recorded November-December 1968; available on *The Velvet Underground*

A gently sad ballad of despair with oneself, which Reed described at the time as being "probably the best song [he'd] written". Sung on the album by Doug Yule, who was teased mercilessly about his performance by Reed, since Yule had no idea what the song was actually about. The "Candy" of the title was Candy Darling, a drag queen and Factory "superstar" from Long Island whose real name was James Slattery. He later died from cancer caused, apparently, by either silicone breast implants or hormone injections (accounts differ). Apart from a few Warhol movies, Candy Darling also appeared in her own stage revue show, *Glamour, Glory And Gold*, in which she played multiple roles, while the ten corresponding male roles were played by the then-unknown actor Robert De Niro. Reed – who was very fond of drag queens – would later refer to Candy again, making her one of the characters in his solo hit 'Walk On The Wild Side'. The song's dissatisfaction with self-image is something uuniversal, as Reed later observed: "I don't know a person alive who doesn't feel that way."

18. Pale Blue Eyes (Reed)

Recorded November-December 1968; available on *The Velvet Underground*

Perhaps Reed's most haunting ballad, it's a delicately arranged song of yearning loss: the relationship described here is doomed, its adulterous nature stated very matter-of-factly. Reed said simply that he'd written it "for someone [he] missed very much", whose "eyes were hazel". It's been recorded by many musicians, but Reed's professed favourite version is by Moe Tucker, which can be found

The Music

on her 1989 solo album *Life In Exile After Abdication*. A certain Lou Reed plays guitar on it.

The lyrics echo both 'I'll Be Your Mirror' and, in the "down for you is up" paradox, the title of a book – Richard Fariña's 1966 cult underground novel *Been Down So Long It Looks Like Up To Me*.

19. That's The Story Of My Life
(Reed)

Recorded November-December 1968; available on *The Velvet Underground*

A rare slice of bounce-along honky-tonk vaudeville, with lyrics that quote from (and refer to) Factory photographer, resident and caretaker Billy Linich aka Name. Reed and

Five great ballads

Despite their reputation as "difficult", "experimental" – in short, hard to approach – the Velvets benefitted enormously from Reed's ability to craft simple, and simply beautiful, ballads.

'Jesus' (Reed, 1968; available on *The Velvet Underground*)

A gently beautiful plea for redemption which surprised even its writer. "When I wrote 'Jesus', I said, 'My God, a hymn!'" Reed observed. It hovers somewhere between folk, country-blues and gospel.

'Some Kinda Love' (Reed, 1968; available on *The Velvet Underground*)

A bluesy (and darkly comic) exhortation to sexual experimentation. Some of the lyrics echo a line from T.S. Eliot's 'The Hollow Men': "Between the idea/And the reality/Between the motion/And the act/Falls the shadow." Reed would later use *Between Thought And Expression* as the title for both his 1992 CD retrospective and his first book collection of selected lyrics. Reed considered Sterling Morrison's guitar part on this track to be one of the finest things he ever did.

'One Of These Days' (Reed, 1969; available on *VU*)

A countryish blues, about being treated badly in love and drunkenly planning an exit, with slide guitar by Yule and Hank Williams-style yodelling by Reed.

'Hey Mr. Rain' (Reed, 1968; available on *Another View*)

There are two versions of this ethereal folk/blues ballad on the album, both dominated by John Cale's droning viola part. The first version is essential; the second somewhat more shambolic.

'Sad Song' (Reed, 1970; available on *Peel Slowly And See*)

How can you possibly resist a love song dedicated to Mary Queen of Scots? Reed would re-record this song for his solo album *Berlin*, when he was talking about divorce, but this version is superior.

Linich became close at around this time, and used to visit gay bars together. As to Linich's opinions on the difference between wrong and right that the song refers to, one should bear in mind something Reed later pointed out: "He also told me I was a lesbian, so you have to take things with a grain of salt." (For an update on Linich/Name's views on life – and everything else – visit Name's "Goat Clinic" at www.billyname.com)

20. The Murder Mystery (Reed)

Recorded November-December 1968; available on *The Velvet Underground*

An experimental track, the song has two sets of "lyrics", recorded and mixed so that one set would emanate from each speaker, with the music in the middle. Sung by the entire band. Reed later explained that he'd been playing around with words "and wondering if you could cause two opposing emotions to occur at the same time". His stream-of-consciousness lyrics were subsequently published as a poem – or rather, two parallel poems – in the winter 1972 issue of *The Paris Review* (#53). One wonders if even Reed knows what it's about, though he later admitted it was an experiment that had failed: "The idea was simple – have two lyrics running at the same time, so you get hit with one monologue in one ear and the other monologue in the other ear, like two guitar parts". But, as Reed explained, "it didn't work, because you couldn't hear either one well enough to hear what was being said".

21. After Hours (Reed)

Recorded November-December 1968; available on *The Velvet Underground*

A song of loneliness, in praise of the solace found in alcohol, it s song for all those whose local bar has become the only bright and friendly place in the world. It is sung by Moe Tucker, making her vocal debut. "It's a terribly sad song, and I didn't sing it because I figured people wouldn't believe me if I sang it," Reed explained. "But I knew Maureen for instance had a very innocent voice". Tucker was so nervous about her vocals that she made everyone but Reed and the engineer leave the studio while she sang. The version on the Valentin mix sounds like more honky-tonk vaudeville; Reed's mix sounds like folk/blues. "I loved afterhours bars", Reed comments in his *Between Thought And Expression* book, going on to relate a telling anecdote about Nico causing a bar fight to break out.

22. Sweet Jane (Reed)

Recorded April-July, 1970; available on *Loaded*

Based around a rhythm riff that's practically a Reed trademark, this verges on the anthemic. The song's "outsider" protagonist (a rock musician) is looking inwards, scrutinizing the lives of his more orthodox friends (a banker and a clerk), perhaps with envy, perhaps not. Following the opening ripple of fairground-ish musak, the line "Standing on the corner, suitcase in my hand" recalls 'Waiting For The Man' in instantly capturing a setting, while the simple down-the-neck/up-the-neck bass riff also conjures memories of the earlier song. An instant classic, and so balls-out simple that it often worked better live than in the confines of this studio cut.

23. Rock & Roll (Reed)

Recorded April-July, 1970; available on *Loaded*

Like most of his generation, Lou Reed discovered rock'n'roll via the radio, and this nostalgic celebration of the medium is practically autobiography (both Reed and Morrison have gone on record to the effect that the music they heard on the radio in their teens gave them a lifeline to hang on to).

First recorded for the "lost" album (a version that would eventually surface on *Another View*), the song has an epic, joyous feel to it – plus some extremely tasteful guitar work. The version on *Another View* features Moe Tucker's great drum fills, and is more delicate than the *Loaded* version; there's also a great demo version on *Fully Loaded*.

24. New Age (Reed)

Recorded April-July, 1970; available on *Loaded*

A song that's practically the screenplay for a movie, this tale of a movie star past her prime and her younger lover's adoration for her is evocative in mood of Billy Wilder's 1950 film *Sunset Boulevard*.

The tone is appropriately mock-epic, approaching gospel territory towards the end. But it's catchy too, with its two key themes: "You're over the hill right now, and you're looking for love" reflected by "Honey, I'll coming running over the hill to you when you want me". Vocals were by Doug Yule, but this is a good instance of him sounding like Reed. The "full-length" version (on *Fully Loaded*) fades with a guitar solo. It is notable as one of the few songs in popular music to namecheck the great Robert Mitchum (to rhyme with "Gee, but I never thought you'd catch him")

25. Stephanie Says (Reed)

Recorded 13 February, 1968; available on *VU*

John Cale's haunting viola announces his presence near the start of this gentle lament of regret. The song pivots on "She's not afraid to die" from the end of a phone conversation, the singer concluding that "it's all in her mind". According to Cale, "Stephanie" was Reed's nickname for Steve Sesnick ("To Lou, everybody's homosexual," John commented). The song would receive its first official outing (in drastically rewritten form) on Reed's 1973 solo album *Berlin*, though by that time Reed had changed the protagonist's name to Caroline. Which didn't affect the rhyme of "So the people ask her" with "It's so cold in Alaska."

26. Ocean (Reed)

Recorded 19 June, 1969; available on *VU*

Originally titled 'Here Come The Waves', this song uses the ocean as an analogy for madness, the protagonist eventually being engulfed by the waves (and/or his own mental processes – perhaps why the lyrics reference Shakespeare's *Macbeth*). The gentleness of mood here, the sweetness of the backing vocals and the maternally embracing bass line make it all the more ominous – not that we are unaware of a sense of threat from the opening.

The closing refrain of "down by the sea" is genuinely haunting, especially when interrupted by a break that sounds – for a hanging second – as if we are about to skid off into a Motown R&B number. There are earlier and later versions of the song, which would surface on *Peel Slowly And See* and *Fully Loaded*; Reed would also re-record the song for his eponymous first solo album in 1972).

27. Temptation Inside Of Your Heart (Reed)

Recorded 14 February, 1969; available on *VU*

Spoof Motown and irresistibly catchy, it also contains Reed's unforgettable theory of physics – "electricity comes from other planets". Not to mention his cod philosophy: "If you going to make it right, you're sure to end up wrong." According to Sterling Morrison, the idle chatter and asides from the participants (himself, Reed and Cale) was recorded unintentionally while they were crammed into a tiny vocal booth waiting to record their backing vocals; somehow, it accidentally ended up on the finished track. If true, then Reed's lead vocal is presumably only a guide track for finished vocals that were never recorded.

It also features a strapped-on doo-doo chorus that anticipated the same year's 'Sympathy For The Devil', from the Rolling Stones, before reaching its apogee on *Transformer*'s 'Walk On The Wild Side'. But all this doesn't really matter – it's still great, exactly the way it is.

28. Andy's Chest (Reed)

Recorded 13 May, 1969; available on *VU*

Reed stated that this song was about the shooting of Andy Warhol by Valerie Solanas, "even though the lyrics don't sound anything like that." In fact, the song is a poetic reverie (its title probably inspired by the famous Richard Avedon portrait of Warhol displaying his scars) that makes no direct mention of the shooting or Warhol's injuries – it's just a deeply affectionate get-well-note from Reed to his one-time mentor.

The version played by the Velvet Underground is minimalist folk/beat-pop; when the song got its first official release on Reed's 1972 solo album *Transformer* it was given a much more lavish treatment, courtesy of its arrangement by Mick Ronson and David Bowie.

29. I'm Sticking With You

(Reed)

Recorded 13 May, 1969; available on *VU*

With vocals by Moe Tucker (aided by Reed and the others), this is a childlike and gently melodic affirmation of friendship/love, that's utterly irresistible. This is one of the few times that a Velvets song has dated due to a contemporary reference (to the Viet Cong), since Reed seldom commented on current affairs. It gained an unlikely and unfortunate afterlife in the 1990s, as the soundtrack for a Hyundai commercial.

30. Ride Into The Sun (Reed)

Recorded May-October 1969; available on *VU*

An exquisite guitar instrumental that starts off sounding like surf music and ends up sounding like The Beatles – just listen to the piano and the drum fill. Versions with vocals can be found on *Peel Slowly And See* and the *Quine Tapes*, where it becomes a song of longing for escape from the city. In all fairness, it works best as an instrumental.

The Music

20 Essential Solo Velvets Tracks

and the stories behind them ...

Lou Reed

Satellite Of Love

Recorded August 1972; available on *Transformer*

The Velvets recorded this first (see *Peel Slowly & See*), but for once Reed's solo attempt is infinitely better. Despite the fact that it's a song about helplessness in the face of a loved one's serial promiscuity, the subject matter is treated in an almost comic way, within the cocoon of a range of pop arrangements.

The banal statement "I like to watch things on TV" becomes one of the great put-down lines of all time as Lou drops it in insouciantly amidst a litany of his partner's infidelities. It also refers back to Bowie's line "Andy Warhol is a gas ... I watch him on TV" from 'Andy Warhol' off the album *Hunky Dory*. Mick Ronson's piano arrangement and David Bowie's backing vocals transform what ought to be a sad song into achingly beautiful pop.

Walk On The Wild Side

Recorded August 1972; available on *Transformer*

The song tracks the sketched-in adventures of a variety of characters, presumably headed towards the New York of the Factory, and nods to literary precedents such as the drifters and grifters of low-down writers such as Jim Thompson and Nelson Algren. It's a stroll across to the darker side of the American Dream. The "back room" mentioned in the lyrics refers to the private bar at Max's where the Warhol crowd hung, being seen, and observing the street life that washed up there.

It's still extraordinary that Reed managed to take such unlikely ingredients (transvestites, rent boys, drugs, oral sex) and cook up a runaway chart hit with them. Credit should go to Herbie Flowers' double-tracked basses, the sweeping strings, the soulful sax solo, and the (anonymous) female chorus. And, of course, to all the daytime radio DJs who spun the record, blissfully ignorant of what "giving head" meant.

Perfect Day (Reed)

Recorded August 1972; available on *Transformer*

This account of an ideal date was sparked by Reed's adulterous relationship with Shelley Albin – hence the awareness in the song that there'll be a price to pay. It became a surprise hit decades after its original release as a result of its inclusion on the soundtrack of *Trainspotting*; the subsequent all-star multi-singer charity version for the BBC's Children In Need appeal helped dispel the druggy associations the film had given it. Although one suspects the BBC hadn't quite cottoned on to the notion that many listeners still think of it as an ode to a monkey on the singer's back rather than a simple love song. Such is Reed's greatness as a song writer. Whichever way the song is read, the chorus ("You're gonna reap just what you sow") retains a chilling ambivalence.

Vicious (Reed)

Recorded August 1972; available on *Transformer*

Reed's hilariously mannered strut – not so much vicious as bitchy, fey and stroppy – was inspired by a comment made to him by Andy Warhol (the opening line), and is rescued from slightness by Mick Ronson's spitting guitar fills. Flashy, grabbing, and a great opening track for an album, which set a tone for the next few years of Reed's solo career. Ouch!

Romeo Had Juliet

Recorded Autumn 1988; available on *New York*

Dirty Blvd.

Recorded Autumn 1988; available on *New York*

While there may be some doubt that Reed was influenced by Leonard Bernstein's adaptation of Shakespeare's tragedy in *West Side Story*, there is little doubt that Reed's vision in 'Romeo Had Juliet' had a direct impact on Baz Luhrmann's streetwise film adaptation of the story in 1996. In both of these songs Reed manages to capture and convey the excitement and energy of the city he loves best without airbrushing its downside in the slightest. Street gangs, crack dealers, drive-by shootings, prostitution, pollution, hopeless poverty, child abuse, homelessness... it's all here, but it still practically makes you feel homesick for the place (regardless of where you're from). Plus, both songs are set to two of rock's most irresistible riffs.

Sword Of Damocles

Recorded April 1991; availoable on *Magic And Loss*

Very few rock songs have been written about cancer, and it would be hard to better this one. Having watched two friends undergoing radiation therapy and suffering protracted , unavoidably painful deaths, Reed here tackles the subject of mortality head on. It's an immensely mature work lyrically, the epic orchestration articulating Reed's frustration and sadness.

John Cale

Paris 1919

Recorded late 1972; available on *Paris 1919*

The highlight of what is perhaps Cale's most essential album: even if you have no idea what this song is about (Europe between the world wars), it really doesn't matter. The lyrics are intriguingly and appropriately surreal, and the melody and singalong chorus confirm Cale's ability to produce some of pop's most compelling tunes.

Fear Is A Man's Best Friend

Recorded Spring 1974; available on *Fear*

A melodic "celebration" of paranoia and despair, the product of Cale's serious drug problems and his disastrous first marriage. The tune slowly degenerates into hysteria, as does Cale's vocal; his adrenaline-driven rage at his own frustration was for real, and it shows.

Guts

Recorded Winter 1974; available on *Slow Dazzle*

Fuelled by booze, drugs and the anger Cale felt at his wife's adultery with Kevin Ayers during the ACNE outing (with Ayers, Nico and Brian Eno), this starts off as gentle rock but grows increasingly disturbing as it progresses. There's real hatred here – much of it directed at himself – and the whole thing eventually collapses into almost incoherent snarling.

Heartbreak Hotel

Recorded Winter 1974; available on *Slow Dazzle*

A standard part of Cale's live repertoire. Cale took Presley's original hit off down a dark alleyway and violently mugged it. Instead of a refuge for the lovelorn, this hotel is a temporary abode of existential despair, if not actually a terror-infested tomb for the damned. Cale's anguished performance is amplified by the gospel-style wailing of the (uncredited) female backing vocalists.

Do Not Go Gentle

Recorded Spring 1989; available on *Words For The Dying*

Flexing his classical muscles on this orchestral adaptation of one of Dylan Thomas's best known poems, Cale produced a work that is both pastoral and challenging, the memorable string motif being truly irresistible. True, the children's chorus is a mite intrusive, but it's still a stunning piece of work.

Dying On The Vine

Recorded Spring 1992; available on *Fragments Of A Rainy Season*

Cale was still struggling with his own drink and drug demons when he and co-writer Larry Sloman came up with this superb tale of a man's realization that his life has come to a dead end: change of some kind is now a must. This version is far better and more powerful than the song's original appearance on *Artificial Intelligence*.

Hallelujah

Recorded Spring 1992; available on *Fragments Of A Rainy Season*

When Cale told Leonard Cohen he planned to cover the latter's Biblical epic of sex and salvation, the poet faxed him literally dozens of verses. Cale culled these down to the ones he preferred and created what is probably the definitive version of the song; though it has been overshadowed somewhat in the public's consciousness by covers by Jeff Buckley and Rufus Wainwright (the latter made familiar to millions via its inclusion in the soundtrack to *Shrek*).

Lou Reed & John Cale

A Dream

Recorded Winter 1989/90; available on *Songs For Drella*

The jewel in *Drella*'s crown, this meandering meditation in the mind of the dying Andy Warhol is one of Reed's finest lyrical achievements, conjuring up the ghost of the artist better than a dozen biographies. Appropriately, Cale's performance delivers an atmosphere that is downright dream-like.

Nico

The Fairest Of The Seasons

Recorded April/May 1967; available on *Chelsea Girl*

An ethereally gorgeous slice of baroque folk-rock, this song was co-written by Nico's then teenage lover Jackson Browne. The delicately sweeping string arrangement and otherworldly vocals turn a fairly straightforward lyric about whether to end a relationship or not into a masterpiece, and a worthy successor to Nico's ballad work with the Velvets.

Frozen Warnings

Recorded October 1968; available on *The Marble Index*

More chanted than sung, this tale of a hermit sounds positively medieval. The arrangement sets Nico's voice almost a capella at the start until Cale's atmospheric, quasi-ambient music rises from the background to embrace her. The song was supposedly inspired by her lover and mentor Jim Morrison (though it's hard to see exactly how).

Janitor of Lunacy

Recorded Spring/Summer 1970; available on *Desertshore*

This is archetypal Nico, her clarion voice ringing out above her pumping harmonium like a demented nun wailing for her lost demon lover. Which is hardly surprising, when you consider that Brian Jones of The Rolling Stones, who

Nico had been involved with, had died the year before. It's impossible to talk about this song without using the term "gothic"; one imagines her performing it in a crumbling turret.

Moe Tucker

Spam Again

Recorded 1988; available on *Life In Exile After Abdication*

A Bo Diddley riff drives along this song about the joys of doing low-paid, mindlessly mundane work for a rich but tight boss, inspired by Moe's days as an employee of Wal-Mart. It's practically a Socialist calypso protest song. "Spam" refers to the canned meat, which was presumably all she could afford to feed her family with on her salary.

Do It Right

Recorded 1988(?); available on *Life In Exile After Abdication*

An insistent honky-tonk piano tune, this has a singalong refrain of very good advice ("Don't act dumb, don't play smart") about personal responsibility and generally getting your act together – presumably intended for Moe's children. It's just as charming as either of her solo spots with the Velvets.

The Velvets' Legacy

It's almost impossible to overestimate the influence of the Velvet Underground upon the rock music of the last forty years. Within a couple of years of the Velvets' demise, both David Bowie and Brian Eno – two of pop music's most innovative pioneers – had publicly acknowledged their debt to the band. And both those gentlemen would in turn, of course, influence almost everything that followed them.

Nor was it just the art-rock bands that fell under the Velvet shadow. The Velvets had a direct impact on the Sex Pistols, as did John Cale's production work (which was arguably in itself a continuation of the Velvets' musical methods). The Pistols covered material by both The Stooges and Jonathan Richman (both produced by Cale), and Cale's production work with Patti Smith on *Horses* was also enormously influential on the whole punk/new wave movement. Of all the late 60s bands, it was only really the Velvets and The Doors that were recognized as as forebears by the punk bands; very few of the indie and grunge outfits that followed punk would take Jim Morrison seriously, but the Velvets still counted – and still do. It's no accident that both REM and Nirvana – neither of whom were known to cover songs by many other artists – both recorded Velvets songs.

You can hear echoes of the Velvets' sound everywhere: in Joy Division and New Order (whose bass player Peter Hook is on record in his admiration for them), Television, Echo & The Bunnymen, Lloyd Cole, Talking Heads, The Smiths, Cowboy Junkies, Jane's Addiction, Simple Minds, The Cure, The Birthday Party, The Jesus & Mary Chain, The Wedding Present, Nick Cave, Massive Attack, Radiohead, The Violent Femmes, The Strokes, The Vines... in short, in pretty much every indie and indie-crossover rock band of the last 30 years, whether guitar-based or not.

Howie Gelb's Giant Sand have continued the Velvets' tradition of unanticipated radical experimentation; the delirious fuzz-tones and apparent chaos of The Jon Spenser Blues Explosion seem determined to take *White Heat/White Light* to its logical conclusion; while the off-the-wall eclecticism of the loose collective (and unclassifiable) Lambchop has it roots in the Velvets' soil.

Many of these bands have recorded their own versions of Velvets material; many more have played it live. The Velvets even had a fashion influence, their all-black ensemble being adopted almost universally as the de rigeur uniform for any band with boho pre-

The Music

tentions. Nico, in turn, became a goth icon, although her bizarre intonation and ability to carry a daunting dirge probably found its greatest successors in Souixie Sue and PJ (Polly Jean) Harvey.

Although it's less obvious, the impact of Lou Reed as a lyricist is also incalculable. Not because he wrote about drugs and alternative sexuality per se, but because in doing so he'd proved that it was possible for rock songs to embrace any subject matter under the sun or moon – to be literate and ambitious and, occasionally, witty. Every songwriter since who has aspired to creating something with a degree of intellectual content owes a debt to Reed, whether it's visible (even to them) or not. It's a fair bet that within the record collections of all of the current crop of interesting lyricists – Sufjan Stevens, Tori Amos, Stephin Merritt, Wayne Coyne – one would find a Velvets album or two. Could Radiohead's 'Creep' have existed without Bob Dylan (who has covered it)? Possibly yes. Without Reed? Probably not.

Today, virtually every month the music press carries some Velvets-related news item, and the world they once inhabited is being repeatedly depicted by Hollywood; it seems entirely possible that their legend may never fade.

Cover Versions

In *The Velvet Underground Handbook* M.C. Kostek lists over 300 known cover versions of Velvets songs – a sum that's increasing daily, and which doesn't include covers of the solo material by Reed, Cale or Nico. Some place the total much higher, and there are at least three volumes in the Heaven & Hell CD series, all of which are exclusively devoted to Velvets covers. In 1998, the Dutch band Bettie Serveert recorded an entire album of Velvets songs. Leaving aside solo versions of Velvets songs by Nico, Reed, Cale and Tucker, here is a round-up of the most notable Velvets covers:

Big Star
'Femme Fatale' (on *Sister Lovers*)

David Bowie
'White Light/White Heat' (on *Ziggy Stardust : The Motion Picture*)

Nick Cave
'All Tomorrow's Parties' (on *Kicking Against The Pricks*)

The Cowboy Junkies
'Sweet Jane' (on *The Trinity Sessions*).

Bryan Ferry
'What Goes On' (on *The Bride Stripped Bare*).

James
'Sunday Morning' (on the compilation *Heaven & Hell Volume I*)

Joy Division
'Sister Ray' (on *Still*)

Lone Justice
'Sweet Jane' (on *I Found Love*)

Thurston Moore

'European Son' (on *The End Of Music As We Know It*)

Mott The Hoople

'Sweet Jane' (on *All The Young Dudes*)

New Order

'Sister Ray' (on the compilation *Like A Girl, I Want You To Keep Coming*)

Nirvana

'Here She Comes Now' (on the compilation *Heaven & Hell Volume I*)

Rainy Day

'I'll Be Your Mirror' (on *Rainy Day*)

REM

'There She Goes Again', 'Pale Blue Eyes' and 'Femme Fatale' (all on *Dead Letter Office*) and 'Afterhours' (B-side of 'Losing My Religion').

The Tom Tom Club

'Femme Fatale' (on *Boom Boom Chi Boom Boom*).

Voice Of The Beehive

'Jesus' (B-side of 'I Say Nothing').

The Wedding Present

'She's My Best Friend' (on *Heaven & Hell Volume I*).

Tributes

Songs about the Velvet Underground

Jonathan Richman

'Velvet Underground'

The Jesus & Mary Chain

'Moe Tucker'

Velvets fans

Jonathan Richman, Robert Quine of The Voidoids, Ric Ocasek of The Cars and Chrissie Hynde of The Pretenders are all known to have seen the (original) Velvets live. They are, of course, not alone. One of the Velvets' support acts was Chris Stein's first band, many years before he founded Blondie.

Bizarrest "Tribute"

The characters Lou and Andy from the UK's BBC TV comedy show *Little Britain*, evolved out of the spoof versions of Lou Reed and Andy Warhol that comedians David Walliams and Matt Lucas had created for *Rock Profiles* and *The Ralf Little Show*. In Matt Lucas and David Walliams' comedy sketches, "Andy" has become a monosyllabic, greasy-haired, wheelchair-bound malingerer who ceaselessly and cack-handedly exploits "Lou", his bizarrely unobservant and rather stupid frizzy-haired social worker.

The Music

Songs (supposedly) about Nico

The Doors
'My Eyes Have Seen You'

Kevin Ayers
'Decadence'

Leonard Cohen
'Take This Longing' and 'Joan Of Arc'

The Stooges
'We Will Fall'

Marianne Faithfull
'Song For Nico'

Part Three:
The Velvet Goldmine

*"Rock'n'roll for me has no limits.
That's one of my points about it"*.

Lou Reed, 1997

On Screen

Tracking down film or video material featuring the Velvets turns in a very mixed bag which – aside from a handful of concert films from Reed's later years and some creditable documentaries put together over the last two decades or so – is, in sum, a disappointment.

Raw footage

All contemporary film footage of The Velvet Underground is of fairly poor quality. Although Andy Warhol, and other underground film-makers, like Barbara Rubin, Jonas Mekas, Ron Nameth and Paul Morrissey, all shot both colour and black-and-white footage of the Velvets performing and rehearsing during 1966 and 1967, most of these films are seldom (if ever) shown, and virtually all of them are thought to be silent (or are simply over-dubbed with recordings from the first album).

The only known definite exceptions are:

• a rehearsal of '**Venus In Furs**' (included on the Lou Reed *Rock And Roll Heart* DVD, listed below).

• *The Velvet Underground: A Symphony Of Sound*: a 20-minute film by Warhol showing the Velvets, with Nico, rehearsing 'Melody Laughter' at the Factory in January 1966 – with the New York police entering at the end to complain about the noise. The film has rarely been shown, and is not commercially available.

• A performance of '**Guess I'm Falling In Love**' from a January 1967 TV show called *Upbeat*. A tape of this may still exist somewhere, but it has not surfaced commercially.

• A short film called *Sunday Morning* by Rosalind Stevenson – a schoolmate of Lou Reed's – was touted by Channel 4 as showing The Velvet Underground rehearsing the song of the same name. In fact, it's simply some very moody silent footage over-dubbed with the track from the first album (which is how any of this silent footage is usually handled when used in documentaries).

• In 1965, CBS News also filmed a feature for its *Walter Cronkite Presents* series on underground film-maker Piero Heliczer entitled *The Making Of An Underground Film*. This included footage of Heliczer jamming (on saxophone) with the MacLise line-up of the Velvets. Heliczer used the soundtrack of this in the same year in his film *Venus In Furs*, which also features John Cale, Sterling Morrison, Lou Reed, Angus MacLise and Barbara Rubin in acting roles.

Films, videos, TV and DVD

LE BATACLAN

French TV; broadcast January 1972; not commercially available.

I'M WAITING FOR THE MAN/BERLIN/THE BLACK ANGEL'S DEATH SONG/WILD CHILD/EMPTY BOTTLES/HEROIN/GHOST STORY/THE BIGGEST, LOUDEST, HEAVIEST GROUP OF ALL/ FEMME FATALE/I'LL BE YOUR MIRROR/ALL TOMORROW'S PARTIES/JANITOR OF LUNACY

The film of the 1972 Paris reunion of Reed, Cale and Nico was broadcast once (with a shortened version broadcast several times that year), but unseen since. Brief clips have surfaced on several other TV programmes, but the fee demanded by the French government – who own the rights – for the whole show has always been deemed too high by other TV companies. Rumour has it that most of the show may since have been erased.

The concert at Le Bataclan in Paris, 1972 with Reed, Cale and Nico remains (if only rarely seen) one of the best pieces of relatively early concert footage, despite post-dating the demise of the Velvets proper

THE SOUTH BANK SHOW: THE VELVET UNDERGROUND

LWT; broadcast April 1986; not commercially available.

A good retrospective evaluation of the band, which chimed with the release of *VU* in 1985 and *Another View* in 1986, it includes 1985 interviews with the Velvets, Nico, Gerard Malanga, Victor Bockris and critic Robert Christgau. Reed was the only one of the Velvets who declined to be interviewed; instead, the show included a brief interview clip taken from another source. There's also archive footage, plus glimpses of both Cale and Nico in solo performance and a few brief clips from the Le Bataclan gig.

ARSENAL

Catalonian TV3; broadcast May 1986; not commercially available.

A Spanish documentary about the Velvets, the cornerstone of which is a lengthy interview with Sterling Morrison (the transcript of which can be found in Albin Zak's book *The Velvet Underground Companion*). Rare music can be heard on the soundtrack, including 'Loop' and 'The Ostrich'.

LOU REED AND JOHN CALE: SONGS FOR DRELLA

Warner Music Vision; VHS video released April 1990; out of print.

Reed and Cale perform their Andy Warhol song cycle in its entirety, directed and photographed by Ed Lachman using a camera team of four. The staging by Jerome Sirlin is simple, with the two men facing each other amid a bank of instruments. The simple but effective stage lighting by Robert Wierzel is set against back projections of Warhol and his work (and visual interpretations of the lyrics, of varying degrees of success). The film version reinforces the fact that this is the work of two artists at the top of their form, whose communication borders on the telepathic. As per usual, while Reed opts for a simple black turtleneck, Cale's look is more outlandish: a black jacket over a white shirt with one of the widest collars ever seen. Coupled with his physical intensity, the look makes him appear deranged and possibly dangerous.

THE VELVET UNDERGROUND: VELVET REDUX MCMXCIII

Warner Music Vision; released 1993, reissued by Rhino 2006; available on Region 1 DVD.

WARNER TRACKLISTING: VENUS IN FURS/SWEET JANE/I HEARD HER CALL MY NAME/FEMME FATALE/I'M STICKING WITH YOU/ROCK & ROLL/I'LL BE YOUR MIRROR/I'M WAITING FOR THE MAN/HEROIN/PALE BLUE EYES/COYOTE/ THE GIFT/HEY MR. RAIN

The Velvet Goldmine

The Velvet Goldmine

RHINO TRACKLISTING: VENUS IN FURS/WHITE LIGHT-WHITE HEAT/BEGINNING TO SEE THE LIGHT/SOME KINDA LOVE/ FEMME FATALE/HEY MR. RAIN/ I'M STICKING WITH YOU/ I HEARD HER CALL MY NAME/ I'LL BE YOUR MIRROR/ ROCK & ROLL/ SWEET JANE/ I'M WAITING FOR THE MAN/ HEROIN/ PALE BLUE EYES/COYOTE

The visual version of the reunion live album, filmed at L'Olympia in Paris, directed by Declan Lowney. The filming itself is quite straightforward (using four cameras) but well done, as is the simple stage lighting. While Reed, Morrison and Tucker all opt for a casual/scruffy look in T-shirts and jeans, Cale wears a dark suit over a zip-fronted jerkin, with a floppy hairstyle that makes him look like a 1940s mad scientist.

For almost all of their audience, this was the first opportunity to see the Velvets live. Cale's viola playing provides much of the visual action (he also alternates between the viola, bass, and organ), but it's Moe Tucker who commands the attention, whether standing at her kit and playing like she's conducting the entire proceed-

That banana (again), this time on a purple and silver metallic finish, on the DVD of the reunion concert at L'Olympia, Paris in 1993

ings or else shyly standing up front to sing with her finger in her ear – a sharp contrast to the solid, impassive figure of Sterling Morrison (who gets a massive cheer when he sings a line on 'I'm Sticking With You'). All of this makes Reed's mannered pose and his expertise in manipulating a concert crowd seem heavy-handed by comparison. For all its musical faults, still an amazing performance.

CURIOUS … THE VELVET UNDERGROUND IN EUROPE

Channel 4; broadcast 1993; not commercially released.

A good documentary about the reunion tour, including some live material and extremely revealing interviews with all four Velvets, plus Czech President Václav Havel (and a smattering of European fans). There's also a great, bluesy solo version of 'Heroin' from Reed, recorded especially for this film.

The programme was screened as the opener for Channel 4's *Velvet Underground Night* in December 1993, which was appropriately titled 'Peel Slowly And See' and hosted by Debbie Harry. Also shown were *Velvet Redux MCMXCIII*, *Songs For Drella*, Warhol's *Chelsea Girls* and *Sunday Morning*. Additionally, there were comments about the influence of the Velvets from Bono, Peter Buck, Kristin Hersh, Peter Hook, Ian McCulloch and Richard Hell. *Chelsea Girls* was introduced by Paul Morley and Paul Morrissey.

JOHN CALE: WORDS FOR THE DYING

Released 1993 on video in USA only (label unknown); out of print.

A short and somewhat bizarre documentary by Rob Nilsson about the making of Cale's orchestral adaptation of Dylan Thomas's poetry. The film follows Cale and Brian Eno to Moscow for the recording sessions, and also shows a visit by Cale to his sick and aged mother in Wales. Eno didn't want to be filmed at all, and is uncooperative throughout; it was at his insistence that the film was only released in the USA.

LOU REED: ROCK AND ROLL HEART

Win Star; released 1998; available on Region 1 DVD.

An excellent – if somewhat reverential – 75-minute-long documentary first shown on American TV in 1997 in Channel 13's *American Masters* series. Directed by Timothy Greenfield-Sanders, the film features extensive archive footage of Lou, the Velvets and Warhol. There's also live footage taken over the years, and interviews with the man himself and a whole host of people connected with him and/or influenced by him, including John Cale, Maureen Tucker, Mary Woronov, Billy Name, Joe Dallesandro, Holly Woodlawn, Gerard Malanga, David Bowie, David Byrne, Dave Stewart, Patti Smith, Thurston Moore, Suzanne Vega, Philip Glass and Jim Carroll, as well as various rock critics and art historians. The documentary follows the story as far as *Magic And Loss*, and also has footage from several scenes of the theatrical production of *Timerocker*. Given how good this film is, it's ironic that it shares its title with one of Reed's worst albums.

The DVD extras include a brief clip of the Velvets performing at the Factory in January 1966 which was originally shown in the documentary *USA Artists: Warhol* (Channel 13). The band runs through 'Venus In Furs' while Edie Sedgwick, Gerard Malanga and Jack Smith dance. The sound quality is pretty dreadful, the vocals so muffled as to be almost inaudible and the dancing fairly embarrassing … but it's still fascinating. There are also biographies of all the interviewees.

JOHN CALE

BBC Wales; broadcast 1998; not commercially released.

A compelling documentary directed by James Marsh, and timed to tie in to the publication of Cale's autobiography. It follows Cale and his literary collaborator Victor Bockris on a sentimental journey to Garnant in Wales, and to Rotterdam for rehearsals of the 1997 dance piece *Nico* by Scapino Ballet. There's archive footage of the Velvets and of Cale's parents, plus shots of Cale and band in rehearsal and in concert, as well as interviews with Lou Reed, LaMonte Young, Billy Name, Brian Eno, Chris Spedding and Marian Zazeela.

The Velvet Goldmine

LOU REED: A NIGHT WITH LOU REED

Eagle Vision; released 2000; available on Region 2 DVD.

SWEET JANE/I'M WAITING FOR THE MAN/MARTIAL LAW/ DON'T TALK TO ME ABOUT WORK/WOMEN/WAVES OF FEAR/ WALK ON THE WILD SIDE/TURN OUT THE LIGHTS/NEW AGE/ KILL YOUR SONS/SATELLITE OF LOVE/WHITE LIGHT WHITE HEAT/ROCK & ROLL

Personnel: Lou Reed (vocals and guitar); Robert Quine (guitar); Fernando Saunders (bass); Fred Maher (drums).

A live set recorded at The Bottom Line in New York in 1983, produced by Bill Boggs and Richard Baker, directed by Clarke Santee with five cameras – none of which intrude on the action. While Reed is enthusiastic about the show in the post-concert footage, the reality is that he and the band turn in a performance which is neither involving or exciting – all the "classics"are treated in an extremely throw-away fashion, and even 'White Light/White Heat' sounds mannered and restrained. They're more alive on the newer material, and there are great versions of 'Women' and 'Waves Of Fear', while Saunders' bass is impressive through-out – but even at its best, the show is merely adequate.

NICO: AN UNDERGROUND EXPERIENCE + HEROINE

Visionary Communications; released 2000; available on Region 0 DVD.

AN UNDERGROUND EXPERIENCE: *I'M WAITING FOR THE MAN/VEGAS/60-40/ALL TOMORROW'S PARTIES/FEMME FATALE/HEROES/SAETA.*

HEROINE: *MY HEART IS EMPTY/PROCESSION/ ALL TOMORROW'S PARTIES/VALLEY OF THE KINGS/THE SPHINX/ WE'VE GOT THE GOLD/MÜTTERLEIN/AFRAID/INNOCENT AND VAIN/FROZEN WARNINGS/FEARFULLY IN DANGER/ TANANORE/FEMME FATALE.*

These two short films are of Nico in concert. Malcolm Whitehead's film *Heroine* records a solo performance at Manchester's Library theatre some time in the 1980s, with the har-monium-playing Nico – accompanied only by a percussionist and a piano player (on 'Femme Fatale' only) – at her most Gothic and doom-laden. Even 'All Tomorrow's Parties', performed a capella, sounds dirge-like. Filmed with only two cameras, neither film nor sound are of the best quality, and the same can be said of the performance.

An Underground Experience is even less fun. Recorded in 1993 in an unnamed small club in Manchester with one camera, Nico – backed by an uncredited but quite good three-piece rock band – looks ancient, haggard and wrecked, wearing a shabby overcoat and chain-smoking cigarettes while she sings. There's also a brief interview with her, though she's fairly dour and uncommunicative, revealing only that she was taking a lot of LSD during her stint with the Velvets. The performance is, ironically, somewhat better than on *Heroine* (although on Bowie's 'Heroes' she sounds like Madeleine Kahn's parody of Marlene Dietrich), but it still makes for uneasy viewing. DVD extras include more interview material from the same gig (more painful viewing), a biography and discography.

NICO: ICON

Éditions À Voir; Released 2001; available on Region 2 DVD.

An excellent documentary by Susanne Ofteringer. It opens with passages that concentrate on Nico's later years as a "middle-aged junkie", before backtracking to her childhood and early career. The sequencing makes the contrast between Nico's youth and her decline all the more appalling. There are interviews with her son Ari Boulogne/Delon, her aunt, Niko Papatakis, Alain Delon's mother, Billy Name, Paul Morrissey, Jonas Mekas, John Cale, Sterling Morrison, Viva, Danny Fields, Jackson Browne, Lutz Ullbrich (Nico's accompanist and lover in the 1970s), her 1980s manager Alan Wise and keyboard player James Young. There are amazing photographs and footage from Nico's early modelling career, plus brief clips from Warhol's *Chelsea Girls*, *An Underground Experience* (see above), Fellini's *La Dolce Vita*, Peter Whitehead's promotional video for 'I'm Not Saying' from 1966, and footage of Nico with Iggy Pop. The film closes with John Cale performing a stark, solo version of 'Frozen Warnings' at the piano.

LOU REED: TRANSFORMER

Eagle Vision; released 2001; available on Region 2 DVD.

One of the TV series *Classic Albums*, this one was directed by Bob Smeaton. It's a surprisingly good documentary that re-examines the *Transformer* album track-by-track, and in great depth. There are interviews with Reed, session men Herbie Flowers and John Halsey, producers David Bowie and Mick Ronson and cover photographer Mick Rock. Engineer Ken Scott isolates musical ingredients on the master tape to demonstrate how the tracks were put together, and Flowers demonstrates the twin-bass overdubbing on 'Walk On The Wild Side'. There are also anecdotes from Gerard Malanga, Joe Dallesandro and Holly Woodlawn, and analysis from musicians Dave Stewart and Lenny Kaye, as well as from journalists David Fricke, Tony Stewart and Timothy Greenfield-Sanders. Throughout his interview, Reed analyzes the contributions of Bowie and Ronson, and praises them effusively.

In addition to some archive footage, Reed performs acoustic versions of 'Vicious', 'Satellite Of Love', 'Walk On The Wild Side' and 'Perfect Day', and recites the lyrics of 'Andy's Chest' and 'Hangin' Round' as if they were poetry. He also segues effortlessly between 'Waiting For The Man', 'Vicious' and 'Dirty Blvd.', just to prove they all use the same chord structure ("See? They're brothers."). There are also clips from the video for the all-star BBC charity version of 'Perfect Day' (but sadly, not the whole thing). DVD extras include more interview material about the Velvets and Warhol, and Reed performing an acoustic version of 'Waiting For The Man'.

The Velvet Goldmine

JOHN CALE: FRAGMENTS OF A RAINY SEASON

FGL/Revenge; released 2003; available on Region 2 DVD.

ON A WEDDING ANNIVERSARY/LIE STILL SLEEP BECALMED/ DO NOT GO GENTLE INTO THAT GOOD NIGHT/CARMEN MIRANDA/CORDOBA/SHIP OF FOOLS/LEAVING IT UP TO YOU/THE BALLAD OF CABLE HOGUE/CHINESE ENVOY/FEAR (IS A MAN'S BEST FRIEND)/DYING OF THE VINE/HEARTBREAK HOTEL/STYLE IT TAKES/PARIS 1919/(I KEEP A) CLOSE WATCH/ HALLELUJAH

The on-screen companion to Cale's live album of the same name, though three tracks shorter in length and probably recorded at a different venue on the same tour – this was recorded at the Palais des Beaux-Arts in Brussels in April 1992, but the live album gives no details as to its venue. The director was Jacquemin Piel, assisted by three cameramen. The lighting is simple, the mood intimate, and Cale absolutely riveting as he performs highlights from his back catalogue unaccompanied except for a Steinway piano or acoustic guitar, his powerful voice carrying the melody. As might have been predicted, his garb is bizarre – a jacket that makes him look like Ichabod Crane, or an 18th-century preacher.

LOU REED: SPANISH FLY – LIVE IN SPAIN

Sanctuary Visual Entertainment; released 2005; available on Region 0 DVD.

MODERN DANCE/WHY DO YOU TALK/VENUS IN FURS/SWEET JANE/JESUS/ROMEO HAD JULIETTE/SATELLITE OF LOVE/ ECSTASY/ THE BLUE MASK/PERFECT DAY/WALK ON THE WILD SIDE

Personnel: Lou Reed (vocals and guitar); Mike Rathke (guitar); Fernando Saunders (bass); Jane Scarpantoni (cello); Tony 'Thunder' Smith (drums).

Produced by Rathke and Saunders, executive producer Reed. Recorded at the Benicassim International Festival in Benicassim, Spain on 7 August 2004.

A relaxed-looking Reed (in glasses) and band amble through a truly career-spanning selection of material in front of a Spanish festival crowd. The guitar solos and jamming are somewhat on the self-indulgent side (the world didn't really need a ten-minute version of 'Romeo Had Juliette'), but Reed's vocal delivery is far more thoughtful and less mannered than in recent years. Scarpantoni's cello adds a dimension missing from simpler guitar-based line-ups, and even though her instrumental histrionics on 'Venus In Furs' aren't really a substitute for Cale's droning viola, it at least seems a nod in the right direction – and Saunders' backing vocals are a delight throughout. All in all, a surprisingly enjoyable set. The DVD also contains a gallery of backstage photographs (by Reed).

Up close and, well, aged. An honest cover for a worthy DVD

LOU REED: LIVE AT MONTREUX 2000

Eagle Vision; released 2005; available on Region 2 DVD.

PARANOIA KEY OF E/TURN TO ME/MODERN DANCE/ECSTASY/ SMALL TOWN/FUTURE FARMERS OF AMERICA/TURNING TIME AROUND/ROMEO HAD JULIETTE/RIPTIDE/ROCK MINUET/MYSTIC CHILD/TATTERS/TWILIGHT/DIRTY BLVD./ DIME STORE MYSTERY/PERFECT DAY

Personnel: Lou Reed (vocals and guitar); Mike Rathke (guitar); Fernando Saunders (bass); Tony 'Thunder' Smith (drums).

Filmed during the Montreux Jazz Festival on 13 July 2000, where Reed made an appearance during the course of his *Ecstasy* tour – half this two-hour set being drawn from that album. And it's a mess. Reed seems off his stride, and far more interested in playing guitar – which he actually does pretty well – than in sticking to the actual song structure. His vocals are a complete throwaway, meandering all over the place with little regard to the tune involved. 'Rock Minuet' is pretty good, with Saunders playing his bass with a bow like an electric cello – but in the main this is definitely not Reed's finest live recording.

THE VELVET UNDERGROUND UNDER REVIEW

Sexy Intellectual Productions; released 2006; available on Region 0 DVD.

Subtitled "an independent critical analysis", this 85-minute long documentary contains no surprises visually, but all the best-known clips of the band are present. The bulk of the film consists of interviews with Moe Tucker and Doug Yule, as well as with Norman Dolph, Billy Name, Velvets expert Sal Mercuri and several rock critics, including Robert Christgau and Clinton Heylin. While it spends the bulk of its time concentrating on the first album, the film is still an excellent career overview.

John Cale film soundtracks

One of Cale's many talents and, presumably, sources of income, has been providing film scores for a range of movies (often French); most major works are detailed under his entry in The Music: Solo Album section of this book. But for quick cinephile reference:

Paris s'éveille (dir. Olivier Assayas), 1991
La Naissance de l'amour (dir. Philippe Garrel), 1993
Antárdida (dir. Manuel Herga) 1995
N'Oublie pas que tu vas mourir (dir. Xavier Beauvois), 1995
I Shot Andy Warhol (dir. Mary Harron), 1996
Eat/Kiss (dir. Andy Warhol, 1965), 1997
Le Vent de la nuit (dir. Philippe Garrel), 1999
The Unknown (dir. Tod Browning, 1927), 1999
Saint-Cyr (dir. Patricia Mazuy), 2000
Paris (dir. Raimin Niami), 2003
Process (dir. C.S. Leigh), 2005

The Velvet Goldmine

Also of interest...

CHELSEA GIRLS

Released 1967; not commercially available.

Warhol and Paul Morrissey's celebrated underground film is virtually two films, since the screen is split vertically down the middle, with two images showing at once. Since none of the people acting here can actually act, the proceedings are almost totally improvised (Warhol's technique was simply to leave the camera running regardless) and the whole thing is pretty tortuous – and plays like a particularly dull home video with terrible sound quality. Of interest to Velvets fans mainly for the lengthy footage of Nico, shown trimming the fringe of her hair and simply posing for the camera with psychedelic lighting effects. Also featuring numerous Factory stalwarts including Ondine, Ingrid Superstar, Eric Emerson, Brigid Polk, Gerald Malanga, International Velvet and Mary Woronov. Although occasionally shown in the small hours on TV, notably as part of Channel 4's *Velvet Underground Night* in 1993, the split screen doesn't work well on the box, and cinema showings (though rare) should be looked out for. However, be warned, this is undiluted Warhol: there's three and a half hours of this material, and it feels like a lifetime in purgatory.

CIAO! MANHATTAN

Plexifilm; first released 1972; available on Region 1 DVD.

John Palmer and David Weisman's underground film is a woolly pile of nonsense, shot in fits and starts over a long period, that acts as the swansong for its star Edie Sedgwick, who died three months after shooting was completed. It's also the best demonstration of what made this "femme fatale" so fascinating. The core of the film consists of Edie – lying half-naked on a waterbed at the bottom of an empty swimming pool – reminiscing about her experiences in New York a few years earlier, which are illustrated with black and white footage taken at the time. She also re-enacts her visits to the methedrine-dealing Dr. Roberts, and her electroshock therapy. While Sedgwick admittedly looks amazing in the 1960s footage, she's also obviously completely out of it on a cocktail of drugs. Knowing Sedgwick's eventual fate makes the whole viewing experience somewhat like watching a traffic accident in slow motion – the more so since Edie herself seems completely aware of her own impending doom.

Barely finished and rarely seen, this tawdry film was exploitation movie-making at its worst, even by underground cinema's standards

VELVET GOLDMINE

Released 1988; formerly available on Region 2 DVD but is currently out of print.

Todd Haynes' glam-rock fantasy is a fable constructed loosely around the early 1970s exploits of David Bowie and Iggy Pop; though it starts out promisingly and has fairly stunning costumes, it soon degenerates into an annoying mess. What makes it of interest here is that the characters who resemble Bowie (played by Jonathan Rhys Meyers) and Pop (played by Ewan McGregor) are both amalgams of the two stars – and McGregor's character also contains elements of a third party, namely Lou Reed. If you know their stories well, then spotting the way they've all been jumbled up is moderately amusing.

I SHOT ANDY WARHOL

MGM; 1996; available on Region 1 DVD.

Former journalist Mary Harron had originally intended to make a documentary about Valerie Solanas for the BBC, but discovered that hardly any footage of Solanas existed, and that there were also very few people willing to discuss her. Instead, Harron made Warhol's would-be assassin the subject of her first feature film as writer and director. Lili Taylor is impressively unlikeable as Solanas, while Stephen Dorff and Jared Harris turn in creditable impressions of Warhol and Candy Darling respectively. Warhol's Factory is enjoyably and evocatively recreated, even if the party scene makes it all seem like a lot more fun than it probably was.

Lili Taylor (right) plays Valerie Solanas and Jared Harris (left) plays Andy Warhol in Mary Harron's *I Shot Andy Warhol* (1996). Here, Solanas is attempting to get Andy to look at her screenplay while he is on the phone; this was, of course, the location at which Solanas would eventually shoot Warhol at point blank range

The Warhol Foundation gave their permission to use reproductions of Warhol silk screens in the film, on the condition that these were destroyed after filming was complete, and Billy Name served as "creative advisor". The party scene features a rock band playing who are obviously intended to be the Velvets, though no actual Velvets music is used. However, John Cale did contribute an orchestral piece to the soundtrack. The film won the Special Jury award at the 1996 Sundance Festival.

PUNK: ATTITUDE

Fremantlemedia; released October 2005; available on Region 2 DVD.

Don Letts' excellent documentary about punk features every major punk band from the Clash and Pistols on down, and is well worth your attention. It includes a brief section on the Velvets as forefathers of punk, with an interview with Cale and fragments of the 'Venus In Furs' rehearsal film. More interestingly, there are also very brief clips of Reed and Nico performing at the 1972 Le Bataclan gig – the only commercial release of this material to date.

FACTORY GIRL

Released March 2007; DVD late 2007.

George Hickenlooper's biopic of Edie Sedgwick was attracting flak even before its release, which as it enjoyed one of the best drip-drip pre-release publicity campaigns of recent years was hardly unsurprising. Lou Reed publicly branded the film-makers as "whoremongers" and scriptwriter Captain Mauzner as an "illiterate retard". In fact, the film is not great, but far better than one might have anticipated, with an amazing degree of visual accuracy, and it paints a fairly rounded portrait of its subject – which means it's also a pretty depressing ride, and probably a dull one if you have no prior knowledge of Warhol's world. Sienna Miller turns

The cult of Edie Sedgwick continues, with Sienna Miller – clearly a better actress than the character she plays – presenting a convincing portrayal, meticulously authentic right down to the last smidgen of eyeliner

in an extremely good performance as Edie, capturing the hollowness and pointlessness behind her glamour, while Guy Pearce's impression of Warhol is positively uncanny (Pearce is now the fourth actor to portray the artist, since David Bowie played Andy in 1996's *Basquiat*, and easily the best).

On the downside, the chronology is somewhat skewed from reality. Warhol is squarely blamed for Edie's decline (which probably isn't entirely fair) and the romance between Edie and Dylan (here portrayed by Hayden Christensen as folksinger 'Billy Quinn') is depicted as being far deeper than it probably was. Dylan threatened to sue for defamation before the film's release, and one can scarcely blame him, since his character here is both dumber and more po-faced than the man himself. So they changed the character's name.

As for the Velvets and Nico, they're reduced to the briefest of cameos, and the casting is truly bizarre – 'John Cale' being downright short and chubby. Also unsurprisingly, no Velvets music is used on the soundtrack. Gerard Malanga acted as one of the film's consultants and he is one of several people who knew Edie interviewed over the closing credits; the DVD contains more interview material.

THE END

In pre-production 2005; expected to be released in 2007.

Tilda Swinton is due to star in director David Mackenzie's biopic of Nico, which will cover the singer's career from her modelling days in Europe and America until her death. Location shooting will take place in Paris, New York, London and Manchester and the script – by *Blade Runner* writers David and Janet Peoples – is said to based partially upon James Young's excellent book *Songs They Never Play On The Radio* (see p.285).

The Velvet Goldmine

In Print and Online

As the Velvets' cult following has grown over the years, so has the number of non-musical publications about them. And, as what once was considered fly-by-night "pop" publishing has gravitated towards serious socio-cultural history, so the Underground have assumed a position in the pantheon which they themselves never doubted. Nevertheless, much of what is written about them largely feeds off the same limited amount of material, and is now hampered by two factors: the declining number of people available to interview (let alone remember) the Velvets' glory days, and the fact that at least Reed and Cale are still producing a fair stream of new recordings themselves, which tend to make retrospective surveys rapidly outdated – if not redundant. Nevertheless, lively (and not so lively) debate continues to flourish on the Internet.

Books By The Velvet Underground

BETWEEN THOUGHT AND EXPRESSION: SELECTED LYRICS

Lou Reed (Penguin Books, 1993; out of print).

This selection of Reed's lyrics includes material from his Velvet Underground days and his solo work – the latest entries being from *Songs For Drella*. There's a short introduction by Reed, and a smattering of anecdotal footnotes to some of the lyrics, most of which are amusing enough to make tracking a copy of this book down worthwhile. Also included are two poems that first appeared in 1976 in *Unmuzzled Ox* magazine – one of which won an award from the Literary Council For Small Magazines, which was presented to Reed by Senator Eugene McCarthy – and two interviews conducted by Reed, with Czech president Václav Havel and novelist Hubert Selby Jr. (of *Last Exit To Brooklyn* fame).

PASS THRU FIRE: THE COLLECTED LYRICS

Lou Reed (Bloomsbury, 2000).

The title is a quote from 'Magic And Loss'. There are a couple of minor works missing, but otherwise this is pretty much Reed's complete lyrical output: all the Velvet Underground material, and his solo work as far as *Ecstasy*. No footnotes this time, but there is a short introduction and several photographs by Reed, plus three unpublished poems and the complete lyrics to *Timerocker*, his H.G. Wells-inspired theatrical collaboration with Robert Wilson. The only drawback to this book is the fact that a wide variety of typographical styles are employed, presumably to make it more visually interesting. Unfortunately, some of them are annoyingly difficult to read.

WHAT'S WELSH FOR ZEN? THE AUTOBIOGRAPHY OF JOHN CALE

John Cale and Victor Bockris (Bloomsbury, 1999).

Cale's account of his life is remarkably candid and thoughtful, and eminent- ly readable. Much of the information here had never been available before, and Cale's insights into his working relationship with Reed over the decades are revealing, to say the least – nor does Cale pull any punches over his own substance abuse and per- sonal shortcomings. An essential read for anyone at all interested in The Velvet Underground or

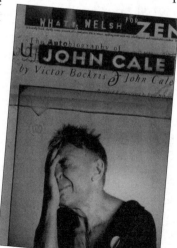

in Cale's extensive solo career. The large format book contains a wealth of rare pho- tographs and artefacts, and was designed by Dave McKean in a style that is both innova- tive and user-friendly.

'69 ON THE ROAD – VELVET UNDERGROUND PHOTOGRAPHS

Doug Yule (Sal Mercuri/Fierce Pup Productions, 1996; out of print).

A signed limited edition of 500 (and thus hard to find), containing photographs of the Velvets taken by Yule in 1969 – though at some point he loans the camera to someone else, since there are shots of the whole band on stage at an outdoor festival in Texas. The photographs themselves are great, but the reproduction and printing isn't – they're very faint and grainy. Yule also con- tributes very little in the way of text: just an extremely brief introduction and a few com- ments on the photos.

Cale wearing his angst on his sleeve once again in a brilliant and memorable jacket design. Rarely has being Welsh seemed so interesting

The Velvet Goldmine

Books On The Velvet Underground

UP-TIGHT: THE VELVET UNDERGROUND STORY

Victor Bockris and Gerard Malanga (Omnibus, 1983; updated edition 1995).

The first proper book to be published specifically about the Velvets, and probably the most evocative. A large format paperback illustrated throughout with amazing photographs (though also published in a text-only edition), peppered with hundreds of first-person reminiscences from all concerned and extracts from Malanga's diaries of the period. Sadly, the book is riddled with inaccurate information, much of which Bockris has corrected in his other books (but not here).

TRANSFORMER: THE LOU REED STORY

Victor Bockris (Simon & Schuster, 1995).

Also published under the title *Lou Reed: The Biography*. Reed apparently disliked Bockris's *Up-Tight* so much that, when he learned of the author's plans to write a biography of himself, he demanded of his musical collaborators that no one should co-operate. In fact, Bockris did an amazing job of research, tracking down family friends, fellow students from Syracuse, Reed's first love Shelley Albin, tour managers and road crew and many more. The cut-off point is shortly after the Velvets' reunion, and the portrait that emerges is that of a man who is exceptionally talented, extraordinarily complex and very, very messed up. It's a great biography, and one that makes its subject more understandable, though no more likeable; needless to say, Reed hates it.

LOU REED & THE VELVET UNDERGROUND

Diana Clapton (Proteus, 1982; out of print).

A large format illustrated biography that goes up as far as *The Blue Mask*. Some great photos, but the prose style is somewhat florid and breathless – though it does contain one interesting ingredient, in a long interview with Barbara Fulk, who was Reed's tour manager between 1972 and 1975.

LOU REED: GROWING UP IN PUBLIC

Peter Doggett (Omnibus, 1991; out of print).

The first in-depth Reed biography ends just prior to the Velvets' reunion. Doggett's approach was solid and workmanlike, and he uncovered much hitherto unknown information. However, this book has since been superseded by the Victor Bockris biography.

THE VELVET UNDERGROUND AND NICO

Joe Harvard (Continuum, 2004).

A personal appreciation of the Velvets' early days and the recording of their first album. A little breathless and somewhat padded, the book scores on the fact that Harvard (a session musician) unearthed some good new information about the actual recording sessions, most of it the result of an interview with Norman Dolph. Prior to this, the addled memories of some of the participants had made the details of the recording extremely hard to fathom.

FROM THE VELVETS TO THE VOIDOIDS

Clinton Heylin (Penguin, 1993; out of print).

Subtitled "A Pre-punk History For A Post-punk World", Heylin's book traces a line of influence from the Velvets through the MC5 and New York Dolls to Jonathan Richman, Television, The Ramones, Talking Heads, Blondie and beyond. Only two chapters on the Velvets (though well-researched), but it's a fascinating read if you're interested in the other bands as well.

ALL YESTERDAY'S PARTIES

Edited by Clinton Heylin (Da Capo Press, 2005).

Subtitled "The Velvet Underground In Print 1966–1970", which says it all. Here you'll find contemporary press coverage of the Velvets, plus a smattering of great visuals from the time, such as posters and promotional material. Given that rock journalism as we know it today was in its infancy in the late 1960s, there are still some interesting insights into the mentality of the times: the straight press largely treats the Velvets purely as an inconsequential adjunct of Warhol, comparing them to "Berlin in the decadent Thirties" or calling them the heirs of Baudelaire, while pieces from the underground press and music magazines like *Crawdaddy* vary between incomprehension and semi-incoherent adulation. On the plus side, there's a good interview with Sterling Morrison by Greg Barrios, as well as pieces by Sandy Pearlman, Lester Bangs and Lenny Kaye.

THE COMPLETE GUIDE TO THE MUSIC OF THE VELVET UNDERGROUND

Peter Hogan (Omnibus, 1997).

Earlier book by the author of the volume you now hold in your hand. Covers the Velvets' output from the recording sessions for their first album through to the release of *Peel Slowly And See*.

THE VELVET UNDERGROUND HANDBOOK

M.C. Kostek (Black Spring, 1989; out of print).

An "ultimate book of facts" put together by Mike Kostek, president of The Velvet

Underground Appreciation Society. Contains rare photos, a chronological history, a staggeringly comprehensive discography, filmography and bibliography. A good book, and even if some of the information here has since been superseded, still well worth tracking down.

PLEASE KILL ME: THE UNCENSORED ORAL HISTORY OF PUNK

Legs McNeill and Gillian Welch (Little Brown, 1996).

This covers the same territory as Clinton Heylin's *From The Velvets To The Voidoids*, with hundreds of first-person accounts of the development of the alternative American music scene between 1967–92. A great piece of documentation, even if the litany of drug casualties makes for depressing reading. The first chapter concerns the Velvets, with a later chapter on their reunion and the death of Nico.

SEDITION AND ALCHEMY: A BIOGRAPHY OF JOHN CALE

Tim Mitchell (Peter Owen, 2003).

A thorough biography of Cale, which goes up to 2002. It's good on the early avant-garde period, and fills in many holes skipped over by Cale's autobiography. There are times that it seems somewhat sketchy, though – and Mitchell's original manuscript is rumoured to have been much longer, but was cut by the publisher simply on the grounds of cost. It's a shame, because Cale certainly deserves the full, comprehensive biographical treatment. Available in paperback, but the limited edition hardback includes a free CD containing a short story by Cale and a short musical piece called 'Imitating Violin'.

LOU REED: WALK ON THE WILD SIDE

Chris Roberts (Carlton, 2004).

One of a seriously useful series of books. The typography is better inside

Large format paperback, subtitled 'The Stories Behind The Songs', which takes an analytical album-by-album, track-by-track approach to Reed's solo career (with a brief preamble about the Velvets). A good selection of photographs (but inserted into the text in somewhat haphazard fashion), and the book makes for a lively read even if you disagree with the author.

BEYOND THE VELVET UNDERGROUND

Dave Thompson (Omnibus, 1989; out of print).

This large format book might as well be titled 'The Velvet Underground In Their Own Words', since it consists almost entirely of direct quotes from band members (plus a few journalists and critical reviews), as well as a smattering of photographs. It follows the story up as far as Reed's *New Sensations* and Cale's *Artificial Intelligence*, with a postscript about the death of Nico.

LOU REED & THE VELVETS

Nigel Trevena (White Light, 1973; out of print).

An early, fanzine-style booklet containing a brief chronology, reviews of the band's albums and Reed's early solo work, an evaluation of Reed as a writer/performer, a selection of Reed quotes and some nice visual material. What makes this of real interest, however, is the inclusion of not only the words to 'The Gift', but also eleven of Reed's early poems.

NICO: THE LIFE & LIES OF AN ICON

Richard Witts (Virgin, 1993).

In the late 1980s Nico asked Witts to write her biography, which she wanted to be called *Moving Target*. She thought it should be more like a novel than a biography, "half true, half not". Instead, Witts has done an excellent job of cutting through Nico's addled self-mythologizing to paint a vivid portrait of an extraordinary woman who lived an extraordinary life, albeit an extremely depressing one. Even before her plunge into a heroin nightmare, Nico was always a tragedy in search of a place to happen.

LOU REED: BETWEEN THE LINES

Michael Wrenn (Plexus, 1993).

Most of Wrenn's book is made up of informative quotes that are straight from the horse's mouth, linked by short narrative pieces from Wrenn. Apart from the quotes, the strength of this large format paperback (which ends just prior to the Velvets' reunion) lies in the fact that it contains a wealth of truly amazing press cuttings and memorabilia from Glen Marks' archive.

NICO: SONGS THEY NEVER PLAY ON THE RADIO

James Young (Bloomsbury, 1992).

Also published under the title *Nico: The End*. Young was Nico's keyboard player throughout the 1980s, and his memoir of her declining years is a touching and extremely humorous account of the chaos that surrounded her both at home and on the road. Shored up by third-rate musicians and fourth-rate management, Nico has little to trade on except her "legend", and the only thing she's interested in trading it for is heroin. Yet although Young readily acknowledges that Nico was "a monster", his affection for her is evident, and he has enough compassion to concede that junkies are "invalids with criminal tendencies". As a study of rock'n'roll at its seediest, most unrewarding and unglamorous, this makes for great reading.

THE VELVET UNDERGROUND COMPANION

Edited by Albin Zak III (Schirmer Books, 1997).

Subtitled "Four Decades Of Commentary", this collection is an entertaining ragbag of articles and reviews from the 1960s onwards, which veers from the interesting to the inane; writers include Lester Bangs, M.C. Kostek and Paul Williams. There are interviews with Morrison, Reed, Nico and Tucker, an exhaustive (and exhausting) discography by M.C. Kostek and Phil Milstein, and written tributes to Morrison on his passing by Lou Reed and Doug Yule. Editor Zak is an assistant professor of music at the University of Michigan.

Also of interest ...

There are literally hundreds of titles in print about the life, work and world of Andy Warhol. The following are a brief selection of books that may be of particular interest to Velvets fans.

ANDY WARHOL'S PHILOSOPHY: FROM A TO B AND BACK AGAIN

Andy Warhol (Cassell, 1975).

POPISM – THE WARHOL SIXTIES

Andy Warhol & Pat Hackett (Harcourt Inc., 1980).

Warhol's own writings – the rambling 'philosophy' was actually transcribed from Brigid Polk's tape recordings – explore every subject under the sun as well as

Every home should have one – and most did back in the 1970s. Quite what the great man's philosophy was remained unclear, but the book was full of Warhol's fascinating meditations on subjects as diverse as purchasing underpants, fame, and making money

his own life, and are a wonderfully enjoyable read: childlike, witty and genuinely touching. His memoir of the 1960s is both fragmentary and biased, but nevertheless fascinating, and is – apart from the occasional catty remark – free of the bitchiness that marred his later diaries. For example, although his memoir contains a fair amount of material about his time with the Velvets, he says absolutely nothing about the way that he and Reed parted company.

ANDY WARHOL: THE FACTORY YEARS 1964–1967

Nat Finkelstein (Canongate Books, 1999).

THE VELVET YEAR: WARHOL'S FACTORY 1965–1967

Photographs by Stephen Shore, text by Lynn Tillman. (Pavilion, 1995).

Both are large format collections of photographs of the Factory era (Shore's in black and white, Finkelstein's in both black and white and colour). Finkelstein's has a few short prose essays by him and an introduction by David Dalton, while Shore's contains anecdotal prose pieces by some of his subjects, including Morrison, Cale and Tucker. Both books contain otherwise unseen photos of the Velvets and Nico, plus shots of most of the key players in the Factory story, and give fascinating insights into Warhol's world.

EDIE: AMERICAN GIRL

Jean Stein, edited with George Plimpton (Alfred A. Knopf, 1982).

Reissued in softcover as *Edie: An American Biography* (Pimlico, 1996).

A meticulous, riveting and brilliantly constructed account of Sedgwick's life and background built up from hundreds of first-person recollections. Stein's book is not only a biography of the troubled model/actress Edie Sedgwick, but also an extraordinarily vivid portrait of her times and world. Not a great deal of material here about the Velvets, but it's an extremely evocative depiction of Warhol and the whole Factory crowd. Even though Edie's life itself reads like an out-of-control Greek tragedy (and is somewhat depressing), this is highly recommended.

A model of biographical research, all told through carefully assembled interviews, with no intrusive authorial/editorial voice

The Velvet Goldmine

FACTORY MADE: WARHOL AND THE SIXTIES

Steven Watson (Pantheon, 2003).

A superbly researched – and lengthy – chronicle of Warhol and his world, concentrating mainly on the period 1960-1968. There's nothing about the Velvets in here that you couldn't find elsewhere, but Watson places them in context with the rest of Warhol's activities. Also, if you wanted one book that would tell you everything you needed to know about the denizens of the Factory, this is the one.

SWIMMING UNDERGROUND: MY YEARS IN THE WARHOL FACTORY

Mary Woronov (Serpent's Tail, 1995).

Former Factory-person and Underground whip-dancer, Woronov's memoir is by turns candid, literary, warm, surreal and harrowing. It evokes the Factory's atmosphere of drug-fuelled desperation

Fanzines

There have been numerous Velvet Underground fanzines over the years, the most impressive of which is *What Goes On*, founded by Phillip Milstein in 1978. Four issues have appeared and a fifth was promised; for back issues and further details, write to M.C. Kostek, c/o The Velvet Underground Appreciation Society, 5721 SE Laguna Avenue, Stuart, FL 34997-7828 USA.

better than almost any other book, and despite the roller-coaster ride through her emotional and sexual problems is occasionally laugh-out-loud funny, particularly on the subject of Nico. Woronov's subsequent career as a successful actress proved that there is life after the Factory, and she brings a humanity to bear on the subject that is frequently absent from other Factory survivors and hangers-on. Not a great deal of material here about the Velvets, but it's still a great read – and contains, according to Lou Reed, the most accurate portrayal of Warhol in print.

Websites

There is no authorised website for The Velvet Underground. But the following are worthy of note:

www.velvetunderground.com is simply a fan website, and not a particularly good one. Of the numerous Velvet Underground fan sites, easily the best is *The Velvet Underground Web Page* (members.aol.com/olandem/vu.html), created and maintained by Olivier Landemaine. Here you'll find an extensive discography (including bootlegs), bibliography and filmography, plus classic magazine articles, photo and audio files (including unreleased live material), and much more, including links to further pages on the individual members. Some of the links don't always work, but it's worth returning to this site frequently – there's enough material to keep you occupied for hours.

The surviving Velvets each have their own official websites. At Maureen Tucker's *Taj Moe Hal* site (www.spearedpeanut.com/tajmoe-hal/) you'll find a biography, a photo album, news pages, FAQs. and a shop where you can (theoretically) buy Moe's albums and T-shirts. In fact, the site – and Moe's PO Box – both seem to be inactive, and recent enquiries by both e-mail and snailmail met with no reply.

Content changes frequently at www.loureed.com, but usually includes a news listing, audio files (of music and interviews), video files, features and a link to an online Reed store. There's also a link here to Enrique Miguel's *Rock And Roll Animal* site (www.arrakis.es/~e.miquel/rnranimal), which Lou presumably considers the best of the Reed fan sites.

The seemingly official www.john-cale.com is a major disappointment, containing only tour and news listings relating to the *Black Acetate* album. Hopefully the site will expand once Cale has some free time to devote to it. Meanwhile, an excellent Cale resource can be found at www.xs4all.nl/~werksman/cale/index.html. Here you'll find an extensive biography, discography, lyrics and sheet music, photos and much more, including a John Cale quiz.

Finally, the best of the many Nico websites would seem to be the one found at smironne.free.fr/NICO/, which has a wealth of material on every aspect of Nico's life and work (including a photo of her grave).

There He Goes Again

The Wisdom Of Lou Reed

"I'm not tasteful. I never said I was tasteful". (1978)

"I work really hard to make my songs sound like the way people really talk. My concerns are somewhat similar to what Sam Shepard and Martin Scorsese are doing, talking about things that people growing up in a city go through. I'm trying for a kind of urban elegance, set to a beat". (1982)

"I don't know why people give me record deals. I think it's because they at least break even, and I think they even make a few bucks while they're at it. I'm a cult figure, but I sell some records". (1989)

"I'm into this for the long haul. I feel I've just started to get a grip on it, what I can do with it, and who I'd like to take with me when I do it. It's really easy in a sense, because the people who like it will go with me, and the people who don't will say I'm full of shit, and more power to them. They don't want me, and I'm not interested in them either. That's okay. I have no problem with that". (1992)

"Warhol said that it's too bad in school they don't have a course about love, like practical stuff. Or maybe one on loss, like what do you do with yourself, who do you ask, where do you turn". (1992)

"Some of the music I like just makes me feel like going out and burning down a house or attacking a politician". (1996)

"I should have been dead a thousand times". (1996)

"I'd have to sit there with people saying, 'Don't you feel guilty for glamourizing heroin, for all the people who've shot up drugs because of you?' I get that to this day, even though I didn't notice a drop-off in the sales of narcotics when I stopped taking things". (1996)

"Three chords is three chords, but there is a finesse to it". (Date unknown)

"Just say that John Cale was the easygoing one and Lou Reed was the prick". (Date unknown)

The Velvets' New York

If ever a band defined the fabric of a city, it was the Velvets. Here we map, for those less familiar with Manhattan, the 40 key Velvet sites.

1 BANK STREET – LaMonte Young lived at # 119 during the 1960s.

2 BARROW STREET – John and Risé Cale lived here in the early 1980s.

3 BLEECKER STREET – John and Risé Cale lived here in the early 1980s.

4 BROOME STREET – The Velvets regularly rehearsed in a loft here in 1966.

5 CAFÉ BIZARRE – West 3rd Street. Where Andy Warhol first met The Velvet Underground.

6 CBGB – 315 Bowery. (Country, Bluegrass and Blues) the club was founded by Hilly Kristal in 1973, and rapidly became the centre of the New York punk movement, a platform for The Ramones, Blondie, Television and Talking Heads. The club closed on 15 October 2006, the final performance being by Patti Smith.

7 THE CHELSEA HOTEL – West 23rd Street. John Cale (with Betsey Johnson) and Nico (for several periods) have both lived here. It remains notorious for many other reasons.

8 CHRISTOPHER STREET – Reed lived here in the 1970s, and again in the 1990s; Cale had an apartment here in the 1990s.

9 CHURCH STREET – LaMonte Young lived here in the mid-1960s, and the Theatre Of Eternal Music rehearsed here.

10 CLUB BABY GRAND – 25th Street. Cale and Reed busked on the sidewalk in front of here in the Summer of 1965.

11 THE DELMONICO HOTEL – 502 Park Avenue, at 59th Street. Scene of the first performance by the Velvets with Nico, in January 1966. The building is now the Trump Park Avenue apartment complex.

12 THE DOM – St. Mark's Place. Venue for the first public gigs of the Exploding Plastic Inevitable show.

13 EAST 2ND STREET – Sterling Morrison lived here in late 1967.

14 EAST 16TH STREET – Nico lived here in 1968.

15 EAST 52ND STREET – Lou Reed lived here with Rachel in 1976; Greta Garbo was one of their neighbours.

16 EAST 63RD STREET & MADISON AVENUE – John Cale lived here with Edie Sedgwick in early 1966.

17 THE FACTORY # 1 (The Silver Factory) – 231 East 47th Street. The Velvets rehearsed here, and many of Warhol's early films were shot here. The building was demolished in 1968.

18 THE FACTORY # 2 – 33 Union Square West. The Factory occupied the 6th floor. Where Andy Warhol was shot by Valerie Solanas.

19 THE FACTORY # 4 – 860 Broadway, the site of Warhol's HQ from 1974.

20 14TH STREET – Cale lived here with Jane Friedman in the late 1970s.

21 450 GRAND STREET – Reed, Cale, MacLise and Morrison shared an apartment on the 5th floor in Autumn 1965 with underground film-maker Piero Heliczer.

22 JANE STREET – Nico and Lou Reed lived together in an apartment here in early 1966.

23 LAFAYETTE STREET – The Velvets performed here in 1965, playing behind the screen at the Lafayette Street Cinémathèque.

24 LAGUARDIA PLACE – John Cale lived here while married to Betsey Johnson.

25 LISPENARD STREET – Cale's first New York apartment, late 1963.

26 LUDLOW STREET – John Cale had an apartment at # 56 during 1964-65. Reed moved in with him in the Summer of 1965, and the Velvets rehearsed and recorded demos here.

27 MAX'S KANSAS CITY – 213 Park Avenue South (at 17th Street).

28 NINTH STREET & FIFTH AVENUE – Maureen Tucker briefly lived here in 1967, until poverty forced her to move back in with her parents in Long Island.

29 PERRY STREET – Lou Reed lived here in 1967.

30 RIVIERA CAFÉ – Sheridan Square. Here Lou Reed informed Sterling Morrison and Moe Tucker that he wanted John Cale fired from the group.

31 SCEPTER RECORDS – 254 West 54th Street. The Velvets recorded the bulk of their first album here. The building subsequently housed the club Studio 54.

32 EAST 55TH STREET – Steve Sesnick's apartment.

33 67TH STREET – Nico and John Cale lived together here (very briefly) in early 1967.

34 30TH STREET – Cale lived here in 1980.

35 28TH STREET & 7TH AVENUE – Reed lived in a loft near Penn Station during 1968-69. According to Morrison, the loft was actually on 31st Street.

36 28TH STREET – Cale lived in an apartment here (between Madison and Lexington) in 1970.

37 WEST 3RD STREET – Reed, Morrison (and occasionally Cale) lived here during 1966-67, sub-letting an apartment above a firehouse. It was known as "Sister Ray House".

38 WEST 10TH STREET – John Cale and Sterling Morrison shared an apartment here in 1966; Lou Reed lived in another apartment two blocks away on the same street.

39 WEST 26TH STREET – The Velvet Underground rehearsed in a former factory here for their 1993 reunion tour.

40 WEST 54TH STREET – Lou Reed lived in the Gotham apartment building here during the 1970s.

Index

Index

Index

Index

Listen Up!

"You may be used to the Rough Guide series being comprehensive, but nothing will prepare you for the exhaustive Rough Guide to World Music . . . one of our books of the year."
Sunday Times, London

ROUGH GUIDE MUSIC TITLES

Bob Dylan • The Beatles • Blues • Classical Music • Elvis • Frank Sinatra
Heavy Metal • Hip-Hop • iPods, iTunes & music online • Jazz • Book of Playlists
Led Zeppelin • Opera • Pink Floyd • Punk • Reggae • Rock • The Rolling Stones
Soul and R&B • Velvet Underground • World Music Vol 1 & 2

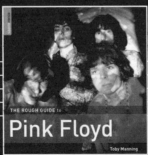

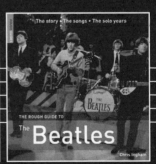

BROADEN YOUR HORIZONS

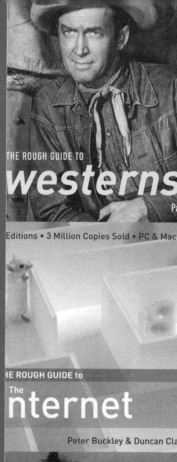

THE ROUGH GUIDE TO
westerns

Pa

Editions • 3 Million Copies Sold • PC & Mac

HE ROUGH GUIDE to
The nternet

Peter Buckley & Duncan Clark

A DIGITAL MUSIC GUI

iPod
Music
Photos
Videos
Extras
Settings
Shuffle Songs

THE ROUGH GUIDE to
iPo
iTun

4 TH EDITION:
COVERS IPOD NANO, VIDE

THE ROUGH GUIDE to
The **Rolling Stones**

Punk

Soul and R&B

THE ROUGH GUI
Blog

Rough Guides presents...

"Achieves the perfect balance between learned recommendation and needless trivia"
Uncut Magazine reviewing Cult Movies

Other Rough Guide Film & TV titles include:

American Independent Film • British Cult Comedy • Chick Flicks • Comedy Movies
Cult Movies • Film • Film Musicals • Film Noir • Gangster Movies • Horror Movies
Kids' Movies • Sci-Fi Movies • Westerns

BROADEN YOUR HORIZONS

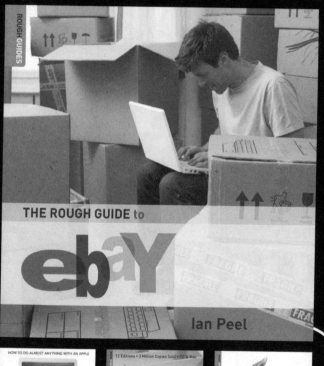

Get Connected!

"Brilliant! ... the unmatched leader in its field"
Sunday Times, London, reviewing The Rough Guide to the Internet

THE ROUGH GUIDE to

ebaY

Ian Peel

A DIGITAL MUSIC GUIDE FOR MAC & PC

iPod
- Music
- Photos
- Videos
- Extras
- Settings
- Shuffle Songs

THE ROUGH GUIDE to

iPods

iTunes & music online

4TH EDITION:
COVERS IPOD NANO, VIDEO IPOD & IPOD SHUFFLE

HOW TO DO ALMOST ANYTHING WITH AN APPLE

Macs & OS X

Peter Buckley & Duncan Clark

12 Editions • 3 Million Copies Sold • PC & Mac

THE ROUGH GUIDE to The **Internet**

Peter Buckley & Duncan Clark

THE ROUGH GUIDE

Website Directory
Shopping Online & Surfing The Net

2007 edition

ROUGH GUIDES

Rough Guide Computing Titles
Blogging • eBay • The iPhone • iPods, iTunes & music online
The Internet • Macs & OS X • MySpace • Book of Playlists
PCs & Windows • Playstation Portable • Website Directory